Intermediate Microeconomics

Intermediate Microeconomics

James P. Quirk
California Institute of Technology

SCIENCE RESEARCH ASSOCIATES, INC.
Chicago, Palo Alto, Toronto, Henley-on-Thames, Sydney, Paris, Stuttgart
A Subsidiary of IBM

Library of Congress Cataloging in Publication Data

Quirk, James P
  Intermediate microeconomics.

  Includes index.
  1. Microeconomics. I. Title.
HB171.5.Q55   338.5   75-34009
ISBN 0-574-19265-4

To my father,
May the next eighty-three years be as rewarding
as the last were.

Contents

Preface

Intermediate Microeconomics is a nonmathematical introduction to the principles of microeconomics. The book developed from my experiences in teaching undergraduate students, generally at the junior or senior level. It reflects my belief that there is a need to emphasize the literary, graphical approach to microeconomic theory, even to students (such as those at Caltech) who possess the mathematical tools to handle a more formal approach; there is just no substitute for the intuition that one acquires with lots of curve-bending. The problem, of course, is to maintain as much rigor as possible, subject to the constraints imposed by the level (or nonlevel) of mathematics used. This text, which uses no mathematics beyond the high school level, is the result.

Compared to other texts currently available, this text emphasizes general equilibrium versus partial equilibrium, especially in the later chapters dealing with applied welfare economics. In the same vein, simultaneous market equilibrium is taken up early in the book in the treatment of the law of supply and demand, and there is an introductory chapter stressing the interrelationships among markets.

Markets for assets and intertemporal decision making are given more detailed treatment than in most texts, and there is in addition a discussion of the determination of the rate of interest in the market for newly produced capital goods. Welfare economics is approached from a general equilibrium point of view, with the revealed preference version of Pareto superiority as the guide to judging among policy proposals. The section on market power includes brief discussions of the Averch-Johnson effect, the prisoner's dilemma, the minimax theorem, and price discrimination. A separate chapter is devoted to uncertainty and the institutions that have developed to mitigate its effects, including analysis of the market for information. The final chapter of the book deals with replenishable and nonreplenishable natural resources. Most of the other topics are standard textual material.

I want to thank the students at Caltech and the reviewers of earlier versions of the book, whose suggestions have been most helpful. Among the reviewers were James R. Jeffers (University of Iowa), John O. Ledyard (Northwestern University), John H. Moore (University of Virginia), R.D. Peterson (Colorado State University), James B. Ramsey (Michigan State University), Hugo Sonnenschein (Northwestern University), and John T. Wenders (University of Arizona). I owe a special debt of gratitude to my colleagues Dave Montgomery, Lance Davis, and Roger Noll for their comments and criticisms, and to Bob Huttenback, who provided the support for typing the book. Bob Bovenschulte of SRA made the original suggestion to me to write the book, and Bruce Caldwell has nursed and encouraged it for longer than either of us would have wished. Gretchen Hargis has been a joy to work with as editor.

I have been especially fortunate to have Georgeia Hutchinson and Aida Demirjian as typists at Caltech. Connie Friedman of the Caltech staff has done just about everything short of actually writing the book; she has been an enormous help. Finally, my wife Shirley made it all worthwhile.

Introduction

Economics has been defined, somewhat facetiously, as "what economists do." In the same vein, *economic theory* may be defined as "how economists think." The way in which economists organize their thinking about society and its problems most clearly distinguishes economics from the other social sciences; the key to an understanding of all of economics is an understanding of the thought processes of economists.

This book is concerned with the branch of economics called *microeconomics*. As the term implies, microeconomics deals with elemental economic units—individual consumers, firms, industries, commodities, and markets. *Microeconomic theory* provides the framework within which the economist describes and analyzes the behavior patterns and interrelationships of these elemental units.

Self-Interest and Incentives

The fundamental conception underlying microeconomic theory is the view of the society as an organism in which *each participant is motivated by self-interest and acts in response to it*. The microeconomist takes as his basic premise, in other words, that the structure of incentives (monetary and otherwise) plays a crucial role in determining the pattern of economic activity in a society. The notion of self-interest and the efficacy of incentives is as fundamental to microeconomics as Newton's laws are to physics.

The objective of microeconomic theory is to explain and predict how the production, exchange, and distribution of goods and services responds to the structure of incentives in a society. That is to say, a prime goal of the theory is to arrive at testable propositions concerning the economic activities of a society. Thus microeconomic theory is, in a formal sense, a scientific theory.

The Nature of Scientific Theory and Its Development

A scientific theory is an attempt to provide a consistent, logical, and testable explanation for a range of phenomena found in reality. Any such theory isolates for study certain objects and the interrelationships among these objects. Empirical observations establish the characteristics of the objects under study, as well as any observable regularities in the interrelationships among them. At the base of the theory, then, are empirical observations.

But reality is infinitely complex. To construct a manageable explanation, the theory abstracts from reality, suppressing all but the most essential features of the objects under study. The theory consists of certain *axioms* concerning the characteristics of the objects and their interrelationships, together with *propositions* that express the implications of these axioms and that can be derived from them by pure logic. The axioms are generally empirically based, describing in abstract form the observed features of the objects; similarly, the propositions are often empirically testable through a confrontation with observations on the objects as they exist in reality.

The ultimate test of the scientific validity of a theory is the extent to which it gives rise to propositions that are verified by observations. But the theory plays a more fundamental role, in providing an understanding of the phenomena it is designed to predict. We are concerned not only with making correct predictions; we also want to understand why the predictions work. The scientific theory provides the logical apparatus for getting at both of these issues.

No scientific theory is ever completed in the sense that its axiom system and its set of testable propositions are completely known, verified, and unchanging over time. The essential reason for this is that by the very nature of a scientific theory, reality has been simplified to make it logically manageable. The process of simplification involved in constructing a scientific theory necessarily introduces distortions into the descriptions of the objects under study. When a theory is first developed, it is designed to explain and predict a rather narrow range of phenomena. The theory is tested through its predictions concerning these phenomena. Given success in these predictions, the theory evolves through wider and wider applications of it. As the range is increased, the probability that the distortions built into the theory will lead to disverification increases. And once empirical tests contradict the propositions of the theory, it is time to reexamine the axiom system to develop a revised characterization of the objects and the interrelationships.

Thus there is a close link between empirical work on the one hand, aimed at both determining the limits of applicability of a theory and specifying more finely the characteristics of the objects of a theory, and theoretical work on the other hand, aimed at restructuring the axiom system so that the testable propositions of the theory jibe with observed results. In a very real sense, the construction and testing of a scientific theory is always an unfinished job. No scientific theory either intends or accomplishes a complete mirroring of the complexities of reality; it is this very complexity that leads in the first place to the construction of the simplified model that constitutes the scientific theory. This is as true, say, of physics as of microeconomic theory.

The Role of Theory in Microeconomics

The objects under study in microeconomic theory are consumers, firms, and markets. The theory postulates certain behavioral rules for consumers and firm managers, and makes certain assumptions about the way in which markets function. Given these axioms, and given subsidiary assumptions concerning the institutional structure of a society (its laws, property rights, customs, and the like), various testable propositions can be derived concerning the operation of the society's economic system.

The behavioral rules for consumers and firm managers that appear in microeconomic theory are derived from the self-interest hypothesis: consumers maximize utility and firm managers maximize profits. The theory postulates in addition that prices are established in markets according to the law of supply and demand. These represent the fundamental axioms of microeconomic theory; all of the testable propositions of the theory ultimately rest on them.

The behavioral rules for consumers and firm managers express, in simplified and abstract form, patterns of behavior by these market participants as they are observed in reality. Similarly, within the theory, markets are reduced to their essence as structures within which bargaining as to the terms of exchange takes place among consumers and firm managers. Given appropriate assumptions as to the preferences of consumers, the technological possibilities available to firms, and the institutional structure of the society, one can derive a set of propositions that express in general form the patterns of economic activity that emerge in a market economy from interactions among these idealized decision makers. These are the testable propositions of the theory.

A basic requirement for any viable scientific theory is that the theory predict at least the general pattern of observed regularities as they appear in reality. Scientific theorizing began historically with attempts to identify the underlying principles that could explain and predict the most common and well-known phenomena—the falling of objects to earth, why certain substances burn, the pattern of the tides. The same is true of microeconomic theory. To illustrate, consider Gresham's law.

Gresham's Law

In the late sixteenth century, Thomas Gresham, an English merchant, formulated what has come to be known as *Gresham's law: Bad money drives the good money out of circulation.* Gresham formulated this statement when he observed that, despite a continuing output of full-bodied silver coins from the British Mint, the coins in circulation were invariably "shaved" (silver being pared from the edges). Gresham's law is simply an observation as to an empirical regularity that he claimed applied to all kinds of money. But this law can also

be viewed as a proposition that follows from the axiom system of microeconomic theory: it expresses an implication of the assumption that individuals follow their self-interest.

Assume that there are two types of money in an economy, both being legal tender (creditors must accept either in payment of debts). If one type of money has more value than the other, then individuals, following self-interest, will pay their bills in the cheaper money and hoard the more valuable. The money that circulates will be the cheaper ("bad") money.

Gresham's law has considerable predictive power. During the U.S. Civil War, "greenbacks" (paper money with no convertibility into gold) replaced gold coins as the circulating medium in the North. While the United States was legally on a bimetallic system during most of the nineteenth century (both gold and silver being minted into coins), a systematic overvaluation of gold at the mint converted this system into a *de facto* gold standard in the latter part of the century (as would follow from Gresham's law) and led to Bryan's famous "Cross of Gold" speech in the 1896 campaign. More recently, silver dollars disappeared from circulation when the silver in the dollar became worth more than a dollar to industrial users. In these and similar cases, the legal tender laws created incentives for individuals to behave in certain ways, and they responded to these incentives.

Gresham's law is one of the simplest illustrations of a testable proposition that can be derived from the axiom system of microeconomic theory. But there are many other such illustrations, of course.

The Instability of Cartels

Charles Schwab, the steel magnate of the early twentieth century, once was asked whether he had heard of agreements to fix prices in the steel industry, and how effective such agreements were. He is reported to have replied that he had heard of such agreements, and that most lasted only as long as it took the participants to get to the telephone to give orders to cheat on the agreement.

When the price of a staple commodity rises, there is invariably a report to the effect that there has been a conspiracy among the firms in the industry to fix prices and output. This certainly can happen, as the OPEC oil cartel illustrates. But economists are generally rather skeptical of conspiracy theories. Predictably, their argument is based on the self-interest hypothesis. Assume that a cartel is formed; that is, a coalition of firms in an industry agrees to act together to raise profits for the group as a whole by splitting markets, limiting competition, restricting output, and raising the price of the industry's product. By combining together, generally the level of profits for the industry can be increased. But once the cartel agreement has been reached, then so long as the other members of the cartel honor the agreement, it is in the self-interest of any given member of the cartel to violate the agreement.

For example, if all firms agree to restrict the output of steel to increase its price, then any one firm increases its own profits by expanding its output to sell it at the higher price. For this reason, economists conclude that in the absence of effective methods to police the cartel agreement and to punish violators, cartels tend to be unstable. To borrow Marx's phrase, a cartel agreement contains the seeds of its own destruction.

Mr. Schwab's comment concerning steel cartels was certainly self-serving (he was head of U.S. Steel Corporation, which accounted for almost 50 percent of U.S. steel output in the early 1900s), but there is an important grain of truth in his statement. When properly qualified, the assertion that cartels tend to be unstable, like Gresham's law, is a testable proposition following from the axiom system of microeconomic theory.

The Meaning of Self-Interest in Microeconomic Theory

Because self-interest plays such a central role in microeconomic theory, it is important that the economist's use of this term be clarified. In the examples just cited, self-interest is identified with the money payoffs from decisions, and in fact many of the testable propositions of microeconomics are concerned with the implications of purely monetary incentives. But self-interest is interpreted much more broadly than this by economists. In microeconomic theory, an individual's self-interest is what the individual views as desirable to him, and is not at all confined to actions that increase the individual's money holdings or wealth.

Thus it is not inconsistent with the notion of self-interest for an individual to turn down a higher paying job that involves more responsibility and more stress; or for an individual to give large sums to charity or to engage in other "unselfish" acts. Behavior consistent with self-interest requires only that the expected consequences of such decisions be preferred by the decision maker to the consequences of alternative decisions that could have been made. Stated in this way, it might appear that any behavior at all could be rationalized as being motivated by self-interest; after all, why would anyone take a certain action if he didn't gain (in some sense) more from that action than from the alternatives available to him?

But of course this line of reasoning presupposes that in making decisions, individuals do so in a "rational" manner, weighing the costs and benefits to them. This is in fact the approach taken in microeconomic theory. A distinctive feature of the theory is that all decision making by consumers and firm managers is assumed to be rational in this sense; consumers and firm managers are assumed to be purposive decision makers whose choices are consistent with their own evaluations of their self-interest. Furthermore, it is assumed that the choices made by these decision makers could be predicted simply from a knowledge of their preferences and the relevant features of the alternatives available to them. This is the "economic man" of microeconomic theory, man as "rational" decision maker.

The economic man of microeconomic theory is an idealization of reality. Human behavior is never as predictable as the economist's theory assumes, nor is it always possible to explain behavior on the basis of self-interest. Economic man is a valuable construct in explaining and predicting certain aspects of the functioning of the society, particularly those relating to the production and distribution of goods and services and their prices. In other areas of human behavior such as family life and other interpersonal relationships, the self-interest hypothesis has limited predictive or explanatory power, and other models of man the decision maker and man the social animal come to the fore.

Property Rights and Self-Interest

There are, of course, restrictions on the expression of self-interest in any society, including restrictions that apply to its economic activities. This is an inevitable consequence of simply living together. Every society develops a set of laws, regulations, and customs that constrain and channel the expression of self-interest. Your ability to express your self-interest in a certain manner means, among other things, that I do not have the ability to keep you from acting in that manner. Rules must be developed, if only by default, to resolve possible conflicts of self-interest and to encourage cooperative activities that further mutual self-interest, if the society is to function efficiently.

We will be particularly concerned with the restrictions and encouragements of self-interest that apply to the production, distribution, and exchange of commodities. In this context, a matter of particular interest is the structure of property rights of a society. Ownership of a commodity really means possession of a certain set of property rights with respect to that commodity, that is, the ability to take certain actions with respect to the commodity that are protected by the laws of the society. Among the most important of such rights is the right to limit access to the commodity on the part of other individuals in the society, which amounts to the legally protected ability to charge others for the use of the services of the commodity (as in renting a piece of land), or to transfer the ownership of the commodity to someone else (as in selling title to a piece of land).

Property rights vary widely from commodity to commodity within a society, and from society to society. Since 1865, property rights in human beings have been abolished in the United States; in many countries, ownership of a tract of land does not include ownership of the mineral resources beneath the soil; in the Middle Ages, ownership of an estate typically did not include the right to sell it; possessing a sum of money available for lending does not include the right to charge "usurious" rates of interest (what is usury varies from state to state); the right to possess a bottle of liquor for sale to others was abrogated during Prohibition (but, interestingly, not the right of a consumer to possess a few bottles at home); and so on.

Many of the most paradoxical results of microeconomic theory arise because of the special nature of the property rights associated with specific commodities. As we shall see, there is strong evidence that by decreasing the number of men and ships employed in ocean fishing, it would be possible actually to increase the harvest of fish on a sustained basis. This strange conclusion reflects the fact that ocean fisheries are *common-property* resources, that is, resources which anyone is free to exploit without being required to pay an access charge—there are no enforceable property rights to the stock of most ocean fish. Common property resources invite exploitation today without concern for tomorrow, since there is no way for an individual fishing firm to capture the future rewards that accrue from practicing conservation today. Similarly, the inability to define and police property rights to underground pools of oil leads to inefficient pumping practices; like ocean fish, oil is in part a common property resource.

What is produced, exchanged, and consumed in a society are bundles of property rights that we call commodities. The pattern of economic activity within a society is closely linked to the structure of property rights of that society, because it is through the acquisition of property rights that self-interest is expressed and incentives operate.

Competition and Self-Interest

In the *Wealth of Nations*, Adam Smith argued that an "invisible hand" guided the self-interest motivated actions of individual consumers and firm managers toward outcomes that are in the interest of society at large. Adam Smith's invisible hand refers to the workings of *competition* in the structure of markets in a society.

It is in the self-interest of each of us to "buy cheap and sell dear," and so economists assume that this is what people in fact try to do. With a single seller of a product, output can be restricted and price increased so that the monopolist exploits his customers to the full in the course of maximizing profits. But with many producers selling the same product, the ability of any one producer to set his price high is constrained by the fact that his customers will buy elsewhere; competition among producers forces each to sell at the level of the firm charging the lowest price. Moreover, competition encourages firms to seek cheaper production methods and to use inputs efficiently. If they persist in using an outmoded, costly technology, they will be undercut by their more efficient rivals. As consumers, we want to buy cheap; but with many consumers of a product, price will be bid up to a level that reflects the demands of those willing to pay the most for the good.

Competition acts to protect individuals from exploitation by monopolistic buyers or sellers, and it provides the incentives for firms to produce goods that are demanded by consumers, as well as moving firms toward the least-cost methods of producing such goods. It should be emphasized that profit-maximizing conduct is crucial to these conclusions; there is nothing "antisocial" about a businessman trying to make as much as he can, so long as he is constrained by the competition of others in the same industry trying to do the same thing. When competition is absent, then problems develop for an economic system—not simply problems in terms of a distorted distribution of income in favor of monopolies, but problems in the sense that there are inefficiencies in the system: either the right mix of outputs is not produced or inputs are used inefficiently.

Admittedly, the question as to whether competition converts self-interest motivated actions into socially desirable results is a complex one, primarily because it involves issues that go beyond science and instead involve ethics. We will spend a considerable portion of this book discussing this question.

Normative and Positive Economics

No doubt you have heard the old one-liner that is resurrected whenever the nation gets into economic difficulties: "Put four economists in a room, and they'll come up with five different opinions." Presumably if the four people were physicists discussing issues related to their field, there would be one agreed-upon, scientific conclusion; does this indicate that economics is not really a science, or is the one-liner just a put-on?

Since there are eighteen chapters to follow that deal with the axiom system and the testable propositions of microeconomics, needless to say, we start with the assumption that there is indeed a scientific basis for microeconomics. While the propositions are neither as specific nor as well tested as comparable propositions in the physical sciences, still they occupy the same status as scientific assertions. Put four

economists in a room, and the odds are strong that they will agree concerning these propositions.

But economists are also called upon to advise government agencies as to the merits of various policies ranging from tax proposals and government-financed energy programs to interest rates. Such measures will affect the distribution of income in the society as well as the pattern of production and consumption of goods and services. It is one thing to predict the outcome of a proposed policy, and quite another to decide whether the policy is desirable in the sense that it is in the "interest of the society at large." The first is a scientific issue, and the second is an ethical issue.

Economists do disagree at times about the effects of a proposed policy, in part because some predictions involve guesses as to political decisions and social trends that are beyond the scope of economics. But most disagreements among economists arise over the issue of what is in the interest of the society at large. Economists with the same approach to scientific issues can have markedly different views on the desirability of a policy. The politics of members of the economics profession ranges from left-wing anarchy to somewhat to the right of Attila the Hun, and these views are reflected in their evaluations of the desirability (as contrasted with the effects) of economic policies.

Disagreements among economists on ethical issues will probably never be resolved; however, over the past twenty to twenty-five years, there has developed a framework within which economists, by more or less tacit agreement, conduct their sometimes acrimonious discussions of ethics. This is the field of *normative economics* (often referred to as *welfare economics*), in distinction to *positive (scientific) economics*.

Like positive economics, normative economics is based on a system of axioms, but these axioms concern ethics. Neither the axioms of normative economics nor the propositions derived from them are verifiable through empirical observations. Anyone is free to accept or reject the conclusions of normative economics as he wishes, simply by accepting or rejecting the axiom system—there are no scientific issues involved.

Since economists play a role in government policy making—and sometimes a major role at that, it is well worth your while to find out how they approach ethical questions. Among other things, we can arrive at some conclusions as to just how effective Adam Smith's "invisible hand" really is. The elements of normative economics are spelled out in chapter 13 of this book, and are then applied to various problem areas in chapters 14 through 18.

The Perfectly Competitive Economy

Chapters 1 through 12 are concerned with explaining the axiom system of microeconomic theory and deriving various propositions from those axioms. The meaning of self-interest is discussed in some detail as is the law of supply and demand. Attention is centered upon the simplest of the theoretical models employed by economists, namely the model of a perfectly competitive economy. Because it is so simplified, the theoretical abstractions employed by economists appear in their starkest form. By zeroing in on the operation of a highly simplified economic system, we can most easily trace the logic of self-interest as expressed through a system of markets. It is essential to understand how a perfectly competitive economy works. When more realistic assumptions are introduced, such as market power, uncertainty, and the like, the logic of the competitive economy still remains central to an understanding of these more complicated systems.

I

The Groundwork

1

The Structure of a Perfectly Competitive Economy

The central problem of economics is how to allocate scarce resources among competing ends. There is no economic problem for a society when goals are not in conflict or resources are so abundant that there is no need to conserve them. Needless to say, the real world is not blessed with either superabundant resources or harmonious goals. Consequently, each society develops a set of institutions to direct the way in which scarce resources are to be allocated. These institutions—the society's "economic system"—determine what goods the society produces, how they are produced, and who obtains them.

A society is distinguished by certain features: (1) natural resources such as water, land, forests, and minerals; (2) a population characterized by its age and geographical distribution, together with its distribution of skills; (3) stocks of man-made resources such as buildings, machinery, and inventories of durable and nondurable goods; (4) a history, which affects not only the preferences of individuals for goods and services, but also the technological know-how available and the distribution of wealth within the society; and (5) an institutional structure of laws, customs, and habits. The economic system operates within the constraints imposed by these fundamental characteristics of an ongoing society.

Real-world economic systems are incredibly complex. To make headway in understanding how they work, we must isolate for study certain crucial features of these systems. This chapter outlines the general structure of the simplest of the market-oriented economic systems, the perfectly competitive economy. We will see how it coordinates the many complex interrelations involved in producing, distributing, and exchanging goods and services in a society.

Markets and Transactions Costs

From the economist's point of view, the interesting thing about the organization of a society is its structure of markets. Self-interest and markets dominate the economist's thinking: self-interest explains how individuals act, and markets provide the arenas in which self-interest is expressed. The more comprehensive the system of markets a society possesses, the richer the economic interrelationships possible within the society.

Economists use the term *market* to refer to the complex of activities through which potential buyers and sellers of goods are brought into contact with one another to engage in purchases and sales of goods. In our society, markets range in sophistication from such highly structured institutions as the New York Stock Exchange to the informality of the garage sale down the block. But common to all markets is the confrontation of potential buyers and sellers, making bids and offers in the process of determining the terms whereby sales take place. It is this central feature of markets that is isolated for study in the economist's theoretical picture of the economic system.

The very existence of markets is evidence that gains can be achieved by the members of a society through exchanging goods and services. Buying and selling are voluntary activities that would not be undertaken unless the gains from these activities outweighed the costs incurred by the market participants; and markets act to facilitate such activities. In fact, it is easy to see that each purchaser or seller of any good must view himself better off by any market transaction to which he is a party; after all, participants engage in such transactions voluntarily. For this reason, purchases and sales do not involve gainers and losers; there are only *gainers*.

The process of engaging in exchange entails costs for sellers and buyers. Such costs are referred to as *transactions costs*. There are costs involved in locating potential buyers or sellers, in identifying the characteristics of goods offered for sale, and (the most pervasive transactions cost) establishing and enforcing property rights to goods. For a number of commodities, markets do not exist, and buying and selling do not take place because the costs of policing agreements between parties outweigh any benefits derived from the agreements. When such transactions costs preclude the development of a market for a commodity, we say that there is *market failure*.

To illustrate, there are potential benefits both to motorists and to the victims of breathing problems in the Los Angeles basin from agreements under which the victims pay motorists to reduce mileage travelled. But the costs of enforcing agreements between individual smog victims and individual motorists exceed the benefits to the victims; hence no market in pollution contracts exists. Instead, the state and federal governments impose regulations on motorists and car manufacturers.

In our analysis of markets, we will follow the usual mode of economists, examining the simplest case first—namely, markets that operate without friction. In these markets potential sellers of a good come into contact with potential buyers of the good and effect transactions (purchases or sales) with no cost associated with the process of exchange itself. It is further assumed that an individual can find a market for any good he wants to buy or sell. We refer to this as the assumption that *there are zero transactions costs in the economy.*

This assumption is unrealistic, and we will have to modify it to capture certain important aspects of market behavior. Identifying and enforcing property rights entails some cost for most commodities. But for the most part in our theoretical discussion of the competitive economy, we will stick to the assumption that markets operate with zero transactions costs.

Uncertainty

It is convenient to adopt a further simplifying assumption: that decision makers, whether consumers or firm managers, have full knowledge of the alternatives available to them, and that they know with certainty the consequences to them of any alternative chosen. This is the assumption of a world of *perfect certainty*. It is considerably easier to understand the workings of an economy operating under perfect certainty than one in which uncertainty is present. Beyond this, an understanding of the certainty case makes more obvious the crucial role played by institutions such as insurance and the futures markets in mitigating problems of uncertainty.

Needless to say, when we assume a world of certainty we are avoiding some of the most difficult problems associated with decision making and markets. These problems will be dealt with in the later chapters of this book.

Stocks and Flows in an Economy

Before describing the structure of markets in a competitive economy, we need to distinguish between *stocks* and *flows* in an economy. In a reservoir, the stock of water is the pool behind the dam, and the water flows from that pool to users below the dam. Water can continue to flow to users indefinitely only if the pool is maintained by an inflow from above the dam, but there is a clear-cut distinction between the size of the pool at a particular time and the flow of water from the pool as a rate per unit of time.

The same distinction holds with respect to economic magnitudes. An economy possesses stocks of natural and man-made resources, together with a stock of human skills. The value of these stocks at a particular time is referred to as the *wealth* of the economy at that time. But these stocks permit a flow of services to the consumers in the economy over future time periods, in the form of labor services; services of buildings, machines, and the like; and goods produced using these services as inputs. The value of the goods and services received by consumers during a given time period is re-

ferred to as the *income* of the economy for that period. Just as with the pool, services can continue to flow only if the stock of resources is replenished while individual resources are wearing out, so that a part of the services of labor, buildings, machines, and so on is required for replacement and maintenance of the existing resource stocks. It is usual to refer to the value of goods and services produced less the value of services employed in replacement and maintenance as the *net income* of the economy for the given time period.

Briefly, stocks are magnitudes that are measured at points in time, and flows are magnitudes measured per unit of time. We have x barrels of oil reserves on January 1, 1976 and we produced y barrels of oil during 1975; the first is a stock and the second is a flow. The possibility of obtaining a flow of services arises only because there is a stock of a resource from which the services flow.

The distinction between stocks and flows is important because markets exist both for resources (or titles to resources) and for the flow of services produced by these resources. The interrelationships among these markets are among the most interesting features of the competitive economy.

Intermediaries and Titles to Resources

In reality, corporations own a substantial share of natural and man-made resources. But corporations in turn are owned by their shareholders. The corporation acts as an *intermediary* between its consumer-owners and the resources to which they indirectly hold title. Compared with individual proprietorships and partnerships, the corporation has developed as a business form primarily because of its economic advantages in raising large amounts of financial capital. These advantages arise because the owners of the corporation have a limited liability for its debts, and the life span of the corporation is independent of the life spans of its individual owners.

Intermediaries exist in many spheres of economic activity. For example, financial intermediaries such as commercial banks and savings and loan associations dominate the markets for business and consumer loans. Financial intermediaries collect funds from individual depositors in order to invest them in loans to business and consumers. They have arisen because of the high transactions costs involved in lending activities when carried on by individual consumers. These costs can be substantially reduced when lending is carried on by a specialized institution such as the financial intermediary.

If we were involved in a detailed description of the institutional structure of our economy, intermediaries would be of central importance to us. Our purpose instead is to acquire an understanding of the way in which markets function to determine patterns of production, consumption, and exchange. In such a study, intermediaries become of secondary importance. As a consequence, we will ignore the role played by intermediaries and assume instead that titles to resources and decisions concerning these resources are in the hands of individuals.

A Perfectly Competitive Economy

In a perfectly competitive economy, title to all resources is vested in private hands; decision-making takes place at the level of individual consumers and firm managers without outside coercion; markets exist for all goods and services; no consumer or firm possesses any market power; and buyers and sellers are *anonymous*, in the sense that they are concerned only with the prices and qualities of the goods being sold, and not with the identities of sellers and buyers.

To simplify our analysis of the market structure of a perfectly competitive economy, it is convenient to assume that all resources are owned directly by individual consumers, who rent the use of such resources to business firms. Consumers occupy center stage in the competitive economy. They own all of the resources; supply all of the labor services; engage in saving, investing, borrowing, and lending; and purchase the final goods produced by firms. Each of these activities involves decision making —arriving at choices from among a set of alternatives. The consumer must also coordinate all of these activities to bring his choices in line with the limitations imposed by his budget.

Firms appear simply as production units, converting inputs into outputs. They emerge as separate decision-making entities because production requires the coordination of a number of distinct activities. In principle, production could take place through agreements arrived at in the market among the individuals engaged in the various separate activities involved in the production process. But the transactions costs associated with implementing these agreements can be reduced substantially through the creation of a coordinating agency, the firm. There are limits to the gains to be achieved through such coordination, and firms specialized to certain products or production processes emerge when agreements between firms cost less to police than concentration of activities within a given firm.

When an individual enters a competitive market, he is informed of the market price for the good in question and, given that price, he decides how many units of the good to buy or sell. He can buy as many units as he wishes (if he has the money) or sell as many units as he wishes (up to the stock he holds) at the going market price. The actions of all individuals participating in the market determine the market price of the good, but each individual's share of the market is so minute that he has no bargaining power. That is, he cannot influence the market price in his favor by his decisions to buy or sell.

A perfectly competitive market is more like the market for winter wheat than like the market for the house you want to buy, where you will probably haggle with the owner about price. It is important to keep this in mind, because in common parlance, we tend to think of competition as overt confrontation among market participants, as when two gasoline stations engage in a price war. A price war is not possible in a perfectly competitive market since either station could sell as much gas as it wanted at the going market price and could sell nothing at a price above the market. Every buyer and every seller is a *price taker* rather than a *price maker*, when perfect competition prevails. A perfectly competitive market is most closely approximated in reality when there are large numbers of buyers and sellers dealing in a good with uniform characteristics, as is the case with winter wheat.

The information that an individual obtains when he participates in a perfectly competitive market is simply the kind of good being traded and the price per unit of the good; no other information is transmitted in the market, and this information is free in the sense that the individual does not have to expend either time or resources to obtain it. Again we are dealing with an idealized situation; as a practical matter, purchasing agents more than pay for themselves because they are able to identify the quality of goods and have information as to prices; in the real world, price and quality information is generally expensive to obtain.

Markets in Resources

At any point in time, we can talk about the distribution of resource ownership among the consumers in a society. With each consumer we can associate the stocks of resources to which he holds title. Summing over all consumers, we account for the existing resource stocks available to the society. Three types of interrelated markets are of interest to us so far as resources are concerned.

First, there is the *market in ownership claims to resources*. Consumers can buy and sell titles to various resources among themselves: land, mineral resources, forests, as well as capital goods such as plant, machinery, and equipment. In the markets in resource titles consumers face consumers as potential buyers and sellers.

Second, there is the *rental market for resource services*, in which the use of a resource such as land is made available to someone else for some specified period of time. Title to the resource remains in the hands of the owner, but use of the resource for the period is acquired by the renter. Since all production in the economy is assumed to take place in firms, consumers owning titles to resources are the suppliers in the rental markets, while firms are the demanders for the use of resources.

Third, we have the *market for newly produced resources*. Certain resources such as buildings and machinery can be produced by business firms, while others are nonproducible.

Resources that can be produced by business firms are referred to as *capital goods.* Business firms producing capital goods sell such goods to consumers (only consumers own titles to resources), thus adding to the stock of resources in the society. In order for the society to increase its stock of capital goods, production of consumer goods must be curtailed (at least in a full employment economy). This means that some consumers must engage in *saving*, spending less than their current income on consumption. Consumer savings represent the demand for currently produced capital goods. In the market for newly produced resources, business firms supply such goods and consumers demand them.

There are some obvious links among these markets. In the first place, the value of the title to an acre of land clearly depends upon the rental that the acre can earn in production, and this criterion for value applies to all resources. Furthermore, there exists a link between the price at which newly produced resources are sold and the value of a unit of an existing resource. If a tractor with certain characteristics can be bought in the new tractor market for $10,000, then the title to an existing tractor with the same characteristics will sell for close to $10,000 as well.

In addition to the links across markets for a given resource, there are links within markets with respect to different kinds of resources. For example, the amount of rent that an acre of land can earn is dependent in part on the rent being charged for the use of tractors; if land gets too expensive, farmers will cultivate land more intensively by using more machinery. Similarly, if land rents get high in a city, business firms will construct skyscrapers rather than one- or two-story buildings, economizing on land and increasing their demands for the use of other resources.

Markets for Ownership Shares in Firms

Titles to resources are not the only assets in a society. Consumers may own business firms by purchasing stock certificates issued by the firms. In the market for outstanding shares, consumers face consumers as suppliers and demanders. The income accruing from ownership of a stock certificate in a certain business firm is the share of the firm's profits represented by the certificate. If we assume that the shareholders' only interest in owning stock certificates is for the income they can earn from them, then the prices of various stock certificates are related in a particularly simple fashion. For a firm that is expected to earn $100,000 in profits per year and has 1,000 shares outstanding, each share must sell at the same price as a share issued by a firm with $1,000,000 in profits per year and 10,000 shares outstanding. To put it another way, the price/earnings ratio of all stock shares must be equal. Keep in mind that we are dealing with a world in which there is no uncertainty. Needless to say, price/earnings ratios differ markedly among shares actually sold on the exchanges precisely because there is so much uncertainty about future earnings.

In addition to the equalization of rate of return over the shares of different firms, there is a further interrelationship between the stock market and the market in titles to resources. Suppose a particular capital good earns a rent of $100 per year (net of all expenses), and the price for title to that capital good is $1,500. Then a share of stock in a firm earning $100,000 per year with 1,000 shares outstanding will sell for $1,500 as well. If the share sold for more than $1,500, consumers would sell shares in order to acquire titles to the capital good offering the same income per year but costing less. This analysis shows that markets for different kinds of assets are closely interrelated, whether such assets represent ownership claims to resources or shares in business firms.

The Lending Market

Consumers can borrow or lend, or (what amounts to the same thing) can issue promissory notes or purchase such notes issued by others. Thus there exists a lending market in which consumers appear as both demanders and suppliers. A consumer issues a promissory note in order to increase his current consumption at the expense of future consumption, while a purchaser of such a note sacrifices present consumption to obtain future consumption.

In a world of certainty, notes issued by consumers offer guaranteed interest income that is equivalent to income earned from ownership of resources or of stock certificates. Again, a close tie exists between the loan market and the markets for other assets. The rate of return earned by purchasing a promissory note must approximate the rate of return that can be earned from owning title to a resource or owning a stock certificate.

The major difference between the loan market and the markets for other assets is that for consumers as a whole, the net amount of assets represented by promissory notes is zero. If one consumer owns a dollar's worth of assets in the form of a promissory note, there must be some other consumer in the society with a liability of a dollar, representing notes he has issued. Applied to the market for loans, the assumption of perfect competition means that any consumer can borrow or lend as much as he wishes at the current rate of interest prevailing in the market. Such a market is said to be a *perfect lending market*.

We have thus far described the skeleton of the structure of markets that relate to assets; it is now time to look at the markets that deal with the flow of currently produced consumer goods and services.

Markets for Goods and Services

The function of business firms is to convert inputs into outputs. Certain inputs represent the services of resources such as buildings, machinery, and equipment. As we have seen, business firms enter the rental markets as demanders for the services of such resources, while consumers owning title to these resources are suppliers. Firms also use as inputs the outputs of other firms, by employing intermediate products (semifinished goods or raw materials) in the production process. Thus beyond participating as demanders in the rental markets for resource services, firms also participate in the *market for intermediate products*, but as both demanders and suppliers.

Just as there is substitution among various resources in production, there is substitution among intermediate products, and so the prices of intermediate products are related to one another. For example, an automobile firm will use leather for upholstery in place of plastics if the price of leather is sufficiently low relative to the price of plastics. Further, intermediate products can sometimes be substituted for resources in production; hence rentals for the use of resources are tied to prices of intermediate products.

Two markets in which consumers face firms are of central importance; these are the *labor market*, and the *market for consumer goods and services*. In a sense, labor is a resource like land and capital goods. But there is one essential way in which labor differs from these other resources. The supply of labor time made available in the labor market depends not only on the income that can be earned by the laborer, but also on the trade-off between income and leisure in terms of the laborer's preferences. Thus things are not quite so simple as in the markets for the use of other resources.

An individual who owns an acre of land presumably will offer the services of that acre at any positive rent (net of expenses) prevailing in the market for use of the land; after all, any rent is better than no income at all from the land. With labor services, the supply forthcoming is sensitive to the wage rate offered on the market, and ultimately reflects preferences by consumers between leisure and income.

As an input in production, labor services are competitive with the services of land, other natural resources, capital goods, and intermediate products. Hence the wage rate prevailing in the market depends upon prices of these other inputs. As rentals for capital goods fall relative to wage rates, labor tends to be replaced by machinery in the production process.

There is a link between the labor market and the markets for assets. Highly skilled labor earns a premium wage because of its higher productivity in production. But to acquire skill, a person must be educated and trained, usually at considerable expense in time and current income. The consumer-laborer may choose to *invest in human capital*—that is, to forego current income in order to acquire more training and thus to increase his earning power in the future. Such a decision involves the same kinds of elements as does saving to acquire newly produced capital goods. In either case, the decision depends upon the consumer's time preferences with respect to income—to what extent is he or she willing to trade off income in the present for higher income in the future?

The decision also depends upon the rate of return that can be earned from investing in human capital relative to rates of return from other investments. If investment in a capital good promises to pay 10 percent per year, while investment in training pays 20 percent, individuals will tend to use their savings (or borrow, if the interest rate is less than 20 percent) to acquire more training, rather than invest in capital goods. Alternatively, individuals owning capital goods will sell them in order to invest their funds in further education. Such decisions tend to bring the rate of return on human capital into line with the rates of return on investment in other assets in the economy.

Finally, there is the *market for consumer goods and services*. Prices of consumer goods and the pattern of production of such goods within the economy reflect both the preferences of consumers and the technology and cost structure of firms, as well as the level and distribution of income among consumers. Firms tend to produce the commodities whose profits are highest, and consumers substitute goods for one another on the basis of their tastes and the relative prices of goods.

Consumer goods are the final stage in the production process. Thus, production costs and prices for these goods incorporate the costs generated at each stage of production. These costs in turn reflect the prices of inputs used in production—labor time, intermediate products, and the services of resources—and thus are directly linked to incomes earned by consumers in their roles as suppliers of labor time and as asset owners.

A shift in consumer preferences clearly affects the entire structure of markets in the competitive economy. Changes in the production pattern for consumer goods also have repercussions in the markets for inputs, which in turn lead to changes in the various asset markets.

The Circular Flow of Economic Activity

The interrelationships among markets, consumers, and firms can be thought of in terms of two simultaneous circular flows: goods and services on the one hand and money payments on the other. Figure 1-1 indicates the nature of these flows.

The inner flow traces the conversion of resource services into consumer goods and newly produced capital goods (including additions to human capital). These final goods are distinguished from intermediate goods, which are inputs for firms. The outer flow traces the flow of money through the system, moving opposite to the flow of goods and services. Outlays by consumers for final goods become the revenues of firms, which are returned to consumers either as wage and rental income or as profits.

The distribution of income among consumers depends in part on the distribution of

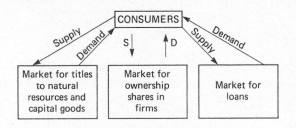

FIG. 1-2   *Asset markets*

three elements: resource holdings, labor skills (human capital), and shares in firms. It also depends on the rentals that are paid for the use of resources and on wage rates, which are determined in the markets for resource services. The prices paid for products in the markets for final goods depend on their costs and on the demands for such goods by consumers. These demands in turn depend in part on the level and distribution of income among consumers. Finally, the prices paid for final goods influence the demand for resource services and hence the rentals and wage rates paid in the market for resource services.

It can be concluded that in a competitive economy, "everything depends on everything else." Admittedly this is not a very helpful statement, but it must be kept constantly in mind as we try to unravel the web of interrelationships in the economy.

Figure 1-2 shows how supply and demand work in the asset markets, where no goods or services are created and no production takes place. Instead, the asset markets redistribute titles to resources, shares in firms, and promissory notes among consumers. Prices prevailing in these markets depend on the earnings from rentals of resources and on profits of firms, as determined in the flow markets of the economy.

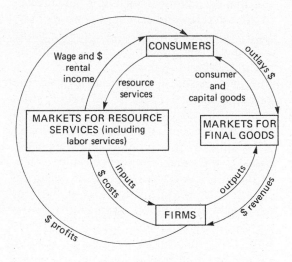

FIG. 1-1   *Circular flows*

The Consumer's Balance Sheet and Income Statement

A convenient way to summarize the status of the consumer relative to the asset and flow markets of the economy is to construct a balance sheet and an income statement. The consumer's balance sheet (fig. 1-3) lists at a point in time the value of all assets owned by the consumer and claims against these assets. The consumer's income statement (fig. 1-4) gives the sources and amounts of income earned by the consumer for the year, together with the consumer's outlays for the year. The balance sheet thus measures the values of *stocks*, while the income statement is concerned with *flows*.

Equity refers to the net worth of the consumer. It is defined as assets less liabilities. The balance sheet always *balances*, since assets equal liabilities plus equity.

January 1, 1976

Assets

Titles to natural resources	$10,000
Titles to capital goods	$20,000
Human capital	$50,000
Shares in firms	$ 5,000
Promissory notes owned by X issued by other consumers	$ 7,000
Total Assets	$92,000

Liabilities

Promissory notes outstanding	$10,000
Equity	$82,000
Total Liabilities plus Equity	$92,000

FIG. 1-3   *Balance sheet for consumer X*

Year Ending December 31, 1976

Income

Rental income—natural resources	$1,000
Rental income—capital goods	$2,000
Wage income	$5,000
Profits	$ 500
Net interest earned on notes	− $ 300
Total Income	$8,200

Outlays

Consumption goods and services	$6,000
Savings	$2,200
Total Outlays	$8,200

FIG. 1-4   *Income statement for consumer X*

In the income statement, total income equals total outlays. These two items balance because savings are defined as the difference between income and expenditures on consumption goods and services. Savings are truly an outlay, since they are used to purchase titles to natural or man-made resources, including human capital. (In the real-world economy, consumer savings often take the form of additions to deposits in financial intermediaries, which in turn invest the savings.)

There is a simple proportion between the sources of income shown in the income statement and the values of the corresponding assets on the balance sheet: income equals 10 percent of the value of the asset. Asset values are determined by the rental incomes that can be earned by the assets. All assets will sell to yield the same rate of return, in this case 10 percent. For simplicity, we have assumed that assets provide constant income streams over time. The more complicated case where income streams vary over time is taken up later in this book.

The rental incomes shown in the income statement are net of maintenance expenses. That is, these amounts are received by consumer X under the assumption that the resources are returned to X at the end of the rental period with no depreciation in value due to usage. For this reason, it is possible to determine the equity position of consumer X as of January 1, 1977 from the data shown in the balance sheet and income statements. Clearly, Mr. X's equity will be $84,200 ($82,000 equity on January 1, 1976 plus $2,200 savings). Precisely how that increase in equity will be distributed among assets (or used to reduce liabilities) cannot be determined from the data given.

Summary

The perfectly competitive economy operates to determine the pattern of production, distribution, and exchange of goods and services for the society through a system of interrelated markets. In the asset markets of the economy, consumers exchange titles to resources, shares in firms, and promissory notes. In the flow markets, firms rent resource services and hire labor services so that they can convert intermediate goods into the final (consumer or capital) goods produced in the economy. Prices in the flow markets help to determine the distribution of income among consumers and the prices of assets. The consumer's balance sheet and income statement provide a summary of his stock-flow situation.

Problems

(These problems are for discussion purposes, as they cannot yet be answered fully with the information provided thus far.)

1. During the 1974 players' strike, the National Football League owners argued that profits ($945,000 per average team in 1973) were not excessive, since NFL teams sell for around $16 million. Thus the investor in an NFL team earns less than 6 percent per year on his investment. Comment on this argument.

   If the argument were accepted, would there ever be a way to identify "excessive" profits? How would you go about determining whether profits in an industry might be "excessive"?

2. There is a theory in economics, going back to at least Karl Marx, that depressions are due to "underconsumption." In its simplest form the argument is this. Only about 70 percent of the value of output is paid in the form of wages; interest, rent, and profits account for the remaining 30 percent. Since wage income is the main source of demand for consumer goods, and since capital goods are demanded primarily to increase the output of consumer goods, there is a fundamental gap between income available to buy consumer goods and the supply of consumer goods forthcoming from the system. This leads to an inherent instability in a capitalistic economy. Comment on this argument.

3. Compared with other countries, the United States has a relatively large stock of capital goods available per laborer employed. Hence this country tends to have an advantage in producing goods that require large capital/labor ratios in production—heavy machinery, chemicals, plastics, and such. What kinds of goods will be "protected" within the United States by tariffs on imports? What will be the effect, on the distribution of income within the United States, of removing such tariffs? Would you expect business leaders or labor leaders to be more in favor of tariffs?

4. We can observe in our society that the dirtiest, most disagreeable and most boring jobs (factory labor, trash removal, janitorial work) tend to pay the least, while the most desirable jobs (movie star, corporation president, TV commentator) pay the most. How do you explain this correlation between job desirability and wages?

5. Under the impact of stricter antipollution standards, new car prices increase. Explain what will happen to used car prices, to rates for renting cars, and to gasoline prices, and why.

The Law of Supply and Demand

A fundamental postulate of microeconomic theory is that prices are established on markets according to the law of supply and demand. Chapter 2 discusses the static and dynamic versions of this law as it applies to a single competitive market, with a distinction drawn between short-term and long-term adjustment processes. In chapter 3, the law is extended to the case of two interrelated competitive markets, using the phase diagram as a tool for analyzing the implications of the law. Included are discussions of elasticity, substitutability and complementarity, and stability of market equilibrium.

2

A Single Competitive Market

In a market economy, prices of goods are determined by supply and demand. Our purpose in this chapter is to convert this rather vague statement into a more precise working tool for the analysis of the behavior of markets.

Market Supply and Demand Schedules

Markets facilitate exchanges between potential buyers and potential sellers of goods. Activities on the market for a particular good determine the price at which it is sold, the number of units bought and sold, and the way in which these units are distributed among potential buyers and potential sellers.

The term *potential* is important in this context. Individuals and firms enter markets with certain notions as to the number of units of various commodities they will buy or sell, *depending on prevailing prices*. If the price of a good is too high, individuals who would have made purchases at lower prices are priced out of the market. If the price is too low, certain sellers will decide to withdraw their goods from sale.

Supply and demand analysis of markets is based on the hypothesis that the forces exerted on the market by potential buyers and sellers determine what the market price will be, and who the actual buyers and sellers will be. At the most primitive level, *market demand* can be interpreted as the forces acting on a market from the point of view of potential buyers, while *market supply* means the forces acting on a market from the point of view of potential sellers. Stated in this way, market supply and demand analysis is simply a convenient way for the economist to classify the forces at work in any given market. The power of supply and demand analysis rests upon a somewhat more specialized interpretation of these terms, however.

We begin with the notion of a *market demand schedule*—a listing (for each price that might prevail in the market) of the amounts that potential buyers are willing to take off the market per unit of time at the prices given. Similarly, a *market supply schedule* is a listing of the amounts that potential sellers are willing to put up for sale per unit of time at each price that might prevail in the market. Table 2.1 illustrates these two schedules.

It is also convenient to graph the market demand and supply schedules (fig. 2-1). The curves labeled $S(p)$ and $D(p)$ are referred to as the *market supply curve* and the *market demand curve* for the good in question. Reading along the $S(p)$ curve, we can determine the

TABLE 2-1   *Market Supply and Demand*
            Schedules

Price* p	Quantity Demanded† D(p)	Quantity Supplied‡ S(p)
$10	0	1,500
$ 8	200	1,200
$ 6	400	900
$ 4	600	600
$ 2	800	300
$ 0	1,000	0

*Price per unit of the good.

†The number of units of the good that potential buyers would take off the market per unit of time *at that price.*

‡The number of units of the good that potential sellers would put on the market per unit of time *at that price.*

number of units of the good that would be supplied at any given price, while the $D(p)$ curve tells us the number of units of the good that would be demanded at any price. If the market price were $6 per unit of the good, then 400 units of the good would be demanded per unit of time while 900 would be supplied. p and q on the graph refer to *price* per unit of the good and *quantity* (number of units of the good), respectively.

In the graph, the demand curve slopes downward to the right, and the supply curve slopes upward to the right: the typical situation in competitive markets. Under certain assumptions, it may be proven that supply curves in a competitive economy slope upward while demand curves slope downward. These assumptions include some restrictions on the technology facing firms, and the hypothesis that, with prices constant, each consumer buys more units of each good if his income is increased.

There are exceptions to the typical situation pictured in the graph. When they arise, they create certain problems. These will cause us difficulties, as the later sections of this chapter will illustrate. Still, in most cases, we will be working with "typical" supply and demand curves.

It should be pointed out that the location and shape of the demand and supply curves for a given good are influenced by variables other than the price of the good itself. Among these variables are prices of other goods, the level and distribution of income among consumers, and the technology of firms. Demand and supply schedules such as in table 2-1 should be viewed as relating quantity demanded or supplied to price of the good, assuming that other variables are held fixed at some preassigned levels. When these variables change, then the demand and supply curves for the given good generally shift their locations and shapes. We will return to this issue later in this chapter.

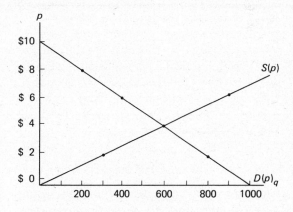

FIG. 2-1   *Market supply and demand curves*

Elasticity of Market Demand and Supply

In classifying market demand and supply curves, a particularly convenient concept is *elasticity*. Economists use many different elasticity measures, such as "own" price elasticity, cross price elasticity, and income elasticity. The purpose of all of these measures is to express the *responsiveness* of quantity demanded (or supplied) to a change in a given variable (such as own price, price of another good, or income).

The elasticity of demand (or supply) for a good, relative to one of these variables is defined as the percent change in quantity demanded (or supplied) of the good per unit of time, for a 1 percent change in the given variable. For example, the ("own") price elasticity of demand for gasoline is the percent change in gallons of gasoline demanded per unit of time, for a 1 percent change in the price of gasoline per gallon. The income elasticity of demand for gasoline is the percent change in gallons of gasoline demanded per unit of time for a 1 percent change in income.

Because elasticities are defined in terms of ratios of percent changes, their measures are *pure* (dimensionless) numbers; units such as quantities and prices cancel out in the calculation. For this reason, it is possible to compare goods in terms of their elasticity measures. Generally, these measures vary along any given demand or supply curve, taking on different values at different points.

Own Price Elasticity of Demand

The most widely used elasticity measure is the ("own") price elasticity of demand, denoted by η_D. Let Δp denote the change in the price of a good, and let $\Delta D(p)$ denote the change in quantity demanded of the good associated with that price change. Then η_D is given by

$$\eta_D = \frac{\text{\% change in quantity demanded}}{\text{\% change in price}} = \frac{\dfrac{\Delta D(p)}{D(p)}}{\dfrac{\Delta p}{p}}. \quad (1)$$

Since the slope of the demand curve equals

$$\frac{\Delta p}{\Delta D(p)},$$

this may also be written as

$$\eta_D = \frac{p}{D(p)} \cdot \frac{\Delta D(p)}{\Delta p}$$

$$= \frac{p}{D(p)} \times \frac{1}{\text{slope of demand curve}} \quad (2)$$

For the "typical" case in which the demand curve slopes downward to the right, η_D takes on values between zero and minus infinity. A distinction is drawn among the following three cases.

1. η_D is between 0 and -1: the demand curve is *inelastic*. For this range of values of η_D, a 1 percent increase in price leads to less than a 1 percent decrease in quantity demanded.

2. η_D is between -1 and minus infinity: the demand curve is *elastic*. For this range of values of η_D, a 1 percent increase in price leads to more than a 1 percent decrease in quantity demanded.

3. η_D equals -1: demand is of *unitary* elasticity. A 1 percent increase in price leads to a 1 percent fall in quantity demanded.

Intuitively then, when demand is inelastic, it is relatively unresponsive to price changes; when demand is elastic, it is relatively responsive to price changes.

The slope of the demand curve in figure 2-1 is −$1/100 units. That is, a $1 decrease in price leads to a 100 unit increase in quantity demanded. Using the elasticity formula, we obtain the values given in table 2-2. (Note that elasticity is a pure number since dollars and units cancel out in calculating η_D.)

For the demand curve in figure 2-1 (with demand schedule given in table 2-2), demand is elastic for high prices and inelastic for low prices; it is of unitary elasticity at the curve's midpoint, $5 per unit. If the market demand curve is a straight line, as in the case depicted, demand is *always* elastic at prices above the midpoint of the curve and inelastic below the midpoint, which is of unitary elasticity.

Although straight-line demand curves are often used for illustrative purposes, they are not in any sense typical. As we will see, demand curves linear in all prices and income are precluded by the axioms of microeconomic theory. At best, a linear demand curve should be viewed simply as a convenient approximation to a true nonlinear demand curve.

The relationship between own price elasticity and expenditures is shown in table 2-3. When demand is *inelastic*, then an *increase in price leads to an increase in the total amount spent on purchases of the good*; when demand is *elastic*, an *increase in price leads to a decrease in the total amount spent on the good*; when demand is of *unitary elasticity*, an *increase in price leads to no change in the amount spent on purchases of the good*.

It is also convenient to identify the polar case where η_D equals zero, and its opposite where η_D equals minus infinity. If η_D equals minus infinity for all quantities, we say that the demand curve is *perfectly elastic*. If η_D equals zero for all prices, we say the demand curve is *perfectly inelastic*.

TABLE 2-2   *Own Price Elasticity of Demand*

Price p	Quantity Demanded D(p)	Demand Elasticity η_D	Own Price Elasticity
$10	0	minus infinity	elastic
$ 8	200	−4	elastic
$ 6	400	−1.5	elastic
$ 5	500	−1	unitary
$ 4	600	− .67	inelastic
$ 2	800	− .25	inelastic
$ 0	1,000	0	inelastic

As figure 2-2 indicates, when demand is perfectly elastic, an unlimited number of units are demanded at the going price, but none at any price above that level. When demand is perfectly inelastic, the same number of units are demanded, whatever the price. When demand is perfectly elastic, quantity demanded is completely responsive to any increase in price, falling to zero for any such increase. At the other extreme, quantity demanded is completely unresponsive to price when the demand curve is perfectly inelastic.

TABLE 2-3   *Expenditures and Own Price Elasticity*

Price p	Quantity Demanded D(p)	Expenditures p × D(p)	Own Price Elasticity
$10	0	$ 0	elastic
$ 8	200	$1,600	elastic
$ 6	400	$2,400	elastic
$ 5	500	$2,500	unitary
$ 4	600	$2,400	inelastic
$ 2	800	$1,600	inelastic
$ 0	1,000	$ 0	inelastic

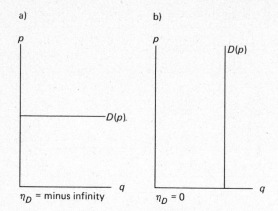

FIG. 2-2   a. *Perfectly elastic demand*
          b. *Perfectly inelastic demand*

Constant Elasticity Demand Curves Generally speaking, the demand curve for a good tends to be more elastic, the more close substitutes there are available for the good. For this reason, demand tends to be more elastic, the more expensive the good is. This correlation is consistent with the case of a linear demand curve, where elasticity increases as price rises.

But in empirical work, to simplify measurement and estimation, it is often assumed that the demand curve has constant elasticity. That is, elasticity of demand is assumed to be the same for every price. A constant elasticity demand curve may be written as

$$D(p) = Ap^\alpha$$

where α is the (constant) elasticity of demand and A is a constant whose value depends upon other prices, income, and the like. In particular, if $\alpha = -1$, the case of unitary elasticity, then the demand curve is a rectangular hyperbola with a constant area under the curve. If

$0 > \alpha > -1$, then demand is inelastic, while if $\alpha < -1$, demand is elastic.

Own Price Elasticity of Supply

Let η_S denote (own) price elasticity of supply of a good, and let Δp denote the change in the price of the good, with $\Delta S(p)$ being the change in quantity supplied due to the change in price. Then η_S is given by

$$\eta_S = \frac{\text{\% change in quantity supplied}}{\text{\% change in price}} = \frac{\dfrac{\Delta S(p)}{S(p)}}{\dfrac{\Delta p}{p}} . \quad (3)$$

For the *typical* case of an upward sloping supply curve, η_S will take on values between zero and (plus) infinity. Again, since the slope of the supply curve equals

$$\frac{\Delta p}{\Delta S(p)},$$

the formula for η_S can be written as

$$\eta_S = \frac{p}{S(p)} \times \frac{1}{\text{slope of supply curve}} . \quad (4)$$

Consider the supply schedule in table 2-4. Graphing the schedule, we can easily verify that

TABLE 2-4   *Supply Schedule*

Price p	Quantity Supplied $S(p)$	Supply Elasticity η_S
$10	800	1.25
$ 8	600	1.33
$ 6	400	1.5
$ 4	200	2
$ 2	0	infinity

Elasticity of Demand: An Illustration

The Cleveland Indians of the American League drew approximately 700,000 fans to their seventy home playing dates during the 1973 baseball season. The Cleveland stadium seats 80,000 per game. Assuming that the owner of the Cleveland club is interested in maximizing his revenue, does this mean that he overpriced tickets to the Cleveland games?

Despite appearances to the contrary (all those empty seats), he might not have overpriced the tickets. It all depends on the location of the demand curve for tickets and its elasticity. With a demand curve such as is depicted in figure 2-3, revenue is maximized at a price of $3 per ticket with attendance of 10,000 per playing date. Attendance could always be increased by lowering the ticket price of course. But with demand inelastic below $3, any price cut leads to a fall in revenue. Empty seats in a stadium might well make sense from an owner's point of view.

In contrast to the case of the Cleveland Indians we have the Cleveland Browns of the National Football League. The Browns play their seven home games each season in the same stadium (Municipal Stadium) that the Indians use for baseball. The Browns sell out all of their home games. Does this mean that the Browns have underpriced their tickets? It should be easy to verify that so long as the demand for football

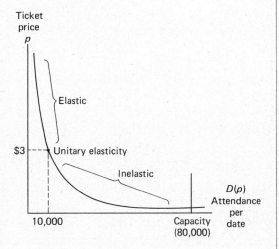

FIG. 2-3 *Demand for tickets*

tickets is elastic (or of unitary elasticity) at the price per ticket where sellouts (80,000 attendance) occur, then the tickets could well be priced to maximize revenue for the Browns' owners. What would be the best evidence that tickets are underpriced? If a secondary market in tickets develops with scalpers selling tickets at prices above the box office rate, then management has underestimated demand; it should have set ticket prices higher.

the slope of supply curve is $1/100 units; using the formula, we find that η_S is as in table 2-4.

For upward sloping supply curves, the elasticity measure η_S is always positive. If η_S is between 0 and $+1$, supply is *inelastic*; if $\eta_S = 1$, supply is of *unitary* elasticity, while if η_S is greater than $+1$, supply is *elastic*. Generally speaking, as price increases, supply tends to become more

inelastic (less elastic), as is the case for the schedule in table 2-4.

It is again of interest to consider the polar cases, the cases of *perfectly elastic* supply where $\eta_S =$ plus infinity, and of *perfectly inelastic* supply where $\eta_S = 0$. Supply curves that are perfectly elastic and perfectly inelastic for all prices or quantities are illustrated in figure 2-4.

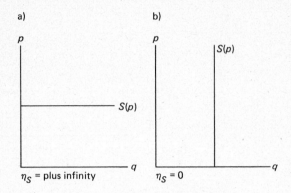

FIG. 2-4   a. *Perfectly elastic supply*
         b. *Perfectly inelastic supply*

Market Equilibrium

Economists use the term *equilibrium* much as physicists do. We say that the market for a particular good is in equilibrium when the forces on the demand side of the market are exactly offset by the forces on the supply side. Specifically, a market price is said to be an *equilibrium price* and the market itself is *in equilibrium*, when the quantity demanded at the price is equal to the quantity supplied at that price. The number of units bought and sold at the equilibrium price is called the *equilibrium quantity*. For the case considered in figure 2-1, equilibrium occurs for $p = \$4$ and $q = 600$.

Equilibrium is a static concept. It describes the state of a market at rest: so long as equilibrium is maintained in a market, neither price nor quantity changes. A substantial part of economic theory deals solely with equilibrium configurations of markets—describing such states and analyzing changes in them after a change in the forces acting on markets. Dy-

namic issues, however, may also arise in the study of a market. For example, a natural question to raise in a dynamic context is whether there is any inherent tendency for price and quantity to move toward equilibrium when the market is initially in a state of disequilibrium.

We might also well ask whether equilibrium exists at all in a given market and whether a market may have more than one equilibrium. In principle at least, it is conceivable that the demand and supply curves for a commodity might not intersect. For example, $D(p)$ and $S(p)$ might both be perfectly inelastic, with $D(p)$ located to the right of $S(p)$. In such a case, no market equilibrium exists. Or $D(p)$ and $S(p)$ may be curves with several intersections, and so several price-quantity pairs would qualify as market equilibriums. Problems associated with the existence and uniqueness of market equilibrium involve technical matters that are beyond the scope of this book; but, generally speaking, the following assertions hold.

1. Given the axiom system underlying the microeconomist's model of a perfectly competitive economy, the existence of an equilibrium in all markets is assured.

2. There is no guarantee that market equilibrium is unique; several price-quantity pairs might represent market-clearing situations.

The Law of Supply and Demand

Taking it as a matter of faith at this point that ensuring the existence of market equilibrium is no problem in a competitive economy, we next turn to the well-known law of supply and demand. This law is usually stated in the popu-

An Example of Market Equilibrium

The notion of market equilibrium is extremely general; it is intended to apply to any commodity. Consider the following example.

It is traditional nowadays for the sports pages to run a story a week or so before the Super Bowl, in which Jimmy the Greek, or some other prominent Las Vegas citizen, announces the point spread between the two teams competing in the game—for example, Pittsburgh favored by 3 points over Minnesota. After the game is played and Pittsburgh wins by 21 points (or loses by 21), there is a critical discussion by the same sports writers about the inaccuracy of the point spread prediction.

This is a misunderstanding of the function of the point spread announcement. The objective in arriving at a point spread is to predict not the outcome of the game, but the market equilibrium in the market for bets on the Super Bowl. These are not completely unrelated of course, but they are not the same thing.

Betting under a point spread works like this. Given that Pittsburgh is favored by 3 points over Minnesota, any bettor can choose to bet on Pittsburgh (that Pittsburgh will win by more than 3 points) or on Minnesota (that Minnesota will lose by less than 3 points, or will win). The bettor puts up $11 to win $10. The $1 difference is the bookie's commission and is called the *vigorish*.

Bookies are not interested in taking any risks on the outcome of the game; they are more than content to collect $11 from a Pittsburgh supporter and $11 from a Minnesota supporter and then pay the winner $20. (If Pittsburgh wins by exactly 3 points, all bets are off.) Thus it is important that the announced point spread not encourage excessive betting on either Pittsburgh or Minnesota; ideally, bets should be exactly balanced.

The point spread will adjust, of course, if too much money comes down on one side or the other, but bets made early still are at the original point spread. Bookies (or the "higher ups" where bookies can "lay off" bets) would far prefer to pick the market-clearing spread than to adjust the point spread. In fact, before the point spread is announced (usually on Tuesday before a game), a selected group of professional gamblers is permitted to bet at the "preliminary" spread to see whether it is close to an equilibrium value.

Don't criticize Jimmy the Greek for missing the Super Bowl score; his job is at once both different and more complicated than simply analyzing football teams. He has to analyze the moods of gamblers all across the country in hopes of coming close to an equilibrium point spread.

---

lar media as *supply and demand determine prices, outputs, and purchases or sales of any good.* This statement can be interpreted to be true by definition (a tautology) since *supply* represents all forces acting on the market from the point of view of potential sellers and *demand,* the forces acting from the side of potential buyers. If all forces are accounted for in demand and supply, then it is true (by definition of terms) that price and quantity are determined by supply and demand.

It is more fruitful, however, to interpret the law of supply and demand as an axiom that describes the operation of markets. This interpretation gives rise to two versions of this law that appear, either implicitly or explicitly, in the professional literature of economics. These can conveniently be classified as static and dynamic.

Law of Supply and Demand (Static)

In any market, the price at which transactions take place is the equilibrium price, and the quantity of the good bought and sold is the equilibrium quantity for that market.

Law of Supply and Demand (Dynamic)

In any market, price is moved by the forces of demand and supply toward the equilibrium level for that market.

To illustrate these versions of the law of supply and demand, we will consider again a "typical" market situation (fig. 2-5). Equilibrium in this market occurs at the price $\bar{p}$ and the quantity $\bar{q}$.

The static version of the law of supply and demand states that the only price at which transactions take place is $\bar{p}$ and when $\bar{p}$ holds, then $\bar{q}$ units are bought and sold per unit of time. Whatever the realism of this version of the law of supply and demand, much of microeconomic theory operates under the assumption that the economy is always at equilibrium. In empirical studies of markets, a common assumption is that the prices and quantities observed are the equilibrium values of these magnitudes. Most of our work in this book will proceed under the assumption that prices and quantities are at their equilibrium levels.

The dynamic version of the law of supply and demand has the following intuitive interpretation. Suppose for some reason that price were not at its equilibrium level. If price is above equilibrium, then quantity supplied exceeds quantity demanded, and price-cutting by sellers (who wish to sell more than the market

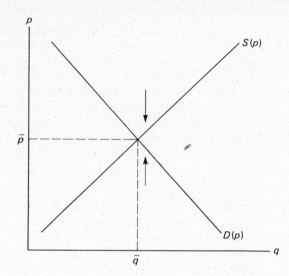

FIG. 2-5   *The law of supply and demand*

will take) forces price down. Such price-cutting persists so long as quantity supplied exceeds quantity demanded; hence price is forced down to its equilibrium level. If price is below equilibrium, then demanders want more units than the market is supplying, and so bids by demanders force price up, again to the equilibrium level.

The Adjustment Process

The process of adjusting to equilibrium through price-cutting by suppliers or bidding up the price by demanders is not consistent with our description of a perfectly competitive market. In a perfectly competitive economy, each buyer and each seller is a price taker; each acts as though he has no influence on prices. Price takers do not cut price or bid up price. This implies that the notion of a perfectly competitive market is a static concept. Only at equilibrium can there be internal consistency between price-taking behavior and the operation of markets in a perfectly competitive economy.

Still, the idea that price falls when quantity supplied exceeds quantity demanded in a market, and rises when quantity demanded exceeds quantity supplied, has considerable predictive content, particularly for the kind of price adjustments that occur in highly organized markets. In the New York Stock Exchange, for example, adjustment of the price of each stock is in the hands of the *specialist*, a broker who accepts buy and sell orders from other brokers, and executes the orders at the prices they specify. His job is to "make a market" in the stock, by buying and selling on his own account to trigger execution of the orders he has on hand. (More importantly from the point of view of incentives, the specialist makes his money by operations on his own account in *making the market*.)

In effect, the specialist is provided with knowledge of the supply and demand schedules for the stock he deals in, and his behavior amounts to lowering price when quantity supplied exceeds quantity demanded and raising it when quantity demanded exceeds quantity supplied. Price adjustments on the stock market are almost instantaneous, and in fact the intuitive version of the law of supply and demand has its greatest predictive power when price adjustments are short term. That is, such adjustments occur quite rapidly, and the supply and demand curves remain unchanged during the process.

In the typical case of a downward sloping demand curve and an upward sloping supply curve, the rule of increasing price when quantity demanded exceeds quantity supplied and decreasing price when quantity supplied exceeds quantity demanded always produces *stability*, in the sense that price moves toward

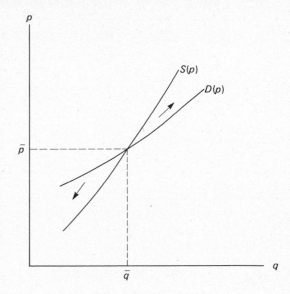

FIG. 2-6   *An unstable market*

its equilibrium level, whatever the initial price in the market is. But when we leave the typical case, problems can arise.

Unstable Equilibrium

In figure 2-6, the $D(p)$ curve slopes upward to the right (quantity demanded increases as price increases), while $S(p)$ still displays the typical supply characteristics. When price is above equilibrium, the price adjustment rule pushes price further away from equilibrium. If price is below $\bar{p}$, the adjustment rule specifies that price should be lowered; again price moves further away from equilibrium. In this case, an equilibrium exists; the static law of supply and demand might well hold, but the dynamic law of supply and demand is violated.

In figure 2-7, there are three points *a*, *b*, *c* at which equilibrium occurs. The points *a* and *c* are *stable* (the dynamic law of supply and

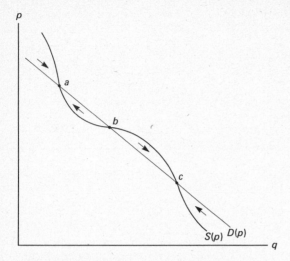

FIG. 2-7   *Multiple equilibrium points*

demand is satisfied), while *b* is an *unstable* equilibrium. In general, when there are multiple equilibrium points in a market, points of stable equilibrium are separated from one another by points of unstable equilibrium.

Because of the very nature of an unstable equilibrium, it would be rare indeed to observe an actual market at such an equilibrium. The slightest disturbance to the market results in a movement of price and quantity away from an unstable equilibrium. For this reason, it is often assumed by economists that the price-quantity pairs observed in markets occur at stable equilibriums, even when we leave the typical case. Generally, this assumption holds throughout this book.

Expectations and Long-Term Dynamic Adjustments—The Cobweb Diagram

An alternative formulation of the adjustment process for a single market emphasizes the role of expectations in production planning decisions. This approach has considerable intuitive appeal as a model of longer term adjustment of markets.

Consider the following situation. In the spring corn farmers must decide how much corn to plant, without knowing for sure what price will prevail in the fall. Their planting decisions thus are based on their expectations of what price they will receive at harvest time. Suppose their price expectations are based on the simple model that still has the best predictive power in the social sciences, namely, "tomorrow will look like today." As a result, the price they expect to prevail at harvest time is the price that they observe at planting time. What are the consequences for the adjustment of the price and quantity of corn over time?

Figure 2-8 illustrates the situation. The $D(p)$ curve is the usual demand curve, relating quantity of corn demanded this period to the current price of corn. The $S(p)$ curve requires a somewhat different interpretation. This curve tells us the bushels of corn that will be supplied *next* period, as a function of the price of corn *this* period. Thus the $S(p)$ curve incorporates the expectations of farmers and their effects on planting decisions.

$\bar{p}, \bar{q}$ are the (long-term) equilibrium price per bushel of corn and output of corn. Suppose $p = p_0$ at time 0. Then farmers will supply q_1 bushels in period #1. q_1 bushels are taken off the market ($D(p) = q_1$) at a price of p_1 in period #1. This leads to a production of q_2 bushels in period #2, which in turn leads to a market-clearing price of p_2 in period #2. The cobweb traces the adjustment of price and quantity over time, and, as can be seen from the diagram, there is convergence over time toward $(\bar{p}, \bar{q})$. In this sense the market is *stable*.

The process of price adjustment in the cobweb case involves changes over time in the

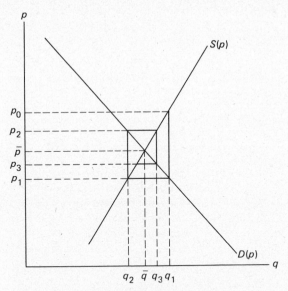

FIG. 2-8   *A stable cobweb diagram*

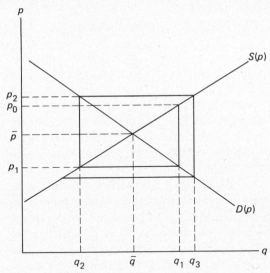

FIG. 2-9   *An unstable cobweb diagram*

quantities of goods supplied, producing a time path of prices that gets closer and closer to equilibrium. In this sense it is a long-term adjustment process. In contrast, the short-term adjustment process discussed in the previous section is assumed to operate so rapidly that transactions at nonequilibrium prices can be ignored. It is of interest that in the long-term cobweb adjustment process, there is no guarantee that the market is stable even in the typical case of upward sloping $S(p)$ and downward sloping $D(p)$, as illustrated in figure 2-9.

In the *explosive* case of an unstable cobweb, price and quantity fluctuate in wider and wider cycles as time proceeds. There is no tendency for price to move toward its equilibrium level, and the dynamic law of supply and demand is violated.

The stability condition for the cobweb adjustment process is easy to see from the dia-grams. Price will converge to equilibrium so long as *the demand curve is flatter than the supply curve*, assuming that the supply curve is upward sloping and the demand curve is downward sloping.

It appears that long-term stability is a much more restrictive condition on markets than short-term stability. This impression is some-what misleading. We have discussed the cob-web adjustment process under the simplifying assumption that farmers expect prices next period to be the same as those this period. There are obvious benefits to farmers from better predictions as to the course of prices, and so the Department of Agriculture and private firms have made sophisticated analyses of price trends and projections. More rapid and more accurate responses to market trends by produc-ers act in the direction of introducing more stability into the cobweb adjustment process.

Movements of
Supply and Demand Curves

Before leaving the case of a single competitive market, some comments are in order as to how equilibrium changes in such a market. This question is directly related to the factors that determine the positioning of the market supply and demand curves. For example, under what conditions will the market demand curve move to the right or to the left?

As noted earlier, the market demand curve for a consumer good reflects the underlying preference patterns of consumers with respect to goods, the distribution of income among consumers, and the institutional structure of the society (including, for example, tax laws). Given changes in these underlying variables, market demand curves for consumer goods will shift. Beyond this, it should be kept in mind that when we center on one market in an economy, we cannot ignore that it is linked into a system of interrelated markets. The position of the market demand and supply curves for a particular commodity depends in part on the prices that prevail in the other markets in the system. When prices of other goods and services change, generally the demand and supply curves for the given commodity will shift their positions in the supply-demand diagram.

Terminology is absolutely crucial in discussing the way markets behave. *Movement along* a given demand (or supply) curve must be distinguished from *movement of* the curve itself (fig. 2-10). We say that there is a *change in quantity demanded*, when there is a movement along a given demand curve, and similarly for supply. We say that there is a *change in demand*, when the entire demand curve moves to a new position. A change in quantity demanded occurs when price changes and the demand curve itself is unchanged. A change

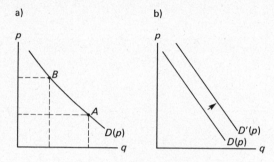

FIG. 2-10   a. *Change in quantity demanded in a move from A to B along the demand curve D(p)*
b. *Change in demand from D(p) to D'(p)*

in demand occurs when there is a movement of the demand curve, as happens when there are changes in consumer preferences, or in the distribution of income, or in the tax laws, or in prices of other goods—in short, when there are changes in any of the variables assumed to be held constant along a given demand curve.

To put this another way, a change in quantity demanded is due to a change in supply, while a change in demand brings about a change in quantity supplied (fig. 2-11).

Comparative Statics

A common application of supply and demand analysis in microeconomic theory arises in predicting the effects, on prices and quantities bought and sold, of external disturbances introduced into a market. Such disturbances include taxes imposed on commodities, price controls, changes in production costs for a good, and the like.

The approach adopted in microeconomic theory to analyze the effects of such disturbances rests on the static version of the law

a)   b)

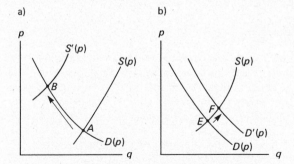

FIG. 2-11   a. *Change in quantity demanded from
                A to B (due to a change in supply)*
            b. *Change in demand (causing
                a change in quantity supplied
                from E to F)*

of supply and demand. In analyzing the effect of a disturbance such as a tax imposed on a commodity, the microeconomist assumes that the market for the commodity was in equilibrium before the tax was imposed, and that the market will be in equilibrium after the tax as well. A comparison is then made between the equilibrium values of price and quantity before and after the tax to determine the impact of the tax. This is the method of *comparative statics*, which amounts to a comparison between equilibrium values before and after a change in some variable. If the variable affects only the supply curve and not the demand curve, then the comparative statics analysis of a change in the variable reduces simply to analyzing the effect on equilibrium price and quantity of a movement of the supply curve with the demand curve held fixed (fig. 2-11a).

When we employ comparative statics analysis in this text, we will be particularly interested in the direction of change of price and quantity following a disturbance, but not in the quantitative magnitudes of such changes. In empirical work dealing with specific industries or mar-

kets, a major part of the researcher's task is to estimate the quantitative characteristics of the demand and supply curves; with such quantitative magnitudes available, comparative statics analysis can be used to estimate not only direction of change but also the magnitude of change. The method of comparative statics analysis is illustrated in the case of OPEC.

Summary

Market demand and supply curves summarize the intentions of potential buyers and sellers to purchase or sell units of a given commodity, as a function of the price prevailing in a market. In the typical situation, the market demand curve is downward sloping while the market supply curve is upward sloping. Various elasticity measures indicate the responsiveness of demand or supply to changes in variables such as own price, prices of other goods, income, and the like. Equilibrium exists in a market when price is such that the market is cleared (demand equals supply).

In its static version, the law of supply and demand asserts that observed prices and quantities sold are equilibrium magnitudes. The dynamic version of this law asserts that forces within a market tend to push price to its equilibrium value. Under a short-term adjustment process in which price is increased when quantity demanded exceeds quantity supplied, and price is lowered when quantity supplied exceeds quantity demanded, the typical case (downward sloping demand, upward sloping supply) is "stable" in the sense of the dynamic version of the law of supply and demand. But if the adjustment process is of the cobweb type, then stability requires that the demand curve be flatter than the supply curve, even in the typical case. Changes in supply bring about movements along a demand curve (changes in the quantity demanded), while changes in demand bring about movements along a supply curve (changes in the quantity supplied).

The Case of OPEC

In early 1975, the OPEC cartel controlled foreign sources of supply of oil for the U.S. economy, offering to supply essentially unlimited amounts at the cartel price of $11/barrel. Domestic supplies of oil, accounting for roughly 60 percent of U.S. consumption, are price sensitive; an increase in the price of oil is required to bring forth more output. The demand-supply situation was as shown in figure 2-12.

D_{US} is the domestic U.S. demand for oil; S_{US} is the domestic supply of oil; and S_{OPEC} is the OPEC supply of oil. Equilibrium occurs at A where the S_{OPEC} curve crosses the D_{US} curve. The equilibrium price of oil is $11/barrel because the *effective* supply curve of oil is the S_{US} curve up to $11/barrel and the S_{OPEC} curve at $11/barrel beyond $\bar{q}_{US}$. The consumption of oil in the United States is $\bar{q}$ barrels, with $\bar{q}_{US}$ supplied out of domestic oil as indicated at B, and with $\bar{q} - \bar{q}_{US}$ representing imports from OPEC.

Oil imports at the cartel price caused balance of payments problems for the United States and other oil importing countries. Several suggestions

were made as to how to reduce U.S. dependence on foreign oil, including (1) a tariff of up to $3/barrel on imported oil; (2) a tax on all oil (domestic and OPEC) of $3/barrel; (3) an import quota, limiting imports of oil to a certain fixed amount per year.

Consider first the effect of a tariff of $3/barrel on OPEC oil. Assuming the OPEC cartel holds to its position of receiving $11/barrel for each barrel sold, the effect of the tariff is to shift the OPEC supply curve up by $3, parallel to itself, as shown in figure 2-13. At $14/barrel to consumers, OPEC producers continue to receive $11/barrel, of course.

The tariff acts as a *change* in the S_{OPEC} curve (the move from the dotted curve to the new S_{OPEC} curve), resulting in a *change in quantity demanded* from A to A'. The effect of the tariff is to increase market price to $14/barrel, reduce the amount of oil consumed, increase the amount of domestic oil supplied, and reduce the amount of oil imported.

Consider the policy of a tax of $3/barrel on

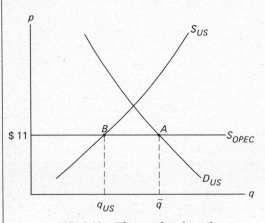

FIG. 2-12 *The market for oil*

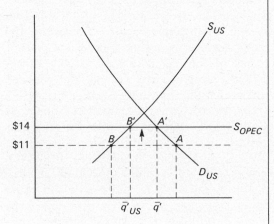

FIG. 2-13 *Tariff on OPEC oil*

all oil, domestic and OPEC. The OPEC supply curve shifts to the perfectly elastic $14 curve as in figure 2-13. The S_{US} curve shifts as follows. Domestic suppliers now require $3 more per barrel than before the tax, in order to obtain the same after-tax income per barrel. Hence the S_{US} curve shifts upward by $3/barrel, parallel to the original S_{US} curve (fig. 2-14).

Both the S_{OPEC} and S_{US} curves shift upward by $3 for every value of q. The new equilibrium price is again $14/barrel, as in the case of the tariff. We indicate domestic consumption by A'' and domestic production by B''. A, B, A', B' are as indicated in figures 2-13 and 2-14. Consumption is identical with the tariff case. What happens to domestic production and imports? There is *no change* in domestic production; after all, domestic producers still get $11/barrel after taxes, which is what they got before the tax was imposed. This lack of change is indicated by the move from B to B''. Imports fall, but not as much as under the tariff (compare B'' with B', domestic production under the tariff).

Finally consider an import quota, limiting imports to some specified number of barrels, but involving neither taxes nor tariffs. The resulting situation is pictured in figure 2-15. Given an import quota of a quantity indicated by the distance FE on the graph, this quota is consistent with equilibrium in the U.S. oil market only if price rises to the point where $D_{US} - S_{US}$ equals the quota. This equality occurs at the price $\bar{p}$ as shown in the diagram. Since $\bar{p}$ is greater than $11/barrel, and only one price can prevail on the market, a valuable property right is created by the quota, namely the right to buy OPEC oil at $11/barrel to sell in the United States at $\bar{p}$ dollars per barrel. These rights can be auctioned by the U.S. government, obtaining fees that should equal $\bar{p} - $11 per barrel. Again domestic output rises and domestic consumption falls.

It is important to note that import quotas are not *alternatives* to price increases. Such quotas always lead to price increases, just as taxes or tariffs do, assuming that price controls and rationing are not used.

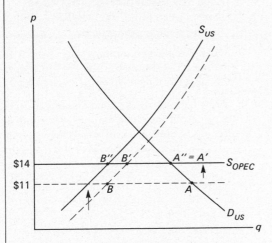

FIG. 2-14 *Tax on OPEC and U.S. oil*

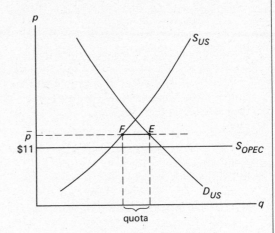

FIG. 2-15 *Import quota*

Problems

1. The market demand and supply schedules for beer by the case are given by the following formulas:

$$D(p) = 1000 - 100\ p$$
$$S(p) = 500 + 100\ p$$

   a. Graph the supply and demand curves and identify the equilibrium price and quantity.

   b. Calculate the elasticity of demand and the elasticity of supply at the equilibrium price.

   c. Assume that a tax of $1 per case of beer is imposed on the brewers of beer. Graph the new supply schedule and determine the new equilibrium price and quantity. (Hint: Before the tax was imposed, brewers were willing to supply 600 cases when $p = \$1$. After the tax is imposed, they will require a price of $2 to supply 600 cases.)

   d. Calculate the percent of the tax that is shifted to the consumer and the percent that is borne by the producer.

2. Show graphically the effect of a per unit tax on the production of a good for the "typical" case. Indicate graphically the part of the tax shifted to the consumer and the part borne by the producer. Next, do the same for these special cases.

   a. Downward sloping demand, perfectly inelastic supply

   b. Downward sloping demand, perfectly elastic supply

   c. Perfectly inelastic demand, upward sloping supply

   d. Perfectly elastic demand, upward sloping supply

Use these special cases to criticize the comment "it really doesn't make much difference how we levy taxes; the consumer ends up paying them anyhow." Finally, identify goods or assets for which cases a, b, c, d probably hold.

3. The minimum wage law is a fixture in our society, but economists often raise objections to this law on the ground that it creates involuntary unemployment among unskilled labor. (There is involuntary unemployment when an individual is willing to work at the going wage, but he can't find a job.)

   Suppose that the demand and supply schedules for unskilled labor are given by

$$D(w) = 100 - 20\ w$$
$$S(w) = -60 + 80\ w$$

where w is the wage rate per hour.

   a. Graph the supply and demand curves for labor and determine the equilibrium wage rate and level of employment.

   b. Suppose that the minimum wage is set at $2 per hour. Determine the amount of involuntary unemployment (in terms of man-hours).

   c. What happens to the total amount of wage earnings for unskilled workers as a group as a result of the minimum wage? Does it go up, go down, or stay constant as compared to the earnings without a minimum wage?

   d. Suppose that you did not know the exact form of the demand or supply curve for unskilled labor. You are asked to conjecture whether imposing a minimum wage will increase or decrease the earnings of unskilled laborers as a group. How would you approach this question, and what would you expect your conclusion to be? Explain how you arrived at your conclusion.

4. Prove that if the supply curve for a good is a straight line through the origin, then the own price elasticity of supply is $+1$ for every positive price.

   Prove that the own price elasticity of demand is unitary for every price if the demand curve is of the form $D(p) = k(1/p)$ where k is a positive constant.

5. The demand curve for gasoline per day in the United States is given by

   $$D(p) = 36,000,000 - (1,000,000)\, p.$$

   The domestic supply of gasoline in the United States is given by

   $$S(p) = 10,000,000 + (666,667)\, p,$$

   where p is the price per barrel. The OPEC cartel offers gasoline in unlimited amounts at $11 per barrel, delivered in the United States.

   a. Graph the domestic demand and supply curves for gasoline, together with the OPEC supply curve. In the absence of any controls on gasoline by the U.S. government, determine the price of gasoline in the United States, the amount and value of imports of gasoline, domestic production of gasoline, and consumption.

   b. Suppose that, in implementing "Project Independence," imports were limited to 4 million barrels per day. What is the new domestic price for gasoline, domestic production, and domestic consumption?

   c. Suppose that the government adopts the policy of taxing gasoline wherever produced, at $2 per barrel. Determine the effects on imports, on domestic production and consumption of gasoline, as well as on the price of gasoline.

   d. Suppose that the government adopts the policy of imposing an import duty on gasoline of $2 per barrel, with no tax on domestic production. Determine the effects on imports, and on domestic production and consumption, as well as on the price of gasoline.

   e. Given the original demand and supply curves for U.S. gasoline production and consumption, suppose that you were the advisor to OPEC, which is interested in maximizing its revenues from the U.S. market. What price would you set for gasoline sold by the OPEC cartel?

6. The demand and supply schedules for wheat are given by

   $$q_{D_t} = 100 - 15p_t$$
   $$q_{S_t} = 50 + 5p_{t-1}$$

   where t denotes the time at which the variable is measured, and q_D and q_S refer to quantity demanded and supplied.

   Determine the long-term equilibrium price of wheat. Given that at time $t = 0$, $p_0 = \$4$, plot the cobweb diagram for wheat for $t = 0, 1, 2, 3, 4$. Use the information from the cobweb diagram to plot price and quantity against time for $t = 0, 1, 2, 3, 4$, and determine whether the wheat market is stable.

7. Street crimes committed by heroin addicts reach such proportions in New York City that a reform administration is voted into office. The new police commissioner undertakes a vigorous program of suppressing the drug traffic, which results in a drastic drop in the supply of heroin. What will happen to the statistics on street crimes?

8. There is a general tendency to overestimate how inelastic demand curves are. For example, the demand curve for medical services is assumed to be essentially perfectly inelastic, since no one

goes to a doctor unless he has to, and really sick people have no choice but to see a doctor, no matter what he charges. Surveys have shown, however, that people with high incomes tend to spend more on medical expenses than do people with low incomes.

Relate demand to income to prove that no demand curve can be perfectly inelastic for every price.

9. "Demand for any commodity tends to be more elastic in the long run than in the short run." Explain why this is true.

10. Advertising is big business in our economy. The defenders of advertising argue that it performs an important role in making information available to consumers. Critics argue that the objective of advertising is to differentiate the advertiser's product from that of his competitors. What would be the consequence of differentiating a firm's product so far as the demand for it is concerned, and why would a firm be willing to do this? (Assume that the total demand for the industry's product is not affected by advertising expenditures.)

3

Several Competitive Markets

The competitive economy is a system of inter-related markets. Disturbances introduced into one market in the economy generally have *spill-over* effects on other markets in the system. If we want to understand and predict the effects of such disturbances, we need to know something about the way in which markets are linked together.

For example, in early 1975, a law was passed to aid the lagging housing industry, providing tax deductions of up to $2,000 for individuals buying newly built houses. Using the tools of chapter 2, we can analyze the effects of this tax deduction on the market for new homes. But certainly the impact of the new law does not end there. What about the market for exist-ing houses? Incentives to purchase newly built homes tend to shift demand away from pur-chase of secondhand houses. And there are repercussions in the market for rental housing, for new and used automobiles, and for other consumer durables as well.

In this chapter we develop some tools that can be used to analyze interrelationships among markets. We will restrict our attention in the main to the case of two markets, but the method of approach can be generalized to more complicated situations. We begin by introduc-ing a concept that is particularly useful in looking at interrelated markets.

Market Excess Demand

Given any price p for a good, $D(p)$ and $S(p)$ denote the quantities demanded and supplied of the good at that price. Market excess de-mand, denoted by $E(p)$, is defined by

$$E(p) = D(p) - S(p).$$

For the example used in figure 2-1, the $E(p)$ schedule is given in table 3-1, and the $E(p)$ curve is shown in figure 3-1.

The market excess demand summarizes in one schedule the state of the market relative to the balancing of demand and supply. When excess demand is positive, demand exceeds supply; when excess demand is negative, supply exceeds demand. Equilibrium in a market occurs when excess demand in that market is zero. In the typical case, where demand slopes

TABLE 3-1 *Excess Demand*

Price	Quantity Demanded $D(p)$	Quantity Supplied $S(p)$	Excess Demand $E(p)$
$10	0	1,500	− 1,500
$ 8	200	1,200	− 1,000
$ 6	400	900	− 500
$ 4	600	600	0
$ 2	800	300	+ 500
$ 0	1,000	0	+ 1,000

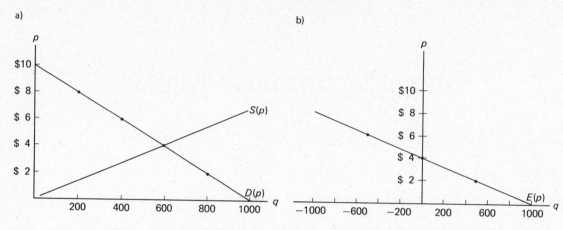

FIG. 3-1   a. *Supply and demand curves*   b. *Excess demand curve*

downward to the right and supply slopes upward to the right, the excess demand curve slopes downward to the right.

Substitutability and Complementarity

Excess demand for any good depends not only on the price of the good itself, but also on variables such as the prices of other goods, tastes of consumers, and the level and distribution of income among consumers. Along a given excess demand curve, all of these other variables are assumed to be held fixed at some levels. But in looking at interrelationships among markets, we are interested in the way in which the excess demand curve for a given good shifts in response to changes occurring in other markets, and in particular in response to changes that occur in the prices of other goods.

As a method of classifying interrelationships among goods, we say that good Y is a *gross*

substitute for good X if the excess demand curve for good X shifts to the right when the price of good Y increases (all other prices, income, tastes, and the like being held fixed). Similarly, good Y is a *gross complement* for good X if the excess demand curve for good X shifts to the left when the price of good Y increases (other things being fixed). Finally, good X is *independent* of good Y if a change in the price of good Y has no effect on the excess demand curve for good X.

These formal definitions have a rough correspondence with the way in which the terms substitute and complement are used in everyday language. We think of goods as being complements if they are consumed together—hot dogs and mustard, cigarettes and matches, beer and pretzels. And we consider goods to be substitutes if they compete with one another in consumption—Fords and Chevrolets, beer and wine, coffee and tea. An increase in the price of Fords shifts the demand curve for Chevrolets to the right; and an increase in the price of beer shifts the demand curve for pretzels to the left. The economist's use of the terms substitutes and complements generally covers these cases as well as cases in which the links between goods are considerably more subtle. Without attempting to read too much into the terminology itself, the notions of gross substitutability and gross complementarity at least offer a convenient way of classifying the links between goods. Figure 3-2 illustrates the two cases.

In figure 3-2 we have labeled the excess demand curve for X with the price p_y per unit of Y. When Y is a gross substitute for X, an increase in p_y from \$1 to \$2 shifts the excess demand curve for X to the right, while the excess demand curve for X shifts to the left in response to an increase in p_y when Y is a gross complement for X. When Y is a gross substitute for X, an increase in p_y thus leads to an increase in the difference between quantity demanded of X and the quantity supplied of X, for every value of p_x, the price per unit of X.

Demand and Supply in Two Interrelated Markets

We will use a numerical illustration to show how the links between two interrelated markets can be analyzed using excess demand curves. The excess demand for X depends both on the price per unit of X, p_x, and the price per unit of Y, p_y, and similarly for Y.

In tables 3-2 and 3-3, excess demands for X and Y are shown for various combinations of values for p_x and p_y. For example in table 3-2 when $p_x =$ \$10, $p_y =$ \$20, excess demand for X is 10 units; that is, quantity demanded of X exceeds the quantity supplied of X by 10 units. From table 3-3, when $p_x =$ \$10, $p_y =$ \$20, excess demand for Y is -5 units, so that quantity supplied of Y exceeds the quantity demanded by 5 units. The tables are graphed in figure 3-3.

Figure 3-3a and b presents excess demand curves for X and Y. Since E_x is plotted against

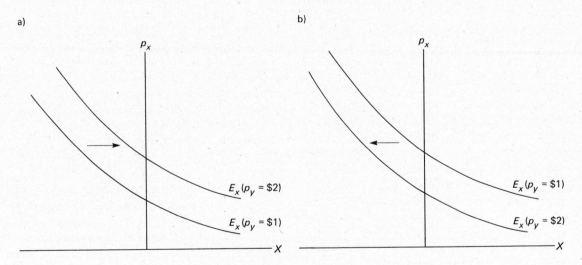

FIG. 3-2   a. *Y a gross substitute for X*   b. *Y a gross complement for X*

TABLE 3-2 *Excess Demand for Good X*

p_x \ p_y	$ 5	$10	$15	$20	$25
$ 5	+ 5	+ 10	+ 15	+ 20	+ 25
$10	− 5	0	+ 5	10	+ 15
$15	− 15	− 10	5	0	+ 5
$20	− 25	− 20	− 15	− 10	− 5
$25	− 35	− 30	− 25	− 20	− 15

TABLE 3-3 *Excess Demand for Good Y*

p_x \ p_y	$ 5	$10	$15	$20	$25
$ 5	+ 5	0	− 5	− 10	− 15
$10	+ 10	+ 5	0	− 5	− 10
$15	+ 15	+ 10	+ 5	0	− 5
$20	+ 20	+ 15	+ 10	+ 5	0
$25	+ 25	+ 20	+ 15	+ 10	+ 5

p_x in figure 3-3a, each E_x curve is labeled with the value taken on by p_y (p_y = $5, $10, . . . , $25). The curve E_x (p_y = $5) in figure 3-3a is simply a plotting of the first column of table 3-2, and similarly for the other E_x curves. In figure 3-3b the curve E_y (p_x = $5) is the plotting of the first row of table 3-3, and similarly for the other E_y curves.

Certain general statements can be made about the characteristics of the E_x and E_y curves. First, each of the E_x and E_y curves slopes down-

ward to the right, as is the case if the demand and supply curves for X and Y are typical. Second, increases in p_y shift the E_x curves to the right, and increases in p_x shift the E_y curves to the right. Thus X and Y are both gross substitutes for one another.

For any given price p_y for good Y, there is equilibrium in the market for X at that price p_x where E_x = 0. Thus if p_y = $5, the market for X is in equilibrium at p_x = $7.50; if p_y = $10, the market for X clears at $10, and

a)

b)

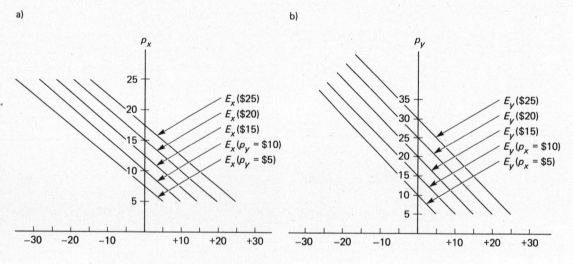

FIG. 3-3 a. *Excess demand for good X* b. *Excess demand for good Y*

so on. But equilibrium for the two markets considered as a system occurs only when there is simultaneous equilibrium in each market. A little checking will verify that the set of prices at which both markets are simultaneously cleared is $p_x = \$15$, $p_y = \$20$.

Clearly, supply and demand are a little more complicated here than in the case of a single market, but we have verified that an equilibrium for the two-market system exists. A little more checking will show that equilibrium in this case is *unique*—at no other set of prices are both markets simultaneously cleared.

The Phase Diagram for Two Competitive Markets

The graphs in figure 3-3 are somewhat unhandy in analyzing the application of the law of supply and demand to a two-market system. We will use figure 3-3 to construct another diagram, one that is easier to work with. This new diagram is referred to as a *phase diagram* and is constructed as follows.

1. Label the axes in a two-dimensional graph as p_x and p_y.
2. Draw a curve showing the combinations of prices (p_x, p_y) for which excess demand for X is zero.
3. Draw another curve showing the combinations of prices for which excess demand for Y is zero.

In figure 3-4 we have plotted the $E_x = 0$ and $E_y = 0$ curves. From tables 3-2 and 3-3 we know that $E_x = 0$ when $p_x = \$10$ and $p_y = \$10$, or $p_x = \$15$ and $p_y = \$20$, and so on. The $E_x = 0$ curve goes through all such points (fig. 3-4). The $E_y = 0$ curve is constructed in a similar manner. The system as a whole is in equilibrium only when both markets are in equilib-

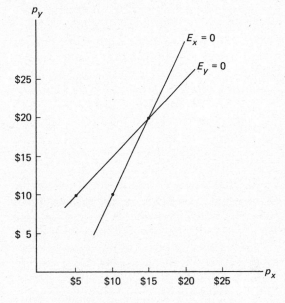

FIG. 3-4 $E_x = 0$, $E_y = 0$ *curves*

rium; in other words, only when $E_x = 0$ and $E_y = 0$ curves cross each other (at $p_x = \$15$, $p_y = \$20$). Figure 3-4 shows that this is the unique equilibrium for the system.

We can convert figure 3-4 into a device for analyzing the short-term dynamic adjustment of prices in the two-market system as follows. As noted earlier, X and Y are gross substitutes for one another. In other words, if we hold p_x fixed, an increase in p_y leads to an increase in excess demand for X, E_x. Similarly, with p_y fixed, an increase in p_x leads to an increase in E_y. Therefore, E_x is positive above the $E_x = 0$ curve and negative below it, while E_y is positive to the right of the $E_y = 0$ curve and is negative to the left of it. This relationship accounts for the signs $(+, -)$ in the phase diagram shown in figure 3-5.

We have added arrows in figure 3-5, which have the following significance. Suppose that the adjustment of prices in the two-market system follows the rules for short-term price adjustment for a single market (discussed in chapter 2): increase price if excess demand is positive and lower price if excess demand is negative. In region I of the phase diagram E_x is negative and so p_x is reduced. This reduction is indicated by the horizontal arrow ◄—. Also in region I, E_y is negative and so p_y is reduced, as indicated by the vertical arrow ↓ . The arrows in the other regions are constructed in the same way.

All of the pairs of arrows point toward the equilibrium $p_x = \$15$, $p_y = \$20$. Whatever pair of prices are set initially in this system, the short-term adjustment rules move them closer to equilibrium. In this case, the system of markets is stable, in the short-term sense. For the system pictured in figure 3-5, the dynamic version of the law of supply and demand holds.

A simple general rule for verifying stability in phase diagrams is that *there is stability if and only if the arrows in each region point toward the equilibrium.*

Stability Conditions for Phase Diagrams In the case of a single competitive market, we have seen from chapter 2 that stability occurs if the excess demand curve for the good is downward sloping. Things are more complicated in the case of two interrelated markets. For example, in the case depicted in figure 3-5, stability depends not only on the fact that the excess demand curves are downward sloping, but also on the fact that the $E_x = 0$ curve cuts the $E_y = 0$ curve from below. To see this, assume the contrary as shown in figure 3-6.

For stability the arrows in each of the regions I, II, III, IV must point toward the equilibrium $(\bar{p}_x, \bar{p}_y)$. This condition is violated in regions I and III; hence the two-market system does not satisfy the dynamic version of the law of supply and demand.

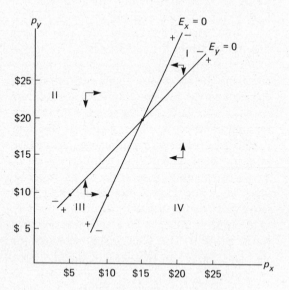

FIG. 3-5   *Stable phase diagram*

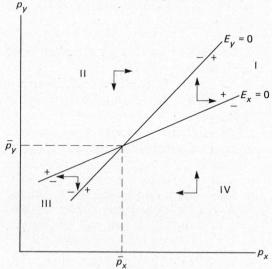

FIG. 3-6   *Unstable phase diagram*

Given that an increase in own price leads to a decrease in excess demand, the stability conditions for various complementarity-substitutability combinations are easily verified.

1. If X and Y are gross substitutes so that the $E_x = 0$ and $E_y = 0$ curves are upward sloping in the phase diagram, then the $E_x = 0$ curve must cut the $E_y = 0$ curve from below.

2. If X and Y are gross complements so that both the $E_x = 0$ and $E_y = 0$ curves are downward sloping in the phase diagram, then the $E_x = 0$ curve must cut the $E_y = 0$ curve from above.

3. If X is a gross complement for Y and Y is a gross substitute for X (or vice versa), then the system is always stable.

The stability condition in the first two cases will be satisfied so long as the *own* price effect is more important than the effect on excess demand produced by a change in the price of the other good.

The same general comments apply to the dynamic law of supply and demand in the context of a two-market system as apply to the case of a single market. In analyzing market behavior, microeconomists typically *assume* that observed prices and quantities occur at stable equilibriums, unless there is convincing evidence to the contrary. The reason for this is that if equilibrium were unstable, then the slightest disturbance would push prices and quantities away from equilibrium. Consequently, the chances of actually observing an unstable equilibrium are minute. As Samuelson has noted, observing an unstable equilibrium is like observing an egg standing on end.† The hypothesis that observed equilibriums are stable in the short-term sense is a powerful tool in the comparative statics analysis of the two-market case, as illustrated in the following example.

---

†P. A. Samuelson, *Foundations of Economic Analysis* (Cambridge: Harvard University Press, 1947).

Skilled and Unskilled Labor— Two Interrelated Markets

Of the many pieces of social legislation passed during the New Deal of the 1930s, the minimum wage law has proved to be one of the most popular and enduring. Since its passage, the law has been extended to cover more and more occupations, and the minimum wage level has been adjusted upward to reflect changes in prices. The most vocal supporters of the minimum wage are the unions, although the earnings of few, if any, union members are actually as low as the minimum wage level.

Think of the labor market as divided into two interrelated markets: the market for skilled labor and the market for unskilled labor. The minimum wage law applies directly to the market for unskilled labor; skilled workers earn in excess of the minimum wage. We want to examine how an increase in the minimum wage rate affects employment and wage rates.

Supply and demand in the market for unskilled

(continued on page 50)

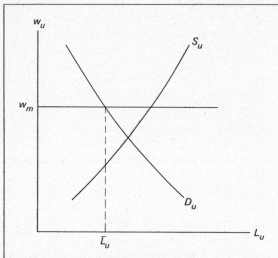

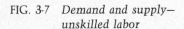

FIG. 3-7   *Demand and supply—
unskilled labor*

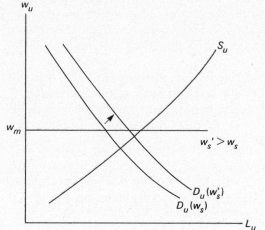

FIG. 3-8   *An increase in the wage for
skilled labor*

labor appear as in figure 3-7. The subscript u refers to unskilled labor. w_u is the wage rate for unskilled labor, and L_u is the number of units of unskilled labor. w_m is the minimum wage rate, assumed to be above the wage that would prevail in the absence of minimum wage legislation. D_u and S_u are the demand and supply of unskilled labor. At w_m, $\bar{L}_u$ units of unskilled labor are hired.

The demand curve D_u depends not only on the wage rate for unskilled laborers but also on w_s, the wage rate of skilled workers. The higher the wage rate for skilled workers, the further to the right is D_u. Thus, an increase in w_s leads to an increase in quantity demanded for unskilled laborers, at any value of w_u, as indicated in figure 3-8. Because no worker can accept a job at less than the minimum wage, the effective supply curve of unskilled labor is perfectly elastic at w_m up to the value of L_u at which the w_m line crosses the S_u curve. Thus excess demand for unskilled labor is as shown in figure 3-9a.

Similarly, the demand for skilled laborers D_s

depends not only on w_s, the wage rate for skilled laborers, but also on w_u, the wage rate for unskilled laborers. An increase in w_u shifts D_s to the right (fig. 3-9b). Excess demand for skilled labor E_s becomes perfectly elastic at w_m because skilled laborers cannot accept jobs at less than the minimum wage, just as is true for unskilled laborers.

Assuming a stable situation in the labor market, the phase diagram looks like figure 3-10. w_u and w_s are both restricted by law to be at least equal to w_m. As shown, equilibrium occurs at A where $\bar{w}_s > w_m$ for skilled laborers and $w_u = w_m$ for unskilled laborers.

Consider now the effect of an increase in the minimum wage rate (fig. 3-11). An increase in the minimum wage to w'_m then produces a shift upward of the flat portions of the original $E_s = 0$ and $E_u = 0$ curves. The new equilibrium is at B, where the wage rate for skilled workers has increased as compared to A (w_s rises from $\bar{w}_s$ to $\bar{w}_s'$) and the wage rate of unskilled workers

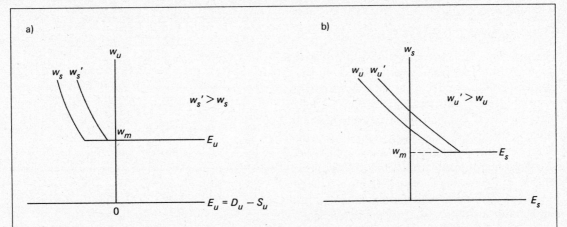

FIG. 3-9   a. *Excess demand for unskilled labor*   b. *Excess demand for skilled labor*

has risen as well (from w_m to w_m').

An interesting feature of the new equilibrium is that for skilled labor, both the wage rate and the level of employment increase. This increase can be verified by noting that with w_u increased from w_m to w_m', the demand for skilled laborers has been shifted to the right. With an unchanged supply curve of skilled laborers, employment of skilled laborers must increase. For unskilled laborers, the wage rate increases (minimum wage has risen), but employment falls. Thus skilled laborers are unambiguously better off with a higher minimum wage, but unskilled workers must trade off jobs for a higher wage.

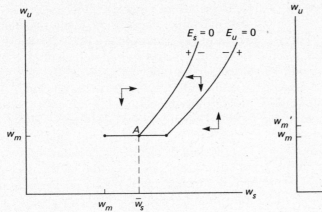

FIG. 3-10   *Phase diagram—skilled and unskilled labor*

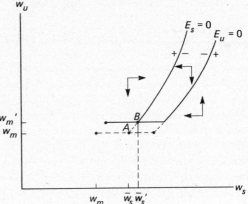

FIG. 3-11   *An increase in the minimum wage from w_m to w_m'*

*Single-Market versus
Multiple-Market Analysis*

Because the competitive economy is a system
of interrelated markets, a disturbance in one
market produces effects on others, which in
turn feed back into the first market. So long
as these effects are small, ignoring them scarcely
affects predictive accuracy, and the single-
market approach (chapter 2) can be aptly used.
Although many applications of microeconomic
theory fall into this category, there is a wide
range of problems for which interactions cannot
be ignored without impairing predictive accuracy. The phase diagram approach provides a
tool for analyzing these situations.

In both their theoretical and empirical work,
microeconomists use the simplest model that
provides acceptable levels of predictive accuracy. The choice of single-market versus multiple-market models is therefore based more on
pragmatic than theoretical considerations.

Individual and Market Schedules

Market demand and supply schedules or curves
are devices for summarizing the aggregate pressures brought to bear on a market by individual
consumers and firms. Underlying these aggregates are the individual supply and demand
curves or schedules reflecting the amounts of
goods that individual consumers and firms wish
to buy or sell at various prices. Suppose we
know these individual schedules. Then to obtain the market schedules, do we simply sum
the individual schedules (as in table 3-4)?

This procedure is valid, *so long as the individual schedules are independent.* By *independent* in this context we mean that each consumer writes down his schedule of quantities

TABLE 3-4 *Individual and Market Demand
Schedules*

Price	Quantity Demanded Consumer #1	Quantity Demanded Consumer #2	Quantity Demanded Consumer #3	Market Quantity Demanded
$1.00	10	7	15	32
.80	18	16	24	58
.60	24	24	28	76
.40	30	26	30	86

demanded, without knowing or caring what the
schedules of other consumers (or firms) look
like. In other words, what anyone else plans
to buy, sell, produce, or consume has no effect
on my own demand or supply schedule. Of
course, other individuals' plans will influence
what I finally decide to buy or sell, since the
aggregate of these plans determine market
prices, and market prices in turn determine my
purchase or sales. But we are referring here to
the *schedule of potential purchases* or *sales*
(my individual demand or supply schedule).
This schedule states what I will buy, *if* the price
is so and so; and under independence the
schedule (but not the market price that will
prevail) will be the same, whatever the schedules of other individuals.

Independence is violated when consumers
try to "keep up with the Joneses," judge quality
by price, or are affected by crowding (as when
a neighbor plays his stereo too loud). Independence is in fact a rather strict requirement on
individual demand schedules. Nevertheless, for
the first half of this book, we will assume that
independence holds, so that market demand
and supply can be obtained through a simple
summation of individual schedules.

Problems created by violation of independence are similar in many respects to the problems associated with pollution. To be successfully resolved, they sometimes require interference in the market system. We will classify violation of independence as an "imperfection" that will be taken up later in the book.

Long-Term Adjustment in Two Markets
The Hog-Corn Cycle

Corresponding to the long-term cobweb adjustment of prices in a single market is the long-term adjustment of prices in two related markets. Generally such an adjustment process is somewhat more complicated to model than the short-term adjustment pictured in the phase diagram. To illustrate the basic principles of long-term adjustment in two markets, we will use one of the first cases investigated using this approach—the corn and hog markets.

Corn is raised for sale primarily to two users: consumers, who use it fresh or canned or frozen, and hog raisers, who use it as an intermediate product to fatten hogs for market. Hogs, of course, are sold as pork for human consumption. Both hog raisers and corn farmers must make plans and decisions concerning production well in advance of the time when their products come to market. To keep market conditions as simple as possible, we will make several assumptions:

1. Both groups base their price expectations on the prices prevailing when they plan production.

2. One hundred pounds of hogs brought to market at time t require α bushels of corn as an input at time $t-1$.

3. The demand by consumers for corn depends only on the price of corn.

4. The demand by consumers for pork depends only on the price of hogs.

5. Producers of corn base their production decisions only on the expected price of corn.

6. Producers of hogs base their production decisions on their expected margin over feeding costs per pound of hogs.

7. The production periods for both corn and hogs are identical.

8. The demand and supply curves are linear.

Even with these assumptions, the model of the corn and hog markets that emerges is somewhat complicated. Using the superscript H to denote hogs and C to denote corn, the demand and supply functions appear as follows:

Corn Market

$$q_{D_t}^C = (a_0 - a_1 p_t^C) + \alpha q_{S_{t+1}}^H \tag{1}$$

$$q_{S_t}^C = b_0 + b_1 p_{t-1}^C \tag{2}$$

$$q_{S_t}^C = q_t^S \tag{3}$$

Hog Market

$$q_{D_t}^H = d_0 - d_1 p_t^H \tag{4}$$

$$q_{S_t}^H = e_0 + e_1(p_{t-1}^H - \alpha p_{t-1}^C) \tag{5}$$

$$q_{D_t}^H = q_{S_t}^H \tag{6}$$

(All constants above are assumed to be positive; q_S and q_D are quantities supplied and demanded.)

(continued on page 54)

The system can be interpreted as follows. Equation 1 gives demand for corn at time t as the sum of consumer demand, $a_0 - a_1 p_t^C$, plus demand for corn as an input for hogs to be produced one period in the future. Equation 2 relates the output of corn at time t to the price of corn at $t-1$, in keeping with the hypothesis concerning price expectations. Equation 3 is the market-clearing condition.

In the hog (pork) market, equation 4 expresses consumer demand for pork. In equation 5, the supply of hogs forthcoming at time t depends upon the expected margin over feeding costs at time $t-1$, namely $p_{t-1}^H - \alpha p_{t-1}^C$. Again, equation 6 is the market-clearing condition.

The basic task is to determine how this system of markets performs over time in the sense of generating price cycles so far as corn and hogs are concerned, and to determine whether there is any inherent tendency for these cycles to "damp down" over time. We will not attempt this analysis for the general case here; instead we will examine a special numerical example of equations 1 through 6:

$$q_{D_t}^C = 100 - 2p_t^C + 3q_{S_{t+1}}^H \tag{1'}$$

$$q_{S_t}^C = 20 + 4p_{t-1}^C \tag{2'}$$

$$q_{D_t}^C = q_{S_t}^C \tag{3'}$$

$$q_{D_t}^H = 200 - 5p_t^H \tag{4'}$$

$$q_{S_t}^H = 40 + 3(p_{t-1}^H - 3p_{t-1}^C) \tag{5'}$$

$$q_{D_t}^H = q_{S_t}^H \tag{6'}$$

Using 3' and 6' and substituting 5' into 1', we have

$$100 - 2p_t^C + 3(40 + 3(p_t^H - 3p_t^C)) = 20 + 4p_{t-1}^C \tag{7}$$

$$200 - 5p_t^H = 40 + 3(p_{t-1}^H - 3p_{t-1}^C). \tag{8}$$

Rearranged, this becomes

$$9p_t^H - 29p_t^C = 0p_{t-1}^H + 4p_{t-1}^C - 200 \tag{9}$$

$$-5p_t^H + 0p_t^C = 3p_{t-1}^H - 9p_{t-1}^C - 160. \tag{10}$$

Long-term equilibrium occurs at $(\bar{p}^H, \bar{p}^C)$ if $p_{t-1}^H = p_t^H = \bar{p}^H$ and $p_{t-1}^C = p_t^C = \bar{p}^C$.

It can be verified from equations 9 and 10 that

$$\bar{p}^C = \frac{3040}{183} = \$16.61,$$

while

$$\bar{p}^H = \frac{7080}{183} = \$38.74.$$

Solving equations 9 and 10 for p_t^H, p_t^C we obtain

$$p_t^H = -.6p_{t-1}^H + 1.8p_{t-1}^C + 32$$

$$p_t^C = -.19p_{t-1}^H + .42p_{t-1}^C + 16.83$$

Suppose that after a period of time in which both markets are in equilibrium, a sudden drought results in a situation (at time 0 in fig. 3-12) where $p_0^C = \$30$, $p_0^H = \$15$. Table 3-5 traces the time path of price adjustment. After

TABLE 3-5   *The Hog-Corn Cycle in Prices*

Time t	p_t^C	p_t^H
0	$30.00	$15.00
1	$26.58	$77.00
2	$13.37	$33.68
3	$16.06	$35.40
4	$16.86	$39.74
5	$16.39	$38.60

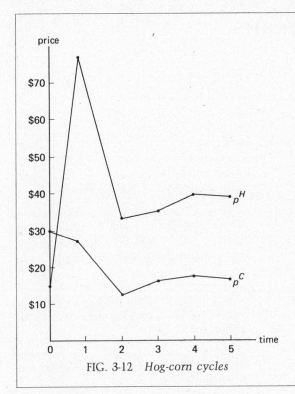

FIG. 3-12   *Hog-corn cycles*

only five periods, the system has returned almost to the equilibrium values ($\bar{p}^C$ = $16.61, $\bar{p}^H$ = $38.74). With the coefficients as specified, the system is stable.

In general, the presence or absence of stability depends on the slopes of both demand and supply curves and on the input coefficient α. It can be verified that stability occurs if in each market the demand curve (in terms of own current price) is flatter than the supply curve (in terms of own lagged price); and if α is large relative to the other coefficients of the model.

Price fluctuations are a part of the process by which equilibrium is reestablished in a stable system of markets. In general, it is necessary to examine the entire system of markets to discover stabilizing tendencies.

Summary

In this chapter, we have tried to indicate the role played by supply and demand analysis as a tool for examining the behavior of interrelated markets. Markets are linked together through complementarity-substitutability relationships. Phase diagrams summarize these properties and permit an analysis of the law of supply and demand (both static and dynamic versions) as they apply to such markets.

In general, stability criteria for the case of two interrelated markets are considerably more complicated than for the single-market case. In particular, single-market stability is neither necessary nor sufficient for stability of a system of two markets. Comparative statics analysis of interrelated markets takes as its typical case a stable system of markets.

Finally, market demand and supply schedules are obtained by summing the corresponding schedules for individual consumers and firms, so long as these schedules are independent.

Problems

1. Given the supply and demand schedules

$$D = 75 - p$$
$$S = 50 + 2.5p$$

write out the formula for excess demand.

a. Graph the demand and supply curves and the corresponding excess demand curves, and identify the equilibrium on the two graphs.

b. A tax of $1 per unit is imposed on the production of the commodity. Graph the new supply curve and the new excess demand curve, and solve for the new equilibrium price and quantity.

2. In a two-market system, suppose that excess demands for goods X and Y are given by the formulas

$$E_x = 100 - 5p_x + p_y$$
$$E_y = 50 + 2p_x - 2p_y$$

a. Construct a table giving excess demands for goods X and Y taking prices $20, $30, $40, and $50 for p_x, and $0, $50, $100, and $150 for p_y.

b. Approximate the $E_x = 0$ and $E_y = 0$ curves from information given in the table, and graph the phase diagram for these two commodities.

c. Determine whether the goods are gross substitutes, gross complements, or independent.

d. Solve graphically for equilibrium, and check the stability of equilibrium.

3. Assume that the formula for excess demand E_x given in problem 2 was derived from the supply and demand relations

$$D_x = 50 - p_x + p_y$$
$$S_x = -50 + 4p_x$$

a. Verify that $E_x = 100 - 5p_x + p_y$ is consistent with these demand and supply schedules.

b. Assume that a tax of $5 per unit is imposed on the production of good X. Graph the new supply curve. Show that the new supply curve is consistent with the formula.

$$S_x = -50 + 4(p_x - 5) \text{ or } S_x = -70 + 4p_x.$$

c. Given this new supply curve, determine the expression for E_x after the tax of $5 per unit is imposed.

d. Construct a new table for E_x, given prices $20, $30, $40, and $50 for p_x, and $0, $50, $100, and $150 for p_y.

e. Plot the new $E_x = 0$ curve, and solve for the new equilibrium prices of goods X and Y. Summarize the effects on prices of the imposition of a $5 tax on good X.

4. Assume that good X is a gross substitute for good Y and that good Y is a gross complement for good X. Assume an increase in own price leads to a fall in excess demand. Plot the resulting phase diagram, and explain why the system is stable.

5. Suppose that goods X and Y are both gross complements, and that an increase in own price leads to a fall in excess demand. Construct two phase diagrams: $E_x = 0$ crosses $E_y = 0$ from below; $E_y = 0$ crosses $E_x = 0$ from below. Discuss stability.

II

The Competitive Economy

Theory of Consumer Behavior

The central figure in the competitive economy is the consumer. Production, distribution, and exchange are geared to satisfy the wants of consumers, as expressed in the form of demands for goods and services in the marketplace. Preferences of consumers as to the timing of consumption play a major role in determining the mix of output between consumption goods and capital goods; and consumers supply the most important input in production, labor services.

In this chapter and the next, we outline the elements of the economist's theory of consumer behavior and consumer demand. Chapter 4 deals with the preferences of the consumer, and chapter 5 is concerned with the characteristics of consumer demands.

4
Modern Utility Theory

The theory of consumer behavior concerns itself with the decision-making process of the consumer—the way he chooses from among available alternatives. The theory is designed to explain and predict the observed demands for goods and services by consumers. As a *positive* (scientific) theory, its axioms and propositions are subject to verification by empirical tests. But the theory of consumer behavior is also used by economists as the basis for judgments as to how well the economic system is functioning. Thus the theory has applications to *normative* (ethical) problems as well. Our concern in the next two chapters is with the scientific aspects of the theory of consumer behavior. But it is important at the outset to distinguish between the positive and normative aspects of the theory.

The Two Basic Postulates of Consumer Theory

The economist's scientific theory of consumer behavior rests on one fundamental postulate concerning human behavior:

The consumer makes choices from among alternatives in a manner that is consistent with his own evaluation of his self-interest.

When properly formalized, this postulate can, in principle, be tested. The modern theory of consumer behavior in economics has developed through specifying, in precise and testable form, not only what is meant by a consumer's "own evaluation of his self-interest" and by "consistency" of choices, but also the implications of these for the observed behavior patterns of consumers. The present chapter outlines the economist's interpretation of the concept of a consumer's "self-interest"; in chapter 5 we turn to the implications of the basic postulate for consumer choices.

In dealing with issues of normative economics, a second postulate is often invoked:

Given that adequate information is available to him, the consumer is the best judge of his own self-interest.

This postulate states a prejudice, value judgment, or "point of view" of the economist, which cannot be tested through observing consumer choices. It is entirely consistent to accept the first postulate on the basis of empirical evidence, while rejecting the second on moral or other grounds. We must be careful to distinguish between these two postulates, especially when they are used together by economists and others concerning policy matters. But the first postulate is a scientific statement, while the second simply states an ethical belief.

Each of the postulates is somewhat controversial. The economist's postulate of consistent, purposeful behavior on the part of the consumer (the first postulate) is at odds with at least some parts of psychological theory, and it must be admitted that the process of testing this postulate is still in its infancy. So far as the second postulate is concerned, the point of view expressed seems to have rather general acceptance in principle, but not necessarily in practice. As is often the case, acceptance of it depends on whose ox is being gored.

For example, in our legal system, contract law operates under the assumption that each of the parties to a contract knows his own interest and follows it. Criminal law, however, punishes "victimless crimes" (such as drunkenness, smoking pot, gambling, and selling pornography) largely on the grounds that these are "inherently" injurious actions, even to those who voluntarily decide to engage in them. To cite another notorious and controversial instance, our welfare system seems to be based on the premise that once one has lost the status of a wage earner, a social worker or bureaucrat should decide which expenditures are in the best interest of the welfare recipient. The point of view underlying our second postulate is expressed even more strongly by Thoreau in *Walden:* "If I knew for a certainty that a man was coming to my house with the conscious design of doing me good, I should run for my life. . . ."

We will defer further discussion of the normative applications of consumer theory until later in this book. Our treatment in the rest of this chapter and the next concerns itself solely with the scientific aspects of the theory.

Substitutability and Consumer Choices

The economist views the consumer as a decision-maker who adjusts his pattern of consumption in accordance with his tastes, his income, and the prices he faces in the marketplace. This viewpoint emphasizes the *substitutability* among goods in satisfying the wants of the consumer. In contrast, the biologist's model of the consumer is an energy machine, with minimum nutritional requirements (for vitamins, protein, calories, minerals, roughage, and the like) to maintain viability. The biologist emphasizes the *constraints* on substitutability that restrict the choices of the consumer.

The biologist's notion of essentials for survival carries over into the distinction in everyday conversation between "necessities" and "luxuries." These terms have no place in microeconomic theory. Consumers have diverse tastes and they satisfy these tastes in different ways. Certainly everyone needs food, clothing, and shelter to survive; but to identify housing as a necessity is to ignore the gradations within this broad category where substitution takes place.

Admittedly, individual consumers are more flexible with respect to certain kinds of goods than with others. The ease with which other goods can be substituted for a given good is reflected in the elasticity of the consumer's demand curve for the given good. Again the factors at work are the tastes of the consumer, his income, and the prices of potential substitutes, as well as the price of the good itself.

Our approach in this chapter is to concentrate on the tastes of the consumer. A starting point in our analysis of consumer tastes is the famous law of diminishing marginal utility.

The Law of Diminishing Marginal Utility

The concept of *utility* in economics goes back at least as far as Jeremy Bentham (1748–1832), an economist, philosopher, and social reformer who developed the utilitarian school of ethics. To Bentham, the utility of an action was the difference between the pleasure enjoyed and the pain suffered as a consequence of the action. Bentham regarded utility (interpreted in this sense) as a magnitude that was in principle measurable, much as body temperature is measurable and in fact comparable among individuals. He was interested in utility as a guide for public policy. His slogan "the greatest good for the greatest number" might be more properly stated as "choose the policy with the greatest utility."

The utility notion was resurrected by the so-called "marginalist" economists of the 1870s, a group of academics whose work revolutionized economic theory. They postulated the law of diminishing marginal utility, which played a central role in their theory of consumer decision-making. To them, utility was a measure of the satisfaction that a consumer receives from the consumption of a commodity. Without attempting to reduce satisfaction to Bentham's notion of pleasure less pain, they defined the *marginal utility* associated with the consumption of a unit of a commodity as the *increase in utility* (satisfaction) that the consumer obtains from consuming an additional unit of it. The *law of diminishing marginal utility* may be stated as follows:

After sufficient units of a commodity have been consumed, the consumer experiences diminishing marginal utility from additional units consumed.

Alternatively, the law reads:

After sufficient units of a commodity have been consumed, each additional unit consumed provides less additional utility to the consumer.

Table 4-1 indicates that the more units of a commodity consumed, the greater the satisfaction afforded the consumer: total utility rises as consumption rises. Marginal utility is the increase in utility associated with consuming one more unit. Thus, the marginal utility of the first unit consumed is 10, of the second unit consumed is 15, and so forth (the first unit adds 10 to the total utility, the second unit adds 15 to total utility, and so on). The law of diminishing marginal utility is illustrated by the decline in marginal utility after the second unit is consumed; that is, the third unit consumed has a smaller marginal utility than the second, the fourth less than the third, the fifth less than the fourth.

The law of diminishing marginal utility may be illustrated graphically (fig. 4-1). Let X denote the number of units of a commodity consumed, and let $U(X)$ denote the utility associated with that level of consumption, while $MU(X)$ denotes marginal utility. Assuming that X is continuously divisible (as water or gasoline are), then the marginal utility at any level of con-

TABLE 4-1   *Total Utility and Marginal Utility*

Units of Commodity Consumed	Total Utility	Marginal Utility
0	0	
		10
1	10	
		15
2	25	
		10
3	35	
		5
4	40	
		2
5	42	

a)

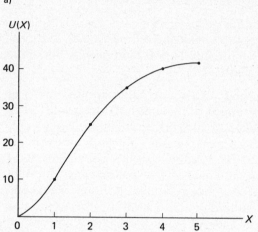

b)

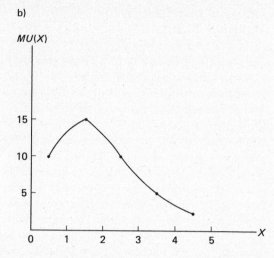

FIG. 4-1   a. *Total utility of X*   b. *Marginal utility of X*

sumption X is simply the slope of the $U(X)$ curve. That is

$$MU(X) = \frac{\Delta U(X)}{\Delta X}$$

where $\Delta U(X)$ is the change in total utility and ΔX is the change in units of X consumed. At $X = 1\frac{1}{2}$, the $U(X)$ curve has an *inflexion point*, the point where marginal utility is maximum, as indicated in figure 4-1b. There is diminishing marginal utility beyond $1\frac{1}{2}$ units of X consumed.

The rationale for the law of diminishing marginal utility is easy to see. An individual who has only a few units of a commodity will tend to apply them to his most pressing needs. As more units are obtained, the needs to which these units are applied are of less and less importance to him, and hence yield less and less increase in utility. For example, if a consumer has only one quart of water per day,

water will be used for drinking purposes only, and the marginal utility of water is high. If the consumer has ten gallons of water available per day, water is used for cooking and perhaps for washing as well as for drinking. Finally, if enough water is available, it is used also for watering the lawn, washing the car, and water fights—activities that are far removed from the notion of water as an absolute essential for human survival.

Marginal Utility and Prices

The law of diminishing marginal utility is of interest because it provides an explanation for the way in which consumers allocate expenditures among goods and services. Consider a consumer who wishes to allocate his income of M dollars between purchases of two goods. Let X and Y denote the number of units of these two goods he purchases. Suppose the consumer faces prices p_x per unit of X and p_y per unit of Y. Then the budget constraint of the consumer may be written as $p_x X + p_y Y \leq M$. (He can spend no more than M dollars on his purchases of the two goods.) We assume that the consumer wishes to reach as high a level of satisfaction as possible; that is, he wishes to maximize utility. The law of diminishing marginal utility implies that the consumer will arrange his purchases of X and Y to satisfy the following condition:

$$\frac{MU(X)}{MU(Y)} = \frac{p_x}{p_y} .$$

The ratio p_x divided by p_y gives the number of units of Y that exchange for one unit of X on the market. For example, if p_x is \$5 and p_y is \$1, then five units of Y would exchange for one unit of X. To see that the ratio of marginal utilities must be equal to the corresponding ratio of prices, suppose that X and Y are purchased in amounts so that the ratio of marginal utilities is less than the price ratio. That is,

$$\frac{MU(X)}{MU(Y)} < \frac{p_x}{p_y} .$$

The consumer has purchased more X and less Y than would be the case if there were equality between the price ratio and the ratio of marginal utilities.

Suppose he now decreases his consumption of X by a small amount, say by ΔX (the change in X). This decreases his utility by the amount of $\Delta X \cdot MU(X)$. ($MU(X)$ is the change in utility due to a one unit change in X, and ΔX is the change in units of X consumed. Thus $\Delta X \cdot MU(X)$ is the change in utility.) But reducing X by the amount ΔX means he can now increase his consumption of Y by an amount

ΔY, where

$$\Delta Y = -\frac{p_x}{p_y} \cdot \Delta X, \ (\Delta X < 0, \ \Delta X > 0)$$

without changing the amount spent in total on both X and Y. This follows because with income fixed at M, we have $p_x \Delta X + p_y \Delta Y = 0$. The increase in utility due to the increased consumption of Y will be $\Delta Y \cdot MU(Y)$. The net change in utility ΔU is then given by

$$\Delta U = \Delta Y \cdot MU(Y) - \Delta X \cdot MU(X)$$

$$= \left(\frac{p_x}{p_y}\right) \cdot - \Delta X \cdot MU(Y) - \Delta X \cdot MU(X)$$

$$= -\Delta X \left[\frac{p_x}{p_y} \cdot MU(Y) - MU(X)\right]$$

$$= -\Delta X \cdot MU(Y) \left[\frac{p_x}{p_y} - \frac{MU(X)}{MU(Y)}\right]$$

But by assumption,

$$\frac{MU(X)}{MU(Y)} < \frac{p_x}{p_y}.$$

Hence

$$\Delta U = -\Delta X \cdot MU(Y) \left[\frac{p_x}{p_y} - \frac{MU(X)}{MU(Y)}\right] > 0.$$

Without spending any more money, the consumer can obtain a higher level of utility by moving his purchases away from X and toward Y until the ratio of marginal utilities equals the price ratio. A similar argument applies if the ratio of marginal utilities is greater than the price ratio. If the consumer wishes to achieve as high a level of utility as possible for any given amount spent, he will adjust his expenditures so that the ratio of marginal utilities equals the ratio of prices.

Recent Developments

The law of diminishing marginal utility has a good deal of intuitive appeal. Once the law was formulated by the "new" economists of the 1870s, it also provided a unifying foundation for a theory of choice by consumers, and so it dominated discussions of consumer behavior in economics for an extended period of time.

For the marginalist economists, utility was a concept as real as the commodities themselves; but as the marginal utility approach spread and became more familiar, certain basic problems arose. First, like the concept of ether invented by the nineteenth century physicists to explain deviations from results predicted by their theory, neither utility nor marginal utility lent itself to empirical measurement. I might accept the law of diminishing marginal utility, but I cannot tell you what the marginal utility of the last glass of wine I consume is; more important, I cannot conceive of a way to measure marginal utility.

Second, and more basic, it is possible to derive all of the conclusions of the marginal utility school—or at least all that can be subjected to empirical tests—without assuming the law of diminishing marginal utility. In a clash between opposing theories, the rules of the scientific game specify, of two theories giving rise to the same consequences, the superior theory is the one that involves the less restrictive assumptions. In scientific theory, this principle is known as *Occam's Razor* ("eliminate all unnecessary assumptions"). This criterion led to the overthrow of the law of diminishing marginal utility in economics.

The modern theory of consumer behavior has developed from the marginal utility approach in two separate but related directions. Generally speaking, one of these developments emphasizes the structure of preferences of a consumer and the way in which these preferences influence the choices a consumer makes. The second development focuses on choices themselves and emphasizes testable propositions concerning them. For the sake of identification, we refer to the first approach as the modern utility theory, and to the second as the revealed preference theory.

Modern utility theory predates revealed preference theory. Important contributions to it were made during the early and middle years of the twentieth century by economists such as Irving Fisher, Eugen Slutsky, J. R. Hicks, and Nicholas Georgescu-Roegen. The axioms of modern utility theory were developed by economists associated with the Cowles Foundation in the early 1950s (including Kenneth Arrow, Gerard Debreu, Leonid Hurwicz, Hirofumi Uzawa, and Tjalling Koopmans). Revealed preference theory was discovered independently by Abraham Wald and Paul Samuelson; later contributions of particular importance were made by Henry Houthakker and Marcel Richter.

The names associated with these two theories indicate the international character of the work done on the foundations of consumer theory—Slutsky was Russian, Hicks English, Georgescu-Roegen Rumanian, Wald Austrian, and Uzawa Japanese. Still it is fair to say that most of the work, particularly since the 1940s, has taken place in the United States, the center for analytical work in economic theory.

We will first discuss the modern utility approach to consumer theory. The revealed preference approach will be taken up in chapter 5, which also deals with consumer behavior.

Commodity Bundles and Substitution

The marginalist economists focused on the utility derived by a consumer from consuming a particular good. In much of the marginalist literature, total utility to the consumer is viewed as the sum of the utilities derived from each commodity consumed. The modern utility theory rejects both the marginalists' notion of utility and the way in which utilities are summed to obtain total utility. In the modern utility theory, the consumer is assumed to possess preferences over market baskets of goods, or commodity bundles. A *commodity bundle* is defined as a listing of the amounts of each of the commodities the consumer consumes. By focusing on commodity bundles rather than on individual commodities, modern utility theory highlights substitution among commodities in terms of the consumer's preferences. The theory views the consumer as making a simultaneous choice of all goods rather than choosing commodity by commodity, as in the marginalist approach.

The modern theory takes the consumer's preferences over commodity bundles as a given. No attempt is made (as there is in the marginalist approach) to relate such preferences to the psychological satisfactions enjoyed by the consumer. The preferences simply exist and have certain properties that can be verified through observations. There is no place in the modern theory for the law of diminishing marginal utility, because this law assumes the existence of a measure of satisfaction, the marginalists' utility, which has no place in the modern theory.

We begin our discussion of the modern utility theory by examining the concept of the consumer's preference ranking over commodity bundles.

Preference Rankings over Commodity Bundles

To explain what economists mean by the notion of a preference ranking, we consider a simple case in which there are two goods available to the consumer, X and Y. Since a commodity bundle in this case is a listing of the amounts X and Y available to the consumer, we can depict commodity bundles in terms of two-dimensional space, as in figure 4-2.

Points A, B, and C are commodity bundles. A is written as $A = (X_0, Y_0)$, B as $B = (X_1, Y_1)$; and C as $C = (X_2, Y_2)$. At A the consumer receives X_0 units of the first commodity and Y_0 units of the second commodity. We assume that between any two such commodity bundles, say A and B, the consumer can express a preference. That is, he can state one (and only one) of the following: A is preferred to B, or B is preferred to A, or A is indifferent to B (neither A preferred to B nor B preferred to A). (Indifference should be viewed as a situation in which the consumer would be willing to let anyone else make the choice between bundles for him.)

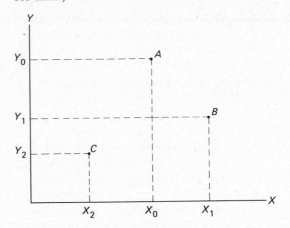

FIG. 4-2   *Commodity bundles*

If the consumer can rank all commodity bundles in this way, then we say that his preferences are *complete* or *total*. It might well be that the consumer simply cannot make a decision between two bundles. For example, suppose your house is burning and you can save either your spouse or your children. This might be a choice you feel you simply cannot make; either alternative is inadmissible, and you would not be willing to let someone else make the choice for you. When such choices occur in real-world situations, the conflict involved may result in a nervous breakdown. The assumption that the preferences of a consumer are complete is restrictive and is undoubtedly violated in particular cases.

Transitivity of Preferences

Preferences of the consumer are also assumed to be internally consistent in the following sense. If the consumer prefers A to B and B to C, then we require that he also prefer A to C. Similarly, if A is indifferent to B and B is indifferent to C, then A is required to be indifferent to C. This property of the preference ranking is referred to as the *transitivity* property. Although human behavior is not necessarily always consistent, what we sometimes regard as inconsistent behavior may still be compatible with transitivity. The tastes of the individual may have changed, or the individual may be considering certain features of alternatives that are not apparent to others.

In experimental work, transitivity of preferences is occasionally violated. Transitivity of indifference is on much weaker ground because of perceptual problems. I may not be able to distinguish between A and B, or B and C, or ... Y and Z, and hence would be indifferent regarding any one pair of alternatives. At the same time, A and Z might well be distinguishable, and within this pair A might be preferred to Z. Consider, for example, distinguishing among lines 1 inch long, 1-1/64 inches long, 1-2/64 inches long, and so on.

Realism of the transitivity postulate is sometimes argued on the basis of the "money pump" notion. Suppose that an individual has intransitive preferences: he prefers A to B, B to C, and C to A. If he is given B, presumably he would be willing to give up B plus some amount of money to obtain A, since A is preferred to B. Having now acquired A, he should be willing to give up A, plus some money, for C, since C is preferred to A. But having acquired C, he should be willing to give up C plus a sum of money to get B.

By running the individual through this cycle, we can pump all of his money from him. Since it seems unreasonable on the face of things that anyone would stand for this, transitivity must hold. This argument, however, has some flaws; for one, it assumes that the individual's preferences are defined independently of his money holdings. Transitivity remains a restrictive condition on individual preferences that will occasionally be violated in practice.

Formation of Preferences

Where do our preferences come from? In general, economists have not had much to say about this question, regarding it as more properly the province of the psychologist, the sociologist, or the anthropologist. Still, it is clear that childhood training, family life, peer group pressures, and the like are important influences on our tastes. Perhaps, the appropriate model of preference formation is one in which the individual learns his preferences, in effect "discovering" his preference ranking through experiments in consumption. The consumer is a dynamic entity, for whom the learning process culminates in a stationary state with fixed preferences. It is this stationary state that represents the economist's model of preferences.

While learning theory has been applied to certain economic phenomena, not much has been done to apply it in a comprehensive fashion to the problem of preference formation. The only significant work that has centered on preference formation in economics deals with the influence of advertising expenditures, and there are few general theoretical results in this area.

Some comments should be made, however, about another aspect of preferences. In the economist's view, the consumer has a preference ranking with respect to specific commodities such as automobiles, books, and food. In contrast, the psychologist tends to think of individuals as motivated by more abstract drives or emotions such as the desire for self-fulfillment, security, and love. These two approaches are not necessarily in conflict.

Instead we can view any commodity on the market as a "bundle of characteristics," each of which is related to the fundamental drives of the individual. What the individual really demands is satisfaction of his basic drives; he achieves this in part through his choices among commodities. Product differentiation through advertising then can be regarded as a process of identifying and highlighting the aspects of a product that appear to satisfy particular drives. The Cadillac is sold not simply as a car but as a status symbol, and the Volkswagen becomes a status symbol of a different type.

The consumer may be viewed as having a set of preferences with respect to certain fundamental characteristics of commodities. These preferences, coupled with the consumer's be-liefs about the bundle of characteristics incorporated into particular commodities, enable us to translate his underlying preference ranking over characteristics into a preference ranking over commodities. The resultant preference ranking is used by the economist as a construct. (This approach was first developed in a systematic way by K. Lancaster.)†

Independence of Preferences

As noted in chapter 3, the market demand schedule for a commodity is obtained by summing the demand schedules of individual consumers (and firms) for the commodity, provided these schedules are independent of one another. Related to this is the notion of *independence of preferences*, sometimes referred to as *selfishness*. When the preferences of any one consumer over the bundles assigned to him are the same, whatever the bundles assigned to other consumers in the economy and whatever the choices of inputs and outputs by firms, there is independence of preferences: each consumer is concerned only with what he himself consumes, and not with what occurs elsewhere in the economy.

Our discussion throughout the first part of this book will operate under the assumption that independence of preferences holds. Problems associated with violation of independence will be taken up in the discussion on externalities in chapter 17. At this point, the importance of the independence assumption is that the preference ranking of the consumer is defined over his own commodity bundles. Thus, the assumption permits a simple graphical representation of the preference ranking.

----

†K. Lancaster, "A New Approach to Consumer Theory," *Journal of Political Economy* (April 1966).

The Indifference Map of the Consumer

Under independence of preferences, the consumer's preference ranking is defined over the commodity bundles assigned to him, with preferences assumed to be both total and transitive. Given any two commodity bundles, the consumer either prefers one to the other or is indifferent between them, and his preferences are internally consistent. We can represent the preference ranking of the consumer in terms of an *indifference map*, a graph of a family of curves, each of which connects commodity bundles that are indifferent to one another. Figure 4-3 illustrates this concept.

Any point lying along the *indifference curve* I_0 is a commodity bundle containing specified amounts of goods X and Y. Any two commodity bundles on I_0 are indifferent to one another; when presented with a choice between any two such bundles, the consumer is willing to let anyone else make the choice for him. I_1 represents another indifference curve. The arrow indicates the direction of preference; each bun-

dle on I_1 is preferred to any bundle on I_0, and each bundle on I_2 is preferred to any bundle on I_1.

Drawing the indifference curves as continuous curves implies that X and Y are regarded by the consumer as *perfectly divisible* commodities; that is, either X or Y is available in as fine a fractional unit as desired. (While "lumpiness," or indivisibility, is certainly an attribute of certain goods, we will ignore this complication in our treatment.) Perfect divisibility, coupled with the assumption of a total preference ranking, also implies that there is an indifference curve passing through every point in the indifference map; we isolated a few of the curves for illustrative purposes.

Finally, the postulate of a total transitive preference ranking implies that indifference curves do not cross one another. If a crossing did occur at bundle A, then A would be indifferent to bundles preferred to bundles indifferent to A, a contradiction to both of these postulates.

As drawn, the indifference curves slope downward to the right, becoming flatter as they move in the X direction. This property reflects the substitutability of Y for X in the consumer's preferences, and is referred to as the law of diminishing marginal rate of substitution.

The Law of Diminishing Marginal Rate of Substitution

Consider a movement along the indifference curve I_0 from $A = (X_0, Y_0)$ to $B = (X_1, Y_1)$, as depicted in figure 4-4. Both A and B lie along I_0, showing that the consumer is indifferent between receiving A or B. Increasing the amount of Y from Y_1 to Y_0 is exactly offset (in terms of the consumer's preferences) by decreasing X from X_1 to X_0.

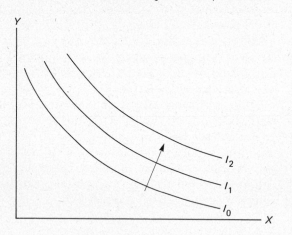

FIG. 4-3 *Indifference map of a consumer*

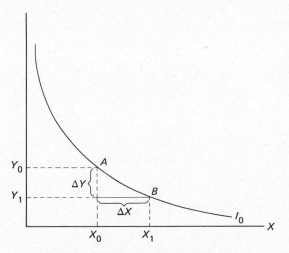

FIG. 4-4 *Marginal rate of substitution*

To put it in different symbols, the change in Y, $\Delta Y = Y_1 - Y_0$, accompanied by the change in X, $\Delta X = X_1 - X_0$, leaves the consumer indifferent. We refer to the ratio

$$- \frac{\Delta Y}{\Delta X}$$

(note the minus sign) as the *marginal rate of substitution (MRS)* of Y for X along the indifference curve I_0. By the marginal rate of substitution of Y for X we mean the number of units of Y that must be substituted for a loss of one unit of X if the consumer is to remain on the same indifference curve. Note two features of the indifference curve:

1. The marginal rate of substitution is positive. If X is increased, then Y must be decreased if the consumer is to remain indifferent.

2. The marginal rate of substitution decreases as X increases. It takes less Y to substitute for a given loss of X, the more X is available to the consumer.

This second property of indifference curves is formalized as the *law of diminishing marginal rate of substitution:*

> *As the number of units of a commodity available to a consumer increases, the marginal rate of substitution of the commodity for any other commodity decreases.*

The law of diminishing marginal rate of substitution asserts that the more you have of a commodity, the easier it is to substitute units of other commodities for a unit of the commodity and remain indifferent. A psychological rationale for the law could be constructed much like the rationale for the marginalists' law of diminishing marginal utility, in terms of the importance of wants satisfied for the consumer. Alternatively, the law can be thought of as providing a rationalization for the observed fact that consumers consume strictly positive amounts of more than one commodity.

Convexity and Indifference Curves

A simpler term and yet one with wide applicability in economic theory may be substituted for "diminishing marginal rate of substitution." This term involves the notion of a *convex set*. In two-dimensional space, a set (of points) is any collection of points in that space. We say a set is convex if, *given any two points in the set, any straight line connecting these points also is in the set.* Consider figure 4-5.

The sets are indicated by the shadings. The first two sets are examples of convex sets, while the third set is not convex (a line drawn between C and D is not in the set). The set of commodity bundles lying on or to the right of an indifference curve (that is, the bundles preferred to or indifferent to any bundle on the curve) appears as in figure 4-5b. We then

a)

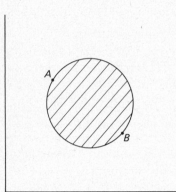

b)

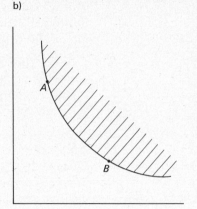

c)

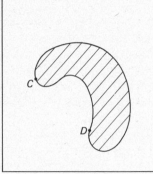

FIG. 4-5   *Three sets of points*

say that the indifference curve *bounds a convex set.* So long as the boundary of the convex set is a smooth curve, this concept expresses the same notion as the law of diminishing marginal rate of substitution.

Commodities and Flows of Services

We have been using the terms *commodity* or *good* to refer to X and Y as they appear in the consumer's preference ranking and his indifference map. These terms should be interpreted as flows of services per unit of time. For example, an individual owns title to an automobile, but he consumes the services provided by the automobile and not the automobile itself. It is these services that enter into the preference ranking as the "good" X or Y.

By adopting this convention, we can view the purchase of a consumer durable good, such as a house or furniture or a car, as an investment decision by the consumer, much like his decision to purchase title to a capital good or an acre of land. In this way we can distinguish between his *consumption choices* as among different flows of services and his *investment choices* as among different portfolios of assets. We defer treatment of investment decisions to chapter 11.

Nonsatiation

To keep our indifference maps as simple as possible, we have assumed that "more is preferred to less" for both X and Y. It is easy to think of examples of cases in which this assumption is violated; in fact it is hard to think of any good for which there is not a point where you would pass up another helping.

Although consumers can and do become satiated with particular goods, economists assume that there is no point of complete satiation for a consumer: whatever commodity bundle is presented to a consumer, there is yet another bundle that he prefers. Economists refer to this as the assumption of *nonsatiation* or the "absence of a bliss point." It excludes from consideration only true ascetics who by definition do have a bliss point and desire nothing more from the world than that.

Ordinal Utility: The Modern Approach

We can now discuss the notion of utility as it is interpreted by economists today when they say "consumers act to maximize utility." The indifference map (including the arrow) shown in figure 4-6 indicates the order of preference among commodity bundles for a consumer.

It is sometimes convenient to attach to each indifference curve an identifying number. The numbers themselves are of no importance, so long as their order corresponds with the order of the indifference curves in terms of preference: the curves higher in the preference ranking receive a higher number. Thus we could assign the number 1 to indifference curve I_1, 7 to indifference curve I_2, 8 to indifference curve I_3, or any other such assignment, so long as the number assigned to I_3 is greater than the number assigned to I_2, which in turn is larger than the number assigned to I_1.

Having assigned these numbers, we can view the indifference map in figure 4-6 as though it were a topographic map, with each point on an indifference curve being a point of equal elevation. That is, we associate with each point on I_1 the number 1, with each point on I_2 the number 7, and with each point on I_3 the number 8. In the modern literature of economics, 1 is then referred to as the "utility" of any commodity bundle lying along indifference curve I_1, 7 is the "utility" of any commodity bundle lying along indifference curve I_2, and 8 is the "utility" associated with any bundle lying along I_3.

Any system of assigning numbers to indifference curves and to the bundles lying on indifference curves which preserves the order of preference among indifference curves would be acceptable as a way of indicating the "utili-

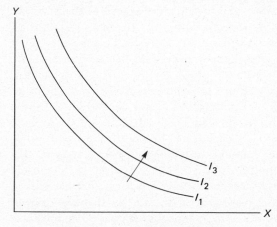

FIG. 4-6   *An indifference map*

ties" of commodity bundles. So the term *utility* is still used in economics, but its meaning is far different from that used in the writings of the marginal utility school. Specifically, *utility* is defined as follows:

The utility of a bundle A is greater than the utility of a bundle B if and only if A is preferred to B, and the utility of A equals the utility of B if and only if A and B are indifferent.

Utility thus turns out to be nothing more than an assignment of numbers to bundles in a way that reflects the preferences of the consumer. In particular, the notion of utility as "satisfaction" or as "pleasure less pain" no longer holds.

Some familiar measures are comparable to the utility of the modern economist. Hardness, for example, is much like preference in being a ranking. One material is harder than another if the first material scratches the second. Any arbitrary assignment of numbers to materials will indicate the degree of hardness, so long as a higher number is assigned to the material that scratches than to the material that is scratched.

Technically, measures such as utility that are arbitrary so long as they preserve a certain underlying ranking or ordering are referred to as *ordinal* measures, and are introduced only for the convenience of dealing with a number-ing system of measurement rather than with the clumsy underlying ranking. It is only the ordering of the numbers and not the quantita-tive differences between them that has mean-ing. Specifically, this means that the law of diminishing marginal utility has no significance in terms of the modern notion of utility.

Marginal Utility and Indifference Curves

Marginal utility, it will be recalled, is defined as the increase in utility associated with con-suming one more unit of a commodity. The marginal utility of commodity X is identified in figure 4-7.

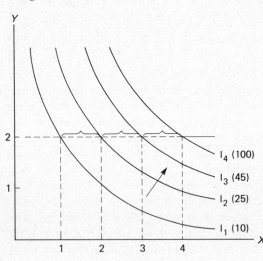

FIG. 4-7 *Marginal utility of X*

Suppose we hold the amount of Y consumed fixed at two units. As we increase the amount of X consumed from one unit to two units, we move from indifference curve I_1 to indif-ference curve I_2. The number in parentheses following each symbol $I_1, \ldots, I_4$ is the utility assigned to these curves. (Any numbers would do, so long as they increase as preference in-creases.) Thus, the marginal utility of the sec-ond unit consumed is 15 (a move from I_1 to I_2), of the third is 20, and of the fourth is 55. If we had assigned the numbers $-1, 0, +1000, +1001$, then marginal utility of the second unit of X would be 1, of the third 1000, and of the fourth 1.

Any such assignment of numbers (in a man-ner that reflects the preference ordering) is valid in terms of the modern concept of utility. In both of the examples, the law of diminishing marginal utility is violated. These examples reflect the different interpretation placed on utility in the modern theory from that of the marginalists. Other than the fact that marginal utility of X is positive when more X is preferred to less X, there is nothing that remains of the marginalists' notion of marginal utility in mod-ern economics.

The Existence of a Utility Measure

One technical point should be mentioned con-cerning the relationship between the modern notion of ordinal utility and preference rank-ings. If commodities are available only in dis-crete units, and so the only feasible points in the X-Y plane are separated from one another, then no difficulties arise in the assignment of utility numbers on the basis of preferences. However, when commodities are infinitely di-visible, there may be no way to convert from preferences to a numerical scale of utility. Work

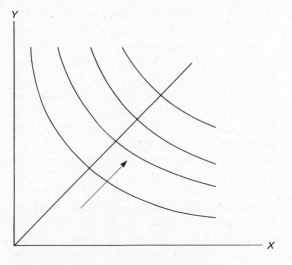

FIG. 4-8 *Indifference map*

during the 1950s by Gerard Debreu identified this problem and provided a solution to it.† While the problem involves highly abstract mathematics, the source of the difficulty can at least be indicated by the following example.

In the indifference maps depicted thus far, the indifference curves have the general shapes and characteristics of isobars on weather maps or curves of equal elevation on topographic maps. Drawing a line from the origin in the indifference map produces a picture as in figure 4-8. An indifference curve passes through each point on the line and every indifference curve crosses the line. In assigning numbers to indifference curves in a manner that reflects the preference ordering, higher numbers must be assigned to points further out on the line, and there are an infinite number of ways to do this. For example, we could let the utility numbers

assigned to indifference curves be the distance from the origin to the points along the line that are on the indifference curves. But this is not necessarily possible for all indifference maps.

Suppose that between any two commodity bundles involving X and Y, a consumer prefers the one with more X. If two bundles have the same amount of X, then he prefers the bundle with more Y. Such a preference ranking is termed a *lexicographic* ranking, since it is much like that found in a dictionary or lexicon. (We first look at the amount of X, and only examine Y if the X components are the same.) There are no indifference curves in such a ranking, since there are no two distinct points indifferent to one another.

Suppose we consider all bundles containing X_0 units of good X (figure 4-9). Each point on the line drawn upward from X_0 is preferred to any point below it on the line, since points below it have a smaller amount of Y. Our assignment of utility numbers must be such that a higher utility is given to points higher on this line. Further, every point on this line must in turn be assigned a higher utility number than that assigned to any point to the left of the line. If X and Y are infinitely divisible, and so at every point on the X axis a line similar to that drawn requires assignment of utility numbers, then there are not enough real numbers to perform this assignment. Hence, for a lexicographic ranking with commodities infinitely divisible, no way exists to convert from the preference ranking to a numerical scale of utility.

Debreu has pointed out that so long as indifference curves satisfy a certain continuity property, the problem associated with lexicographic rankings can be avoided. (This property is that the set of bundles preferred to or indif-

†G. Debreu, "Representation of a Preference Ordering by a Numerical Function," in *Decision Processes*, ed. Thrall, Cooms, and Davis (New York: Wiley, 1954).

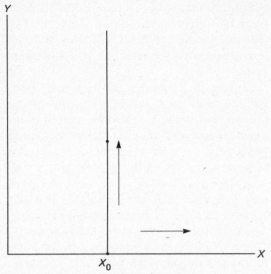

NOTE: The arrows denote direction of preference.

FIG. 4-9   *Lexicographic ranking*

ferent to any bundle contains its boundary, and the set of bundles to which any bundle is preferred or indifferent also contains its boundary.) Suffice it to say that the indifference maps used in this book always satisfy this condition, so that it is always possible to convert from a preference ranking to an assignment of utility numbers.

Money Illusion and Consumer Preferences

In our discussion of consumer preferences we have implicitly assumed the "absence of money illusion." *Money illusion* exists when the preferences of a consumer are influenced by the prices of goods and services he consumes. For example, there is a story to the effect that when the first home permanents went on the market in the 1940s, they were priced at 25¢ a kit. They didn't sell. After some market research, the price was jacked up to $1 a kit. Sales soared. In effect, consumers, lacking information about the product, judged quality by price. The product at $1 per kit was no different from the product at 25¢ per kit, except for the price, which consumers used as a measure of the value to them of the product.

In modern utility theory, the preferences of a consumer are defined over commodity bundles, independently of the prices at which such commodities sell. The home permanent example is not covered by our analysis. One can think of similar cases where money illusion is present, and the approach of modern utility theory breaks down. Most of these cases arise because of lack of information on the part of the consumer as to the qualities of the product, rather than because of a systematic tendency on the part of consumers to practice money illusion. We will regard them as aberrations that tend to be corrected as information becomes available.

It is important to distinguish between money illusion or its absence as a characteristic of preferences, and choices that reflect money prices. If we ask "would you prefer a Cadillac or a Volkswagen," the natural answer (whatever your preference ranking over cars) is the Cadillac. Even if you prefer Volkswagens, why not take the Cadillac, sell it, and buy a Volkswagen (plus several thousand dollars of other goods)? The semantic problem arises because in the question "would you prefer . . . ," *prefer* is interpreted to mean "choose." A preference ranking is the economist's description of the *tastes* of a consumer, while *choices* of course reflect not only the underlying tastes but also prices and the income of the consumer. It is tastes (as described by the consumer's indifference map) that are assumed to be independent of prices, not choices.

Interpersonal Comparisons of Utility

For Jeremy Bentham, it was completely natural to say that "Mr. A attains a higher level of utility than Mr. B." Bentham thought of utility as a concept that is measurable and comparable among individuals in much the same way that wealth or income can be measured and compared among individuals. The modern approach to utility rejects both the "measurability" and the "interpersonal comparability" of utility. For any one individual, we can say that "bundle W provides more utility than bundle Z," because this means precisely that bundle W is preferred by the individual to bundle Z. But we cannot say that "bundle W is preferred to bundle X by more than bundle X is preferred to bundle V," because such comparisons assume a utility measure that does more than simply reflect the *order* of preference among bundles. In this sense modern utility lacks "measurability," even for a single individual.

In order for utility to be comparable among individuals, there would in addition have to exist a zero and a unit measurement (like our measurements of distance) for utility that applied to each individual. Both are lacking in the modern concept of utility, and the utility scales used for different individuals need have no connection at all with one another. They simply reflect the order of preferences for each individual.

Because normative economics is based on the theory of consumer behavior, including the specification of consumer preferences outlined in this chapter, it lacks any standards to judge whether "Mr. A has a higher level of satis-faction than Mr. B," which is the way that Bentham would interpret the statement "Mr. A has a higher utility than Mr. B." When we turn to a study of normative economics later in this book, the consequences of this situation will become quite apparent. The propositions of normative economics turn out to concern ways in which everyone in the society can be made better off by a certain action, rather than ways in which the losses of certain groups are "more than offset" by the gains of other groups. Interpersonal comparisons are rejected throughout the entire body of modern normative economics.

Summary

In this chapter, we have described the general characteristics of the tastes of the consumer, as they are viewed by the economist. The tastes are represented by a preference ranking over commodity bundles assigned to the consumer. The preference ranking is *total* (all bundles can be compared in terms of preference or indifference), and *transitive* (consistent). In our treatment we have assumed that preferences are *independent* of the amounts of commodities assigned to other consumers or of activities by firms, and are characterized by *absence of money illusion* in the sense that prices of commodities do not influence the preference ranking.

The indifference map of the consumer gives a graphic portrayal of the preference ranking, with indifference curves sloping downward to the right and satisfying the *law of diminishing marginal rate of substitution* (indifference curves bound convex sets). The concept of utility used in economics is simply an assignment of numbers to commodity bundles in such a way that the order of preference among bundles is preserved. Utility is neither measurable nor comparable among consumers.

Problems

1. The utility for a consumer associated with a bundle containing x units of X and y units of Y is equal to the product (that is, $U = xy$).

   a. Draw the indifference curves for the consumer for $U = 100$, $U = 400$.

   b. Verify that more is preferred to less for both X and Y, assuming positive amounts consumed of both goods.

   c. Verify that the law of diminishing marginal rate of substitution holds.

   d. Suppose that the utility numbers assigned to bundles are determined by the formula $U = \sqrt{(xy)}$. How does the change in the formula for U change the indifference map? (Hint: draw the indifference curves for $U = 10$ and $U = 20$, and compare with the original curves for $U = 100$ and $U = 400$). Explain in terms of the notion of utility as an ordinal measure.

2. Plot the indifference maps for each of the following preference rankings. Comment on the correspondence between the resulting indifference maps and the assumptions employed in the chapter.

   a. I can't stand either peanut butter or jelly alone; but peanut butter and jelly sandwiches turn me on.

   b. X and Y are good substitutes for me. Double X and, if Y is halved, I'm just as well off.

   c. The thing I look for in a friend is honesty; of course, as among honest people I like those with a sense of humor.

   d. I could care less whether you have Coors or Budweiser, so long as it's beer.

   e. Plot the indifference curve of a miser, relating money and "all other goods."

3. A husband comes home on Friday and says: "My God—hamburger again?" His wife replies, "You liked hamburger on Monday, Tuesday, Wednesday, and Thursday—and Friday you don't like hamburger?" Does the economist's theory of preferences cover the case of this husband?

4. "The law of diminishing marginal utility as applied to money argues that income taxes should be levied on a progressive basis rather than simply proportionately to income." Point out the fallacies in this line of reasoning, in terms of modern utility theory.

5. Take one section of today's paper and examine the ads. What is the purpose of the ads? Are they designed primarily to provide price and quality information for the reader? Are they designed to change the preferences of the reader? Are they designed to change the reader's conception of how the commodity might help to satisfy his or her basic drives? Is there a systematic difference among commodities in these respects, and do you have some ideas about what causes these differences?

5

The Theory of Consumer Demand

The indifference map of the consumer describes his tastes or preferences. The choices of the consumer are determined in part by his tastes and in part by the constraints imposed upon choices by his limited income and by the prices of goods and services. In discussing the tastes of the consumer, a consistency requirement was imposed—namely, that preferences be transitive. A consistency requirement is imposed on choices as well.

Consistency and Choices

The basic consistency requirement on choices is that the consumer act according to his perception of his self-interest. We interpret this to mean:

> Given a choice from a set of commodity bundles, the consumer chooses the bundle belonging to the set that is highest on his preference ranking.

This amounts to saying that a consumer's choices are consistent with his preferences. Equivalently, given an assignment of utility numbers to bundles, the consumer chooses the bundle in the set that has the highest utility: *the consumer maximizes utility.*

As noncontroversial as the axiom of consistency of choices might appear, in fact there

are some aspects of this assumption that are not at all obvious. To illustrate, consider a game in which an individual is told that an urn contains sixty black balls and forty red balls. A ball is selected at random, and the individual is paid $1 if he correctly guesses the color of the ball but nothing if he is wrong. Ten such trials are to be run, with balls replaced in the urn after being drawn. The individual is asked to state the rule he will use in making his guesses. A remarkably large number of people will use the rule "guess black 60 percent of the time, red 40 percent of the time." The correct rule, of course, is to guess black all of the time. The choices of an individual guessing black 60 percent of the time are not consistent with his preferences (more money preferred to less). The point is that the axiom of consistency of choices assumes that consumers can in fact correctly assess the alternatives available to them in terms of their preferences. When computations of one kind or another are involved in such assessments, or when other informational problems arise, observed choices can violate the condition of consistency.

The rule of maximizing utility underlies all of consumer theory in economics. In this chapter we will discuss the implications of utility maximization in the simplest possible setting. We consider the case of a consumer with a given amount of income to be allocated between purchases of two goods, X and Y. We will put off until later questions relating to how income of the consumer is determined, or how choices are made between consumption and saving, or how the consumer decides what portfolio of assets to hold. Our basic objective is to see how utility maximization permits us to derive certain testable propositions concerning the properties of consumer demand schedules.

The Consumer's Budget Set

Let p_x denote the price per unit of good X; let p_y denote the price per unit of Y; and let M denote the income of the consumer. We assume that X and Y are purchased in perfectly competitive markets, so that each consumer treats the prices of X and Y as fixed constants, independent of the amounts of either good purchased. The budget constraint for the consumer can be written as follows:

$$p_x X + p_y Y \leq M.$$

This constraint says that the amounts spent by the consumer on X and Y cannot exceed the income available to the consumer. In other words, borrowing is excluded. This constraint, together with the constraint that X and Y can be purchased only in nonnegative amounts, leads to a graph of the consumer's *budget set* (fig. 5-1).

The shaded area represents the set of commodity bundles available to the consumer under the budget constraint. The budget equation $M = p_x X + p_y Y$ is graphed by locating the intercepts along the X and Y axes. We refer to the graph of this equation as the *budget line*, while the shaded area is the consumer's *budget*

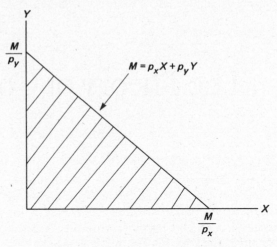

FIG. 5-1   *The consumer's budget set*

set. The X intercept tells us the maximum number of units of X the consumer can purchase with his income M, and the Y intercept the maximum number of units of Y. Because prices and income are independent of the amounts purchased of X and Y, it follows that the budget equation is a straight line through the X and Y intercepts.

The X intercept of the budget line is solved for by setting $Y = 0$ in the budget equation. Hence, the X intercept is M/p_x. Setting $X = 0$ gives the Y intercept as M/p_y. Note that the slope of the line is equal to the negative of the Y intercept divided by the X intercept; hence the slope of the "budget line" is given by $-(p_x/p_y)$.

There is an interesting feature of the set of bundles available under the budget constraint. If we double both prices, and also double income, the available set of bundles does not change. The intercepts remain the same, while the equation of the budget line is unchanged as well. In other words, the budget line and budget set depend only on *relative prices* and *the purchasing power of income.* Once the consumer knows the ratio of (1) price of X to price of Y, (2) income to price of X, and (3) income to price of Y (how much his income will purchase in terms of X and Y), then he knows the set of bundles in the budget set.

Utility Maximization

Suppose we now superimpose the consumer's indifference map on the graph of the budget set (fig. 5-2). The consumer is faced with a choice from among the commodity bundles that lie in the budget set. Which does he choose? If his choices are consistent with his preferences, he picks the bundle that lies on the highest attainable indifference curve within the budget set. This bundle is $(\bar{X}, \bar{Y})$—the "utility-maximizing" bundle for the consumer.

In the situation we are examining, a certain amount of income, M, is assumed to be available for spending on consumption this period. The consumer is assumed to have decided already how much to save for the future; hence the alternative to spending is not to add to saving, but rather to throw income away. For this reason, it is not surprising that the utility-maximizing bundle lies on the budget line. The consumer spends all of his income in maximizing utility as long as he is not satiated with goods X and Y. The indifference map as drawn exhibits nonsatiation; in fact, more is preferred to less for either X or Y.

The utility-maximizing choice occurs not only on the budget line, but also at a point of tangency between the budget line and the highest indifference curve that touches the line, the indifference curve I_2. The tangency condi-

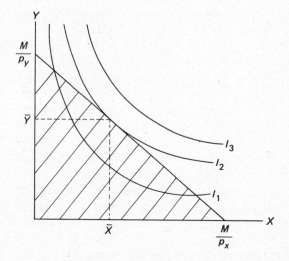

FIG. 5-2 *Utility maximizing*

tion characterizes a utility-maximizing choice so long as there are positive amounts of both X and Y in the utility-maximizing bundle. We will take this as the typical case.

We have already noted that along an indifference curve, the marginal rate of substitution between X and Y is defined by

$$MRS = -\frac{\Delta Y}{\Delta X}$$

where $\Delta Y/\Delta X$ is the slope of the indifference curve. The tangency condition between the budget line and the highest attainable indifference curve thus reduces to the condition

$$MRS = \frac{p_x}{p_y}$$

where MRS is the absolute value of the slope of the highest attainable indifference curve. MRS is interpreted as the number of units of Y that must be obtained to offset the loss of one unit of X, given that the consumer remains on the same indifference curve. p_x/p_y gives the number of units of Y that can be obtained in the market in exchange for one unit of X. (If $p_x = \$3$, $p_y = \$6$, then one unit of X exchanges for one-half unit of Y.)

The tangency condition thus implies that the consumer adjusts his consumption of X and Y in such a way that the substitutability of Y for X in terms of his personal preferences (his MRS) is equated to the substitutability of Y for X in terms of the market exchange rate between these two goods. Note that since all consumers face the same prices in perfectly competitive markets, MRS between X and Y is the same for all consumers purchasing positive amounts of these goods.

Consumer Demand Functions

Thus far in this book we have talked in terms of demand schedules and demand curves, relating quantity demanded to "own" price. Now we can deal with things a little more generally. The quantity demanded of X depends on the price per unit of X, the price per unit of Y, income M, and the tastes of the consumer. Given the tastes of the consumer (as displayed in his indifference map), we define the *demand function* for X as a listing of the quantities of X demanded for all values of p_x, p_y, and M. Similarly, the demand function for Y is a listing of quantities of Y demanded for all combinations of values for p_x, p_y, and M.

How do we determine what quantities of X and Y will be demanded for any given values of p_x, p_y, and M? We plot the budget set associated with the given prices and income, and determine the utility-maximizing choice of a bundle. The quantities of X and Y appearing in the utility-maximizing bundle are then the quantities demanded by the consumer of the two goods for the given prices and income. What this amounts to saying is that by superimposing the indifference map on the budget set (as in figure 5-2), we can in principle determine the demand functions for both X and Y by varying prices and income and reading off the corresponding utility-maximizing quantities. For the remainder of this chapter, we will explore the properties of such demand functions.

Homogeneity of Degree Zero of Consumer Demand Functions

We first consider the effects of a proportionate increase in the prices of X and Y and in income. Suppose p_x, p_y, and M are all doubled. Then both relative prices p_x/p_y and the purchasing power of income, M/p_x and M/p_y, are left unchanged. But this means that the budget set remains unchanged as well. This outcome can be verified directly from the fact that the slope and the intercepts of the budget line remain as before.

Furthermore, since the preference ranking of the consumer is characterized by absence of money illusion, the indifference map is unaffected by *any* changes in prices and income. It immediately follows that the utility-maximizing bundle is unchanged by proportionate increases in prices and income. This characteristic is referred to as *homogeneity of degree zero of consumer demand functions*.

The quantity demanded by a consumer of any good is unchanged by an equal proportionate increase in all prices and income.

Homogeneity of degree zero is simply a shorthand expression to characterize any function that has the property whereby multiplying all the arguments of the function by a positive constant leaves the value of the function unchanged. Examples of consumer demand functions for X that satisfy homogeneity of degree zero include the following.

$$X = \frac{ap_x + bp_y}{M} \qquad (1)$$

$$X = p_x^a \; p_y^b \; M^{-(a+b)} \qquad (a, b \text{ are constants.}) \quad (2)$$

In both equations 1 and 2, replacing p_x by $2p_x$, p_y by $2p_y$, and M by $2M$ results in no change in X.

But suppose that the demand function for X is linear, as in

$$X = a_0 + a_1 p_x + a_2 p_y + a_3 M. \qquad (3)$$

Multiplying p_x, p_y and M by 2 we get

$$X = a_0 + 2a_1 p_x + 2a_2 p_y + 2a_3 M.$$

Clearly, linear demand functions do *not* satisfy homogeneity of degree zero. Consequently, the use of straight-line demand functions (as in chapters 2 and 3) is, strictly speaking, incorrect. As noted earlier, they are to be regarded as approximations to the true nonlinear demand functions; they are used only for illustrative purposes.

Homogeneity of degree zero of demand functions has some interesting implications. As we are all too well aware, there has been worldwide inflation over the past few years. Without attempting to identify the causes of this inflation, we might ask what its costs are to consumers and how they arise. Our analysis indicates that if all prices and all incomes increased proportionately during an inflation, there would be no *real* impact on consumers; they would continue to purchase the same bundle of goods and would remain at the same level in their preference rankings on the same indifference curves. The costs of inflation arise precisely because not all prices and incomes rise together. The differential rates of growth of prices and incomes cause a redistribution of purchasing power from those on relatively fixed incomes to those whose incomes are derived from occupations where prices and wages are rising most rapidly.

Recognition of this fact has led to experiments involving "indexing," which is in essence public policy aimed at ensuring a rough equality of growth rates in all incomes during inflation, through contracts specified in terms of dollars of constant purchasing power rather than in terms of current dollars. Indexing has been used in Brazil and has been suggested by a number of economists as a means to offset inflation in the U.S. economy.

Response of Quantity Demanded to Income Changes

Consider next what happens when the prices of X and Y remain unchanged but income increases. What can be said about the amounts of X and Y that will be demanded? In figure 5-3, when income increases (say from M' to M''), the intercepts along the X and Y axes increase. Because the slope of the budget line is determined by the price ratio only, and because this ratio has not changed, the new budget line is parallel to the old one. We plot in the two utility-maximizing choices for the consumer.

Let X' denote the amount of X demanded when $M = M'$, and X'' denote the amount of X demanded when $M = M''$, and similarly for Y. Then when income increases, the amounts demanded for both X and Y increase. Is this true for all goods and for all consumers? Clearly

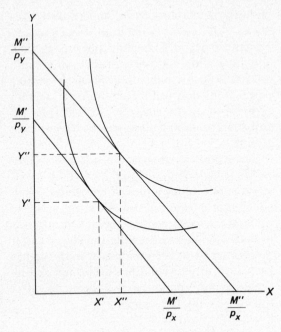

FIG. 5-3   *Quantities demanded and changes in income*

A good is said to be *inferior if, when income increases, prices being held fixed, the quantity demanded of the good declines.* In figure 5-4, X is an inferior good (at least for the income range between M' and M") while Y is a normal good.

The issue of which goods are inferior and which goods are normal rests on the consumer's tastes or preferences. What is inferior for one consumer may be normal for another, and a good may be inferior for one range of prices and income, but normal for another range. We can, however, impose some limits on the extent of inferiority of commodities for a given consumer.

It cannot be the case for any consumer that all goods are inferior; at least one good must be normal.

The reason for this limitation is that the utility-maximizing bundle always lies on the budget line and so all of income is spent. In-

it is not. We know that, as income goes up, people tend to switch from low priced cars to more expensive models, and to substitute steak for hamburger, and generally to buy higher quality goods. Similarly, interest in professional baseball compared to pro football has declined over the past twenty years partly because baseball has traditionally been a lower-income, blue-collar sport, while the upper middle classes are football freaks. As the average level of income has risen in the United States, the shift from baseball to football has followed.

Normal and Inferior Goods   We define a commodity as being a *normal good if, when income increases, prices being held fixed, the quantity demanded of the good increases.* The situation depicted in figure 5-3 applies to normal goods.

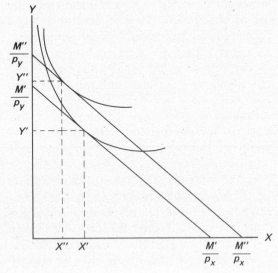

FIG. 5-4   *X an inferior good, Y a normal good*

creasing income while holding prices constant means that there must be at least one good for which quantity demanded increases. Not all goods can be inferior.

Income-Consumption Curve If, for given prices for goods X and Y, we permit income to vary over a broad range of values, we will generate what is known as the consumer's *income-consumption curve.* This curve traces the responsiveness of quantities demanded of goods to income changes.

If the income-consumption curve rises to the right (as in figure 5-5), both goods X and Y are normal. If X is inferior, the curve will turn back on itself to the left; while if Y is inferior, the curve will fall to the right. When we deal with broad groups of commodities (such as food, clothing, shelter, entertainment, and medical expenses), and compare expenditures for various income classes in a society, the curve

typically rises to the right; that is, each of the broad groupings of commodities tends to act as a normal good. When the classes are broken down to specific commodities, and to specific grades of commodities, then inferiority begins to appear in the income-consumption curve.

To illustrate, consider the budget data in table 5-1. These data are used by the Department of Labor in constructing and revamping the consumer cost of living index. Except for social security taxes, which are fixed by law as a function of income, all of the broad categories rise with rises in income. All five components of consumption are normal goods, although as a percent of income before taxes, food and other (personal care, out-of-pocket medical and health costs, and so on) fall, while housing and clothing rise.

Response of Quantity Demanded of a Good to a Change in Its Own Price

We next consider the effect on quantities demanded of X and Y of a change in the price of X, assuming that income and the price of Y remain fixed. Figure 5-6 depicts the resulting changes in the utility-maximizing choices of X and Y. Note that the intercept along the Y axis remains unchanged, while the intercept along the X axis varies inversely with changes in p_x.

The change from p_x' to p_x'' represents an increase in the price of X, with income and the price of Y remaining fixed. As shown in figure 5-6, the effect of this change is to decrease the quantity of X demanded from X' to X", and also to decrease the quantity of Y demanded. Additionally, the consumer is "worse off" since he ends up at a lower indifference curve following the increase in the price of X than he formerly was able to achieve.

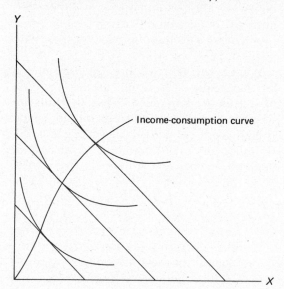

FIG. 5-5 *Income-consumption curve*

TABLE 5-1   *Annual Expenditures by Income Classes*
Urban United States, Autumn 1973

Expense Items	Lower Budget $	Lower Budget % of total	Intermediate Budget $	Intermediate Budget % of total	Higher Budget $	Higher Budget % of total
Income	*$8,181*	*100*	$12,626	100	$18,201	100
Social Security	492	6	647	5	647	4
Income Tax	724	9	1,607	13	3,080	17
Net Income	6,965	85	10,372	82	14,474	79
Savings	385	5	609	5	1,024	6
Consumption	6,580	80	9,761	77	13,450	74
Food	2,440	30	3,181	25	4,020	22
Housing	1,627	20	2,908	23	4,386	24
Clothing	596	7	995	8	1,456	8
Transportation	563	7	1,014	8	1,315	7
Other	1,354	17	1,661	13	2,273	12

SOURCE: *Monthly Labor Review*, U.S. Department of Labor, April, 1975.

The increase in the price of X changes the market rate of exchange between X and Y and in addition reduces the purchasing power of income. These two effects can be analyzed separately. First, the increase in the price of X, with the price of Y fixed, tends to move the consumer toward substituting Y for X. X is relatively more expensive than formerly; hence Y becomes a more attractive alternative for the consumer. If this were all that happened, then an increase in the price of X would lower the quantity demanded of X *and* increase the quantity demanded of Y.

But there is a second effect of the price increase. Since X is more expensive than before, and since the money amount of income has not changed, the consumer has become "poorer" in terms of purchasing power. The importance of this aspect of the price increase depends upon how important X is in the consumer's market basket. For someone who spends most of his income on food, an increase in the price of food has an important influence on the purchasing power of the consumer's income, while for someone who spends, say, 10 percent of his income on food, the purchasing power effect is much less. In either case, however, the reduction in purchasing power is much like a decrease in money income with prices fixed.

What is the effect of this reduction in real purchasing power of income on the quantities of X and Y demanded? This depends on whether X or Y are normal or inferior goods. If both goods are normal, then the effect will be to decrease the amounts purchased of both commodities. If X is an inferior good, then the effect is to *increase* purchases of X. We conclude that the effect on quantities demanded of X and Y because of an increase in p_x depends on the relative strengths of the two forces operating on the consumer—the force operating in the direction of substituting Y for X as X becomes relatively more expensive, and the force operating on both X and Y through the fall in the purchasing power of

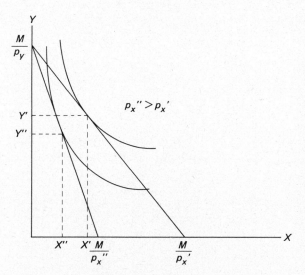

FIG. 5-6   *Quantities demanded and change in* p_x

income. We refer to the first of these as the *substitution effect*, and to the second as the *income effect*.

The Substitution Effect and the Income Effect   The two forces operating on quantities demanded because of an increase in the price of X can be identified as in figure 5-7. In the original situation, the utility-maximizing choice is the bundle A on the indifference curve I_2. With p_y and M unchanged, the effect of increasing p_x is to rotate the budget line downward to the left, about the unchanged Y intercept. The new utility-maximizing choice is the bundle C on the indifference curve I_1.

An increase in the price of X makes X relatively more expensive compared to Y than before, and reduces the purchasing power of the consumer's income. But suppose that when the price of X increases, the consumer is given sufficient additional income so that he can remain on the indifference curve I_2. Then,

because of the change in the price ratio p_x/p_y, the consumer would pick the bundle B on I_2. (Note that the budget line through B is parallel to the budget line through C, reflecting the higher price of X; and the budget line is tangent to I_2 at B.) Since the consumer remains on I_2, he has suffered no loss of purchasing power. Hence we have been able to isolate the substitution effect of the increase in the price of X in the move from A to B, that is, the change from the bundle (X', Y') to the bundle (X^*, Y^*). The substitution effect tells how the consumption of X and Y are altered in response to a higher price of X, assuming that the consumer remains on the same indifference curve.

Of course, the consumer is not actually compensated by an increase in income when the price of X increases. What happens is that he moves from the bundle A to the bundle C. For purposes of analysis, we can think of the move from A to C in terms of both the changes

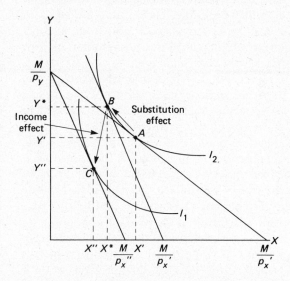

FIG. 5-7   *The substitution effect and the income effect (X, Y normal)*

in quantities demanded due solely to a change in relative prices (the move from *A* to *B*) and the change due to a fall in the purchasing power of income (the move from *B* to *C*). The move from *B* to *C* is the *income effect* of the increase in the price of *X*. It isolates the change in consumption of *X* and *Y* due solely to the fact that an increase in the price of *X* lowers the purchasing power of income for the consumer. The lower purchasing power is indicated by the fact that at the higher price of *X*, the consumer can now achieve only the indifference curve I_1, which is lower in the preference ranking than I_2. Again note that the move from *B* to *C* is a move along the income-consumption curve of the consumer, given the higher price of *X* and the fixed price of *Y*.

As indicated in figure 5-7, the substitution effect (the move from *A* to *B*) leads to a substitution of *Y* for *X* when *X* becomes relatively more expensive than before. This is always the case in a two-good world. The income effect is more ambiguous. In the case pictured, both *X* and *Y* are normal goods, and so the income effect acts to reduce the consumption of both *X* and *Y*. This need not be the case, of course. If either *X* or *Y* were inferior, then the income effect associated with a fall in the purchasing power of income would lead to an increase in consumption of the inferior good.

In figure 5-8, *X* is an inferior good, while *Y* is normal. As in figure 5-7, the substitution effect increases the consumption of *Y* at the expense of *X;* that is, Y^* is larger than Y' while X^* is less than X'. However, the income effect (the movement from *B* to *C*) results in an increased consumption of *X* (the change from X^* to X''), while the consumption of *Y* falls from Y^* to Y''. *X* is an inferior good, while *Y* is a normal good.

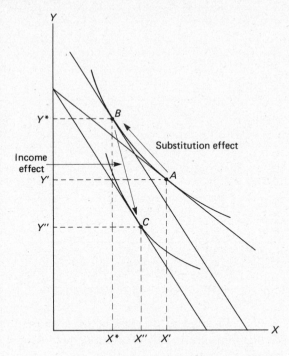

FIG. 5-8   *The substitution effect and the income effect (X inferior, Y normal)*

Giffen Goods   The case of a downward sloping demand curve for a good has been identified earlier as the typical case in economic theory. In figures 5-7 and 5-8, consumption of *X* is less in bundle *C* than in bundle *A*. Both graphs are consistent with the typical case. But cases can arise in which an increase in the price of *X* leads to an increase in the consumption of *X* in the utility-maximizing bundle. These are regarded as oddities; in fact, it is difficult to find empirical examples of this phenomenon. When an increase in the price of a commodity leads to an increase in the quantity demanded of the commodity, it is called a *Giffen good*.

The name derives from that of an English

economist who investigated living conditions among the Irish peasants in the late nineteenth century. He discovered that potatoes, the staple of the Irish diet, were a strongly inferior good. Furthermore, the Irish peasants were so poor (ranking only with the Poles among Europeans) that few substitutes for potatoes were available. The importance of potatoes in the Irish diet is indicated by the devastating effects of the potato famine of the 1840s, which drastically reduced the Irish population both directly through starvation and indirectly through emigration. Given a fall in the price of potatoes, there would be little substitution of potatoes for other goods by the peasants. Because potatoes are strongly inferior, and so important an element of consumption expenditures, the increase in purchasing power associated with a fall in potato prices generates a large income effect in the direction of decreasing the consumption of potatoes. The two together could well lead to a decrease in consumption of potatoes as the price of potatoes falls (although it is not clear from the data available whether this was in fact true in Ireland at that time).

The case of a Giffen good is illustrated in figure 5-9. Here the income effect (movement from B to C) is so strongly inferior for good X that the substitution effect is overwhelmed, and at point C, the quantity demanded of X, X'', is larger than the original quantity demanded, X', even though the price of X has increased.

The Giffen good case is regarded in the economic literature as a theoretical oddity. Certainly any argument posited on the assumption that the good in question is a Giffen good would be regarded as weak indeed, unless considerable empirical evidence were available to support the claim.

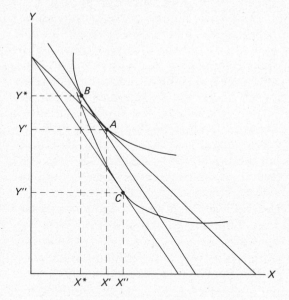

FIG. 5-9   *The case of a Giffen good*

Net Substitutes and Net Complements   Many concepts in economic theory can be illustrated, without too much distortion, by two-dimensional graphs. However, problems can arise in generalizing from the two-good case to the case of many goods. This point is raised because the simple conclusion concerning the substitution effect (that an increase in the price of X, with the price of Y constant and with the consumer staying on the same indifference curve, always results in a substitution of Y for X) does not hold quite as simply when there are more than two goods. It is always true that along a given indifference curve, increasing the price of X (with other prices fixed) decreases the amount of X at a utility-maximizing point. However, it is not necessarily true that the consumer will substitute each and every other good for X.

Goods X and Y are said to be *net substitutes* for one another if, when the consumer remains on a given indifference curve, an increase in the price of X leads to a substitution of Y for X. X and Y are said to be *net complements* for one another if, along a given indifference curve, an increase in the price of X leads to a fall in Y at the utility-maximizing point.

When there are two goods, they are always net substitutes, as indicated by the graphical analysis of the last sections. Along a given indifference curve an increase in the price of X leads to less X and more Y being consumed, when utility is maximized. When there are more than two goods, then the law of diminishing marginal rate of substitution (indifference curves bound convex sets) implies that a least one other good must be a net substitute for any given good. Thus, it is consistent with the theory of consumer behavior for X to be a net substitute for Y, Y a net complement for Z, and Z a net substitute for X.

The notions of net substitute and net complement are symmetric—X a net substitute for Y implies that Y is a net substitute for X. Because of this, there is at least one net substitute for each of the goods X, Y, and Z, as required by the law of diminishing marginal rate of substitution.

Along a given indifference curve, an increase in the price of X leads to at least one other good being substituted for X, but it is not required that all other goods be net substitutes for X.

The term *net substitute* is to be contrasted with the idea of a gross substitute, introduced in chapter 3. For a consumer, X and Y are *gross substitutes* if an increase in the price of X leads to an increase in the quantity demanded of Y. X and Y are net substitutes if, *along a given indifference curve*, an increase in the price of X leads to an increase in the quantity demanded of Y. The term *gross* is used to denote the fact that both the income effect and the substitution effect are taken into account in the relation between X and Y; with "net" substitutes, only the substitution effect is taken into account. It turns out that if X and Y are normal goods, net complementarity implies gross complementarity; and if X and Y are inferior goods, net substitutability implies gross substitutability. In other cases, the gross relationships between goods depend upon the quantitative importance of income and substitution terms.

Deriving the Consumer's Demand Curve   To return to the basic device economists use in analyzing markets, we might summarize how the consumer's demand curve for X is derived from utility maximization. The demand curve for X displays the quantities demanded of X as a function of the price of X, assuming income and other prices are held fixed. By varying the price of X, we can read off the utility-maximizing quantities of X associated with these prices. Transferring these to a price-quantity diagram (fig. 5-10), we obtain the demand curve for X.

M and p_y are fixed in value. As p_x takes on the values p_{x_1}, p_{x_2}, p_{x_3}, the quantity demanded of X takes on the values X_1, X_2, X_3. The resulting plot of quantities demanded against prices gives the demand curve for X, D_x. The demand curve is written as $D_x(p_y, M)$, because the location of the curve depends upon the values taken on by the price of Y and income. As p_y and M vary, the demand curve shifts. If X and Y are gross substitutes for the consumer, an increase in the price of Y shifts the demand curve for X to the right; if they are gross complements, the curve shifts to the left when the price of

a)

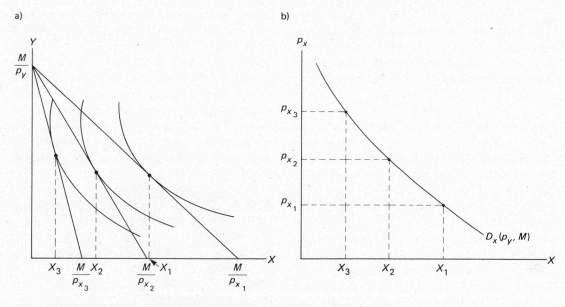

b)

FIG. 5-10   *Derivation of the demand curve for X*

Y goes up. If *X* is a normal good, an increase in income shifts the demand curve to the right; if *X* is inferior, an income increase shifts the demand curve to the left. As drawn, *X* exhibits the typical downward slope. If *X* were a Giffen good, the demand curve would slope upward to the right.

Summary of Utility Maximization and Consumer Demand

The modern utility approach takes as a fundamental postulate that consumers make choices in a manner consistent with their preferences; consumers act to "maximize utility." Under the assumption that consumers face competitive markets for the goods that they purchase, and with a given income available for spending on consumption goods, utility maximization leads to certain testable propositions concerning consumer demands. The most important of these are the following.

1. An equal proportionate increase in all prices and income leaves quantities demanded of all goods unchanged. (Consumer demand functions are homogeneous of degree zero).

2. If a commodity is a normal good, then the demand curve for the commodity displays the typical property of sloping downward to the right.

3. Only in the case of an inferior good can the demand curve violate the "typical" property. (corollary to 2)

It should be emphasized that the Giffen good case of upward sloping demand requires not only inferiority, but also that the resulting income effect be sufficiently strong to offset the substitution effect, which always acts in the direction of reducing quantity demanded of a good in response to an increase in its price.

Compensated Demand Curves

The observed demand curve of a consumer reflects both the income and substitution effects of price changes. Still it is possible in principle to estimate separately the income and substitution effects and, with sufficient data, to construct for a consumer his income-compensated demand curve. This curve relates quantities demanded of X to the price of X, assuming that the price of Y is fixed and that income for the consumer is varied so that the consumer remains on the same indifference curve. The process of generating an income-compensated demand curve is illustrated in figure 5-11.

With the price of Y fixed at p_y, and with income at M, X_1 units of X are demanded at a price of p_x. When the price of X is increased to p_x', p_y fixed, income has to increase to M' in order for the consumer to remain on the indifference curve I_1. Given an income of M', the consumer chooses to consume X_2 units at a price per unit of p_x'.

Transferring these choices to a price quantity diagram, we obtain the demand curve of figure 5-11b. The location of the demand curve is indicated by $D_x(p_y, I_1)$. p_y is held fixed along the curve, as is the level of preference along the indifference curve I_1.

The main interest in income-compensated demand curves arises from their relationship to consumer's surplus.

a)   b)

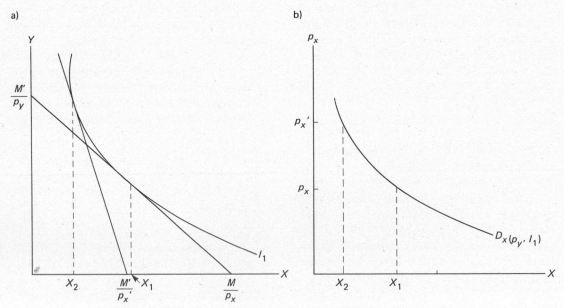

FIG. 5-11   *Derivation of the income-compensated demand curve for X*

Consumer's Surplus

Given a price $\bar{p}_x$, let $\bar{X}$ denote the level of consumption associated with $\bar{p}_x$ on the income-compensated demand curve. Then the area under the curve up to $\bar{X}$ can be interpreted as the amount of income that would be required to compensate the consumer for the loss of $\bar{X}$ units of X, while maintaining the consumer on the given indifference curve I_1.†

The consumer buys X in a competitive market; hence he pays the market price $\bar{p}_x$ per unit of X purchased, and his total expenditures on X are simply $\bar{p}_x\bar{X}$. The difference between the amount of income that would be required to compensate the consumer for the loss of $\bar{X}$ units of X, and what he actually pays to obtain these units is called *consumer's surplus*, and is illustrated in figure 5-12.

The shaded area (consumer's surplus) is the difference between the area under the compensated demand curve up to $\bar{X}$ and the area representing total expenditures on X, namely the rectangle with horizontal distance $\bar{X}$ and vertical height $\bar{p}_x$. The consumer obtains a "surplus" through the operation of competitive markets, because he does not give up as much as he would be willing to, in order to obtain the specified number of units of X.

We will return to the notion of consumer's surplus in our discussion of normative economics in chapter 13. The main thing to keep in mind at this point is that consumer's surplus is a valid measure of the gains to a consumer in a competitive market in the general case only when measured relative to the income-compensated demand curve. Calculating con-

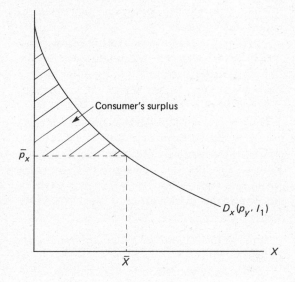

FIG. 5-12   *Consumer's surplus*

sumer's surplus by using the observed demand curve of the consumer instead (that is, the demand curve along which p_y and M are constant) is valid only in the empirically uninteresting case in which a 1 percent increase in income is accompanied by exactly a 1 percent increase in the consumption of all goods.

The Weak Axiom of Revealed Preference

It was mentioned in chapter 4 that recent work on consumer demand has followed two different approaches—the "modern utility" approach, which investigates the implications of utility maximization for choices, and the "revealed preference" approach, which focuses on the choices themselves. We next briefly sum-

---

†Strictly speaking, it is the *change* in this area associated with small changes in p_x (and thus X) which can be so interpreted.

marize the revealed preference approach to consumer demand.

Suppose that a consumer facing competitive markets with a given income chooses bundle A in his budget set. Let B be any other bundle that lies in the budget set of the consumer. Then A is said to be *revealed preferred* to B. The choice of A when B was available "reveals" that the consumer prefers A to B.

There is a simple consistency condition on choices developed independently by Abraham Wald and Paul Samuelson.† This condition is known as the *weak axiom of revealed preference:*

> Suppose that A and B are two different commodity bundles. If A is revealed preferred to B, it is never the case that B is revealed preferred to A.

The weak axiom asserts that if in some price-income situation on competitive markets, A is chosen when B is in the budget set, then the only price-income situation in which B could be chosen is one in which A is *not* in the budget set, assuming A and B are different bundles.

Figure 5-13 shows situations in which the weak axiom is satisfied and in which the weak axiom is violated.

The line through A is the budget line when A is chosen by the consumer, and the line through B is the budget line when B is chosen by the consumer. Figure 5-13a illustrates the case in which A is chosen when B is available (B is in the budget set bounded by the budget

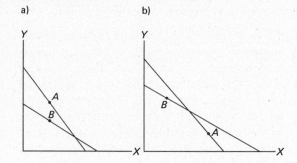

FIG. 5-13   a. *Weak axiom satisfied*
              b. *Violation of the weak axiom*

line through A), and B is chosen when A is not available (A is outside the budget set bounded by the line through B). Hence the weak axiom is satisfied. In figure 5-13b, A again is chosen when B lies within the budget set bounded by the line through A, but B is chosen when A is available as well, hence violating the weak axiom.

Of special interest is the relationship between the weak axiom of revealed preference, a postulate concerning the *choices* of a consumer, and the view of the consumer as a utility maximizer. The following two results hold.

1. If a consumer maximizes utility subject to his budget constraint, and if the consumer's indifference map is characterized by nonsatiation and by the law of diminishing marginal rate of substitution, then the choices of the consumer will satisfy the weak axiom of revealed preference. This holds, however many goods there are.

2. Assume there are only two goods. If the choices of a consumer satisfy the weak axiom of revealed preference, then the con-

†A. Wald, "On Some Systems of Equations in Mathematical Economics," *Econometrica* 19 (1951).

P. Samuelson, *Foundations of Economic Analysis* (Cambridge: Harvard University Press, 1947).

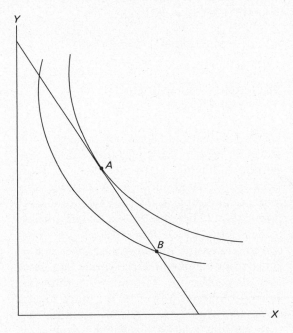

FIG. 5-14 *Revealed preference and utility
          maximization*

wise *B* would not be the utility-maximizing choice.

We will not attempt here to provide a proof of the second result, which in any case holds only for the case of two goods.

When we go to the case of an arbitrary number of commodities, a somewhat more complicated condition on consistency of choices is required to establish that the consumer acts "as if" he were maximizing utility. The condition in the many goods case goes under the name of the *strong axiom of revealed preference* and was first formulated by H. Houthakker, a prominent American economist.† The strong axiom of revealed preference may be summarized as follows:

> Let $A_1, A_2, \ldots, A_n$ denote any n commodity bundles, of which at least two are different. Suppose that A_1 is revealed preferred to A_2, A_2 is revealed preferred to A_3, ..., A_{n-1} is revealed preferred to A_n. Then it cannot be the case that A_n is revealed preferred to A_1. This holds for n = 2, 3, ...

As is immediately apparent from a reading of the strong axiom, the weak axiom of revealed preference is the special case of the strong axiom when the number of commodity bundles being compared is reduced to two. We might briefly summarize the relationship of the strong axiom to utility maximization.

1. If a consumer maximizes a utility function subject to a budget constraint, where the utility function satisfies nonsatiation and the law of diminishing marginal rate of substitution, then the choices of the consumer

sumer's choices are consistent with the hypothesis that the consumer acts to maximize utility.

The argument underlying the first result is summarized briefly in figure 5-14. If we assume that the consumer is a utility maximizer, then in choosing *A* with the given budget set, there is an indifference curve tangent to the budget line at *A*, as indicated. But if *B* is available when *A* is chosen, then *B* must lie in that budget set, and hence the indifference curve through *B* must lie below the indifference curve through *A*; *B* must have a lower utility than *A*. It immediately follows that if *B* is chosen in some situation, *A* cannot be available; other-

†H. Houthakker, "Revealed Preference and the Utility Function," *Economica* 17 (1950).

satisfy the strong axiom of revealed preference.

2. If the choices of the consumer satisfy the strong axiom, then they are consistent with the hypothesis that the consumer acts to maximize utility.

Both of these propositions hold, whatever the number of goods.

An Algebraic Statement of the Weak Axiom

It is often useful to work with the weak axiom in algebraic form. The statement of this axiom is quite simple.

Suppose that a bundle $A = (X^a, Y^a)$ is chosen in a certain price-income situation (with competitive markets) when a different bundle $B = (X^b, Y^b)$ lies in the budget set. Let p_x^a, p_y^a denote the prices in this situation. To say that B lies in the budget set when A is chosen means that B is no more expensive than A at prices p_x^a, p_y^a. Thus A is *revealed preferred* to B when

$$p_x^a X^a + p_y^a Y^a \geqq p_x^a X^b + p_y^a Y^b$$

(B costs no more than A at prices prevailing when A is chosen.)

Let p_x^b, p_y^b be the prices prevailing when B is chosen. Then if A and B are different bundles, the weak axiom states that A is *not* available when B is chosen or, equivalently, A is too expensive; that is

$$p_x^b X^a + p_y^b Y^a > p_x^b X^b + p_y^b Y^b .$$

Formally, the weak axiom is the following.

$$p_x^a X^a + p_y^a Y^a \geq p_x^a X^b + p_y^a Y^b$$

implies

$$p_x^b X^a + p_y^b Y^a > p_x^b X^b + p_y^b Y^b$$

assuming that $A \neq B$, where

$$A = (X^a, Y^a), \ B = (X^b, Y^b).$$

Individual and Market Demand Curves

While it is possible to devise experimental situations in which verifiable propositions concerning individual consumer demand functions can be tested, most of the data available to the economist appear in the form of market information. Therefore, it is of some interest to determine which properties of individual consumer demand functions carry over to market demand functions representing aggregates over all consumers. Assuming independence among consumers as well as the other axioms of modern utility theory, and assuming that each consumer has a preassigned amount of income, then the following general results hold.

1. Market demand functions exhibit homogeneity of degree zero in all prices and incomes.

2. Suppose that a certain good is a normal good for each consumer. Then the market demand curve for that commodity slopes downward to the right.

3. Even though each consumer satisfies the weak axiom of revealed preference, it does *not* necessarily follow that the market demand functions will satisfy the weak axiom, and similarly with respect to the strong axiom.

The significance of the third result is that, except in unusual circumstances, it is not legitimate to think of an aggregated market demand function as though it were derived from some underlying preference ranking representing a "consensus" of the consumers in the society. The diversity of tastes and income positions of the consumers in a society simply cannot be ignored in the analysis of forces operating on the market.

Food Stamps versus Income Supplements

The revealed preference approach offers a convenient way to analyze a number of economic problems. Consider a comparison between a policy of cash grants to welfare recipients and a food stamp program. Under simplified conditions, we will show that for the same value received by the welfare recipient, the cash grant approach is preferable to the food stamp program, in that the recipient is on a higher indifference curve with the cash grant than with food stamps.

Let X denote units of food purchased by the recipient, with Y denoting units of "other goods" purchased. p_x and p_y are the per unit prices of X and Y, and M is the recipient's income. Under a food stamp program, the recipient is in effect provided with a subsidy of s dollars per unit of food purchased, and so the price per unit of food to the recipient is $p_x - s$. Let the superscript "0" denote quantities purchased under the food stamp program. Then, given nonsatiation, we have

$$(p_x - s)X^0 + p_y Y^0 = M. \qquad (1)$$

Under a program of income supplements, the consumer receives a cash grant of G dollars, but faces the prices p_x, p_y for food and other goods. Let the superscript-"1" denote quantities purchased under the cash grant program. The budget constraint is the following.

$$p_x X^1 + p_y Y^1 = M + G. \qquad (2)$$

In particular, assume that the grant G is equal to the subsidy received under the food stamp program, so that $G = sX^0$. Then from (1) we have

$$p_x X^0 + p_y Y^0 = M + G,$$

which, from (2), implies

$$p_x X^1 + p_y Y^1 = p_x X^0 + p_y Y^0.$$

At prices prevailing under the cash grant program, the welfare recipient could have chosen the bundle (X^0, Y^0) chosen under the food stamp program. Because the price of X to the recipient differs in the two cases with the price of Y unchanged, the utility-maximizing bundle (X^1, Y^1) differs from (X^0, Y^0). But this means that (X^1, Y^1) is revealed preferred to (X^0, Y^0); hence (X^1, Y^1) is on a higher indifference curve than (X^0, Y^0). (Recall that (X^1, Y^1) is revealed preferred to (X^0, Y^0) if $p_x X^1 + p_y Y^1 \geqq p_x X^0 + p_y Y^0$; $(X^1, Y^1) \neq (X^0, Y^0)$.) The cash grant program is superior to the food stamp program, from the point of view of the welfare recipient.

While this conclusion is derived under the assumption that prices p_x, p_y are unaffected by the kind of welfare program adopted, in fact a similar conclusion follows even when prices adjust to different demands in the two cases assuming a competitive economy. See chapter 13 for a discussion of this issue.

Summary

This chapter has presented an outline of the positive (scientific) aspects of the economist's theory of consumer behavior. Modern utility theory postulates the existence, for the consumer, of a preference ranking whose properties are incorporated into the indifference map of the consumer. The consumer is assumed to act in a manner consistent with his preferences; that is, he acts to "maximize utility." Assuming that (1) the consumer faces competitive markets for the goods he purchases, (2) he has a preassigned amount of money income to spend, and (3) his preferences are nonsatiated, it can be concluded that equal proportionate increases in prices and in income leave quantities demanded of all goods unchanged. If a good is normal, then the demand curve of the consumer for that good displays the typical property of being downward sloping to the right. These are the major testable propositions of consumer theory.

The analysis of the effect of an increase in the price of a good on quantities demanded involves two separate forces acting on choices—the *substitution effect* and the *income effect*. An increase in the price of X, with the price of Y and with income constant, leads to a substitution of Y for X, along a given indifference curve. This is the substitution effect. The income effect measures the change in quantity demanded of X and Y due to the effect on the purchasing power of income of an increase in the price of X. The income effect moves quantity demanded in the direction of the price change if a good is inferior, but opposite to this direction if the good is normal. Only in the case of an inferior good can the consumer's demand curve be upward sloping; but this upward slope occurs only if the income effect is large relative to the substitution effect. When this occurs, the good is called a *Giffen good*. Giffen goods are exceptional; there is little, if any, empirical evidence of their existence in our economy.

Income-compensated demand curves have the property that the area under such a demand curve measures the amount of income the consumer is willing to give up to obtain any specified number of units of the good. Deducting actual expenditures for the good we obtain *consumer's surplus*.

The weak axiom of revealed preference is a consistency condition on the choices of the consumer. If the consumer acts to maximize utility under nonsatiation and assuming that indifference curves bound convex sets, then the weak axiom is satisfied. The strong axiom of revealed preference implies that the choices of the consumer are consistent with the hypothesis that the consumer acts to maximize a utility function.

Market demand functions are homogeneous of degree zero in all prices and all incomes; and the market demand curve for a good is downward sloping to the right if, for each consumer, the good in question is normal.

Problems

1. Suppose that the utility function of a consumer is of the form $U = XY$.

   a. Plot the indifference map for $U = 50, 100, 200$.

   b. $p_x = \$1$, $p_y = \$1$. Draw in the income-consumption curve for the consumer. Verify that X and Y are normal goods.

   c. With $p_x = \$1$, $p_y = \$1$, let $M = \$20$. Determine the utility-maximizing choices of X and Y.

   d. Suppose $p_x = \$2$ while $p_y = \$1$, $M = \$20$. Determine the new utility maximizing quantities, and identify the substitution effect and the income effect of the change in p_x.

   e. Sketch in the demand curve for X, assuming that $p_y = \$1$, $M = \$20$.

   f. Are X and Y gross substitutes for one another? Explain why.

2. Suppose that in question 1 we replace the utility function by $U = (XY)^2$. Show that the indifference map is unchanged except for the utility numbers assigned to indifference curves. What effect is there on the quantities demanded of X and Y for given values of M and the prices of X and Y? Explain in terms of the meaning attached to utility by economists.

3. A gasoline tax of 10¢ per gallon is to be imposed in order to conserve fuel. The present consumption of gasoline is 500 gallons per year per person. The government does not want anyone to be worse off because of the tax; it simply wants consumers to conserve fuel. Consequently, the government will return the proceeds of the tax to consumers in the form of lump-sum payments. Using the indifference map, indicate how the correct amount of rebate should be calculated to offset the gasoline tax for an average consumer. Is it more or less than $50 per person per year?

   As a practical matter, what are the difficulties with using such a method to determine the amount of the rebate? Are there any incentive problems?

4. Suppose that there is a sales tax of 50 percent on goods X and Y, the only two goods in the economy. Compare the effects of such a sales tax on quantities demanded and on the level of preference achieved, with the effects of a 33⅓ percent tax on income. Use the indifference map and budget set of the consumer to derive your results.

   What special assumption is being employed in this chapter that biases the results you obtain? Explain what differences you would expect in your conclusions if this assumption were dropped and why.

5. A standard argument against applying an excise tax on food is that people in the low-income brackets are hurt most by such a tax. Suppose we define the "hurt" suffered by a consumer as the amount of income he would have to be paid in order to return him to the indifference curve he was on before the tax was levied. Do you think that, measured in this way, "hurt" implies that low-income people are "hurt more" by a tax on food than are rich people? Explain in terms of income and substitution effects of the tax increase.

6. Check each of the following to determine whether the choices satisfy the weak axiom of revealed preference.

a. With $M = \$20$, $p_x = \$1$, $p_y = \$1$, the choice is $X = 15$, $Y = 5$; with $M = \$20$, $p_x = .50$, $p_y = \$2$, the choice is $X = 10$, $Y = 7.5$.

b. With $M = \$20$, $p_x = \$1$, $p_y = \$1$, the choice is $X = 10$, $Y = 10$; with $M = \$20$, $p_x = .50$, $p_y = \$3$, the choice is $X = 20$, $Y = 3\frac{1}{3}$.

c. With $M = \$20$, $p_x = \$1$, $p_y = \$1$, the choice is $X = 5$, $Y = 15$; with $M = \$20$, $p_x = \$2$, $p_y = .50$ the choice is $X = 8$, $Y = 8$.

Theory of Firm Behavior

The past two chapters have summarized the elements of the economist's theory of consumer behavior. Given an underlying pattern of tastes (represented by the consumer's indifference map), the consumer's demands for goods and services arise out of utility maximization, subject to the consumer's budget constraint.

In chapters 6 through 8, we look at the supply side of the markets for goods and services. Our approach roughly parallels the approach taken with respect to consumers. Chapter 6 summarizes the characteristics of the technology available to firms—the alternative ways in which inputs can be converted into outputs. In chapter 7, the costs of a competitive firm are discussed. For any given level of output, the firm chooses that method of producing the level of output that minimizes its costs. Chapter 8 deals with profit-maximizing choices of the firm as to input-output mixes, and identifies the properties of the firm's demand curves for inputs and its supply curve of output.

6

The Theory of Production

For the economist, *production* simply means the conversion of inputs into outputs, and a *firm* is any organization that engages in production—specifically, planning, coordinating, and supervising it. Historically, the firm emerges as a distinct decision-making entity when division of labor and specialization of machinery occur, with a corresponding increase in the problems of coordinating the activities involved in production. According to the economist's model, the firm is a decision-making unit that chooses, on the basis of profit maximization, among the input-output combinations available to it.

Profit Maximization and the Firm

The fundamental postulate that economists use in their model of the firm is that *firms are operated so as to maximize profits.* This assumption should be thought of as not just a cynical view of the motivation of business management, but as a direct consequence of the motivations of the consumer as stockholder.

Stockholders and Profit Maximization

The firm is owned by its stockholders. It is assumed that stockholders are concerned only with the flow of income they receive from their shareholdings (and the market price of their shares), but not with other aspects of the firm's operations. With minor qualifications, this appraisal of stockholders' attitudes toward firms appears to be realistic.

Suppose, in addition, that stockholders exercise effective control over the hiring and firing of the managers of firms. It follows that the firm manager operates simply as an agent of the owners, which amounts to saying that his job is to operate the firm as a profit-maximizing entity. If—through ignorance, lack of attention to work, or because he employs a criterion other than profit maximization—the manager fails to achieve the highest profits possible, presumably the owners will replace him. The manager then maximizes profits not because he has a warped set of values, but because his living depends upon his furthering the interests of the owners of the firm.

The assumption that owners exercise effective control over the hiring and firing of managers of firms makes sense in the case of closely held corporations. But in large corporate firms, ownership is often divorced from control of the firm. Stockholders are widely dispersed; they have varying amounts of information about the activities of the firm, and are often willing to sign over their proxies to the "inside" group of managers who actually run things. Direct communication among stockholders is expensive, and stockholder revolts to throw out the insiders are relatively rare.

But when firms are run inefficiently, stockholders can always "bail out" by selling their shares, thus raising the costs of financial capital to the firm and putting pressure on the management to improve its operations. Moreover, the presence of poorly run firms in an industry invites entry into the industry by competitors—a threat to the very existence of the inefficient firms.

In brief, pressures do build up in the real world, if a firm is operated in a manner that deviates significantly from the profit maximization norm. The economist's postulate of profit maximization as an ongoing criterion for the operation of a firm may be viewed as an idealization that reflects tendencies inherent in the real-world adjustment of firm decision-making to the interests of the owners of the firm.

Profits

Despite its apparent simplicity, the rule of maximizing profits has some hidden snares, especially those related to the meaning of the term *profits*. There is one school of thought in economic theory, deriving from Joseph Schumpeter and Frank Knight, that reserves the term solely to refer to the income earned by innovative firms operating in a world of uncertainty; and there are strong arguments to justify this position, as we shall see. In our treatment of the firm in the first part of this book, we are assuming a world of certainty in which the menu of alternatives available to the firm is known and unvarying. We will follow the usual practice in the economic literature of identifying profits with the earnings assigned to the owners of the firm.

The theory developed in this chapter applies to the special case in which the firm's activities over time are repetitive, each period duplicating the previous one, with no overlap between periods in production or sales activities. Under these special conditions, maximizing profits comes to mean maximizing the net cash flow of the firm (receipts minus outlays) for the current period.

Like the consumer, the firm is an ongoing entity that makes plans over an extended period of time into the future. By telescoping the firm's activities into one period, we do some violence to the decision problems that the firm faces. A similar criticism applies to the theory of consumer behavior developed in chapters 4 and 5. In chapter 11, we will return to the specific problems that arise for the consumer and the firm in an intertemporal setting.

Production Processes

Because the mechanical and chemical processes used by firms in modern society are incredibly complex, we can speak only very generally of the technology available to a firm. Fortunately, only a few aspects of this technology appear to be crucial for an overview of the way in which the firm links into the system for allocating resources in the society.

We will restrict our attention, in the main, to a technology in which several inputs are used to produce a single output. A starting point in our analysis of the technology is the concept of a *production process*.

A production process is a schedule that, for given fixed proportions of all inputs, lists the outputs associated with various levels of use of that mix of inputs.

This definition is different from common usage in which production process refers to the various steps through which raw materials go in the course of being transformed into a semi-finished or finished product. In our description of a production process we suppress all of the detail concerning the way in which inputs are converted into outputs. We preserve for attention only the properties that are relevant to the choice of inputs to use in producing a certain number of units of the output.

For example, assume that only capital services (K) and labor services (L) are used in producing some product (X). The following is a production process:

Production Process #1

K	L	X
1	1	10
2	2	20
3	3	35
4	4	45

In this production process, capital and labor services are used in the fixed proportions of one unit of capital to one unit of labor. Another production process might be represented by the following:

Production Process #2

K	L	X
2	1	15
3	1½	25
4	2	40
5	2½	55

In this case, capital and labor services are used in the fixed proportions of two units of capital to one unit of labor. (Implicit in these examples is the assumption that a given number of units of the raw material is converted into one unit of the finished product in each process. Alternatively, we can view the input K as including the raw material input into production.) These two production processes can be diagrammed as in figure 6-1.

The point labelled a along process #1 is intended to indicate that one unit of capital and one unit of labor are required to produce ten units of output in the process identified in our first schedule; b is associated with twenty units of output, and so on. We have drawn a line from the origin through the points a, b, c, and d to indicate the fixed proportions (1:1, capital to labor) in process #1. A similar interpretation applies to points a', b', c', d' along the process #2 line, where the fixed proportions are 2:1, capital to labor.

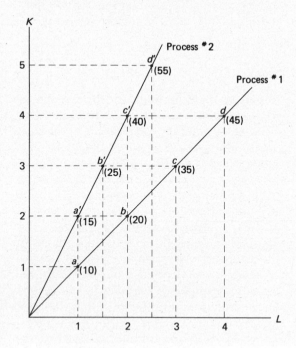

FIG. 6-1   *Production processes*

Constant Returns to Scale, Independence, and Divisibility

Three assumptions are often made concerning the properties of production processes—namely, constant returns to scale, independence, and divisibility.

Constant returns to scale. Multiplying all inputs by the same positive constant means that output is multiplied by the same constant. In particular, doubling all inputs doubles output, and halving all inputs halves output.

Independence of production processes. If two or more production processes operate simultaneously within a firm, output from any one process depends only on the inputs to it, not on the level at which any other process operates.

Divisiblity. Output from any process can be expanded or contracted to any arbitrary degree by a proportional expansion or contraction of all inputs used in the process.

In both the technological literature and the writings of economists, constant returns, divisibility, and independence are often assumed. There are cases where one or more of these properties do not hold, however. For example, constant returns are not present for either process #1 or process #2 in figure 6-1. We will return to these exceptions a little later in this chapter.

Suppose we initially assume that all three conditions characterize production processes. Divisibility means that every point along a process line is a feasible input-output combination. Because of the constant returns to scale assumption, doubling the distance from the origin along any process line results in a doubling of output. In figure 6-2 along process line A, point a (representing the input requirements for one unit of output) is halfway between the origin and point b (representing input requirements for two units of output), and one-third of the way between the origin and point c (representing input requirements for three units of output). The same applies for the process lines for processes B and C.

Postulating independence of production processes, together with constant returns to scale and divisibility, implies that processes can be "combined" in a particularly simple fashion to produce any given level of output. This combining involves the notion of adding points in two-dimensional space. Suppose that we wish to add the points (2, 1) and (1, 2), where the first component is units of labor services and the second is units of capital services. The sum of the two points is simply (3, 3); that is, we add each component separately.

Adding the points (1, 2) and (2, 1) to obtain the point (3, 3) is done graphically (fig. 6-3).

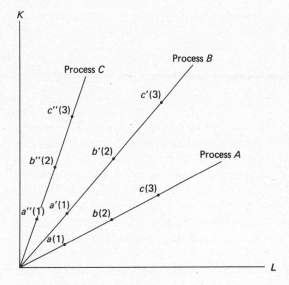

FIG. 6-2   *Constant returns to scale*

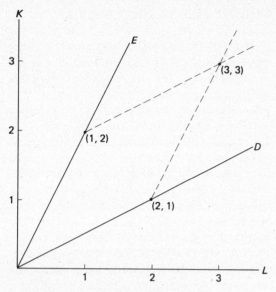

FIG. 6-3   *Adding two points in two-dimensional space*

process *A* and process *C*, every point lying on the straight line between *b* and *b''* is a feasible way to produce two units of output.

For the production map in figure 6-2, combinations of processes *A*, *B*, and *C* appear as in figure 6-5.

Efficient and Inefficient Production Processes

We say that a production process is *inefficient* if there exists another feasible process (or a combination of feasible processes) that, for any given output, uses no more of any input, and less of some input In figure 6-5 consider point *a'* on process *B*. To produce one unit of output at *a'* involves using more of both labor and capital than is required to produce one unit of output at point *a'''*, which lies on the line between *a* and *a''*. Clearly, *a'* is an inefficient

Draw the lines *D* and *E* from the origin through these two points. Beginning at (2, 1), draw the dotted line parallel to *E*. Beginning at (1, 2) draw the dotted line parallel to *D*. Where these two dotted lines intersect is the point (3, 3), representing the sum of (2, 1) and (1, 2).

In figure 6-4 points *b* and *b''* represent outputs of two units operating only process *A* or process *C*. But under independence, two units may be produced by operating process *A* at *a* and process *C* at *a''*, leading to point *b'''*. It is easy to verify that *b'''* lies halfway along the straight line connecting *b* and *b''*. Similarly, two units of output can be produced by operating process *A* at one-half unit of output and process *C* at one and one-half units of output, resulting in a point lying halfway between *b''* and *b'''*, and so on. In brief, it turns out that by combining

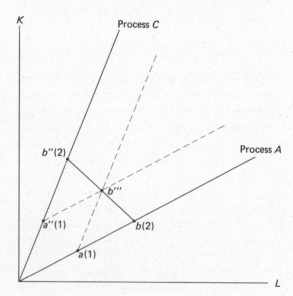

FIG. 6-4   *Combining production processes A and C*

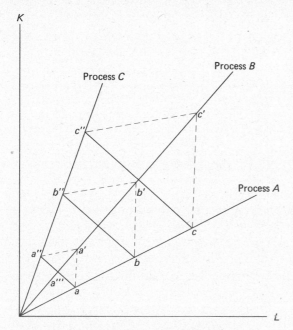

FIG. 6-5 *Combining production processes A, B, and C*

The Production Map of the Firm   In the economist's view, the technology available to a firm consists of a wide range of different production processes. Restricting attention only to efficient processes and combinations of such processes, we obtain a graphical representation of the firm's technology as in figure 6-6. In this figure, we have constructed two curves by connecting points along efficient process lines, such that output is constant. Along the $X = 1$ curve, output is one unit, and output is two units along the $X = 2$ curve. As the number of processes increases, the straight-line segments in the first graph are replaced by a smooth curve, as in the second graph. The curves bound convex sets, because inefficient processes are eliminated from consideration. If the curve representing $X = 1$ "bulged" in the opposite way, independence and divisibility combined with constant returns would imply that points along the bulge are in fact inefficient.

A graph of the firm's technology (such as figure 6-6) is called its *production map*. We refer to any curve along which output is a constant as a *production isoquant* of the firm. Once the firm has determined which output level to produce, then the problem for the firm is to determine which point along the given isoquant (that is, which production process) will lead to the highest profit. The production map shows the extent to which alternatives exist for the firm manager.

From the economist's point of view, the firm is not a black box into which inputs are fed and from which output emerges according to some predetermined rule specified by the engineer. Instead, the input-output mix associated with a firm is the result of a deliberate choice by the firm manager from among a range of possible alternatives.

method of producing one unit of output. A similar argument applies to points b' and c', as well as to all points lying on the process B line or on the dotted lines connecting process A to process B and connecting process C to process B. Clearly, process B is inefficient.

All processes that are not inefficient are said to be efficient. Both process A and process C are efficient, as are all processes representing combinations of process A and process C.

Given that inputs are costly, no profit-maximizing firm would choose an inefficient production process. Hence, the only production processes that are relevant for decision making by a profit-maximizing firm manager are efficient processes, such as A or C or combinations of these two.

a)   b)

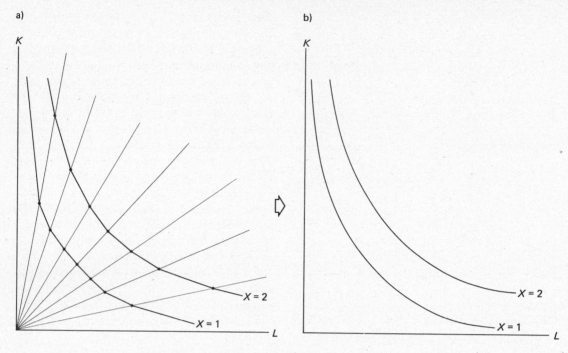

FIG. 6-6   *The production map of the firm*

The Production Function of the Firm

There are some obvious parallels between consumer theory and production theory. Just as the indifference map is the graphical representation of the tastes of the consumer, the production map is the graphical representation of the technology of the firm. Similarly, indifference curves are curves along which utility for the consumer is constant, while production isoquants are curves along which output for the firm is constant. Indifference curves are thus the "level curves" of the utility function, and isoquants can be viewed as the "level curves" of the firm's *production function*. This function can be viewed as a schedule that associates with each combination of inputs the

maximum output attainable by the firm from that combination of inputs. The term *maximum output* is used to indicate that inefficient production processes are excluded from the firm's production process.

For a single-product firm employing only capital and labor as inputs, we can express the production function symbolically as $X = F(K, L)$. X is the number of units of output, and F is the rule that expresses the maximum number of units of output obtainable when the firm employs K units of capital services and L units of labor services. A description of the firm's technology (at least with respect to efficient production processes) then amounts to a description of the properties of the firm's production function.

a)

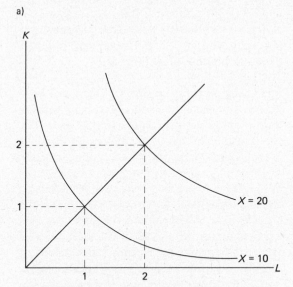

b)

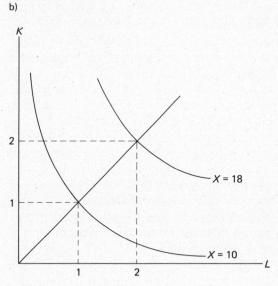

Three main features of the firm's production function are of interest. These involve *returns to scale, returns to a variable input,* and *substitutability among inputs.*

Returns to Scale

Thus far, we have assumed that the technology facing the firm is characterized by constant returns to scale, and so doubling all inputs doubles output. But other cases are conceivable. The technology is characterized by *decreasing returns to scale*, if when all inputs are multiplied by a constant greater than one, output is multiplied by a smaller positive constant. Under *increasing returns to scale,* multiplying all inputs by a constant greater than one results in a multiplication of output by a larger positive constant.

Under constant returns to scale (fig. 6-7a), the process using a ratio of one unit of labor to one unit of capital (and any other process) has the property that doubling the amounts of

c)

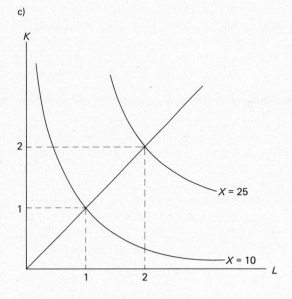

FIG. 6-7   *Constant (a), decreasing (b), and increasing (c) returns to scale*

capital and labor results in a doubling of output. Under decreasing returns to scale (fig. 6-7b), doubling the amounts of capital and labor leads to a less than doubling of output; while under increasing returns to scale (fig. 6-7c), output is more than doubled when the capital and labor inputs are doubled. When we say that a production map exhibits decreasing returns to scale, we mean that there are decreasing returns along every production process line, and similarly for constant or increasing returns. The concept of "returns to scale" applies *only* to the case where *all* inputs are changed in equal proportions. In figure 6-7, it is implicitly assumed that capital and labor services are the only inputs of the firm.

What is the view of the economist concerning the returns to scale properties of real-world production functions? If there is independence of production processes, then we will observe only constant returns to scale or increasing returns to scale in real-world technologies. Assume that, by using a certain mix of inputs, it is possible to produce a certain number of units of output. Suppose we then wish to double this output. One straightforward way of doing this is to set up a new production line alongside the old, duplicating the input mix of the original production line and presumably duplicating its output as well. This means that the technology always is capable of performing at least as well as constant returns to scale. Any production process characterized by decreasing returns to scale would then be ruled out of the production map as being inefficient. But this argument assumes independence of production processes, of course.

The returns to scale properties of real-world production functions can deviate from the constant returns case, given indivisible inputs or absence of independence of processes. While engineers often take constant returns to scale as the standard case, this assumption presupposes perfect divisibility of inputs and independence of production processes.

Increasing Returns to Scale   There are well-known situations in which increasing returns follow almost directly from physical laws. The simplest and perhaps clearest illustration of this is the case of a pipeline. The carrying capacity of a pipeline is approximately equal to the area of a cross section of the pipeline times the speed at which the fluid moves through it. But the cross section of a pipeline is equal to the area πr^2, where r is the radius of the cross section. Similarly, the amount of material required in order to construct the line is directly proportionate to the circumference of a cross section multiplied by the distance of the pipeline, where the circumference is equal to $2\pi r$. Suppose we double the radius (r) of the pipeline. Then the new circumference is $4\pi r$, but the new cross section area is $\pi(2r)^2 = 4\pi r^2$. In this situation, doubling the input (the circumference) results in quadrupling the output (the area).

This is a clear-cut case of increasing returns to scale that result from the most efficient use of materials in constructing a pipeline. Of course, it is possible to double output of the pipeline by constructing a second pipeline next to the first one, and in this way achieve constant returns to scale. But this alternative is obviously an inefficient use of inputs and hence will be excluded from the production map; only efficient processes appear on the map.

Increasing returns to scale are also often associated with "lumpy" inputs, that is, inputs for which perfect divisibility does not hold. As the scale of operations of a firm increases, lumpy inputs such as specialized labor and machinery can be employed more efficiently within the firm, leading to a more than proportionate increase in output for a proportionate increase in inputs. Lack of divisibility of inputs is the most important source of increasing returns to scale.

Decreasing Returns to Scale While the technology always performs at least as well as constant returns, given independence of processes, the independence condition can be violated as well. The more production lines in a firm, the greater the number of lines of communication that must be monitored and controlled, and the more complicated are planning and coordinating of production. Such activities affect the input-output performances of the lines. Independence of processes is an idealization of the real-world technology. When it is violated, production processes can exhibit decreasing returns to scale.

Returns to a Variable Input

Returns to a variable input refer to the effects on output of changes in one input with other inputs being held fixed. The distinction between returns to scale and returns to a variable input can be illustrated in terms of the production function in table 6-1. The entries are the

outputs associated with various combinations of inputs. Thus with one unit of labor services and one unit of capital services, the maximum output attainable is 100 units; with $L = 2$, $K = 3$, $X = 232$ units, and so on. The production function here exhibits constant returns to scale; equal proportionate increases of both capital and labor lead to the same proportionate increase in output.

On the other hand, assume that capital is fixed at one unit. Then the first column of the table gives the returns to the variable input, labor, as L varies from one to four units. If labor is fixed at three units, then the third row of the schedule gives the returns to the variable input, capital, as K varies from one to four units. One feature of the schedule is that for any given amount of the fixed input, each additional unit of a variable input increases output, but the rate of increase falls as more and more units of the variable input are added. This is a special case of the law of diminishing marginal productivity.

The Law of Diminishing Marginal Productivity The marginal product of labor MP_L is defined as the increase in output from adding an additional unit of labor, with all other inputs held fixed. Symbolically,

$$MP_L = \frac{\text{change in output}}{\text{change in labor}}$$

$$= \frac{\Delta X}{\Delta L} \text{(with } K \text{ held fixed)}.$$

The marginal product of capital MP_K is then

$$MP_K = \frac{\Delta X}{\Delta K} \text{(with } L \text{ held fixed)}.$$

In terms of the production function of table 6-1, marginal products of labor and capital are

TABLE 6-1   *Production Function F(K, L)*

L \ K	1	2	3	4
1	100	128	144	158
2	164	200	232	256
3	207	266	300	330
4	249	328	365	400

TABLE 6-2   *Marginal Product of Labor (MP$_L$)*

L	MP_L $K = 1$	MP_L $K = 2$	MP_L $K = 3$	MP_L $K = 4$
1	100	128	144	158
2	64	72	88	98
3	43	66	68	74
4	42	54	65	70

TABLE 6-3   *Marginal Product of Capital (MP$_K$)*

K	1	2	3	4
MP_K for $L = 1$	100	28	16	14
MP_K for $L = 2$	164	36	32	26
MP_K for $L = 3$	207	59	34	30
MP_K for $L = 4$	249	79	37	35

as in tables 6-2 and 6-3. (We assume that output is zero with $L = 0$ or $K = 0$.)

The marginal product of labor schedule is constructed as follows. With capital fixed at one unit, the first unit of labor increases output from zero to 100 units; hence MP_L for $L = 1$, $K = 1$ is 100. The second unit of labor increases output from 100 to 164, hence $MP_L = 64$ for $K = 1$, $L = 2$. The first column of table 6-2 is constructed by determining the increase in output from adding one unit of labor, with K fixed at 1, and similarly for the other columns. A similar interpretation applies to the rows of table 6-3. Along the first row we have the marginal products of capital for $L = 1$ while K takes on values 1, 2, 3, 4.

Both tables illustrate the *law of diminishing marginal productivity:*

> *Regardless of the returns to scale, as more and more units of a variable input are added to fixed amounts of other inputs, a point is reached after which the marginal product of the variable input continues to decline.*

In tables 6-2 and 6-3, there is diminishing marginal productivity for both labor and capital for all input levels. But this is not necessarily the only case of interest. In table 6-4, the marginal product of the second unit of labor is greater than that of the first, but there is diminishing marginal productivity from $L = 3$ on;

hence the law of diminishing marginal productivity holds.

The law of diminishing marginal productivity is taken by economists as a basic postulate concerning production functions. There are various rationalizations for the law. The simplest is that, because of the lumpiness of the fixed inputs, for a time adding more units of a variable input might result in a rise in marginal product of the variable input; but as we add more units of the variable input, we decrease the number of units of the fixed input available *per unit* of the variable input. This decrease hampers increases in output.

For example, with two shovels available, a second laborer who was hired might have the same (or perhaps even higher) marginal product as the first. But certainly a third laborer added to the two shovels will have a lower marginal product. It is important to emphasize in this regard that we are assuming *homogeneous* inputs. That is, all units of labor services are

TABLE 6-4   *Diminishing Marginal Productivity of Labor*

K	L	X	MP_L
1	0	0	
1	1	10	10
1	2	30	20
1	3	40	10
1	4	45	5
1	5	48	3

assumed to be identical, and similarly for capital services. Changes in marginal products are due to changes in the combinations of these homogeneous inputs, not to differences in the units of inputs themselves.

Marginal Product and Average Product Given a fixed amount of other inputs, the law of diminishing marginal productivity (of labor) can be illustrated as in figure 6-8. The first graph shows a "total product" TP curve obtained by plotting output, X, against labor employed, L, assuming other inputs are fixed. Treating labor as a divisible input, then

$$MP_L = \frac{\Delta X}{\Delta L}$$

is the change in output per unit change in labor,

and MP_L can be interpreted as the *slope* of the TP curve. The TP curve has an inflexion point at L_0, which is the point where the slope of the curve is a maximum, following which MP_L (= slope of TP curve) falls. This is indicated in the second graph, with MP_L attaining a maximum at L_0.

We define the average product of labor, AP_L, as total product per unit of labor. Thus

$$AP_L = \frac{X}{L}.$$

Graphically this means that for any value of L, AP_L is equal to the slope of a line drawn from the origin of the first graph to the TP curve. Note that AP_L increases up to the point L_1 and falls thereafter. It is also clear that when AP_L is a maximum, then the slope of a line

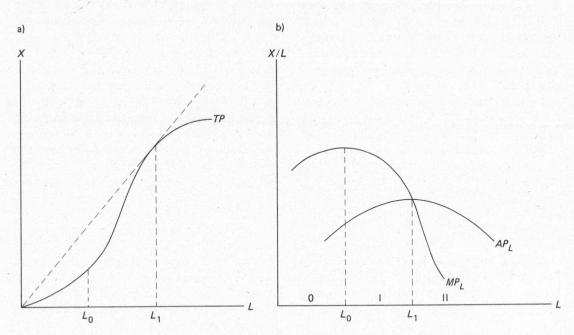

FIG. 6-8   a. *Total product curve*
b. *Marginal and average product curves*

drawn from the origin to the *TP* curve is equal to the slope of the curve itself. Thus we have

$$AP_L = MP_L \text{ at } L_1,$$

where AP_L is a maximum. This is indicated in the second graph as well.

The relationship between MP_L and AP_L is the following:

1. So long as AP_L is rising, MP_L is greater than AP_L.

2. So long as AP_L is falling, MP_L is less than AP_L.

3. $MP_L = AP_L$ at the maximum of the AP_L curve.

If AP_L is increasing, X is increasing faster than L. But this can occur only if an additional unit of L adds more to output than the average product of laborers hired to that point. Hence $MP_L > AP_L$. When AP_L is falling, X is increasing slower than L, which implies that $MP_L < AP_L$.

Three regions have been identified in figure 6-8b. In region 0, MP_L is increasing due to the lumpiness of the fixed inputs. Diminishing marginal productivity sets in in region I, but AP_L is still increasing, with $MP_L > AP_L$. In region II, both AP_L and MP_L are falling. It is of some interest that under competitive conditions in input and output markets, the hiring of labor occurs only in region II.

We will return to this relationship in the succeeding chapters. It should be emphasized that while we have singled out labor for consideration in this section, the same comments apply to any variable factor of production.

The Law of Variable Proportions   A generalized version of the law of diminishing marginal productivity is known as the *law of variable proportions:*

> *Regardless of the returns to scale, if one or more inputs are held fixed, a point is reached after which equal proportionate increases in all other inputs leads to a less than proportionate increase in output.*

This law asserts that if, say, plant capacity is held fixed, then beyond some point doubling all other inputs leads to a less than doubling of output. This effect holds under constant, increasing, or decreasing returns to scale.

Substitutability Among Inputs

Under constant returns to scale, divisibility, and independence of production processes, any production isoquant is a curve that bounds a convex set. When we leave the case of constant returns, things are not so simple. Because the extent to which decreasing (or increasing) returns prevail along a process line may differ for different processes, independence of processes does not necessarily guarantee convexity of isoquants, even if a production map has all processes exhibiting decreasing (or increasing) returns to scale. Instead, we make the explicit assumption that, *whatever the returns to scale properties of the production map, isoquants are smooth curves that bound convex sets.*

This assumption corresponds to the assumption concerning indifference curves in the theory of consumer behavior. It concerns the way in which substitutability among inputs operates in production. For any level of output, the more units of a given input employed in production, the easier it is to substitute other inputs for the input in question.

In figure 6-9, at each point $A = (L_0, K_0)$, $B = (L_1, K_1)$, $C = (L_2, K_2)$, output is ten units.

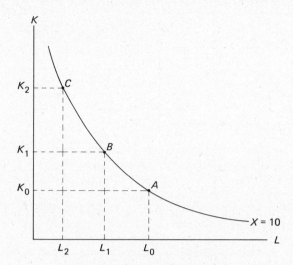

FIG. 6-9   *Substitutability along a*
production isoquant

Suppose that the distance from L_2 to L_1 is the same as that between L_1 and L_0. Then to replace $L_0 - L_1$ units of labor, while maintaining output at ten units $K_1 - K_0$ additional units of labor are required. To replace $L_1 - L_2$ ($= L_0 - L_1$) units of labor requires adding $K_2 - K_1$ units of capital, if output is to stay at ten units. Note that $K_2 - K_1$ is greater than $K_1 - K_0$. Labor is a better substitute for capital, the more capital is employed in production, just as capital is a better substitute for labor, the more labor is employed in production, assuming output is fixed.

The Law of Diminishing Marginal Rate of Technical Substitution   Let ΔL = change in labor, ΔK = change in capital, along a given isoquant. Then the ratio $- \Delta K / \Delta L$ (note the minus sign) is referred to as the *marginal rate of technical substitution of capital for labor.*

$$MRTS = - \frac{\Delta K}{\Delta L}$$

along a given isoquant. This ratio, which is the absolute value of the slope of the isoquant, decreases (gets closer to zero) as L increases. The assumption that isoquants bound convex sets is equivalent to the *law of diminishing marginal rate of technical substitution of capital for labor:*

> Along any production isoquant, the marginal rate of technical substitution of capital for labor decreases as the amount of capital is increased.

An equivalent (and simpler) statement is that along any production isoquant, labor becomes a better substitute for capital, the more units of capital that are employed. This law describes the way that the marginal products of capital and labor behave along any given isoquant.

Let ΔX = the change in output brought about by changes ΔL in labor and ΔK in capital. Then

$$\Delta X = MP_L \Delta L + MP_K \Delta K;$$

that is, the change in output equals the increase in output due to adding one unit of labor (MP_L) times the number of units of labor added (ΔL) plus the increase in output due to adding one unit of capital (MP_K) times the number of units of capital added (ΔK). But along any isoquant, $\Delta X = 0$. It thus follows that

$$- \frac{\Delta K}{\Delta L} = \frac{MP_L}{MP_K}$$

or, equivalently,

$$MRTS = \frac{MP_L}{MP_K}$$

along any isoquant, so that the *marginal rate of technical substitution of capital for labor turns out to be equal to the ratio of the marginal product of labor to the marginal product of capital.* The law of diminishing marginal rate of technical substitution thus asserts that as we increase the amount of capital employed along an isoquant, the ratio of the marginal product of labor to the marginal product of capital falls.

Substitutability among Inputs—A Polar Case
To some extent, the production maps we have developed in this chapter represent an idealization of the technological possibilities available to the firm in the real world. We have assumed that firms are aware of a wide range of production processes, which can be combined to generate the smooth isoquants shown in the production map.

At the other extreme from the economist's picture of the technology is the view of the firm as a "black box," with inputs being fed in and outputs spewing out according to a fixed engineering formula. In a black box firm, the manager is simply a supervisor, making sure that inputs are combined in the predetermined proportions. The production map for a black box firm is shown in figure 6-10.

Economists refer to the situation depicted in the graph as *fixed proportions*. Under fixed proportions, there is only one production process available to the firm. As indicated in the graph, a usual black box assumption is constant returns to scale; in the case depicted, there are constant returns to the process with fixed proportions of one unit of capital to one unit of labor. Given that there is one unit of labor, the firm can only productively employ one unit of capital; any more capital is redundant. This is the case where there is no substitutability at all among inputs, and hence no decision problem as to the best mix of inputs to use in production. The method of production is the same, whatever are the relative costs of capital or labor services.

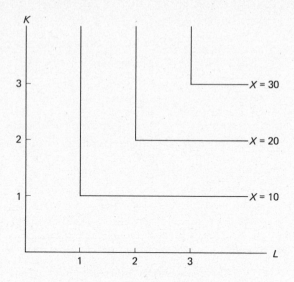

FIG. 6-10   *Production map for a "black box" firm—fixed proportions*

There is some surface appeal to the view of the firm as a black box, with its corollary that engineers rather than business school graduates are best suited to operate firms. However, the empirical evidence is overwhelmingly against this view. Admittedly, any given firm has probably "explored" only a small part of its production map, and in that sense the pictures presented in this chapter give an oversimplified view of the substitution possibilities available to the firm. But when input prices change so that incentives are created for economizing on the use of costly inputs, firms can and do change their production processes. We are all familiar with the dramatic instances, such as the replacement of rubber by synthetics in the production of tires, nylon stockings ousting silk, aluminum cans replacing "tin" cans, or computers taking over the jobs of office workers. But the process of substitution is much more pervasive than that, and does not rely at all on major new innovations, although innovations are of course encouraged by changes in the relative costs of inputs. The fixed proportions case has little predictive value.

Interrelationships among Inputs

Beyond the issue of substitutability among inputs is the issue of the extent to which inputs cooperate or compete with one another in production. Two inputs may be said to cooperate if an increase in the amount of one input results in an increase in the marginal product of the other. The inputs are competitive if an increase in one results in a fall in the marginal product of the other. In regard to labor and capital services as inputs, the marginal product of labor depends on both the number of units of labor employed and the number of units of capital, and similarly for capital.

The first column of table 6-5 gives MP_L for $L = 1, 2, 3, 4$, assuming $K = 1$. The second column gives MP_L for $K = 2$. Reading across any row in the MP_L table, it is easy to see that capital cooperates with labor because MP_L for any value of L is larger, the greater the amount of capital employed. Similarly, reading down any column in table 6-6 shows that labor cooperates with capital in increasing its marginal product.

We say that two inputs are *normal* if they cooperate with each other; that is, an increase

TABLE 6-6   *Marginal Product of Capital*

K	1	2	3	4
MP_K for $L = 1$	100	28	16	14
MP_K for $L = 2$	164	36	32	26
MP_K for $L = 3$	207	59	34	30
MP_K for $L = 4$	249	79	37	35

in one input increases the marginal product of the other. If the marginal product falls when the other input increases, we say that they are *competitive*. For the production function displayed in tables 6-5 and 6-6, both capital and labor are normal inputs. There are few general statements that can be made concerning the presence or absence of "normality" among inputs. However, the following does hold for two inputs.

> If there are only two inputs employed in production, and if there are constant returns to scale with production isoquants bounding convex sets, then both inputs are normal.

Unfortunately, this result does not carry over to the case of many inputs. Even under constant returns to scale, competitive inputs can be present if there are more than two inputs.

Homogeneous and Homothetic Production Functions

Certain special classes of production functions are often employed in both theoretical and empirical work in microeconomics. Thus the production function is often assumed to be *homogeneous*. Given the production function $F(K, L)$, it is said to be homogeneous of degree k if, given any positive constant t,

$$F(tK, tL) = t^k F(K, L).$$

For example, $F(K, L) = K^a L^b$ is homogeneous

TABLE 6-5   *Marginal Product of Labor*

L	MP_L for $K = 1$	MP_L $K = 2$	MP_L $K = 3$	MP_L $K = 4$
1	100	128	144	158
2	64	72	88	98
3	43	66	68	74
4	42	54	65	70

of degree $a + b$. The condition of constant returns to scale for every production process is equivalent to the assertion that the production function is homogeneous of degree 1, that is,

$$F(tK, tL) = tF(K, L)$$

for every positive t. When the production function is homogeneous, then there are increasing returns to scale when k is greater than 1, and decreasing returns to scale when k is less than 1. With a homogeneous function, the returns to scale are the same along any process line in the production map.

Homogeneous production functions have one other interesting property.

> Along any process line in the production map, the marginal rate of technical substitution between capital and labor is the same, whatever the level of output; along any straight line from the origin of the production map, the slopes of all isoquants are identical.

This is the defining property of a *homothetic* production function, of which homogeneous production functions form a special class. When a production function is homothetic, we need know only the production process employed (but not the level of output) to determine the marginal rate of technical substitution between inputs. This relationship will be of some importance to us in chapters 7 and 8 when we take up questions concerning the way in which demands for inputs by the firm vary as the level of output of the firm changes.

Summary

The economist's view of the firm's technology is summarized in the production map of the firm, which in turn is the graphical representation of the firm's production function. Inefficient production processes are excluded from the production map. Under independence of processes, the production map exhibits constant or increasing returns to scale. It is assumed that the law of diminishing marginal rate of technical substitution holds, and so production isoquants bound convex sets. Returns to a variable input are governed by the law of diminishing marginal productivity, while returns to collections of variable inputs are governed by the law of variable proportions.

The average product and marginal product of a variable input are related to one another by these rules:

1. If AP is rising, $MP > AP$.

2. If AP is falling, $MP < AP$.

3. $MP = AP$ at the maximum value of AP.

Inputs can be classified as normal (cooperative) and competitive. In the special case of constant returns to scale with two inputs, the law of diminishing marginal rate of substitution implies that the inputs are normal.

Problems

1. It is well known that productivity per worker in the U.S. economy rises most rapidly in the first months of an economic upswing; and that productivity rises least (or actually falls) as full employment is reached. The explanation usually given is that as the economy moves toward full employment, the least productive members of the work force become employed. Construct an alternative explanation.

2. a. "Cooking with gas makes sense; it uses one-third less energy than electricity." Is cooking with gas more "efficient" than cooking with electricity?

   b. The engineer's measure of efficiency of a machine is the ratio of energy output to energy input. Can a 10 percent efficient machine be "efficient" in the economist's sense when a 20 percent efficient machine is not? Explain in terms of the production map of the firm.

3. For each of the following production functions, construct an output table for $K, L = 1, 2, 3, 4$.

   a. $X = \sqrt{KL}$
   b. $X = K^2 L$
   c. $X = K + L$
   d. $X = $ minimum of K or L

   Sketch in the $X = 1$ isoquant for each production function. Comment on returns to scale, whether inputs are normal or competitive, whether the law of diminishing marginal productivity holds, and whether diminishing marginal rate of technical substitution between inputs holds.

4. In its crudest form, the Malthusian argument goes as follows. Population has a "tendency" to grow at a geometric rate, while the food supply increases only at an arithmetic rate. Hence there is a built-in tendency toward famine and war. Explain the role played by the law of diminishing marginal productivity in this argument. (Malthus was among the first to discover a variant of this law.)

5. "U.S. workers are superior to workers in other countries, as is evidenced by the higher productivity per worker in the United States relative to other countries."

   "The long era of continued high growth in productivity in the United States is near an end, since agriculture and manufacturing in the United States are becoming less important than the service industries."

   Comment on these two statements. Explain your grounds for agreement or disagreement.

6. "While prices of most goods have gone up drastically since 1960, your telephone company has been hard at work keeping costs down; the dedication of telephone employees and management is reflected in the low prices of telephone services."

   What else is reflected in the relatively low prices of telephone services? In general, assuming all input prices increased proportionately, where would you expect to find the largest and the smallest increases in costs per unit of output during a period of growth in population and output?

Appendix

Linear Programming and the Production Map of the Firm

The problem of identifying efficient production processes is simple enough in the case of two inputs, but when there are large numbers of inputs, there can be real difficulties in specifying the production map of the firm. This is one of a wide range of problems where *linear programming* has been employed.

A linear programming (LP) problem has the following mathematical form:

Choose values of $x_1, x_2, \ldots, x_n$ so as to maximize

$$c_1 x_1 + c_2 x_2 + \ldots + c_n x_n \left(= \sum_{i=1}^{n} c_i \, x_i \right)$$

subject to

$$a_{11} x_1 + a_{12} x_2 + \ldots + a_{1n} \, x_n \leq b_1$$
$$a_{21} x_1 + a_{22} x_2 + \ldots + a_{2n} \, x_n \leq b_2$$
$$\vdots$$
$$a_{m1} x_1 + a_{m2} x_2 + \ldots + a_{mn} x_n \leq b_m$$

where

$$x_1 \geq 0, \, x_2 \geq 0, \ldots, x_n \geq 0.$$

In this problem, the c_i's, the a_{ij}'s and the b_j's are all constants. Consequently, the LP problem is one of maximizing a linear function subject to a set of linear inequality constraints. Note that there are n x's and $m + n$ inequality constraints. In general, $m \neq n$.

Associated with any LP problem is the *dual* problem, namely minimize

$$b_1 y_1 + b_2 y_2 + \ldots + b_m y_m = \sum_{j=1}^{m} b_j \, y_j$$

subject to

$$a_{11} y_1 + a_{21} y_2 + \ldots + a_{m1} y_m \geq c_1$$
$$\vdots$$
$$a_{1n} y_1 + a_{2n} y_2 + \ldots + a_{mn} y_m \geq c_n$$
$$y_1 \geq 0, \, y_2 \geq 0, \ldots, y_m \geq 0.$$

The y's are referred to as the *dual* variables relative to the x's.

Note that in the dual problem, the coefficients of y's in the objective function ($\Sigma b_j y_j$) are the constants on the right-hand sides of the first m inequality constraints of the LP problem. The constants on the right-hand side of the first n inequality constraints in the dual are the c_i's, the coefficients of the x's in the objective function of the LP problem. Finally, the a_{i1} coefficients in the first constraint of the dual are the coefficients of x_1 in the constraints of the LP problem; the a_{i2} coefficients in the second constraint of the dual are the coefficients of x_2 in the LP problem; and so on. These are the defining characteristics of the dual problem.

The *basic theorem of linear programming* is this:

A solution exists to an LP problem if and only if a solution exists to the dual problem; further, if a solution exists to the LP problem, then the maximum value of $\Sigma c_i x_i$ equals the minimum value of $\Sigma b_j y_j$.

Linear programming is an important management tool because there exist efficient algorithms, such as the "simplex" technique, for finding numerical solutions to large-scale LP problems. Our interest is not in that direction; instead we are interested in the economic interpretation that can be placed on LP problems and their duals. Consequently, we will illustrate the LP approach in the simplest possible context, where solutions can be derived graphically.

Consider the following problem. A firm producing a single output has available to it two production processes, characterized by constant returns, divisibility, and independence. The processes use capital and labor in fixed proportions. The firm has available to it certain limited amounts of capital and labor. The problem is to maximize output for the firm.

Let x_1, x_2 denote the outputs using processes number 1 and number 2. a_{1j} is the number of units of labor required to produce one unit of output in process j, $j = 1, 2$; and a_{2j} is the number of units of capital required to produce one unit of output in process j, $j = 1, 2$.

Then the LP problem becomes

$$\max x_1 + x_2$$

subject to

$$a_{11}x_1 + a_{12}x_2 \leq L_0$$
$$a_{21}x_1 + a_{22}x_2 \leq K_0$$
$$x_1 \geq 0, x_2 \geq 0$$

where L_0, K_0 are the number of units of labor and capital available to the firm. The problem can be interpreted as "maximize output subject to the constraints that no more than L_0 units of labor or K_0 units of capital can be employed by the firm."

Note again that process 1 uses a_{11} units of labor and a_{21} units of capital to produce one unit of output, while process 2 uses a_{12} units of labor and a_{22} units of capital to produce one unit of output. Thus the first constraint says total labor employed is no more than L_0 units, and the second that total capital employed is no more than K_0 units.

The dual problem is

$$\min y_1L_0 + y_2K_0$$

subject to

$$a_{11}y_1 + a_{21}y_2 \geq 1$$
$$a_{12}y_1 + a_{22}y_2 \geq 1$$
$$y_1 \geq 0, y_2 \geq 0.$$

The variables y_1 and y_2 in the dual problem are interpreted as the implicit valuations to the firm of a unit of labor services and of a unit of capital services, these valuations being in terms of units of output. Such values are called the *shadow prices* of labor and capital. Thus $y_1 = 1$, $y_2 = \frac{1}{2}$ means that a unit of labor has a value to the firm of one unit of output, while a unit of capital has a value of one-half unit of output. That is, the firm would be willing to give up one unit of output to obtain one more unit of labor services, and one-half unit of output to obtain one more unit of capital services.

The dual is to be interpreted as the choosing of values to assign to labor and capital services so as to minimize the value of the resource stocks, subject to the constraint that the capital and labor used in process number 1 to produce one unit of output must be assigned a value of at least one unit of output, and similarly for process number 2. Then the basic theorem of linear programming asserts that the minimizing value of the resource stocks equals the maximum output of the firm from those stocks. The importance of the dual to the firm manager is that the values determined by it are the amounts that the manager should be willing to spend to obtain additional units of the resources.

In the LP problem, a distinction is drawn between effective and ineffective constraints. If, at the maximizing values $(\bar{x}_1, \bar{x}_2)$, a constraint holds as an equality, then the constraint is said to be *effective*; if it holds as a strict inequality, then it is *ineffective*. There is a simple rule relating the values to be assigned to labor and capital to ineffective constraints: If the labor constraint is ineffective, then $y_1 = 0$; if the capital constraint is ineffective, then $y_2 = 0$. This rule expresses the intuitive notion that

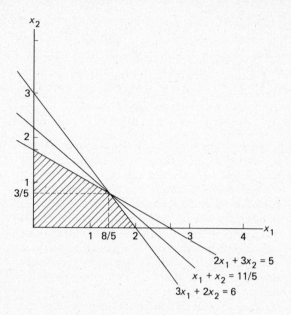

FIG. 6-A1   *LP problem*

if there is excess labor when output is maximized, then additional labor has no value to the firm, and similarly for capital.

A numerical illustration is the following:

$$\max\ x_1 + x_2$$

subject to

$$2x_1 + 3x_2 \leq 5$$
$$3x_1 + 2x_2 \leq 6$$
$$x_1 \geq 0,\ x_2 \geq 0.$$

Thus the two processes available to the firm are processes in which two units of labor combine with three units of capital to produce one unit of output; and three units of labor combine with two units of capital to produce one unit of output. The firm has five units of labor and six units of capital available.

Plotting the constraints and the objective function, we obtain figure 6-A1. The shaded area represents the feasible region as specified by the con-

straints. The maximum of output $x_1 + x_2$ occurs at the point A where $x_1 = 8/5$, $x_2 = 3/5$.

Consider the dual:

$$\min\ 5y_1 + 6y_2$$
$$\text{s.t.}\ 2y_1 + 3y_2 \geq 1$$
$$3y_1 + 2y_2 \geq 1$$
$$y_1 \geq 0,\ y_2 \geq 0.$$

As shown in figure 6-A2, the shaded area indicates the feasible region for the dual variables, the implicit valuations of labor (y_1) and capital (y_2). The minimizing value occurs at $y_1 = 1/5$, $y_2 = 1/5$. This means that the firm should be willing to spend as much as the value of one-fifth unit of output to obtain an additional unit of either capital or labor, since this is what either of them would add to the output of the firm. Note that both the labor and capital constraints in the LP problem were effective; if one were ineffective, the value of the corresponding resource would be zero. Note also that minimum of $5y_1 + 6y_2 = 11/5$; equal to the maximum of $x_1 + x_2$, $11/5$.

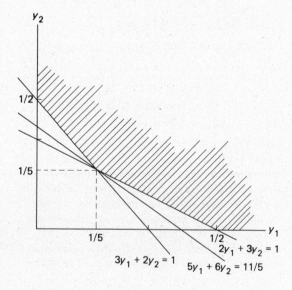

FIG. 6-A2   *Dual problem*

7

The Costs of the Firm

The production map displays the menu of alternative production processes available to the firm. From it the firm manager chooses the input-output mix that maximizes the profits of the firm. Whatever output level is chosen, profit maximization implies that the output be produced at as low a cost as possible. It is convenient to look first at the way in which a firm's costs are determined, before examining the choice of a profit-maximizing output level. This chapter deals with the costs of the firm.

Opportunity Cost

The economist uses the term *cost* in a more general sense than its usual one. For him, the cost of an action is the *opportunity cost:* the *value of the best available opportunity forgone because of the action.* For example, consider the cost of a college education to a student who is paying his own way. A year's expenses such as tuition, activity fees, and books might total $4,000. These cash outlays are a part of the opportunity cost of college, because if they were not incurred, then the $4,000 could have been spent on other goods and services. But these are not the only elements of opportunity cost in this situation. A student spending four years in college forgoes the income he could have earned during this time if he had worked

instead. Suppose that forgone income from work (above room and board) runs a maximum of $4,000 per year. Then assuming it is equally distasteful either to work or to attend class, the opportunity cost of the college education is $32,000 (4 years × $8,000 per year), plus interest.

To justify itself as a financial investment, the college education would have to return $32,000 (plus interest) above what could be earned without a college degree in the years following graduation. The evidence strongly suggests that this criterion is met, so that over and above the cultural advantages of college, higher education makes sense on purely financial grounds. But the point of this simplified example is this. In trying to decide whether to enroll in college, the prospective student should include the $4,000 per year in forgone income as one of the costs of his decision. Economists take "cost" to mean opportunity cost, because opportunity cost is the relevant measure for a decision maker contemplating an action.

To take another example, during the 1930s, the Roosevelt administration employed millions of workers on WPA projects ranging from raking leaves to creating murals for public buildings. The WPA came under scathing attack as a waste of public funds. What was the "cost" to the economy of a typical WPA project?

If the only alternative to WPA projects for the workers was the unemployment rolls, the opportunity cost was zero—there were no valuable opportunities forgone because of the WPA activity. In such circumstances, any public benefits at all for WPA projects would provide a justification for such projects.

In a competitive economy, factors of production such as labor, and capital are paid their opportunity costs. If there is some industry in the economy where steamfitters are paid their maximum rate of $10/hour, then steamfitters of like ability will be paid $10/hour in every industry. Competition is critical in arriving at this conclusion. Monopolistic constraints can drive a wedge between opportunity cost and the market price of a factor. For example, unions can establish wage rates that exceed the best alternative opportunities available to a union member; as a result, there are more applicants for union jobs than there are jobs available. The existence of monopoly also can influence the opportunities available to a factor of production. In professional sports, the reserve clause means that the best alternative employment for a baseball player is not to play for another team, but to work outside baseball. Consequently, star players earn less than they would if there were competitive bidding for their services on the part of all baseball teams.

We will ignore the effects of monopolistic imperfections in our discussion in this chapter. Instead, we will assume that all input markets are perfectly competitive in the sense that buyers and sellers alike take market prices as given, independent of the quantities of input services bought and sold. Under this assumption, the market price for the services of any input is equal to the opportunity costs of the input.

Distinguishing Short-Run from Long-Run Costs

It is traditional in economic theory to draw a somewhat artificial distinction between the short run and the long run. By the *short run* we mean a situation in which a firm operates within a given industry with fixed plant capacity. By the *long run* we mean a situation in which all of the incentives available to the firm are exploited; in particular, the firm is free to choose the levels of all inputs (including plant capacity) and to move from industry to industry.

The short-run/long-run dichotomy is artificial because it implicitly assigns an arbitrarily high cost to adjusting plant capacity or entering and leaving industries in the short run, while ignoring the costs of adjusting the levels of other inputs. Adjustment costs vary from input to input and from industry to industry, and involve intertemporal aspects that complicate the analysis. To keep things as simple as possible, we will follow the traditional short-run/long-run approach, but it is important not to read too much into the terminology. Long-run and short-run adjustments occur at each point in time, and astute firm managers take both into account simultaneously.

We will continue to maintain the distinction between stock and flow decision-making. Titles to all resources (including plant) are in the hands of consumers, and so firms make decisions only as to renting plant capacity, hiring inputs, and setting output levels. Thus, the short run should be interpreted as a situation in which the firm has contracted for the use of a specific plant, and chooses the best input-output mix for that plant. In the long run, the firm shops around in the rental market for plants, as well as in the markets for other inputs.

This means that in the short run, the number of firms in an industry is fixed; in the long run, new firms can be created and old firms destroyed. In the short run, the law of variable proportions characterizes the technology; in the long run, returns to scale come to the fore.

Costs in the Short Run

In the case of short-run costs, a distinction is drawn between fixed costs and variable costs of a firm.

Fixed and Variable Costs

As the terms imply, fixed costs are independent of the level of output of the firm, while variable costs vary with the output of the firm. Among fixed costs are the maintenance costs incurred to protect plant and equipment from wear and tear due solely to aging; executive salaries contracted for in the past to be paid in the current period; and rents, contracted for in the past, that must be paid regardless of the firm's operations. Variable costs include the cost of raw materials, production labor costs, and outlays arising from rentals geared to the use of inputs in the current period.

The importance of the distinction between fixed costs (often called "sunk costs") and variable costs is that *fixed costs are irrelevant for decision making*. This may also be stated as *sunk costs don't count*. After all, fixed costs represent water over the dam. These expenditures have already been contracted for in prior periods, and no decision now is going to alter the firm's obligation to pay them. (We assume that the firm will in fact honor its obligations.

The possibility of default will be deferred to later chapters concerned with uncertainty.)

Although fixed costs never enter into choosing among alternatives representing positive amounts of output, the firm may find that it loses less by shutting down completely (in which case its loss equals its fixed costs) than by operating at a positive output level. We will be a bit more precise about this in chapter 8.

Cost Minimization in the Short Run

The basic postulate that underlies the determination of the costs of the firm is the following:

> *Given any level of output, the firm chooses the production process that minimizes costs for that output.*

The firm's cost of producing a certain output is then interpreted simply as the minimum cost of producing that output.

We restrict our attention to the case of competitive input markets. For concreteness, assume that there are two variable inputs, labor services and capital services (machinery), combined with a fixed plant—the short-run case. Let w denote the wage rate per unit of labor services, and let r denote the rental rate per unit of capital services, both rates per unit of time. We will take the fixed cost of the firm to be the contractual rental payment for the use of the plant facilities. Total cost for the firm, TC, may be written as

$$TC = FC + VC$$

where FC is fixed cost and VC is variable cost. VC in turn is given by

$$VC = wL + rK$$

with L denoting the number of units of labor

services hired and K denoting the number of units of capital services rented. Note that in contrast to our discussion in chapter 6, we are now dealing with a technology involving three inputs—capital services K, labor services L, and plant services P. Output X is then given by the production function $F(K, L, P)$. In the short run, P is fixed while K and L can vary. In the long run, K, L, and P are all variable inputs. The short-run production isoquants for the firm are then isoquants along which P is held fixed.

The relationships between VC or TC and the two inputs are indicated in figure 7-1. This graph displays the *iso-cost* lines for the firm—lines along which the variable (and total) cost of the firm is a constant. (Since $TC = FC + VC$, and FC is constant, therefore when VC is constant, TC is constant as well.) Suppose we set variable cost at VC_0 dollars. With capital renting for r dollars per unit, we could rent a maximum of VC_0/r units of capital with VC_0 dollars available. Similarly, VC_0/w represents the maximum number of units of labor that could be hired. Since w and r are independent of the number of units of the two factors hired, the iso-cost line associated with VC_0 dollars is drawn by connecting these two intercepts. A similar argument applies for the VC_1 and VC_2 iso-costs lines. Note also that the slope of any iso-cost line equals $-(K$ intercept$/L$ intercept$)$ $= -w/r$.

Consider next the choice of a production process to minimize short-run cost for a given output $X = X_0$. Superimpose the production isoquant $X = X_0$ on figure 7-1. We obtain the graph shown in figure 7-2. To produce the output X_0' at the lowest possible cost, the firm must choose the production process, along the isoquant $X = X_0$, that is associated with the lowest value of VC. It is clear from the graph

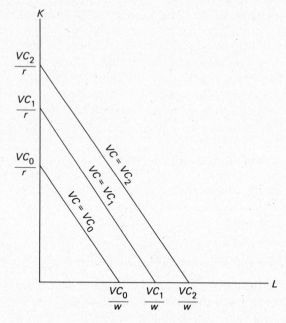

FIG. 7-1   *Iso-cost map*

that this occurs at $(\bar{L}, \bar{K})$, where there is a tangency between the isoquant and the iso-cost line $VC = VC_1$. At a tangency, the slope of the isoquant equals the slope of the iso-cost line. Thus $MRTS = w/r$; equivalently, $MP_L/MP_K = w/r$. (Recall from chapter 6 that the marginal rate of technical substitution between capital and labor is equal to (MP_L/MP_K).)

Given any output level, the firm employs capital and labor services such that the ratio of their marginal products equals the ratio of their per unit costs.

Expansion Path of the Firm   If we perform this operation for all possible output levels, we obtain a curve called the *short-run expansion path* for the firm, giving the combinations of

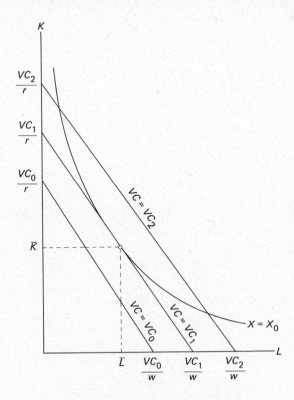

FIG. 7-2 *Cost minimization*

Short-Run Cost Curves for the Firm

Once the short-run expansion path of the firm has been determined, the cost curves for the firm can be immediately derived as in table 7-1 and figure 7-4, where $w = \$1$, $r = \$1$, and fixed cost is assumed to be $10. It should be recalled that we are assuming that the firm operates in a short-run situation, with fixed plant. Hence beyond some point, the law of variable proportions applies. Because of the lumpy fixed input (plant), there are increasing returns to capital and labor in moving from isoquant $X = 10$ to $X = 22$ (fig. 7-4). Beyond

input hirings that represent cost minimization for the firm, as a function of output, for the given plant capacity available to the firm. The shape of the short-run expansion path reflects the substitutability among production processes at different output levels, given the plant capacity. Thus it might be the case, as indicated in figure 7-3, that for low output levels, relatively capital-intensive processes are employed, while for high outputs, the firm shifts to relatively labor-intensive processes. (One production process is said to be more capital-intensive than another one if the ratio K/L is larger in the first than in the second process.)

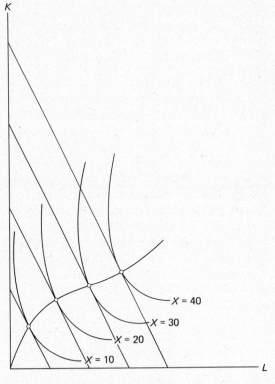

FIG. 7-3 *Short-run expansion path of the firm*

TABLE 7-1   *Short-Run Costs*

Cost Min. Point	Output	Units of Labor	Units of Capital	VC	FC	TC
a	10	4	6	$10	$10	$20
b	22	7	10	$17	$10	$27
c	30	15	12	$27	$10	$37
d	35	22	16	$38	$10	$48

that point, proportionate increases in K and L lead to less than proportionate increases in X.

Turning to the costs themselves, table 7-2 summarizes relevant cost information. *ATC* is average total cost (*TC* divided by output, *X*); *AVC* is average variable cost (*VC* divided by output); and *AFC* is average fixed cost (*FC* divided by output). *MC* is marginal cost, defined as *the increase in total cost brought about by increasing output by one unit*. In symbols,

$$ATC = \frac{TC}{X}, \ AVC = \frac{VC}{X},$$

$$AFC = \frac{FC}{X}, \ MC = \frac{\Delta TC}{\Delta X}.$$

In the table we approximate *MC* by dividing the increase in total cost by the increase in output for the points for which data are given.

Relationships between Average and Marginal Costs   Figures 7-5 and 7-6 show the firm's short-run cost curves, based on table 7-2. The

TABLE 7-2   *Total, Average, and Marginal Costs*

X	TC	ATC	VC	AVC	FC	AFC	MC
10	$20	$2.00	$10	$1.00	$10	$1.00	
22	$27	$1.23	$17	.77	$10	$ .56	$ .58
30	$37	$1.23	$27	.90	$10	$ .33	$1.25
35	$48	$1.37	$38	1.09	$10	$ .28	$2.20

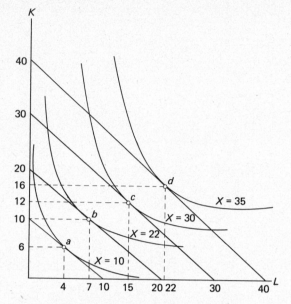

FIG. 7-4   *Deriving short-run costs*

first graph is a plot of *TC*, *VC*, and *FC* against *X*. The *TC* curve is parallel to the *VC* curve, lying above it by the constant amount of *FC*. Using the first graph, *ATC* can be interpreted as the slope of a line drawn from the origin to the *TC* curve; *AVC* and *AFC* have similar interpretations with respect to the *VC* and *FC* curves. *MC* is then the slope of either the *TC* curve or the *VC* curve (they are parallel) for any value of *X*.

Per unit cost measures are shown in figure 7-6. The rules that apply to such graphs play important roles in the economist's theorizing, but are quite simple and straightforward.

1. *AFC* declines as output increases.

2. The *AVC* curve reaches its minimum at point *a*, at a lower level of output than point *b* where the *ATC* curve attains its minimum.

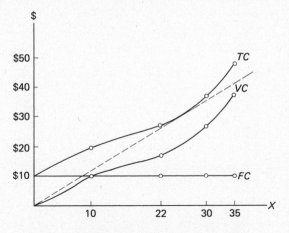

FIG. 7-5   *Short-run total costs, variable costs, and fixed costs*

3. The *MC* curve crosses the *AVC* curve at its minimum point *a* and crosses the *ATC* curve at its minimum point *b* as well.

4. The *MC* curve is rising as it passes through the minimum points of the *AVC* curve and the *ATC* curve.

Properties 3 and 4 require some discussion. *MC* is defined as the increase in total cost brought about by increasing output by one unit or, equivalently, *MC* is the increase in variable cost due to a one unit increase in output.

Suppose *ATC* is falling as output increases. Then *MC* lies below *ATC*. Why? *ATC* is defined as total cost divided by the number of units of output. If *ATC* falls when one unit is added to output, then that unit must add less to total cost than the average cost per unit of output before the unit was added. The same argument applies to *AVC*. Hence we conclude that when *ATC* is falling, *MC* is less than *ATC*, and if *AVC* is falling, then *MC* is below *AVC*.

Similarly, if *ATC* is rising, *MC* is above *ATC*; if *AVC* is rising, *MC* is above *AVC*. It follows that *MC* = *AVC* at *a*, the minimum point on the *AVC* curve, and *MC* = *ATC* at *b*, the minimum point on *ATC*.

Further, *MC* must rise to the right as it passes through the *AVC* curve, since the *MC* curve is below the *AVC* curve when it falls, and above the *AVC* curve when it rises, and similarly for the *ATC* curve. The same point can be made by noting that the slope of a line drawn from the origin to the *TC* curve in figure 7-5 equals the slope of the *TC* curve at *b* where *ATC* is a minimum.

One other feature of figure 7-6 should be noted. The vertical axis is designated in terms of $/unit of output, which represents the units

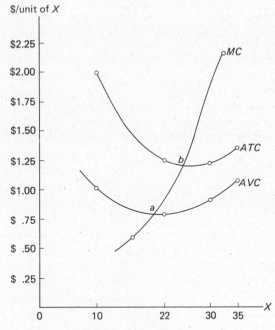

FIG. 7-6   *Short-run average and marginal cost curves of the firm*

in which *ATC*, *AVC*, *AFC*, and *MC* are measured. We can, however, represent *total* dollar amounts (*TC*, *VC*, *FC*) in terms of areas. Thus at any point on the *X* axis, drawing a line to the *ATC* curve and completing the rectangle gives an area equal to *TC*, as illustrated in figure 7-7.

Let ATC_0 denote *ATC* when $X = X_0$. The crosshatched region in figure 7-7 has an area equal to *TC* when $X = X_0$, since the horizontal distance is X_0 units of output, while the vertical distance is ATC_0 dollars per unit of output. The area $= ATC_0 \cdot X_0 = TC_0$, total costs at X_0. Similar areas enable one to calculate *VC* and *FC* for any level of output. In particular, since *FC* is constant for any output level, the *AFC* curve cuts off rectangles of constant area for any values of *X*.

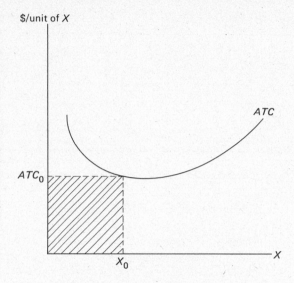

FIG. 7-7   *Total cost as an area*

Costs and the Law of Variable Proportions

The U-shaped *ATC*, *AVC*, and *MC* curves represent the typical case that economists work with in their analysis of firm behavior in the short run. The rationale underlying the use of these U-shaped curves as a typical case should be noted. *ATC*, *AVC*, and *MC* fall within a certain range of outputs because we have implicitly assumed that the given plant capacity is a lumpy fixed input that promotes increasing returns to the variable inputs for a range of output levels.

In the production map from which our example was drawn (fig. 7-8), such efficiencies occur between the first and second isoquants. Note that output more than doubles in going from the first iso-cost line to the second, even though variable costs double along the second line. This means that the firm has not yet begun to feel the effects of the law of variable proportions; doubling the variable inputs (*K* and *L*) more than doubles output for fixed plant.

Beyond the $X = 22$ isoquant, the law of variable proportions begins operating. As a result, increasing the variable inputs proportionately leads to a less than proportionate increase in output.

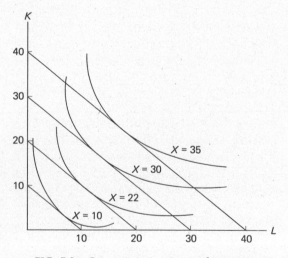

FIG. 7-8   *Cost minimization and outputs*

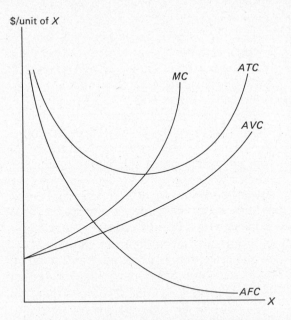

$/unit of X

MC

ATC

AVC

AFC

X

FIG. 7-9 *Short-run costs with diminishing returns to variable inputs*

The law of variable proportions implies that the *ATC* curve must rise to the right beyond some level of output. It is also entirely possible that the law of variable proportions begins operating immediately on costs. Hence the cost curves of the firm could appear as in figure 7-9.

When the law of variable proportions applies immediately, then *AVC* rises to the right over all output levels, and *MC* is above *AVC* for every positive output. In other respects, however, the rules relating average and marginal costs still apply.

Factor Costs and the Elasticity of Substitution

For given costs *w, r* per unit of labor services and capital services, the short-run cost curves of the firm can be derived from the short-run expansion path for the firm. In particular, at each level of output we can determine the cost-minimizing capital/labor ratio for the firm.

Suppose that market conditions change, causing the factor price ratio *w/r* to change and therefore also the slope of the iso-cost lines facing the firm. In dealing with this change in market conditions, the cost-minimizing firm adjusts its capital/labor ratio at each level of output. This adjustment results in a new expansion path and a new set of short-run cost curves for the firm.

The impact that a change in the wage/rental ratio has on marginal cost of the firm depends on the ease with which factors can be substituted for one another. In general, the more easily factors can be substituted, the less will a change in the wage/rental ratio change the marginal cost of the firm. An increase in the price of labor, for example, can be partly offset by a shift to more capital-intensive processes.

A measure of the ease of substitutability of inputs one for another is provided by the notion of *elasticity of substitution*, which we denote by σ. Formally, σ is defined by

$$\sigma = \frac{\% \text{ change in the capital/labor ratio}}{\% \text{ change in the marginal rate of technical substitution}} .$$

(The changes referred to in this formula occur along a given isoquant.)

The marginal rate of technical substitution in turns equals MP_L/MP_K. A cost minimizing firm chooses K and L so that $MP_L/MP_K = w/r$. Hence for a firm facing competitive input markets, σ may be written as

$$\sigma = \frac{\% \text{ change in the capital/labor ratio}}{\% \text{ change in the wage/rental ratio}} .$$

That is, $\sigma = \dfrac{\Delta\left(\dfrac{K}{L}\right) \Big/ \dfrac{K}{L}}{\Delta\left(\dfrac{w}{r}\right) \Big/ \dfrac{w}{r}} .$

The larger σ is, the larger the percent change in the capital/labor ratio in response to a 1 percent change in the wage/rental ratio. Thus σ gives an indication of the sensitivity of costs to a change in factor prices.

In empirical work in economics involving the estimation of the production functions of firms and industries, the simplifying assumption is often made that the elasticity of substitution is constant for all output levels and for all capital/labor ratios. Such a production function is called a *CES* (constant elasticity of substitution) function. Under constant returns to scale and with only two inputs (K and L), the formula for a *CES* production function is given by

$$X = A(\alpha K^{(\sigma-1)/\sigma} + (1-\alpha)L^{(\sigma-1)/\sigma})^{\sigma/(\sigma-1)}$$

where A is a positive constant and $0 < \alpha < 1$. When $\sigma = 1$ (a 1 percent increase in w/r leads to a 1 percent increase in K/L), the *CES* production function reduces to the *Cobb-Douglas* form

$$X = AK^{\alpha}L^{1-\alpha}.$$

For the three input case (K, L, and P), the *CES* function becomes

$$X = A(\alpha_1 K^{(\sigma-1)/\sigma} + \alpha_2 L^{(\sigma-1)/\sigma} + \alpha_3 P^{(\sigma-1)/\sigma})^{\sigma/(\sigma-1)}$$

where

$$\alpha_1 + \alpha_2 + \alpha_3 = 1.$$

Long-Run Costs

In the long run, the firm is free to choose the plant capacity it wishes, as well as the levels of other inputs. The choice of plant capacity or other inputs depends of course on the output level desired. Given an output level, the firm chooses an optimal plant capacity. Within that plant capacity, the choice of other inputs to employ follows the rule of minimizing short-run cost.

In the long run, all inputs are free to vary. Hence long-run costs are related to the returns to scale that characterize the technology, in contrast to the central role played by the law of variable proportions in short-run costs. As in the short-run case, it will be assumed that the firm operates in perfectly competitive input markets, so that the firm can rent as many units of any input (including plant capacity) as it desires at the going market price for the input. Because the firm is making choices with respect to *all* of the inputs it hires, there are no long-run fixed costs. *In the long run, all costs are variable.* In particular, the contractual rental payment for use of the plant, which is a fixed cost in the short run, becomes a variable cost in the long run. Keeping this in mind, we define long-run total costs as follows.

Long-run total cost for a firm for a given level of output is the total cost associated with the least cost combination of inputs (including plant capacity) required to produce that level of output.

Similarly, long-run marginal cost is the increase in long-run total cost associated with increasing output by one unit; long-run average cost is long-run total cost divided by the number of units of output.

In a short run, the mix of inputs changes as we increase output and the firm moves along the short-run expansion path associated with a given plant. In the long run, generally all inputs (including plant) vary as output is increased.

Long-Run Cost Curves

The short-run cost curves of the firm give the costs associated with various output levels, for a given plant capacity. A similar set of curves can be developed for the long-run case, giving costs associated with various output levels, allowing all inputs (including plant capacity) to vary. There is a close connection between the short-run cost curves of the firm and its long-run cost curves; as we shall see, the long-run cost curves are envelope curves built up from the underlying short-run curves.

The characteristics of the long-run cost curves of the firm depend in large part on the returns to scale properties of the firm's production function. We will consider separately the cases of constant returns to scale, increasing returns, and decreasing returns.

Constant Returns to Scale

As noted in chapter 6, constant returns to scale and homogeneity of degree 1 of the production function are equivalent. That is,

$$F(tK, tL, tP) = t \cdot F(K, L, P)$$

for any positive t. (Multiplying all inputs by t multiplies output by t.) Furthermore, homogeneous production functions are homothetic, so that the marginal rates of technical substitution among capital, labor, and plant are the same for all output levels, given fixed ratios of K, L, and P.

Given fixed prices for K, L, and P, the firm uses the same proportions of these inputs to minimize cost for any output level. For example, if K, L, and P are combined together in proportions 1: 2: 2 to produce some output level at minimum cost, then the same proportions will be used to produce any other output level

at minimum cost. And because there are constant returns to scale, the total cost associated with 10 or 100 units of output is just 10 or 100 times the total cost of producing 1 unit of output, assuming input prices are fixed.

It follows that under constant returns to scale the long-run total cost ($LRTC$) curve of the firm is simply a straight line through the origin (fig. 7-10). But we can also think of the $LRTC$ curve as an envelope curve built up from the short-run "plant" cost curves, as in figure 7-11.

The least cost method of producing X_1 units is to use plant 1 with (short-run) total cost curve TC_1; at X_2, plant 2 with total cost curve TC_2 is the cost-minimizing choice. The $LRTC$ curve is obtained by linking together these cost-minimizing points; hence the short-run curves are tangent to the $LRTC$ curve at the outputs

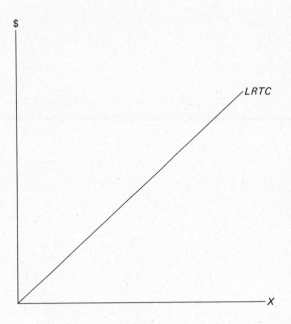

FIG. 7-10 *Long-run total cost under constant returns*

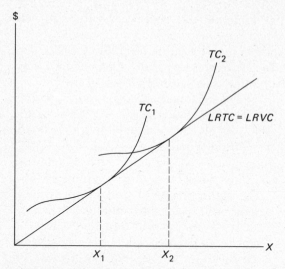

FIG. 7-11   *Long-run total cost and plant cost curves*

at which the plants are employed. By the nature of the *LRTC* curve it follows that at X_1, *LRTC* equals short-run total cost (TC_1) of plant 1; long-run average cost equals short-run average total cost of plant 1; and long-run marginal cost equals short-run marginal cost of plant 1 as well. Finally, note that the tangency of TC_1 to the *LRTC* curve occurs at the minimum of average total costs for plant 1.

Long-run total cost (*LRTC*) can be expressed by the equation

$$LRTC = aX$$

when *a* is the total cost of producing one unit of output and *X* is the level of output. Doubling all inputs doubles output, and there is no cheaper way to double output than by doubling all inputs. In the long run, all costs are variable so that *LRTC* = *LRVC*. Long-run average cost (*LRAC*) is given by

$$LRAC = \frac{LRTC}{X} = a.$$

Thus, long-run average cost is constant for every level of output. Similarly, long-run marginal cost (*LRMC*) is equal to *a*, since increasing output by one unit increases long-run total cost by *a* dollars. Equivalently, the slope of the *LRAC* curve is constant at *a* dollars; hence *LRMC* = *a* for every *X*.

Figure 7-12 shows that for plant 1 ATC_1 = *LRAC* and MC_1 = *LRMC* at X_1, with ATC_1 a minimum at X_1.

Constant Costs for the Firm   Constant returns to scale, coupled with competitive input markets, lead to *constant costs* for the firm (that is, constant *LRAC* for every output level). The assumption of competitive input markets is important. If the firm finds that increasing its output (and thus its input hiring) causes the market price of the input to rise, then increases in output would be associated with a rising *LRAC* even under constant returns to scale. But with competitive input markets, the firm can hire as many units of the inputs as it desires at the going market price.

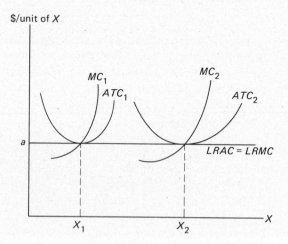

FIG. 7-12   *Long-run average and marginal costs under constant returns*

It might be well to emphasize that the cost curves of the firm are drawn from the perspective of the manager of the firm, reflecting the way that such costs enter into his decision making. Thus it might be the case that every firm in an industry operates under constant returns and faces competitive input markets, so that the firms operate under constant costs. But the industry could be the sole purchaser of some specialized input. This would mean that as the industry expands output, the price of the specialized input increases. The industry would face increasing costs, despite the fact that each firm in the industry operates under constant costs. In a competitive industry, each firm represents such a negligible fraction of total output for the industry that in its decision making it ignores the effects of its decisions on industry output. This accounts for the possible paradox of increasing costs for the industry with constant costs for the firm. We will return to this issue in chapter 10.

Increasing Returns to Scale If the firm operates in perfectly competitive input markets, increasing returns to scale are associated with decreasing costs. That is, *LRAC* falls as output is increased, since doubling all inputs results in a more than doubling of output.

The increasing returns case is pictured in figure 7-13. Once again, the *LRTC* curve is built up from the short-run (plant) cost curves that minimize cost for each level of output. The plant with cost curve TC_1 provides the least cost method of producing X_1 units, and the plant with cost curve TC_2 minimizes the cost of producing X_2 units. *LRTC* at any output is equal to the short-run total cost of the plant which produces that output at minimum cost.

Under increasing returns to scale, the tangency of a short-run cost curve to the long-run curve does *not* occur at a minimum of average

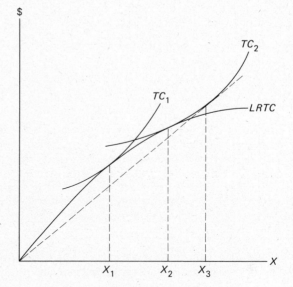

FIG. 7-13 *Long-run total costs and increasing returns to scale*

total cost for the plant. In figure 7-13, the minimum of average total cost for plant 2 occurs at $X_3 > X_2$, as indicated by the tangency of a line from the origin to the TC_2 curve.

A characteristic of increasing returns to scale (with competitive input markets) is that plants are operated "in the long run" at levels of output less than the short-run output where average cost for the plant is a minimum. This situation is illustrated in figure 7-14. The *LRTC* curve increases at a decreasing rate, which is reflected in the falling *LRAC* curve. The *LRAC* diagram again indicates that the plant cost curves are tangent to the *LRAC* curve at average costs that are higher than the minimum for each plant size. In producing an output of X_1 units, the firm finds it most advantageous to rent a plant with "excess capacity" in the sense that the minimum of AC_1 occurs at an output larger than X_1. Smaller or larger capacity plants will have *higher* cost of producing X_1 units.

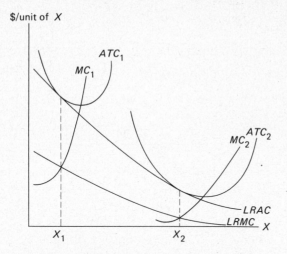

FIG. 7-14   *Long-run average and marginal costs under increasing returns to scale*

The *LRAC* curve turns out also to be an "envelope" curve. This curve is obtained by connecting the points on the *ATC* curves of plants with the lowest short-run average total costs to produce each output level. The *LRMC* curve is constructed by using the rule that *LRMC* at X_1 is equal to MC_1, the short-run marginal cost of plant 1, the optimal plant to produce X_1 units. This holds because TC_1 is tangent to the *LRTC* curve at X_1. Similarly, *LRMC* at X_2 is equal to MC_2. Connecting all such points, we obtain *LRMC*. Under increasing returns to scale, *LRMC* is below *LRAC* for every output level. In the special case where the production function is homogeneous, *LRMC* falls as output increases under increasing returns to scale.

Decreasing Returns to Scale Under decreasing returns to scale, the *LRTC* increases at an increasing rate as output rises. The tangencies

of plant total cost curves to the *LRTC* curve occur at outputs higher than those that lead to minimum short-run average cost. The *LRAC* rises with output, and the *LRMC* lies above *LRAC* for every output level. The long-run average and marginal cost curves are shown in figure 7-15. (Once again, in the special case of a homogeneous production function, *LRMC* increases as output increases.)

Combining the constant, increasing, and decreasing returns cases, we obtain the U-shaped long-run average cost curve shown in figure 7-16. For outputs less than X_2, increasing returns hold; beyond X_2 there are decreasing returns; and at X_2 constant returns prevail. It is only

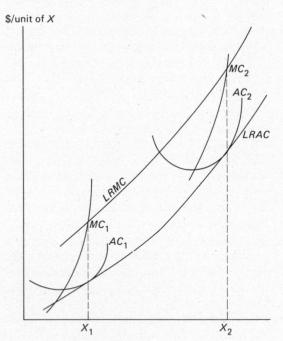

FIG. 7-15   *Long-run average and marginal costs under decreasing returns to scale*

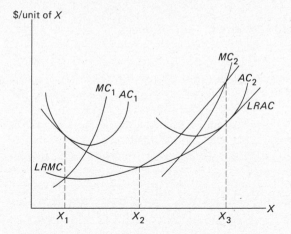

$/unit of X

FIG. 7-16   *U-shaped long-run average cost*

at X_2 that the minimum of short-run average cost for the plant equals *LRAC*. Moreover, at X_2 we have short-run marginal cost = *LRMC* = *LRAC* = short-run average cost. The *LRMC* curve lies below *LRAC* to the left of X_2 and above it to the right of X_2.

Long-Run Costs versus Short-Run Costs

By the very manner in which the *LRTC* curve is constructed, short-run total cost for any level of output can never be less than long-run total cost. This rule applies to average cost as well. It reflects the simple fact that in the long-run situation, the firm manager has a wider choice of options than in the short run; hence he can always do at least as well as he does in any short-run decision.

Note also that the short-run marginal cost curves are steeper at all output levels than is the *LRMC* curve; that is, the short-run marginal cost curves cut the *LRMC* curve below the

LRMC curve. While infinitesimal changes in output lead to the same increase in total cost both in the short run and long run along the *LRMC*, finite increases in output increase costs more in the short run than in the long run.

Summary

Because the firm is operated to maximize profits, it minimizes the cost of whatever output it chooses to produce. The cost curves of the firm are derived by determining the cost-minimizing combination of inputs to produce any given output.

In the short run, plant size is fixed. As a consequence, the law of variable proportions operates to ensure that beyond some level of output, average costs rise—both average variable cost (*AVC*) and average total cost (*ATC*). Marginal cost (*MC*) is below *ATC* when *ATC* is falling, and above it when it is rising. The same relation holds between *MC* and *AVC*. Consequently, *MC* equals *ATC* at the low point of *ATC*, and *MC* equals *AVC* at the low point of *AVC*. Average fixed cost falls for every increase in output. When factor prices change, the cost curves of the firm change as well, with the sensitivity of marginal cost to changes in factor prices being governed by the elasticity of substitution.

In the long run, all costs are variable. The *LRTC* curve is an envelope curve that associates with each output the minimum cost of producing that output. Plant *TC* curves are tangent to the *LRTC* curve at outputs such that the plants represent the least cost alternatives for producing such outputs. Under constant returns to scale with competitive input markets, *LRAC* = *LRMC* = constant for all output levels. Under increasing returns to scale with competitive input markets, *LRAC* falls as output increases, and *LRMC* is below *LRAC* for every output. Under decreasing returns to scale, *LRAC* rises with output, and *LRMC* is above *LRAC* for every output.

Problems

1. a. The Milwaukee Brewers are said to have paid Henry Aaron over $200,000 for the 1975 baseball season. The rules of baseball provide that a player under contract cannot play for any team other than the one holding his contract; he may, however, take a job outside baseball. Is Henry Aaron receiving more or less than his opportunity cost?

     Suppose the baseball rules were amended so that any team could bid for his services. What happens to Henry Aaron's opportunity cost? Would you expect him to receive more or less than his opportunity cost in this new situation?

   b. Why do movie stars and athletes often "hold out" or "walk out" while negotiating contracts, but college professors rarely do?

   c. An acre of land is used only for wheat production. Contrast the variability of the price of an acre of such land with the price of an acre of land that can be used for producing several crops.

2. "The high capital/labor ratio in the United States relative to other countries is a direct reflection of the inventiveness of American technicians with its accompanying increase in the productivity of capital." Present an alternative explanation for the high K/L ratio in the United States.

3. Public utilities are regulated in the United States on the basis of "fair rate of return" on investment. Therefore, the fee schedule for electricity, gas, and water services is set high enough that the utility earns, say, 6 percent on all physical capital invested in producing the utility services. How would you expect such a rate setting system to affect the choice of production processes by utilities? Present an argument that elimi-

nating such a system will reduce the cost of producing electric, gas, and water services.

4. Following is a production function for a firm that employs two inputs, plant P and labor L, to produce output X. Assume that $X = 0$ for $P = 0$ or $L = 0$.

L \ P	1	2	3	4
1	100	125	140	150
2	125	200	230	270
3	140	230	300	320
4	150	270	320	400

Assume that the wage rate of labor is $10 per unit, while the rental per unit of plant is $15. Sketch the $LRTC$, $LRAC$, and $LRMC$ curves on the basis of the corresponding short-run curves for $P = 1, 2, 3, 4$.

5. Sketch the short-run and long-run costs curves that seem to fit the following cases. Explain why you have drawn the curves as you have.

   a. Hospital costs are high because, while the case load at a hospital varies widely from month to month, the hospital finds it necessary to maintain its nursing staff at a constant level, and nursing costs account for over 60 percent of total hospital costs.

   b. To protect small town and "neighborhood" banks, most states have enacted "branch banking" laws restricting the number of branches that can be set up by a bank.

   c. Electric power is a regulated industry in every state, because the generation of electric power is assumed to be a "natural monopoly."

   d. Barbershops.

8

Profit Maximization and the Competitive Firm

The competitive firm is managed so as to maximize the firm's profits. Under the simplifying assumptions made earlier, we identify profits with net cash flows in the current period—that is, revenue minus cost. Further, we assume that production and sales of the firm are simultaneous, and so the firm carries neither inventories nor backlogs of orders, and has no sources of revenue other than sales of its product.

Recall that for the perfectly competitive firm, the price per unit of the firm's output is treated by the firm as fixed, independent of the number of units produced and sold by the firm. Let p denote the price per unit of output and X the output of the firm. Then we can define the following revenue measures.

Total Revenue, Average Revenue, and Marginal Revenue

Total revenue (TR) is revenue received by the firm; average revenue (AR) is the revenue received by the firm per unit of output; and marginal revenue (MR) is the addition to the firm's revenue brought about by producing one more unit of output. Under the assumption that the firm faces a perfectly competitive output market, it immediately follows that

$$TR = pX$$
$$AR = \frac{TR}{X} = p$$
$$MR = \frac{\Delta TR}{\Delta X} = \frac{p\Delta X}{\Delta X} = p.$$

That is, the average revenue received per unit sold is simply the price per unit of output, and the additional revenue gained by producing one more unit of output is also the price per unit of output. Curves representing these magnitudes appear in figure 8-1.

A firm that has market power, as in the case of a monopoly, takes into account the effect of its output on market price. For such a firm, the expression for $MR = (\Delta TR/\Delta X)$ becomes

$$MR = \frac{p\Delta X + X\Delta p}{\Delta X}$$

where Δp is the change in market price due to a change ΔX in the firm's output. The competitive firm ignores the effects of its output on price and hence regards Δp as equal to zero.

Profit Maximization by the Competitive Firm

Profits are defined as total revenue minus total cost, and the firm is assumed to choose the

a)

b)

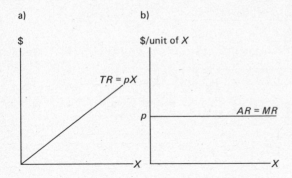

FIG. 8-1   a. *Total revenue for the competitive firm*
          b. *Average and marginal revenue for the competitive firm*

level of output (and the production process to produce the specified level of output) that maximizes profits for the firm. To show graphically what is going on, superimpose the total cost curve of a firm with U-shaped average costs on the total revenue graph as in figure 8-2. Profits π are given by $\pi = TR - TC$. Hence at any value of X, the vertical distance between the TR curve and the TC curve denotes profits for that level of output. When output is less than $\underline{X}$ or more than $\overline{X}$, then profits are negative. The point at which a maximum of profits occurs is the level of output X_0 where the slope of the TC curve is equal to the slope of the TR curve—that is, $MC = MR$.

We can also illustrate the choice of a profit-maximizing output level in terms of a graph that plots X against \$/unit of X, superimposing the curves representing ATC, AVC, and MC on the AR, MR graph, as in figure 8-3. The points $\underline{X}$ and $\overline{X}$ are identified as in figure 8-2. Profits are zero both at $\underline{X}$ and $\overline{X}$ since $ATC = AR$ at these points. That is, average total cost per unit equals average revenue per unit; hence profits are zero. The profit-maximizing output of X_0 is the output at which the marginal

cost curve crosses the marginal revenue (= average revenue) line. Total profits at X_0 are given by the area of the shaded rectangle. The area equals profits because the length of the rectangle is X_0, the number of units produced, while the height of the rectangle is given by the difference between AR and ATC_0, the average cost at the output X_0. Thus the height of the rectangle is average profits per unit of output (when output is X_0), and the area is average profits per unit times the number of units produced, or simply, total profits.

Marginal Revenue = Marginal Cost

The condition that profits are maximized at X_0 where $MC = MR$ requires further discussion. First, MR is the slope of the TR curve, while MC is the slope of the ATC curve, as noted earlier. Hence, point X_0 can be viewed as the output level where the slope of the TR curve equals the slope of the TC curve.

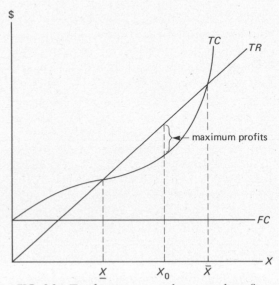

FIG. 8-2   *Total revenue, total cost, and profits*

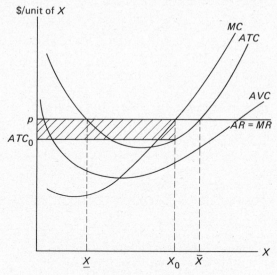

FIG. 8-3 *Average revenue, average cost, and profits*

To show that profits indeed are a maximum at X_0, suppose that output is less than X_0, with MC below MR. MR $(=p)$ gives the increase in revenue from producing one more unit, while MC gives the increase in cost from producing one more unit. To the left of X_0, with MC less than MR, increasing output by one unit would add more to revenue than to cost; hence profits increase by increasing output by that unit. So long as MC is less than MR, we are not at a profit-maximizing output. Similarly, assume that the firm produces to the right of X_0, where MR is less than MC. Then by reducing output by one unit, we reduce cost by the amount MC and reduce revenue by the amount MR. Since MC is greater than MR, we can increase profits by *reducing* the level of output. It immediately follows that when profits are maximized, $MR = MC$ as at X_0.

Two qualifications to this conclusion should be noted. First, the argument just given assumes that the MC curve is rising to the right as it passes through the MR line. If the MC curve crosses the MR line twice, then it is only the point where the MC curve rises to the right that represents the point of maximum profits. Second, we have assumed that the firm will choose a positive output level in maximizing profits. But it might be that the firm is better off, given the price and the firm's costs, to shut down operations completely and suffer a loss equal to fixed costs.

At the point X^* in figure 8-4, $MC = MR$, but $MR = AR$ lies below the average variable cost curve. Thus at X^* total revenue $(=pX^*)$ is *less* than total variable cost$(=X^* \cdot AVC(X^*))$. The firm loses more than its fixed costs, since at X^* it has to pay not only its fixed costs but also the difference between variable costs and revenue. Its revenues do not cover even its variable costs of operation. Consider in contrast a decision to shut down the firm. Then losses are equal to fixed costs. Clearly, the profit-maximizing (loss-minimizing) decision for the firm is to shut down.

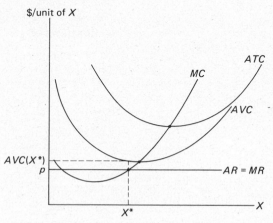

FIG. 8-4 *The shut-down decision for the firm*

Recall that the MC curve crosses the AVC curve at the minimum point of the AVC curve. Then so long as the AR line lies below the minimum point on the AVC curve, the profit-maximizing decision for the firm is to shut down. If AR is above the minimum of AVC, then the firm will produce a level of output such that MR = MC.

Summarizing this discussion, we arrive at the following as the profit-maximizing rules for the competitive firm.

The profit-maximizing output for the firm is either (1) zero, if price is less than the minimum of average variable cost; or (2) the output level where MC = price, given that price is higher than the minimum average variable cost and that the marginal cost curve is rising to the right.

For completeness we note that if price equals the minimum of average variable cost, the firm is indifferent between operating at zero output or at the output where average variable cost is a minimum. In either case, the firm's losses are equal to its fixed costs. Note that the rules concerning profit maximization hold under both short-run and long-run conditions.

Existence of a Profit-Maximizing Output

Can we guarantee that a profit-maximizing output (zero or positive) exists for the firm? This question arises because it is possible to conceive of situations in which the firm finds that profits increase indefinitely as output is increased. Suppose, for example, that AVC falls continually as output increases, as in figure 8-5. So long as AVC falls, MC lies below AVC. If AVC falls continually as output increases, then there will be no point at which MC = price *and*

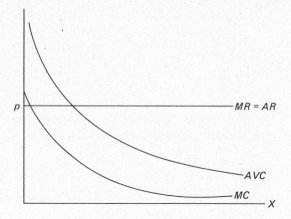

FIG. 8-5 *Nonexistence of a profit-maximizing output for the firm*

MC is rising to the right. To put it another way, profits are always larger the more output is produced. Thus in the case pictured, there is no profit-maximizing output.

The situation pictured in figure 8-5 arises under long-run conditions when there are increasing returns to scale with competitive input markets. We can immediately conclude that *perfect competition in the output market for a firm in the long run is incompatible with increasing returns to scale and competitive input markets.* Perfect competition in the long run requires constant or decreasing returns to scale beyond some level of output for the firm.

Under short-run conditions, however, the firm's plant is fixed, and the law of variable proportions ensures that beyond some point, proportional increases in variable inputs yield less than proportionate increases in output. Translated into cost curves (assuming that the firm operates in perfectly competitive input markets), this law means that the AVC must turn up beyond some finite level of output.

Supply and Demand for the Firm and Profit Maximization

Assume that the technology available to each firm is such that the firm is a price taker in both the input and the output markets. Given any prices for inputs and for output, the rule of profit maximization determines the amount of output supplied by the firm. Once we know the profit-maximizing output level for the given prices of inputs and output, we can determine the number of units of each input hired by finding the combination of inputs that minimizes the cost of producing the profit maximizing output. Another way of saying this is that the rule of profit maximization, applied to a competitive firm, enables us to determine the demand and supply schedules of the firm—the demand schedules for inputs to be hired and the supply schedule of output to be produced.

As in the case of consumer theory, our concern is with the responsiveness of quantities demanded and supplied to changes in prices of inputs and outputs. We consider first the impact of an equal proportionate increase in the prices of all inputs and output.

Homogeneity of Degree Zero of the Firm's Demand and Supply Schedules

Suppose that, given the prices p_0 per unit of output, r_0 per unit of capital, and w_0 per unit of labor services, the profit-maximizing firm chooses to produce X_0 units of output, employing L_0 units of labor and K_0 units of capital. Then we have the situation pictured in figure 8-6. VC_0 is the variable cost associated with an output of X_0 units:

$$VC_0 = w_0 L_0 + r_0 K_0.$$

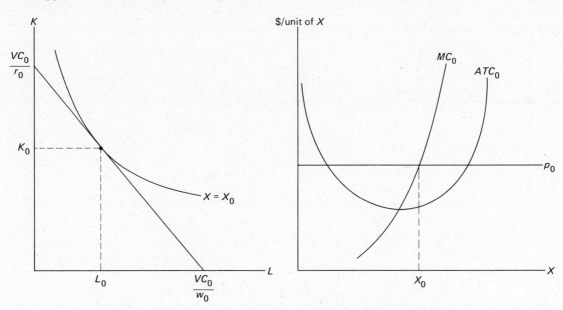

FIG. 8-6 *Profit maximization and input-output choices*

Suppose we now double all prices, and so (p_0, r_0, w_0) is replaced by $(2p_0, 2r_0, 2w_0)$. Under this new set of prices, the iso-cost lines of the firm have slope $-2w_0/2r_0$, which reduces to $-w_0/r_0$. In other words, doubling all prices leaves the slope of the iso-cost lines unchanged. Since the production isoquants are independent of prices (depending instead only on the technology), the input combination (K, L) that minimizes cost for any X remains the same as before. In particular, under the new prices, the firm chooses (K_0, L_0) if it wishes to produce X_0 units of output. Hence the new variable cost associated with X_0 units of output is given by

$$2w_0L_0 + 2r_0K_0 = 2VC_0.$$

It is clear that variable cost for every output level doubles when all prices are doubled. This implies that marginal cost (which equals the change in VC for a one unit change in X) also doubles, at each output level. Since we are assuming that p_0 doubles as well, clearly the new profit-maximizing output will still be X_0, with the units of inputs hired thus remaining (K_0, L_0). Doubling all prices leads to the same choices of inputs and output for the firm, as shown in figure 8-7.

The new MC and ATC curves are labelled MC', ATC'. $MC' = 2MC_0$ for every value of X, and MC' crosses the new price line $2p_0$ at X_0, the same level of output at which $MC_0 = p_0$. Thus the profit-maximizing output level

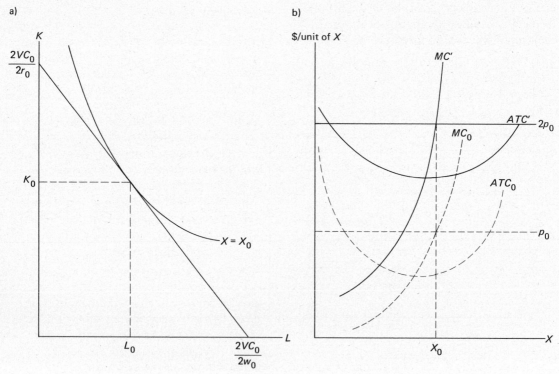

FIG. 8-7   *Effects, on input-output choices, of doubling all prices*

remains unchanged following a doubling of all prices. As indicated in figure 8-7a, the profit-maximizing choice of inputs remains K_0, L_0.

What is the effect of a doubling of all prices on profits of the firm? Here we must distinguish between short-run and long-run effects. Under short-run conditions, a part of the costs of the firm are fixed costs. Since these costs are unaffected by changes in input or output prices, ATC' (the new average total cost curve) is less than $2ATC_0$ at each value of X. In fact $ATC' = AFC_0 + 2AVC_0$. This means that total profits more than double in the short run when AFC_0 is nonzero. In the long run, all the costs of the firm are variable costs, and therefore ATC doubles when all input prices double. In the long run, a doubling of the prices of inputs and outputs leads to a doubling of profits.

We have obtained the following basic result concerning the supply schedule of output and the demand schedules for inputs for a competitive firm:

Under either short-run or long-run conditions, demand and supply schedules for the competitive firm are homogeneous of degree zero in the prices of all inputs and output; that is, an equal proportionate increase in all input prices and in the price of output leaves quantities demanded of inputs and quantity supplied of output unchanged. Profits are increased more than proportionately in the short run, but increase proportionately with prices in the long run.

We next examine the way in which the supply curve of output for the firm is derived.

The Short-Run Supply Curve of Output for the Competitive Firm

Looking first at short-run decision making, the supply curve of output is derived directly from the rule of profit maximization by the firm. A simple result holds:

The short-run supply curve of the competitive firm is the marginal cost curve of the firm, for the portion of the marginal cost curve that lies above the minimum of the average variable cost curve and that slopes upward to the right.

Given that all input prices are fixed, the short-run supply curve of the firm specifies the number of units of output that will be supplied as a function of the price per unit of output. Consider figure 8-8a. The graph indicates various prices for output and the corresponding profit-maximizing outputs chosen by the firm. At p_1 the firm chooses output X_1; at p_2, X_2; and so on. Positive output levels are determined by setting marginal cost equal to price, but then the marginal cost curve rising to the right (above the minimum of AVC) is the supply curve of the firm, as indicated in figure 8-8b. There is a discontinuity at p_5—the firm is indifferent between an output of zero and the output X_5. Below p_5 the output is zero.

Recall that the MC curve is derived from cost minimization for each output level. Hence a change in input prices will shift the MC curve, as will a change in the underlying technology (the firm's production map).

One fundamental verifiable proposition follows from the identification of the firm's supply curve with its marginal cost curve.

An increase in the market price of a produced good always leads to an increase in the quantity supplied of that good in the short run by every firm producing the good, given that (a) price is above the minimum of average variable cost; (b) the firm operates under competitive conditions in both the input and the output markets, and (c) other prices and the firm's technology are fixed.

a)

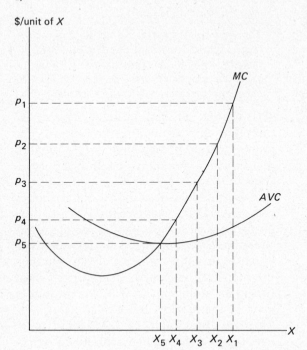

b)

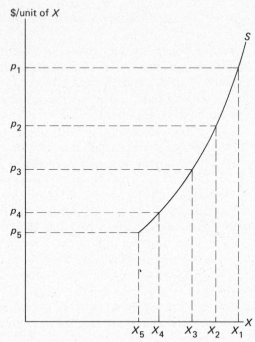

FIG. 8-8   a. *Short-run marginal and average variable cost*
b. *Short-run supply curve of the firm*

The Long-Run Supply Curve of Output for the Competitive Firm

The basic argument used in the short run applies to the long-run supply curve as well. Under competitive conditions, the (long-run) supply curve is the (long-run) marginal cost curve, but some comments are in order concerning the implications of this.

Under constant returns to scale, the firm is indifferent to the amount of output it supplies, so long as market price equals $LRAC$, which in turn equals $LRMC$. If price is above $LRAC$, the firm produces an unlimited amount; while if price is below $LRAC$, the firm produces nothing. Hence market price is equal to the $LRAC$ of any firm that actually produces a positive output of the good, and the supply curve of output is perfectly elastic, as indicated in figure 8-9.

If increasing returns characterize the technology, perfect competition breaks down, as noted in chapter 7. Hence the long-run supply curve is not defined for this case.

Under decreasing returns (fig. 8-10a), the $LRMC$ is the firm's long-run supply curve. In the U-shaped case (fig. 8-10b), $LRMC$ above the minimum of $LRAC$ (and sloping upward to the right) is the supply curve. In figure 8-10b, $LRMC$ for $X \geq X_0$ is the long-run supply curve.

The long-run supply curve of the competitive firm is the $LRMC$ curve of the firm, for that portion

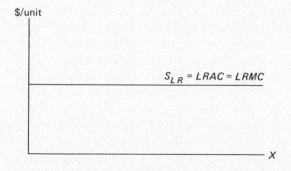

FIG. 8-9 *Long-run supply curve of the firm under constant returns to scale*

of the *LRMC* curve that lies above the minimum of *LRAC* and that slopes upward to the right; if *LRAC* is constant, the long-run supply curve is *LRMC* (=*LRAC*).

Short-Run and Long-Run Elasticity of Supply One interesting consequence of the identification of the firm's long-run supply curve with *LRMC* is the following proposition:

> *The long-run supply curve of the competitive firm is always more elastic than the short-run supply curve.*

For any given percent increase in price of output, there is a larger percent increase in quantity supplied if the firm optimally adjusts its plant size than if it operates with a fixed plant capacity. This follows from the fact that short-run *MC* is steeper than *LRMC*. Given an increase in the price of output, the long-run quantity supplied increases more than does short-run quality supplied.

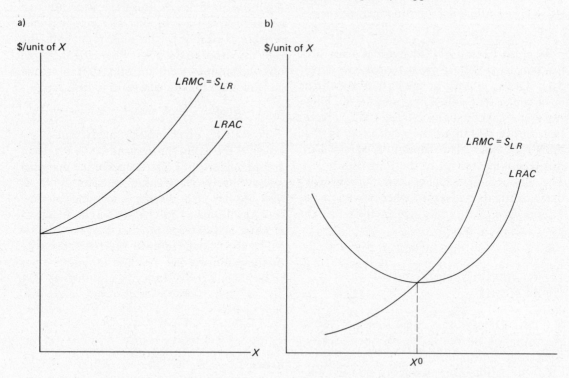

FIG. 8-10 *Long-run supply—decreasing returns (a) and U-shaped LRAC(b)*

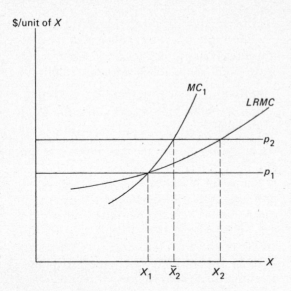

$/unit of X

FIG. 8-11   *Short-run and long-run marginal cost*

of output should be chosen so that marginal revenue equals marginal cost. A similar condition holds in the hiring of inputs. We define the *marginal revenue product* of labor, MRP_L, as the increase in revenue due to hiring one more unit of labor, all other inputs being fixed. Since the marginal product of labor MP_L is the increase in output from adding one more unit of labor, other inputs being fixed, and since the firm sells its output in a competitive market at the fixed price of p dollars per unit of output, it follows that $MRP_L = p \cdot MP_L$.

We will argue that if profits are maximized, then labor should be hired to the point where the marginal revenue product of labor equals its marginal cost, defined as the increase in cost due to hiring one more unit of labor, other inputs being fixed. Because the firm hires in a competitive labor market, the marginal cost of labor is simply w, the wage rate. Thus the rule, hire labor to the point where the marginal revenue product of labor is equal to its marginal cost, reduces for the competitive firm to:

Choose L such that $p \cdot MP_L = w$.

To see why this condition holds, and to see how it is related to the demand curve for labor, consider figure 8-12. The shapes of the marginal and average product curves in figure 8-12a reflect the law of diminishing marginal productivity as discussed in chapter 6. The marginal product and average product curves of figure 8-12a are translated into marginal revenue product and average revenue product curves in the second graph simply by multiplying MP_L and AP_L by p, the price per unit of output. (Recall that

$$AP_L = \frac{X}{L}$$

hence $$ARP_L = \frac{pX}{L}$$

= revenue per unit of labor.)

Profit Maximization and Input Hiring

We next examine the implications of profit maximization for the hiring of inputs, taking labor as an illustration.

Given that the firm produces a positive output, profit maximization specifies that the level

At p_1, in figure 8-11, the optimal plant size has associated with it the marginal cost curve MC_1. $LRMC = MC_1$ at the output X_1 which is, of course, both the short-run and the long-run profit-maximizing output level. When price increases to p_2, output increases to $\bar{X}_2$ *in the short run*; when plant capacity is adjusted to this new price, output of the firm rises to X_2. The same argument applies even more strongly in the constant returns case, where any increase in price leads to an unlimited increase in output in the long run.

a)

b)

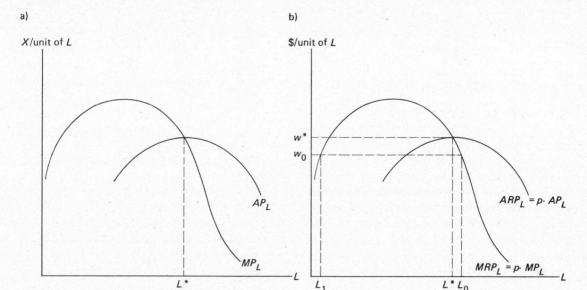

FIG. 8-12   a. *Marginal and average product of labor*
b. *Marginal revenue product and average revenue product of labor*

Given the wage rate w_0, we wish to show that profit maximization implies that L_0 units of labor will be hired. The argument goes as follows. Suppose L were chosen less than L_0 such that $MRP_L > w_0$. Then adding one more unit of labor increases revenue by MRP_L, which is greater than the increase in cost w_0. Hence profits increase if we add more labor; this holds so long as $MRP_L > w_0$. Similarly, if $L > L_0$, then $MRP_L < w_0$, and decreasing labor hiring increases profits. Thus profit maximization implies $MRP_L = w_0$. There are two values of L, L_0 and L_1, that satisfy this condition; however, at L_1 adding more laborers increases profits. Hence L_1 cannot be a profit-maximizing choice. It follows that labor will be hired to the point where $MRP_L = w$, *given that the MRP_L curve slopes downward to the right.*

There is one other qualification to the rule, of equating MRP_L with w. At L^*, ARP_L is a maximum and $ARP_L = MRP_L$. Suppose $w =$

w^*. Then setting $MRP_L = w^*$, we have $L = L^*$, and total payments to labor equal $w^* L^*$. But total revenue for the firm equals $ARP_L \cdot L$, for any value of L, since $ARP_L = pX/L$; thus $ARP_L \cdot L = pX$. At L^*, $ARP_L = MRP_L = w^*$, hence total revenue of the firm, pX, is equal to $w^* L^*$. In short, at L^*, labor costs exhaust all of the revenue of the firm. For L less than L^*, labor costs exceed the firm's revenues. This amounts to saying that for L less than L^*, the firm's revenue is less than variable costs. But if revenue is less than variable costs, the profit-maximizing decision is to shut down the plant, and to hire zero units of any variable input.

All this can be summarized as follows:

Profit maximization under perfect competition in the input and output markets implies that any variable input is hired in the amount such that the marginal revenue product of the input equals its per unit cost, assuming that (1) the marginal revenue product curve slopes downward to the right and (2) marginal revenue product does not exceed average revenue product.

Short-Run Demand Curves for Inputs

The results of the previous section apply directly to the derivation of the firm's demand curve for input services. The demand curve for input services, say labor services, gives number of units of labor hired as a function of its wage rate w, assuming that the price per unit of output p and the rental per unit of capital r are fixed. We consider first the special case in which labor is the only variable input.

The Case of One Variable Input   The demand curve for labor is the MRP_L curve, for the portion of the curve that slopes downward to the right, and lies below the maximum of ARP_L, as pictured in figure 8-13. Given any w, $w \leq w^*$, profit maximization implies that labor is hired to the point where $MRP_L = w$ (with MRP_L sloping downward to the right). Hence we can read off the MRP_L curve the number of units of labor demanded for any such w. For $w > w^*$, $D_L = 0$, which means that there is a discontinuity at w^*, as indicated by the dotted line, with $D_L = 0$ above w^*.

The case of several variable inputs is more complicated.

The Case of Two Variable Inputs   From the analysis of the last section, one may be tempted to conclude that the marginal revenue product curve of an input is always its demand curve (subject to the qualifications noted). Unfortunately, this conclusion holds only in the case of one variable input. The problem is that the demand curve for an input specifies quantities

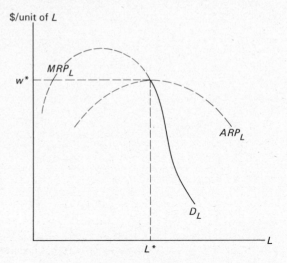

FIG. 8-13   *Demand curve for labor (one variable input case)*

demanded of the input as a function of the hiring price per unit of the input, assuming *prices* of other inputs and the *price* of output are fixed. In contrast, the marginal revenue product curve gives the increase in revenue from adding units of the input, assuming that the *quantities hired* of other inputs are fixed. So long as there is only one variable input, changes in the price of the input have no effect on quantities hired of *other* inputs; but once there are two or more variable inputs, a change in the price of one input generally will change the quantity hired not only of that input but also of other inputs as well.

Throughout the following illustration for the case of capital, we assume that both capital and labor services are variable inputs of production, with plant held fixed. We examine the effects on the hiring of K and L as the rental rate for capital r changes, with w and p held fixed.

Figure 8-14 illustrates input hiring with prices

a)

b)

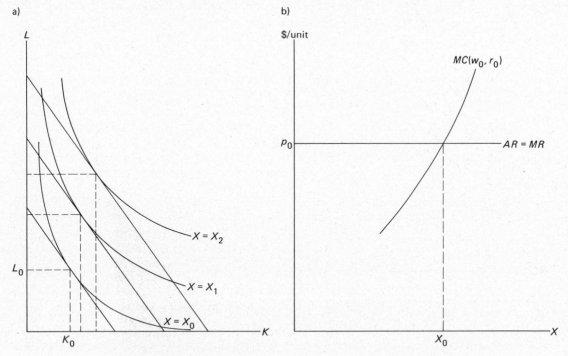

FIG. 8-14   *Profit-maximizing input-output determination for* (r_0, w_0, p_0)

(w_0, r_0, p_0). Given w_0, r_0, cost minimization determines the marginal cost curve $MC(w_0, r_0)$. Given the price p_0, a profit-maximizing output occurs at X_0, which implies in turn that L_0 and K_0 are the firm's choices of units of labor and capital to hire. Suppose r decreases from r_0 to r_1 with w and p still at the values w_0, p_0. The situation graphed in figure 8-15 results. The reduction in r from r_0 to r_1 flattens the isocost lines in figure 8-15a relative to figure 8-14a. This change in turn shifts the marginal cost curve to the right, leading to the choice of a new profit-maximizing output X_1, with corresponding inputs L_1, K_1 as indicated. Thus the points (r_0, K_0) and (r_1, K_1) lie on the demand curve for capital (D_K), given that $w = w_0$ and

$p = p_0$, as shown in figure 8-16. Note that the D_K curve is not the marginal revenue product curve of capital, because at (r_1, K_1) the number of units of labor hired is not the same as at (r_0, K_0).

Substitution between Inputs along an Isoquant   To determine the properties of the short-run demand curves for inputs, it is necessary to explore in more detail the properties of the firm's production map. With output fixed at X_0 units, figure 8-17 shows the cost-minimizing combinations of capital and labor for the price pairs (r_0, w_0), (r_1, w_0) where r_1 is less than r_0. The decrease in the rental price of capital from r_0 to r_1 results in a shift from

a)

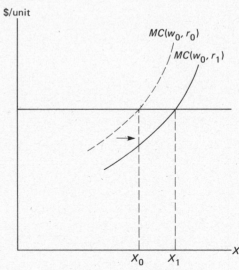

b)

FIG. 8-15 *Profit-maximizing input-output determination for (r_1, w_0, p_0)*

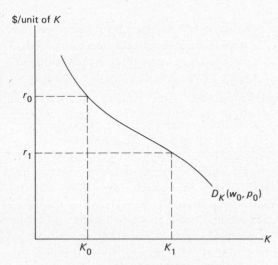

FIG. 8-16 *Demand curve for capital*

$A = (K_0, L_0)$ to $B = (K_1, L_1)$ along the isoquant $X = X_0$, where $K_1 > K_0$, $L_1 < L_0$. This looks much like the substitution effect discussed in chapter 5, and in fact the same kinds of comments made there hold in this case as well. In particular, *along any isoquant, a decrease in the price of an input, with other input prices held fixed, leads to an increase in the amount of the first input used at a cost-minimizing point.*

If there are only two variable inputs, then the amount of the second input used falls along an isoquant when the price of the first input is decreased. When there are just two variable inputs, both are net substitutes in production in this sense. When there are more than two inputs, a fall in the price of one input leads to a decrease in the amount used of at least one other input, along an isoquant, but not all

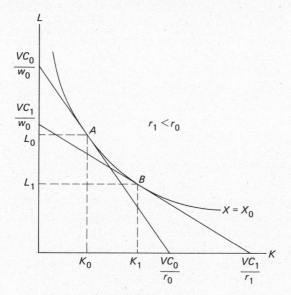

FIG. 8-17   *Substitution of inputs along*
an isoquant

inputs must be net substitutes. This follows so long as the marginal products of all inputs are positive. In order for output to remain constant, when we use more of one input we necessarily use less of some other input.

Downward Sloping Short-Run Demand Curves for Inputs   A decrease in the price per unit of capital services leads to an increase in the quantity of capital demanded, *if output is held fixed.* But we have already noted that a fall in the price of capital shifts the marginal cost curve of the firm and hence leads to a different profit-maximizing output. What is the effect of a decrease in the rental rate for capital services on the quantity demanded of such services, taking into account the change in output that occurs?

An interesting general result can be derived:

A decrease in the price of an input, with other input prices and the price of output held fixed, results in an increase in the amount of the input hired when short-run profits are maximized.

To put it briefly, *the short-run demand curve of a competitive firm for any input slopes downward to the right.*

We will not attempt to prove this proposition in the general case. Instead, we will outline the proof for the special case where inputs are *normal;* that is, an increase in capital increases the marginal product of labor and an increase in labor increases the marginal product of capital. When inputs are normal, the argument that demand curves for inputs are downward sloping goes as follows.

When r falls from r_0 to r_1 (w fixed at w_0), then capital is substituted for labor along any isoquant in order to satisfy the cost-minimization condition,

$$\frac{MP_K}{MP_L} = \frac{r_1}{w_0}.$$

Thus, in figure 8-18, the fall in r shifts the capital/labor combination from $A = (K_0, L_0)$ to $B = (K_1, L_1)$, when output is fixed. But the decrease in r also shifts the MC curve leading to a change in the profit-maximizing output, say, from X_0 to X_1. We want to show that the new profit-maximizing point must lie to the right of C so that more capital is demanded at the lower value of r.

Note that at A,

$$\frac{MP_K}{MP_L} = \frac{r_0}{w_0}$$

while at C,

$$\frac{MP_K}{MP_L} = \frac{r_1}{w_0}$$

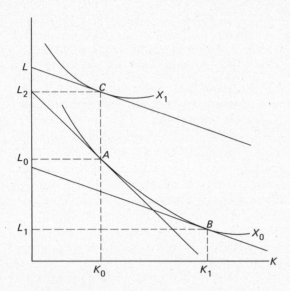

FIG. 8-18   *Effect of a fall in r on K and L*

Long-Run Demand Curves for Inputs

Long-run demands for inputs by the firm have much the same characteristics as short-run demands except for the constant returns case. We have already seen that under constant returns to scale, the supply curve is perfectly elastic at the $LRMC = LRAC$ level. At any price above $LRMC$, the firm expands output indefinitely while at any price below $LRMC$, the firm drops out of production. The long-run demand curve for the services of capital (the same applies to any input) has the properties that, at the value of r for which $LRMC = p$, demand for capital is perfectly elastic; for r below that level, the demand becomes indefinitely large, while for r above that level, demand is zero. The reason for this is that if r falls (with p and w fixed), the firm can make indefinitely large profits by increasing its hiring both of capital and labor proportionately. If r increases, $LRAC$ rises for every level of output; hence $LRAC$ is greater than p and the firm shuts down.

The cases of decreasing returns or of a U-shaped long-run cost curve look much like the short-run case, at least in terms of the properties of the demand curves for inputs. The only important distinction between the short-run and long-run cases is that the *long-run demand curves for inputs are more elastic than the short-run demand curves*, paralleling the higher elasticity of the long-run supply of output relative to short-run supply. Under increasing returns, of course, competition breaks down; hence long-run demand curves for inputs are not well defined for the competitive firm.

where $r_1 < r_0$. Hence in order for a point like C to be attained, the ratio MP_K/MP_L at C must be smaller than the ratio MP_K/MP_L at A. But at C, we have the same capital (K_0) as at A, and more labor. Because of diminishing marginal productivity, MP_L is less at C than at A. MP_K at C is certainly larger than at A, however, because $K = K_0$ both at A and at C, while L is larger at C than at A, and capital and labor are normal inputs. This means that MP_K/MP_L at C is larger than MP_K/MP_L at A; hence C cannot be a profit-maximizing capital/labor combination. The same argument applies for points lying to the left of C, which establishes the fact that a fall in the price per unit of capital leads to an increase in the quantity of capital demanded by the profit-maximizing firm. As noted above, this result can be extended even to the case in which capital and labor are not normal inputs, but this is beyond the scope of this book.

Summary

We can briefly summarize our findings with respect to demand and supply curves of the competitive firm as follows:

1. The short-run supply of output curve for the firm is the firm's *MC* curve, for the portion of the curve that lies above the minimum of the *AVC* curve and rises to the right.

2. The long-run supply of output curve for the firm is the firm's *LRMC* curve under constant and decreasing returns to scale; if *LRAC* is U-shaped, then the long-run supply curve is the portion of *LRMC* that lies above the minimum of *LRAC* and rises to the right.

3. The long-run supply of output curve is always more elastic than the short-run supply of output curve.

4. The short-run demand curve of the firm for any input slopes downward to the right.

5. The long-run demand curve of the firm for any input slopes downward to the right except under constant returns to scale. Under constant returns, the demand curve is perfectly elastic at the price per unit of the input such that *LRMC* = price per unit of output.

6. The long-run demand curve for any input is always more elastic than the short-run demand curve.

7. Doubling all prices (input *and* output) leaves the amount demanded of any input by the firm unchanged and leaves the output of the firm unchanged, in both the short and the long run.

8. Doubling all prices (input *and* output) doubles profits in the long run and more than doubles profits in the short run.

Problems

1. The production function for a firm is given by $X = \sqrt{P \cdot L}$, where P is plant and L is labor. Assume $w = \$1$, $q = \$4$ where q is the price per unit of plant. Let p denote the price per unit of output.

    a. Derive the short-run and long-run supply curves for the firm.

    b. Derive the short-run demand curve for L, assuming that P is fixed at one unit, and that the price per unit of output is $8.

    c. Derive the demand curve for L, assuming that both P and L are free to vary, with price per unit of output equal to $8.

    d. Verify that long-run supply of output and long-run demand for labor are both more elastic than short-run supply and short-run demand.

2. Contrast the effects on the firm's short-run supply curve of:

    a. a property tax levied on plant

    b. an excise tax per unit of output

    c. a percentage tax on profits

    d. a license fee to operate the business

    e. the social security tax treated as a percentage tax on wages (with half paid by the employer and half by the employee)

3. In the short-run, general inflation has the effect of shifting income toward stockholders relative to other classes of consumers. How might you explain this phenomenon?

4. The Environmental Protection Agency has two alternative policies under consideration for conserving on natural gas as an input used in production. The first involves rationing, limiting any firm to the amount of natural gas consumed in the current period. The second involves placing a per unit tax on any usage of natural gas above current levels. Assuming that the firm uses only labor and natural gas as variable inputs with a fixed plant, contrast the effects of these two policies on the supply curve of the firm, for outputs above the current level. Show that the supply curve under rationing lies above the supply curve under the tax, and explain why.

5. A plant employs skilled and unskilled labor as its variable inputs. Unskilled labor earns the federal minimum wage rate. Discuss the effects of an increase in the minimum wage on (a) the demand curves for skilled and unskilled labor and (b) the supply curve of output.

Theory of Input and Output Markets

The individual actors in the competitive economy are consumers and firms. Each consumer decides on the commodity bundle he will consume, acting to maximize utility subject to his budget constraint, and treating the market prices of goods and services as given. Each firm chooses an input-output combination so as to maximize profits, again taking the market prices of inputs and outputs as given. Our discussion over the past five chapters has been concerned with deriving the properties of the demand and supply functions of individual consumers and firms operating in perfectly competitive markets.

While individual consumers and firms treat market prices as given, the law of supply and demand asserts that such market prices are in fact determined by the demands and supplies of consumers and firms in the aggregate. Our objective over the next few chapters is to spell out the implications of the law of supply and demand for competitive markets. In chapter 9 we examine competitive markets for outputs, and in chapter 10 we examine competitive markets for inputs.

9
Competitive Markets for Outputs

A starting point in our analysis is the notion of a competitive industry. By a *competitive industry* we mean a collection of competitive firms who account for the total production and sale of some specified homogeneous product. A product is *homogeneous* if consumers cannot distinguish between the product sold by any one firm in the industry and that sold by any other firm in the industry. Thus, within a competitive industry, firms are "anonymous"; consumers are unconcerned about the identity of any firm in the industry.

Each firm in the competitive industry is assumed to face the same market prices for inputs and outputs, with a single market price in each market. Beyond this, firms are assumed to be independent: the supply and demand schedules of any one firm are assumed to be the same, whatever are the supply and demand schedules of other firms or consumers. We also assume independence of consumers, with consumer demand and supply schedules being unaffected by the supply and demand schedules of any other decision makers in the economy.

Our analysis of competitive markets will deal separately with the implications of the law of supply and demand as it applies to the short run and to the long run. As noted earlier, in the short run it is assumed that the costs of adjusting the capacity of plants or of moving from industry to industry are so large as to preclude such changes. In the short run, the competitive industry consists of a fixed number of firms operating with given technologies and with given plant capacities.

In the long run, adjustment costs for the firm are zero. Firms can enter or leave industries and can choose to change their plant capacities at will. We also assume that costs of acquiring information as to the currently feasible technology are zero, so that every firm has available to it the production possibilities available to any other firm.

All of these abstractions—the competitive industry, the short run, and the long run—are obviously idealized concepts. They are convenient devices for isolating certain features of reality for study. Entry and exit are never as costly as in the economist's concept of the short run, nor as costless as in the economist's notion of the long run. Industries in the sense of the competitive industry do not conform to industries as used in statistical studies of the real-world economy. The differences are important enough that most of the conclusions we will derive in this and the succeeding chapters must be reexamined in the later parts of this book in attempting to apply them to the functioning economy. But some significant aspects of reality are highlighted in the notion of a competitive industry operating either in the short run or in the long run, and it is these that we wish to examine in the simplest possible framework.

Short-Run Equilibrium in the Market for Outputs

We will restrict our attention to markets for consumer nondurable goods and services. The purchase of consumer durables (such as houses) is treated as an investment decision on the part of the consumer, and will be discussed in chapter 11. It should be noted, however, that we intend our analysis to cover the purchase of the *services* of a consumer durable (such as renting a house).

> *Short-run equilibrium for a competitive industry occurs when the market for the industry's product is cleared, assuming utility maximization by consumers and profit maximization by the firms in the industry, each firm operating with fixed plant capacity.*

The consumer enters the market with a certain money income and a set of preferences with respect to commodities. Following the approach of chapter 5, these get translated into demand functions for commodities, relating quantities demanded of commodities to the prices that prevail on the market. Aside from the exceptional case of a Giffen good, the demand curve for any commodity by each consumer slopes downward to the right.

The aggregate demand curve for any consumer nondurable or service is then obtained by summing the demand curves of the individual consumers. Unless the Giffen case dominates, the aggregate demand curve for the good will slope downward to the right.

Following the analysis of chapter 8, the short-run supply curve for each firm in the competitive industry is the firm's marginal cost curve, for that portion of the curve that slopes upward to the right and lies above the minimum of AVC. We obtain the aggregate supply curve for the good by summing the supply curves of the individual firms. The aggregate supply curve will then also slope upward to the right.

Let x denote the amount of the consumer nondurable or service that is consumed by a typical consumer or produced by a typical firm. Then d_x is the amount demanded by the typical consumer, and s_x is the amount supplied by the typical firm. D_X is the aggregate demand by consumers and S_X is the aggregate supply by firms, where $X = \Sigma x$. The resulting market demand and supply curves are derived as in figures 9-1 and 9-2.

In figure 9-3, we have arrived back at the typical market demand and supply curves first discussed in chapter 2. But now it is possible to interpret the characteristics of these curves explicitly in terms of maximizing conduct by market participants. The law of variable proportions, coupled with profit maximization by firms, gives rise to a market supply curve that slopes upward to the right; and the assumption that the commodity is not a Giffen good for any consumer guarantees that the market demand curve slopes downward to the right.

Furthermore, an increase in the incomes of consumers has predictable consequences for movements of the market demand curve. In particular, if all consumers view the good as a normal good, then increases in consumer incomes shift the demand curve to the right. If, for all consumers, the good is inferior, the market demand curve shifts to the left follow-

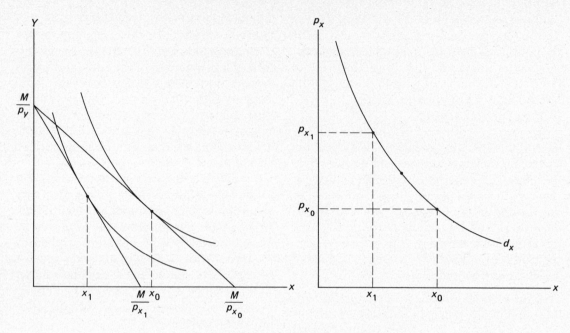

FIG. 9-1   *Demand curve of a consumer*

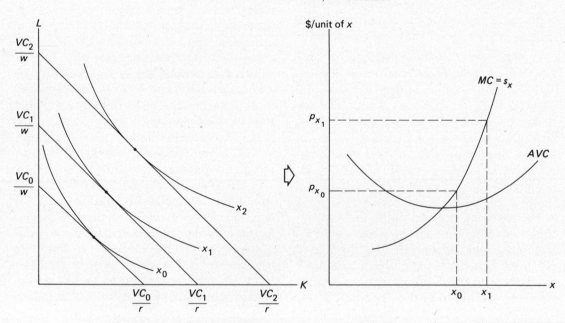

FIG. 9-2   *Supply curve (MC) of a firm*

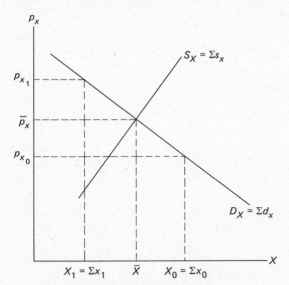

FIG. 9-3 *Short-run equilibrium—consumer nondurable good or service*

ing an increase in consumer incomes. In cases where the good is normal for some consumers and inferior for others, the movement of the demand curve depends upon the size of these offsetting effects. Movements of the market demand curve in response to changes in the prices of other goods are determined by whether the goods are gross substitutes or gross complements in terms of the preferences of consumers.

The market supply curve shifts in response either to changes in input prices or to other changes in costs such as taxes or subsidies imposed by the government. As we have seen from chapter 8, if all inputs are normal, then an increase in the price of any input shifts the market supply curve upward—less is supplied at any market price. Any tax that increases variable cost for firms results in an upward shift of the market supply curve; but if the tax affects only fixed costs, then the supply curve is unchanged.

Elasticity of the market demand curve is related to the substitution and income effects. The larger the substitution effect for each consumer for a given good, the more elastic the demand curve for that good at a given quantity demanded. The same holds for the income effect, so long as the good is normal. Thus the demand for a good is more elastic, the better the substitutes available for the good; and, in the case of a normal good, the demand is more elastic the more responsive is demand for the good to changes in income and the more important is the good in the consumption pattern of consumers. When the good is inferior, the income effect acts to offset the substitution effect: the more important is the income effect, the less elastic is demand for the good.

Elasticity of the market supply curve reflects the characteristics of the technology facing the firm. The weaker the law of variable proportions is, the more elastic the supply curve. This amounts to saying that the elasticity of the supply curve depends upon how important the fixed plant capacity is in increasing marginal cost as output increases. If, as seems likely, the influence of plant capacity makes itself felt mainly at high output levels, then we would expect the supply curve to show decreased elasticity at higher output levels.

Market equilibrium occurs in figure 9-3 at $(\bar{p}, \bar{X})$, where market demand equals market supply. Because each consumer and each firm faces the same market price, the following results hold.

1. Market price equals marginal cost for each firm in the industry.

2. The marginal rate of substitution (*MRS*) between any two consumer nondurable goods or services is the same for all consumers buying these goods, and is equal to

the ratio of market prices for the goods, which in turn is equal to the ratio of the marginal costs of the goods.

At the margin, firms are indifferent between producing one more unit of the good and not producing that unit; and consumers are indifferent between an additional unit of X and the fraction of a unit of Y that can be purchased with the money saved by not consuming a unit of X. These conclusions are closely related to the fact that in a competitive economy, goods and services (including the services of inputs) sell for their opportunity costs. We will return to this relationship in chapter 12.

Long-Run Equilibrium in the Markets for Outputs

In the long run, firms are free to contract or expand plant capacity, and to move from industry to industry. The prior commitments that restrict choices in the short run are no longer binding in the long run. In the short run, firms act to maximize profits within the restrictions imposed by given plant capacities; in the long run, all of the incentives afforded to self-interest by the structure of competitive markets are fully exploited.

Equilibrium occurs in the short run when markets are cleared, given the fixed plant capacities of firms. The notion of long-run equilibrium for a competitive industry is an attempt to capture the characteristics of a situation in which there is no incentive for any firm to move from industry to industry or to change its plant capacity, nor for consumers to alter their pattern of purchases. So long as the technology, consumer preferences, and the structure of prices remains constant, under long-run equilibrium there is neither entry nor exit of

firms, and the output of each firm remains unchanged over time. In contrast, short-run equilibrium is a transitory phenomenon; generally incentives exist for firms to make changes, once short-run commitments (to a given plant or to a given industry) that create adjustment costs are eliminated. In our discussion of long-run equilibrium, we will assume that there are no entry or exit barriers for firms; however, the organizational expenses associated with creating a firm require some attention.

Normal Profits and the Organization of Firms

Under short-run conditions, the number of firms in an industry is fixed, and there is no need to inquire into how firms come into existence or are liquidated. But in the long run, the creation and dissolution of firms play a central role in the process of adjusting to equilibrium.

In order to bring a firm into existence, expenses are incurred for one-time organizational activities such as bringing potential investors together, choosing a location for the plant, setting up a managerial structure, and hiring executives. Only after these preliminary stages of organization are complete can the firm operate as an ongoing entity.

The organizer of a firm is referred to as an *entrepreneur*; he expends time and money to create the firm. His activity is like investing in that he incurs costs today for the purpose of obtaining income in future periods. Investment in organizing a firm is undertaken only under the same conditions as investment in any other asset: the rate of return on organizational expense must be at least as high as the rate of return that could be earned on any other asset of comparable riskiness. As we shall see in chapter 11, in a world of certainty, all assets earn the same rate of return, including organizational activities. Given the organizational expenses associated with a particular firm, we define *normal profits* for the firm as the amount of money that, if paid annually, would earn the entrepreneur the market rate of return on investment in organizing the firm. If it costs $1 million to organize a firm and the market rate of return on investment in assets is 10 percent, then normal profits for the firm are $100 thousand per year.

We will treat normal profits as a cost to the firm that must be paid if it is to survive in the long run. The term *excess profits* then refers to any earnings of the firm above normal profits. Only when excess profits exist in an industry is there an incentive for entry of new firms into the industry.

Equilibrium Conditions

Long-run equilibrium for a competitive industry occurs when the market for the industry's product is cleared, given that the number of firms in the industry and the output of the industry are such that there are no incentives for entry or exit of firms, or for changes in the plant capacities of firms.

One defining characteristic of the long run is that each firm has complete knowledge of the technology currently feasible to convert inputs into the product of the industry. It thus follows that in long-run equilibrium, *the market price of a good produced in a competitive industry must be equal to its long-run average cost of production (including normal profits in such cost), which is identical for every firm in the industry.*

The idea behind this statement is the following. Since each firm has full knowledge of the technology, then for any given output (and with given prices of inputs), each firm would choose the same plant capacity and mix of inputs. That is, each firm in the industry has the same long-run cost curves. If price were above long-run average cost (including normal profits in such cost), then there would be excess profits and hence an incentive for firms to enter the industry. If price were below long-run average cost, there would be incentives for exit. But in long-run equilibrium, no such incentives can exist. It follows that in long-run equilibrium, price equals long-run average cost, which is identical for each firm in the industry.

Furthermore, each firm in long-run equilibrium acts to maximize profits. This means that the firm chooses an output level for any market price such that price equals long-run marginal cost. The long-run marginal cost curves are identical for all firms in the industry. Hence we conclude that in long-run equilibrium, *market price is equal to long-run marginal cost, which is the same for every firm in the industry.*

Long-run profit maximization by the firm implies the choice of some specific plant capacity, given the market price. Within that plant, the firm chooses the mix of other inputs that maximizes profits. This means that in long-run equilibrium for the industry, the firm maximizes both long-run and short-run profits. Hence, in long-run equilibrium, *the market price equals short-run marginal cost for the plant capacity chosen as optimal in the long run, with short-run marginal cost being the same for every firm in the industry.*

Finally, free entry and exit for the industry implies in addition that *price per unit of output equals the minimum of long-run average cost, which is identical for every firm in the industry.* Each firm must operate at the minimum of its long-run average cost curve, since if price were above the minimum of long-run average cost, a firm could enter the industry, choose

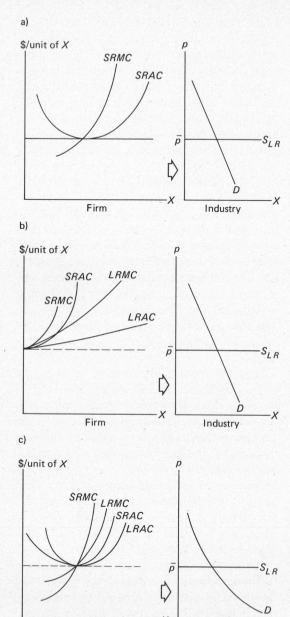

a)

b)

c)

FIG. 9-4   *Long-run equilibrium—constant returns
to scale (a), decreasing returns
to scale (b), and U-shaped costs (c)*

a plant size at the minimum of *LRAC*, and make excess profits. If price were below the minimum of *LRAC*, each firm would earn less than normal profits and there would be an incentive to leave the industry.

These propositions are illustrated in figure 9-4 for the cases of constant returns to scale and decreasing returns to scale as well as the case of a U-shaped long-run average cost curve, assuming competitive input markets. The cost curves identify average and marginal costs for the firm, both in the short run and in the long run. The firm's long-run supply curve is its *LRMC* curve, subject to the usual qualifications, and its short-run supply curve is the *SRMC* curve. The industry long-run supply curve, S_{LR}, is to be interpreted as the quantity supplied by the industry as a function of price per unit of output, given that all incentives for entry or exit or changes in plant capacities are fully exploited within the industry. Thus the long-run industry supply curve is *not* obtained by summing the supply curves of a fixed number of firms in the industry, as is the case in the short run; instead, the long-run industry supply curve reflects entry and exit of firms as well.

The S_{LR} curve is perfectly elastic at the minimum of *LRAC* for each firm, regardless of the properties of the firm supply curves. This elasticity reflects the arguments given above—entry will occur whenever the market price is above the minimum of *LRAC*, and exit if price is below *LRAC*. When price equals the minimum of *LRAC*, industry output is perfectly elastic, since any number of units of output can be supplied through changes in the number of firms in the industry, each earning just normal profits.

So we conclude that whatever the returns to scale (except for increasing returns, which are incompatible with a competitive industry), in long-run equilibrium price equals the minimum of *LRAC* for any firm in the industry. Because the long-run supply curve is perfectly elastic, market demand has no influence on long-run equilibrium price; instead, market demand determines only the number of firms in the industry.

To briefly summarize the properties of long-run equilibrium:

1. *Market price = long-run marginal cost = short-run marginal cost = minimum of long-run average cost = minimum of short-run average cost, all of which are identical for every firm in the industry.*

2. *Except for the case of constant returns to scale, where firm size is indeterminate, every firm in a given industry chooses the same plant size; under decreasing returns to scale, each firm is infinitesimally small.*

3. *Whatever the returns to scale, the industry performs "as if" there were constant returns to scale, since the long-run equilibrium price is the same whatever the level of demand. Similarly, each firm operates "as if" there were constant returns to scale "in the small," since at the output levels and plant sizes chosen, firms operate at the minimum of long-run average costs.*

4. *In long-run equilibrium, every firm earns precisely normal profits; there are no "excess profits" in any industry.*

In short-run equilibrium, excess profits arise in various industries because of the adjustment costs that hamper movement of firms among industries to meet changing demands. Again, in the short run, firms might operate either above or below the minimum of long-run (and short-run) average costs. In long-run equilibrium, resources are allocated in a manner such that no change could result in a lowering of per unit production costs for any goods, given the state of technology and the structure of consumer preferences.

Economies and Diseconomies External to the Firm but Internal to the Industry

There is one major real-world qualification to the third conclusion of the last section. Expanded output of the industry may create technological efficiencies or inefficiencies for the firms in the industry. The classic examples are the effects associated with crowding. Consider an industry that is concentrated in one small geographic region. Expansion of industry-wide output may create smoke and other air pollution problems that reduce output from a given mix of hired factors for each firm in the industry—an example of a diseconomy due to expansion of industry output. As an example of a corresponding economy, if the industry employs certain highly specialized inputs, say skilled laborers, then an increase in industry output may create interactions among them that lead to the discovery and implementation of more efficient production methods for all firms in the industry.

In microeconomic theory, these effects are referred to as *economies or diseconomies external to the firm that are internal to the industry.* The technological efficiencies (or inefficiencies) could not be accomplished by any one firm increasing output on its own, with industry output constant; it is the increase in *industry* output that produces the effects. In this sense the effects are *external* to the firm; that is, they are beyond the firm's control. The economies are *internal* to the industry because they are controlled by changes in industry output, and the gains or losses are captured within the industry by the constituent firms. (Note that we are interested in changes in the technologies facing firms and *not* changes in the prices of inputs. The S_{LR} curve is drawn with all input prices fixed.)

Firms ignore potential economies or diseconomies due to the expansion of industry output, since changes in industry output rather than in the output of the firm trigger such effects. At any given industry output, each firm operates in the long run at the minimum of *LRAC*. But with external economies or diseconomies, *LRAC* for the firm *depends* on the level of industry output.

Certain external economies or diseconomies may be *irreversible*. That is, future changes of industry output may well leave the technology unchanged. In the example involving interactions among skilled laborers, the technological improvements discovered by such interactions are still available to firms even if industry output later declines. The S_{LR} curve then becomes time-dependent in that the position of the curve depends on the history of demand and price for industry output, and not simply on the present price.

The issue of external economies and diseconomies can be of importance in real-world applications of the notion of long-run equilibrium. The assumption of independence of firms specifically excludes such effects, since the input-output choices of firms depend only on market prices and not on the activities of other firms, when independence holds. Thus the logic of our analysis is intact; but the empirical relevance of the independence assumption is at least questionable. We will examine this problem in more detail in chapter 17.

Further Comments on Long-Run Equilibrium: Consumer Demands

Our discussion of long-run equilibrium has centered on the behavior of firms that results in the characteristic long-run supply curve of perfect elasticity. But a parallel treatment can be accorded long-run demands by consumers. The consumer's short-run demand curve relates quantities demanded to prices, assuming a given portfolio of assets for the consumer. As in the case of the firm, adjustment costs are assumed to preclude changes in the asset portfolio in the short run. In the long run, however, the consumer is free to modify his asset portfolio as well as his demands for nondurable goods and services. The consequence is that *the consumer's long-run demand curve is more elastic than his short-run demand curve.* Quantity demanded of any good is more sensitive to price changes if the consumer is free to adjust all of his purchases (including assets) than if he is constrained to a given asset portfolio.

To illustrate, an increase in the price of gasoline leads to a short-run fall in the amount of gasoline consumed, as other goods and services are substituted in the consumer's budget for automobile transportation—assuming the consumer continues to own his existing automobile. In the long run, there may be substitution of a compact car for the existing car, or the second car may be sold, further reducing the consumption of gasoline. Similarly, an increase in the price of natural gas has an impact in the short run by reducing fuel consumption for home heating; in the long run, consumers invest in insulation, an asset whose rate of return has increased because heating costs have risen.

As in the case of long-run supply, long-run demand is an attempt to capture the notion of a situation in which, for the consumer, there are no further incentives to exploit. Given his preferences and the prices prevailing on the markets for goods and services and for assets, long-run demands represent the best adjustment by the consumer to his situation.

The Use of Long-Run Equilibrium in Economic Analysis

In many ways, the concept of long-run equilibrium is the most confusing and controversial notion in microeconomic theory. During the 1930s, critics of the New Deal complained that government manipulation of the economy was hampering the adjustment of the system to a long-run full employment equilibrium. Keynes's response to the critics was that "in the long run, we're all dead." Certainly long-run equilibrium is never quite achieved in any market, in that profitable opportunities are always being discovered or are only partially exploited. Still, with appropriate qualifications, long-run equilibrium can be a useful tool of economic analysis.

To illustrate, your broker tells you: "Buy stock X; I've heard that there is a favorable announcement in the wind." The microeconomist argues that any such advice should be treated with a great deal of scepticism. If your broker really does have access to some hot inside information, then clearly there are other "insiders" who know about it, as well as other clients to whom your broker is giving advice. Hence a reasonable conclusion is that a number of people have already acted on the basis of the "inside tip," and the market price of the stock already reflects the forthcoming favorable news. In the jargon of Wall Street, the market has already "discounted" the announcement, before it is made public.

This is really a long-run equilibrium argument, here applied to the stock market. The economist assumes that all profitable opportunities have already been exploited. It turns out that in the case of the stock market at least, the economist's view has considerable predictive accuracy; the market *does* discount most "inside" information. As a working hypothesis, the view of the stock market as being in more or less perpetual long-run equilibrium has a lot of merit. In large part, the reason for this is that the stock market is one of the best examples of a "frictionless" market, operating as it does with thousands of full-time specialists and with an institutional structure geared to quick responses to changes in demand and supply.

There is no requirement that adjusting to a long-run equilibrium take a "long" period of time; adjustment may be almost instantaneous, as in the case of the stock market. Long-run equilibrium on any market is simply the state of the market that would prevail if the frictions interfering with the exploitation of incentives in the "short-run" were absent. The speed of adjustment of a market to long-run equilibrium depends upon the frictions that are present in the market and upon the costs associated with bypassing or eliminating them. These vary widely from market to market.

Long-run equilibrium is not intended as a description of the observed characteristics of the typical market in an economy. Economists are well aware of the idealized nature of the concept. But long-run equilibrium allows the economist to see what the full implications of the incentive structure of a market truly are.

It allows him to predict changes that will occur on the market as adjustment costs are overcome, and it focuses his attention on the nature and importance of such adjustment costs. Used in this fashion, it can be a powerful analytical tool.

Summary

The market demand curve for a consumer nondurable good or service is the sum of the demand curves for the commodity over all consumers, assuming independence of consumers. The short-run market supply curve is the sum of the short-run marginal cost curves of firms in the competitive industry producing the product, for the portions of such curves rising to the right and lying above the minimum of AVC, again assuming independence. The short-run equilibrium price equates short-run demand and supply, with price being equal to marginal cost for every firm in the industry. Demand and supply curves have the "typical" properties in the short-run case, so long as the good is not a Giffen good.

The long-run supply curve for any produced good is perfectly elastic at the minimum of $LRAC$ for each firm in the industry, again assuming independence. In the long run, each firm earns "normal profits," providing a rate of return on organizational expenses equal to the market rate of return on other assets. Consumer long-run demands are more elastic than short-run demands, reflecting the increased ability to respond to price changes when asset portfolios (as well as purchases of nondurable goods and services) may be adjusted. Long-run equilibrium is an idealized concept in which all of the incentives available to decision makers are fully exploited. It is a state toward which the market will move, as adjustment costs are overcome. Adjustment to long-run equilibrium need not be a lengthy process, depending instead on the time required to bypass or eliminate the frictions that give rise to adjustment costs.

Problems

1. Discuss the process by which adjustment both to short-run and long-run equilibrium takes place in each of the following examples.

   a. After World War II, the private automobile and the commercial airliner intruded into the passenger market for railroads, and this intrusion has continued up to the present time.

   b. The baby boom of the late 1940s and 1950s was followed by the introduction of the pill and the legalizing of abortion. Discuss the impact on the market for encyclopedias.

   c. In the late '50s, Elvis Presley came along, followed by the Beatles. By 1970, it looked as though no one was ever going to get a haircut again. Consider the continuing impact these styles have on the barbershop industry.

2. Henry Ford revolutionized the automobile industry around 1915 by introducing the assembly line and a standardized product, the Model T—you could get any color you wanted as long as it was black. Show the effects of such a cost reduction in terms of the short-run and long-run firm and industry graphs.

3. During the oil embargo by the Arab states in 1973–74, it was discovered that there was a shortage of oil refineries in the United States. Multinational corporations like Exxon, Shell, and Mobil had built their newest refineries abroad. According to industry spokesmen, this shortage indicated that changes had to be made in U.S. environmental laws to encourage investment in U.S. refineries since if it were profitable to invest in the United States, the companies certainly would have done so. Analyze this argument in "short run" and "long run" terms.

4. Let the demand curve for a competitive industry be given by $D(p) = 100 - 5p$.

   Assume that the production function for each firm in the industry is $x = \sqrt{L \cdot P}$, where x is output, L is the number of units of labor, and P is the number of units of "plant." The wage rate per unit of labor is \$1, and the rental per unit of plant is \$2. In the short run there are ten firms in the industry, each with $P = 1$.

   a. Graph the short-run total cost curve, and the short-run average total cost, average variable cost, and marginal cost curves.

   b. Graph the short-run industry supply curve, and determine equilibrium price and quantity for the industry.

   c. Calculate short-run profits per firm.

   d. Graph the long-run supply curve for the industry and determine long-run equilibrium price and quantity for the industry.

5. a. Show graphically the short-run and long-run effects on price and quantity of an excise tax on a good produced by a competitive industry.

   b. Prove that in the short run, a tax on profits is borne entirely by firms but that in the long run the tax is shifted to consumers.

10
Competitive Markets for Inputs

The theory of consumer behavior developed in chapters 5 and 6 deals with the case of utility maximization by a consumer who is endowed with a given money income. But in a market economy, the consumer's income is in fact derived from his sale of labor services, from rentals on the capital goods and resources to which he owns title, and from profits earned by firms in which he owns shares. Thus the income of the consumer is as much a decision variable for him as is the commodity bundle he chooses to consume.

The choices consumers make with respect to the labor and capital services they will provide to firms, when aggregated, determine the supply side of the market for inputs. The demand side is accounted for by the aggregated choices of profit-maximizing firms who employ such inputs in production. In this chapter we discuss short-run and long-run equilibrium in the market for inputs.

Short-Run Equilibrium in the Market for Inputs

Labor Services

The most important source of consumer income is the sale of labor services, which account for roughly 70 percent of personal income in the U.S. economy. Two related aspects of income from the sale of labor services can be viewed as separate decision problems for the consumer. First, how much in the way of labor services should the consumer offer on the labor market? Second, how much should be invested by the consumer in "human capital" (that is, in improving the quality of the labor services he possesses)? We will put off dealing with the second question until chapter 11; here we look only at the choice problem involved in the decision to supply labor services of a given quality.

The Leisure-Consumption Choice for the Consumer Along with his choice of a bundle of goods and services to consume, the consumer makes choices with respect to the level of his income by deciding on the number of hours to work and the number of hours of leisure to enjoy. We will consider the case of a consumer who possesses a certain stock of labor skills accumulated through training and experience. In the short run, this stock of labor skills is fixed, but the consumer can decide on the number of hours of such skilled services to offer on the labor market per period.

In order to continue to use two-dimensional graphs, suppose that the goods and services consumed are represented by a "composite good" to be denoted by C (consumption), with a price of p dollars per unit. Let L denote the number of labor hours supplied per day, with w being the wage rate per hour of labor services. Then $\ell = 24 - L$ is the number of hours of leisure per day. We assume that the consumer has an indifference map of the usual type, defined over consumption and leisure. For a consumer who derives all of his income from sale of labor services, the budget constraint is

$$pC \leq wL,$$

or equivalently,

$$pC \leq w(24 - \ell).$$

(Total expenditures on consumption must be no more than income.)

The utility-maximizing consumer combines consumption and leisure to achieve the highest attainable indifference curve. This combination results in the usual condition of tangency of the indifference curve to the budget line, as indicated in figure 10-1. The consumer can enjoy a maximum of twenty-four hours of leisure per day, which accounts for the leisure intercept of the budget line. Working twenty-four hours per day provides an income of $24w$, which can purchase $24w/p$ units of the consumption good. This is the C intercept of the budget line. The slope of the budget line is $-(w/p)$, where w/p is the wage rate per hour in units of consumption (the "real" wage rate.)

Thus at the utility-maximizing choice $(\bar{\ell}, \bar{C})$, the marginal rate of substitution between consumption and leisure equals the real wage rate per hour. The number of hours of labor supplied, $\bar{L}$, equals $24 - \bar{\ell}$, as indicated in the graph.

Note that doubling w and p leaves the budget line unchanged, and thus leaves the choice of C and L unchanged; hence the supply of labor hours is homogeneous of degree zero in all prices. When w is changed, with p fixed, then

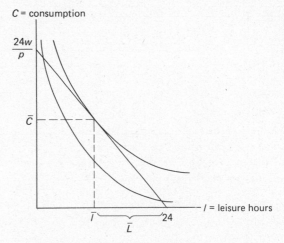

FIG. 10-1   *The leisure-consumption choice*

the budget line rotates about the leisure intercept of 24 hours. (Twenty-four hours of leisure are always available, whatever the values of w or p.) An increase in w leads to changes in the consumption-leisure choice that can be analyzed in terms of the familiar income effect and substitution effect.

The Income and Substitution Effects of an Increase in the Wage Rate   In figure 10-2, at the wage rate w_0, the consumer chooses the leisure-consumption bundle $A = (\ell_0, C_0)$; at the higher wage rate w_1, the choice is $D = (\ell_1, C_1)$. The increase in the wage rate has the effect of increasing the slope of the budget line, which continues to pass through the leisure intercept of 24 hours per day. If the consumer remained on the same indifference curve I_0 following the increase in the wage rate, he would choose the bundle $B = (\ell^*, C^*)$.

The substitution effect is indicated by the change from A to B. Given the higher wage rate, the consumer substitutes consumption for leisure along I_0. The reason for this is that

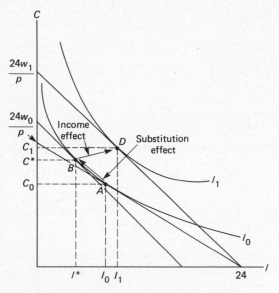

FIG. 10-2 *Income and substitution effects
in the leisure-consumption choice*

leisure becomes more expensive when w increases; each hour of leisure enjoyed now costs the consumer w_1 dollars in foregone income, as compared to w_0 dollars before the increase in w. The income effect is represented by the change from B to D. The graph illustrates the case where both leisure and consumption are taken to be normal goods, so that the increase in income associated with the increase in w leads to an increase in both leisure and consumption.

Assuming that both leisure and consumption are normal goods, it follows that an increase in the wage rate (with the price per unit of consumption fixed) leads to an increase in units consumed of the consumption good—both the income effect and the substitution effect work toward an increase in C. But the effect on leisure is ambiguous in the general case. An increase in w leads to a decrease in leisure

demanded through the substitution effect, but to an increase in leisure demanded through the income effect. If the substitution effect dominates, a higher wage rate leads to less leisure or, equivalently, an increase in the number of labor hours supplied. If the income effect dominates the substitution effect (as is the case in figure 10-2), a higher wage rate leads to more leisure and fewer labor hours supplied. In the second case, the supply curve of labor for the consumer is backward bending, as shown in figure 10-3.

The Backward Bending Supply Curve of Labor Services   As drawn in figure 10-3, the labor supply curve S_L is upward sloping for w less than w^* and is backward bending for w greater than w^*. The intuitive idea behind the backward bending labor supply curve is this. For low values of w, income and consumption levels are low for the consumer. Low-income consumers find consumption a very good substitute for leisure, and hence the substitution

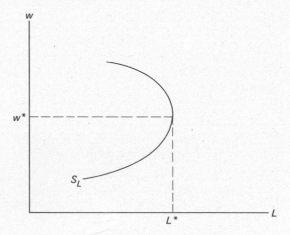

FIG. 10-3 *Backward bending supply curve
of labor services*

effect dominates the income effect so far as the demand for leisure (supply of labor hours) is concerned. So long as w is less than w^*, increases in the wage rate bring forth more labor hours supplied so that income (and consumption) continue to increase as the wage rate is increased. However, beyond some sufficiently high value of w (and correspondingly high levels of income and consumption), it takes a larger amount of consumption to substitute for a given amount of leisure, and the substitution effect becomes less important relative to the income effect. Above w^*, the income effect dominates.

We do not mean to imply that for every consumer, the supply curve of labor is backward bending for w sufficiently large. It might be the case that the substitution effect dominates the income effect at all wage levels for a consumer. But what is important to keep in mind is that the decision to supply more labor hours involves a cost in terms of leisure foregone; there is nothing "irrational" in the decision of a consumer to respond to an increase in the wage rate by decreasing his hours of work in order to enjoy more leisure.

Finally, it might be argued that our approach is somewhat unrealistic in that the typical worker is not offered the kind of leisure-consumption choices implied by the indifference map. On most jobs, the worker is hired for a forty-hour week, and is offered only an "all or nothing" choice; if he takes the job, he works forty hours, and is not permitted the kind of fine adjustment between leisure and consumption shown by the tangency condition in figure 10-1 or 10-2. The use of rules specifying fixed hours of work arises because of problems of coordinating activities within a business firm, and has the effect of limiting choices available to workers.

A more realistic model of the labor market would be one in which the hours of work (forty hours per week) are roughly the same for all firms, but working conditions differ from firm to firm. In such a model, workers choose between alternative job opportunities offering different combinations of income and "leisure on the job." The implications of such a (realistic) model do not differ significantly from those already derived; the quantity of effective labor power offered on the market by a consumer is responsive to the income and substitution effects associated with consumption-leisure choices. The consumer expresses such choices by moving from firm to firm rather than by changing the number of nominal hours of labor power supplied.

Short-Run Equilibrium in the Market for Labor Services   Given a skill class of labor services and assuming independence among firms, the short-run market demand curve for such services is obtained by summing the short-run demand curves of firms employing workers in that skill class. Figure 10-4 shows the derivation of the demand curve for labor services by a typical firm, using the approach of chapter 8.

The supply of labor services by a consumer is derived as in figure 10-5. Assuming independence among consumers, the market supply curve is obtained by summing the supply curve of consumers. The resulting short-run equilibrium is shown in figure 10-6.

Short-run equilibrium occurs in the market for labor services when that market is cleared. The market supply curve of labor services shifts in response to changes in the prices of consumer goods, the direction of the shifts depending upon the importance of income and substitution effects. (Note that in figure 10-2, an increase of w with p fixed is equivalent to a

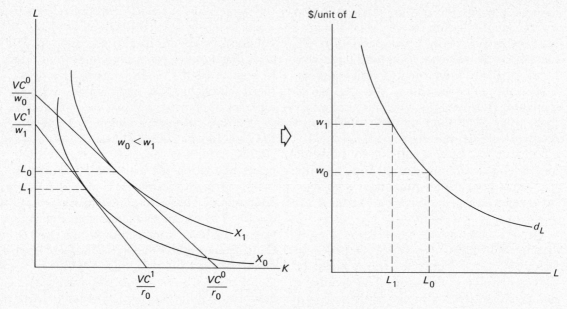

FIG. 10-4 *Demand for labor by the firm*

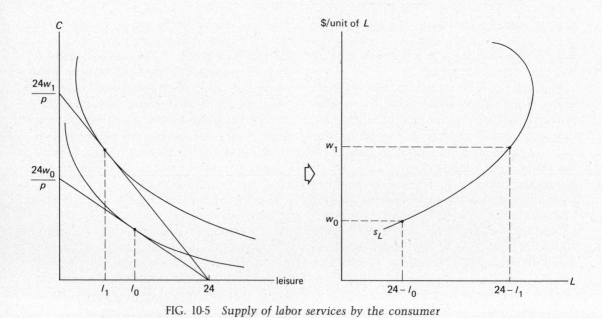

FIG. 10-5 *Supply of labor services by the consumer*

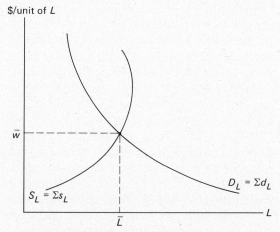

FIG. 10-6   *Short-run equilibrium in the labor market*

sumption equals the "real" wage rate, that is, the wage rate measured in units of consumption. The marginal rate of substitution between leisure and consumption is the same for all consumers supplying the given kind of labor service.

3. The supply of and demand for labor services are homogeneous of degree zero in all prices.

The peculiarity of the short-run labor market relative to other markets we have discussed is that equilibrium may not be unique or "stable," as illustrated in figure 10-7.

At the equilibrium ($\bar{w}_2$, $\bar{L}_2$), demand exceeds supply above equilibrium and supply exceeds demand below equilibrium (for $w > \bar{w}_1$). The arrows indicate the direction of change of the

corresponding decrease in p with w fixed, and so the effects of a change in p on labor hours supplied can be traced out just as the effects of a change in w were.) The market demand curve for labor services shifts as prices of other inputs or prices of outputs change. The market demand curve for labor services is downward sloping to the right, but the sign of the slope of the market supply curve depends upon the relative importance of the income and substitution effects of an increase in the wage rate.

Because all consumers and all firms face the same wage rate in the market for labor services, the following conditions hold at a short-run equilibrium:

1. The wage rate per hour of labor equals the marginal revenue product of labor hired for each firm in the economy.

2. Labor services are supplied by each consumer up to the point where the marginal rate of substitution between leisure and con-

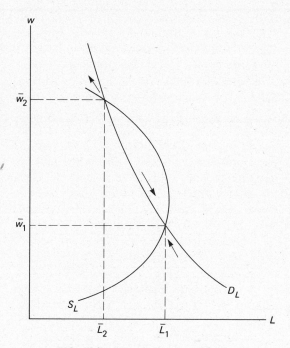

FIG. 10-7   *Nonunique equilibrium*

wage rate under the rule "raise the wage rate when excess demand is positive and lower the wage rate when excess demand is negative." In contrast, $(\bar{w}_1, \bar{L}_1)$ is a stable equilibrium.

Services of Capital Goods and Resources

In the rental markets for capital goods and resources, consumers holding title to such assets rent their use for specified periods of time to firms. A distinction can be drawn between gross and net rentals. The *gross rental* paid by a firm is the contractual rental payment for use of a capital good or resource for a certain period of time. The *net rental* is the gross rental less depreciation that occurs due to use of the asset. For example, assume a capital good that is worth $1,000 and for which a gross rental of $200 per year is charged. If at the end of the year, the capital good has depreciated in value to $900 because of its employment during the year, then the net rental is $100 per year, equal to the $200 gross rental less $100 depreciation.

In the short run, the stocks of all capital goods and natural resources in the economy are fixed in amounts, and asset portfolios of consumers are fixed as well. Thus each consumer holds title to given stocks of capital goods and natural resources. The consumer is interested only in deriving as large an income as possible from his asset holdings. This means that the consumer should be willing to accept any positive net rental for the hire of the assets to which he holds title rather than allow them to lie idle. As a consequence, the short-run supply curve of services of capital goods or natural resources for any consumer is perfectly inelastic at any positive net rental for the services of these assets.

On the demand side, firms view the services of capital goods and resources much like the services of labor. The firm hires such services

to the point where the marginal revenue product of the service equals the gross rental charged per unit of the service, resulting in the demand curve shown in figure 10-8. Assuming independence on the part of both consumers and firms, short-run market demand and supply curves are obtained by summing the individual demand and supply curves as in figure 10-9.

In figure 10-8, d_K is the demand curve for capital services K for a typical firm. To keep the notation as simple as possible, we assume that there is no depreciation due to use of capital goods so that gross rental and net rental are equal, both being denoted by r. In figure 10-9, s_K is the supply of capital services for a typical consumer. S_K and D_K are the market supply and market demand of capital services respectively.

Because S_K is perfectly inelastic in the short run, the equilibrium rental $\bar{r}$ is determined solely by demand; and the equilibrium quantity of capital services $\bar{K}$ is determined solely by supply. The equilibrium rental will increase if there is an increase in the prices of other inputs (assuming that all inputs are normal), or if there is an increase in output prices (again assuming that all inputs are normal).

Long-Run Equilibrium in the Market for Inputs

In long-run equilibrium all of the incentives afforded to market participants in a competitive economy are fully exploited. This exploitation applies to the input markets as well as to the markets for outputs. We have seen in chapter 9 that in long-run equilibrium, every produced good sells at a price equal to the minimum of *LRAC* of producing the good, with the long-run supply curve of any produced good being perfectly elastic at that price. A similar kind

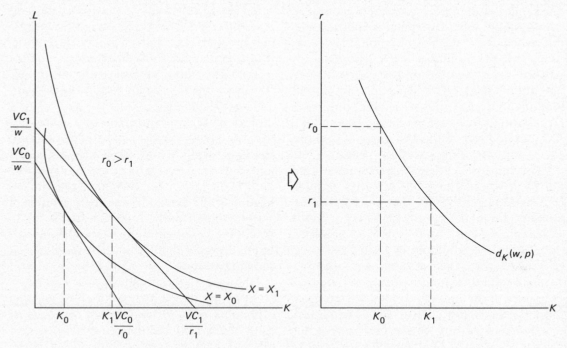

FIG. 10-8   *Demand by a firm for services of a capital good*

of conclusion holds in the input markets.

Consider first the demand side of input markets. The long-run market demand curve for any input is a curve along which the prices of all other inputs and the prices of outputs are all held fixed. The long-run demand curve then relates the quantity demanded of an input to its price, assuming that demanders are free to vary all inputs (including plant capacity) and to move from industry to industry.

All industries operate under constant costs in the long run. Therefore, given the prices of other inputs and the price of an industry's product, the long-run demand curve for any input is perfectly elastic at that price for the input such that the minimum of $LRAC$ for the industry equals the per unit price of the industry's product. No units of the input are

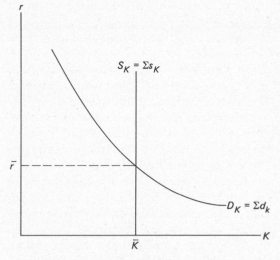

FIG. 10-9   *Short-run equilibrium in the market for services of a capital good*

demanded at any price for the input above that level, and an unlimited number of units would be demanded if the price for the input were such that the minimum of *LRAC* for the industry is less than the price of the industry's product. Briefly, *the long-run demand curve for any input is perfectly elastic at that price for the input such that the minimum of LRAC for any industry using the input equals the price per unit of the industry's output.*

This conclusion is hardly surprising. Because of free entry and exit, all industries perform in the long run "as if" they were operating under constant returns to scale, facing competitive input markets. Fix the price of an industry's product at the minimum of *LRAC*, assuming $r = r_0$, $w = w_0$. Then if w is greater than w_0, average cost for the industry must rise. But with the price of the industry's product fixed, each firm in the industry earns less than normal profits, and industry output falls to zero, together with its demand for labor services. If w is less than w_0, then every firm in the industry can earn excess profits and entry occurs resulting in an indefinite expansion of output and of the demand for labor services. This leads to the perfectly elastic long-run demand curve for any input.

On the supply side a similar phenomenon is at work. Capital goods (including human capital) are produced goods; hence in the long run such goods sell at prices equal to the minimum of *LRAC* of producing them. If we fix the prices of all other inputs and of outputs (including the market interest rate), and allow the rental for the services of a capital good to vary, then the resulting curve is the long-run supply curve of services of that capital good. At any rental such that investment in the capital good earns more than the market rate of interest, the long-run supply is infinite; at any rental such that investment in the capital good

earns less than the market rate of interest, no investment will take place. Thus we conclude that the *long-run supply curve for the services of a capital good (including human capital) is perfectly elastic at that rental such that investment in the capital good earns the market rate of interest.*

With both long-run demand curves and long-run supply curves perfectly elastic, long-run equilibrium in the input markets occurs only if the curves are perfectly elastic at the same market rental for the input. Furthermore, looking at the demand and supply analysis of a single input market does not enable us to determine how many units of the input will be hired, even if equilibrium exists, as indicated in figure 10-10.

The reason for the indeterminacy in figure 10-10 is that the problem we are investigating is solvable only in the context of a general equilibrium model of the economy, that is, a model that takes into account the interrelationships among all markets in an economy. We have carried our analysis as far as it will go in a partial equilibrium framework; general equilibrium is taken up in chapter 12.

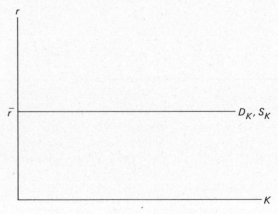

FIG. 10-10   *Long-run equilibrium for capital services*

Economic Rent and Quasi-Rents

Our discussion of long-run equilibrium in the input markets has been confined to the case of produced inputs such as capital goods and human capital. These are certainly the most important kinds of inputs in terms of their share of total input earnings in the economy. But certain distinctive inputs—such as unique human talents and abilities and strategic geographic locations—cannot be produced to order. The economic system can turn out trained physicists in response to demand, but geniuses like Einstein and Newton appear on the scene in a manner that is beyond the explanations offered by the economic laws of production. We can reclaim land, but the special climatic advantages of the Imperial Valley of California still remain. Distinctive inputs require special treatment in our analysis of input markets.

In classifying the earnings of factors of production such as capital, land, and labor, economists use the term *economic rent* to mean *any earnings over and beyond what is required to bring forth the services of the factor of production.* The term has wide applicability. For example, any positive net rental earnings of capital services in the short run are economic rent. Owners of capital goods are willing to hire out the services of these assets at any positive net rental rather than forego such earnings; the services of capital goods are in perfectly inelastic supply in the short run. In either the short run or the long run, the owner of a piece of property in the Imperial Valley should be willing to rent out that property at any positive net rental, and so his earnings represent economic rent either in the short run or in the long run.

In the case of capital services, the long-run situation is quite different from the short-run. In the long run, the stock of capital goods adjusts to the demand-supply situation; consumers will not invest in capital goods unless the rental earnings of such goods are such that consumers can expect a rate of return on their investment equal to the market rate of interest. As the stock of capital goods changes in the long run in response to prices, so does the flow of capital services offered on the market and the rentals paid for such services. Earnings such as short-run net rentals of capital goods are referred to as quasi-rent. By a *quasi-rent* we mean *earnings of a factor of production that are economic rent in the short run, but are converted in the long run into necessary payments required to bring forth the services of the factor.* For reproducible inputs such as capital goods and human capital, all economic rents are quasi-rents. Only for inputs with distinctive, nonreproducible qualities is economic rent both a long-run and short-run phenomenon.

Under a competitive organization of markets, inputs are paid their marginal revenue products. All labor of a specified skill is paid the same wage rate, equal to MRP_L. Suppose a firm employs a specially talented individual whose MRP is greater than that of other workers. Then competition among firms, bidding for the services of this individual, will force his wage rate to the level of his MRP. Similarly, an individual who owns a particularly productive piece of land will find the rent on it bid up to its MRP. The special earning capabilities associated with distinctive skills or with unique locational advantages will be captured by the owners of such assets. A department store located on the best corner in town will earn no more on its investment than a store on a back street; it is the owner of the land on which the department store is located who captures the extra revenues, not the firm. Similarly, superior management talent does not result (in the long run) in higher profits for a firm; instead, the salary of the manager rises until such excess profits are eliminated.

This process of long-run adjustment of earnings of inputs with differential advantages underlies the traditional theory of land rent.

Land Rent

The classic case of economic rent being earned by owners of a factor of production in the long run is land. By the early 1800s the classical economists (Malthus, West, and Ricardo) had already developed a theory of land rent based on differences in the qualities of land. The essence of that theory is the assumption of inelastic supply, in the long run, of various grades of land.

The story told by Malthus and Ricardo goes as follows. When a country is sparsely populated, only the best quality land is employed in production. With a tiny population, there is land enough for all, and no one would be willing to pay for the use of a piece of land. As population grows, the demand for agricultural produce grows, and soon all the best land is taken. As it becomes necessary to use second-best land, economic rent develops on the best land, the rent per acre representing the difference between net profit per acre on the best land and net profit per acre on the second-best land. Economic rent is paid by farmers to owners of the best land equal to the difference in net profit between the two grades of land; if any rent less than this were charged, there would be an incentive for farmers to shift away from the second-best to the best land. On the other hand, no one would be willing to pay more than the difference in net profit in rent.

To illustrate the way in which economic rent arises because of differences in the fertility of

TABLE 10-1   *Output per Acre by Grade of Land*

Land\Labor	Grade A	Grade B	Grade C	Grade D	Grade E
1	100	90	70	50	20
2	180	160	130	70	30
3	240	210	150	80	38
4	280	230	160	87	43
5	300	248	168	92	46
6	310	255	173	95	48

land, consider the case in which there are five grades of land, labeled A, B, C, D, and E. Table 10-1 summarizes outputs of wheat per acre from each grade of land, for various levels of labor employed on the land. Suppose that wheat sells for $1 per bushel and that labor costs $20 per unit. What can be said about the economic rent that is generated?

To begin with, we know that labor is hired to the point where the marginal revenue product of labor equals the wage rate. The marginal product schedule of labor for each grade of land can be constructed in the usual way from table 10-1. Given a price of wheat of $1 per bushel and a wage rate of $20 per laborer, the profit-maximizing farmer would employ 5 units of labor on grade A land, 4 on grade B, 3 on grade C, 2 on grade D, and 1 on grade E, as shown in table 10-2. These figures determine the *intensive* margin of cultivation, that is, the level of use of other factors to employ on given grades of land.

At the prices for wheat and labor shown in table 10-2, it just pays to use land of grade E; income after labor costs is zero on land E. The extensive margin of cultivation is reached at land E; any land less fertile than land E would not be employed for production, given the prices of wheat and labor. We refer to grade E land as *land on the extensive margin of cultivation.*

How does economic rent arise? Using tables

TABLE 10-2 *Marginal Revenue Product of Labor*

(price of wheat = $1/bushel; wage rate = $20/laborer)

Labor\Land	Grade A	Grade B	Grade C	Grade D	Grade E
1	$100	$90	$70	$50	$20
2	$ 80	$70	$60	$20	$10
3	$ 60	$50	$20	$10	$ 8
4	$ 40	$20	$10	$ 7	$ 5
5	$ 20	$18	$ 8	$ 5	$ 3
6	$ 10	$ 7	$ 5	$ 3	$ 2

10-1 and 10-2, the net income for each grade of land (sales of wheat minus cost of labor) can be calculated as follows:

Grade A:

300 bu. × $1/bu. − 5 lab. × $20/lab. = $200

Grade B:

230 bu. × $1/bu. − 4 lab. × $20/lab. = $150

Grade C:

150 bu. × $1/bu. − 3 lab. × $20/lab. = $90

Grade D:

70 bu. × $1/bu. − 2 lab. × $20/lab. = $30

Grade E:

20 bu. × $1/bu. − 1 lab. × $20/lab. = $0

These net incomes represent the rentals per acre that would be earned by each of the grades of land reflecting the differences in fertility. For example, an owner of an acre of grade D land would accept nothing less than $30 for the use of the land for a year since an alternative always available to him is to farm the land himself and earn $30. Farmers will be willing to pay up to $30 per year to use grade D land; at any rental less than $30 they make a higher profit than on grade E land.

To return to the Malthus-Ricardo story, as population increases, the price of food increases, thus leading to more intensive cultivation of fertile land and to the use of poorer and poorer land: both the intensive and extensive margins of cultivation are increased. Both of these changes increase the rents earned by owners of land. Hence a basic conclusion of the classical economists is that the "progress of society" tends to distribute income more and more in favor of landlords at the expense of the other classes of society. What is particularly onerous about this is that land rents are not payments needed to bring forth the services of land, but instead represent "unearned income," from society's point of view. The fact that land of various qualities is in perfectly inelastic supply, both in the short run and in the long run, makes the income "unearned." In brief, the income is economic rent.

It should be pointed out relative to the classical conception of land rent that land is not necessarily in perfect inelastic supply; by draining and filling and irrigating, we can increase the supply of land along with that of other inputs. And we can improve the productivity of the soil by investment in fertilizers, terracing, and the like. Land is not quite as unique an input as the classical economists would have us believe.

Profits

Finally, some comments should be made about the role played by profits in the competitive model. We identified profits as the earnings that are assigned to the owners of the firm, representing a return to them for their investment in organizing the firm. The manager of the firm does not participate in profits; instead, that person is treated as a skilled laborer whose salary is determined by the same forces of supply and demand that determine the wage rate for other classes of laborers.

We will have to reexamine the role of profits when we look at a world in which uncertainty exists. Only in such a world does it make sense to talk about profits as the earnings of the successful innovator, as in Schumpeter, or as the earnings of the risk-taker, as in Frank Knight. The problems associated with uncertainty are discussed in chapter 16.

Summary

The income of the consumer is determined in part by his choices with respect to consumption and leisure. Assuming both are normal goods, then the supply curve of labor is upward sloping if the substitution effect of a wage increase dominates the income effect. At sufficiently high wage rates, the income effect may dominate the substitution effect, accounting for the "backward bending" portion of the labor supply curve. The consumption-leisure choice is such that the marginal rate of substitution between consumption and leisure equals the purchasing power of the hourly wage rate in terms of units of the consumption good. The supply of labor is homogeneous of degree zero in all prices.

Economic rent is defined as any payment to a factor of production beyond that required to bring forth the services of the factor. All positive *net rentals* to capital goods and resources represent economic rent in the short run to such factors. In the long run, the net rentals earned by reproducible capital goods and resources are such that investment in any such good yields the market rate of return, with the price of the good equal to the minimum of *LRAC* of producing the good. Hence economic rents vanish in the long run for reproducible capital goods and resources, that is, the short-run economic rents are quasi-rents.

Economic rent persists in the long run for distinctive inputs that are in long-run fixed supply. The rent earned by a plot of land is determined by the productivity of the land relative to other grades of land, and by the level of demand for the products that can be raised on it. Inputs are employed on any piece of land until the last "dose" of them generates a marginal revenue product equal to its marginal cost. This point determines the "intensive" margin of cultivation of land. Grades of land are employed to the point where the poorest grade of land in cultivation pays no profits. Such land represents the "extensive" marginal land.

In a world of certainty, profits are simply the earnings assigned to the asset organizational expenses.

Problems

1. The utility function of a consumer is of the form

$$U = C\ell$$

   where C is unity of consumption and ℓ is leisure. Let $w = \$2/\text{hour}$ and let $p = \$5$, where w is the wage rate and p is the price per unit of consumption.

   a. Determine the choice of C and ℓ for the consumer.

   b. Are C and ℓ normal goods?

   c. Sketch the supply curve of labor for the consumer for $w = \$1, \$2, \$3, \$4, \$5$.

   d. What happens to income of the consumer as w varies from \$1 to \$5? Is there a general rule that applies to all consumers?

2. The Malthusian approach to the labor market argues in essence that the long-run supply curve of unskilled labor is perfectly elastic at a "subsidence" wage rate. Present a defense and a criticism of this viewpoint, noting especially the difference between the "short run" and the "long run" so far as factors operating on the supply of labor are concerned.

3. Indicate the effects on the short-run supply of labor of an increase in the social security tax rate. Identify the income and substitution effects associated with the tax increase. Are there any conditions under which an increase in the tax rate would lead to a fall in receipts by the Social Security Administration?

4. Given the table of outputs per acre by grade of land (table 10-1), determine the intensive and extensive margins as well as the rents earned by each grade of land in the following cases, where w is the wage rate and p is the price per bushel of wheat:

   a. $w = \$40$ $\quad p = \$2$
   b. $w = \$10$ $\quad p = .50$
   c. $w = \$70$ $\quad p = \$1$

   Is there any general rule concerning land rents and extensive and intensive margins suggested by a and b above and by the discussion concerning tables 10-1 and 10-2?

5. Discuss the short-run and long-run consequences of a system of taxes whereby 100 percent of all quasi-rents are taxed away by the government.

11
Intertemporal Decision Making and the Market for Assets

Up to this point, we have ignored the intertemporal aspects of decisions by consumers and firm managers—that is, decisions that take into account not only the consequences for the current period, but also consequences in future periods as well. The theory that has been developed thus far is particularly appropriate to a world in which decisions taken in the current period are determined only by the current payoffs from these decisions. In this chapter we consider both the way in which future payoffs from decisions influence decision making in the current period, and the structure of markets that links current decision making with future payoffs from decisions.

The Decision to Save

The consumer enters the marketplace on any day possessing a certain preference ranking over alternatives and endowed with a stock of assets—titles to various resources, holdings of shares in different firms, labor skills acquired through previous training, and a net stock of promissory notes (notes he owns issued by others minus notes he has issued owned by others). He has a number of choices to make, including whether to alter his list of assets; which firms to contract with for the rental use of his resources; how much in the way of labor

services to supply for the day; what bundle of consumer goods to purchase; and how much to save for future periods.

All of these choices are to be made simultaneously by the consumer in such a manner as to maximize utility. We have already discussed the way in which consumers make choices with respect to current consumption and with respect to supplying labor services and the services of capital goods. We next examine the decision concerning how much to save in the current period.

The Consumer's Time Preferences

The approach we will adopt to dealing with the decision as to how much to save in the current period can in fact be extended to an arbitrary number of periods into the future; but for simplicity, we will restrict our attention to the problem of deciding how much to save today in order to consume more tomorrow. In other words, we will examine the saving decision in the case of a two-period planning horizon.

As in chapters 4 and 5, we assume that the consumer possesses a preference ranking over commodity bundles that consist of amounts to be consumed today and amounts to be consumed tomorrow. In order to continue to use a two-dimensional graph, we will represent the bundles of goods available today and tomorrow by "composite goods," which can be viewed as single magnitudes.

Suppose C_1 represents consumption today, while C_2 represents consumption tomorrow. Then the consumer's indifference map specifying his time preferences is assumed to appear as in figure 11-1. As drawn, the indifference curves have the properties postulated in chapter 4. The arrow indicates the direction of preference; more of either C_1 or C_2 is preferred to less.

The law of diminishing marginal rate of substitution also characterizes the indifference map. For clarity, we will use the term *marginal rate of time preference* to refer to the marginal rate of substitution between C_1 and C_2. Thus along any indifference curve, the marginal rate of time preference (MTP) is defined by

$$MTP = -\frac{\Delta C_2}{\Delta C_1}$$

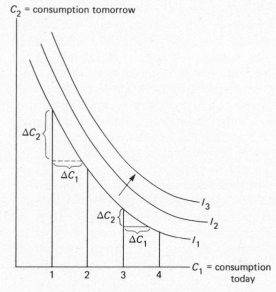

FIG. 11-1   *The consumer's indifference map with respect to timing of consumption*

Diminishing marginal rate of time preference ("indifference curves bound convex sets" as in the graph) is then to be interpreted as meaning that *along any indifference curve, consumption tomorrow becomes a better substitute for consumption today, the larger is consumption today.* In effect, the marginal rate of time preference expresses the willingness of the consumer to sacrifice consumption tomorrow in order to increase consumption by one unit today; this willingness declines as consumption today increases.

Impatience and Patience   There is a long tradition in economics holding that consumers are typically "impatient" or "myopic"; that is, in some sense, consumers tend to value current consumption higher than future consumption. Perhaps the leading exponent of this point of view was Irving Fisher, an early twentieth cen-

tury American economist who ranks as one of the dominant figures in the development of modern economic theory. Fisher's main argument for impatience is based on the uncertainties of the future. After all, who can be sure that he will be around tomorrow to consume what he saved today? This argument introduces elements we are specifically excluding from the competitive model, since we are assuming that each consumer knows, *with certainty*, what the consequences of his choices are, including his ability to consume in the future. This is obviously unrealistic, especially with respect to choices concerning future periods, but it is important to understand the workings of a "certainty" world before attempting to explore the special problems created by uncertainty.

Is there any reason to expect a tendency for consumers to exhibit impatience when they are absolutely certain of what the future holds? The answer, at least in terms of the current state of economic theory, is that there is not; impatience appears to be closely tied to uncertainty about the future. Interestingly enough, however, recent work by Tjalling Koopmans indicates that if a consumer makes plans over an infinite future and if his preference ranking over commodity bundles extending into the indefinite future can be represented by a utility function, then the consumer's preferences must exhibit some amount of impatience. Koopmans's result does not apply to planning over a finite number of periods; hence the general theory of consumer behavior does not imply that the consumer planning over a finite horizon will exhibit impatience. Still, for classifying preferences with respect to the timing of consumption, the concept of impatience is of interest.

For the case of a two-period planning horizon with one consumption good, a consumer is said to be impatient if, when $a > b$, he prefers the bundle (a, b) to the bundle (b, a) where the first component of each bundle is his consumption today and the second component is his consumption tomorrow. For example, a consumer who prefers $(2, 1)$ to $(1, 2)$ is impatient; he prefers consuming two units today and one unit tomorrow to consuming one unit today and two units tomorrow. As we shall see, this amounts to saying that a consumer is impatient if, at a zero interest rate, he prefers to consume more in the present than in the future.

Figures 11-2 and 11-3 illustrate "impatient" and "patient" preferences. Note that in the first graph, points lying to the right of the $C_1 = C_2$ line are on higher indifference curves than transposed points lying to the left of the line; for example, $(1\frac{1}{2}, \frac{1}{2})$ is on a higher indifference curve than $(\frac{1}{2}, 1\frac{1}{2})$, and so on. The reverse is true for the case of patient preferences shown in the second graph.

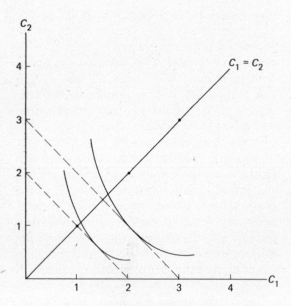

FIG. 11-2   *Impatient preferences*

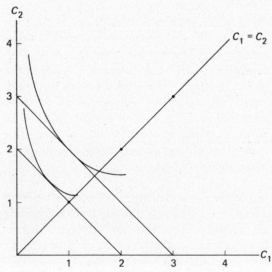

FIG. 11-3   *Patient preferences*

The Consumer's Budget Constraint

We next turn to the opportunities afforded the consumer in the marketplace. From his decisions as to the supplying of services of capital goods and of labor, the consumer knows with certainty that his income today is some fixed amount M_1 dollars, while his income tomorrow will be the fixed amount M_2 dollars. His decision with respect to spending or saving does not influence these amounts of income. We are also assuming that the consumer faces a perfect lending market, in which he can borrow or lend as much as he wants at the market rate of interest of i percent per day.

Let S denote saving out of today's income. (If S is negative, then S represents the dollar amount of borrowing the consumer does today.) C_1 is the number of units of the consumption good consumed today, and C_2 is the number of units of the good consumed tomorrow. p_1 and p_2 denote the per unit prices of the good today and tomorrow. We assume that the good cannot be stored, so that consumption today equals the number of units purchased today and similarly for consumption tomorrow.

Then the budget constraint for the consumer may be derived from the condition that if the consumer plans only over a two-day period (today and tomorrow), then he must pay off tomorrow any debts incurred today, and he will spend tomorrow any savings he accumulates today. Hence we have

$$S = M_1 - p_1 C_1 \qquad (1)$$

This equation simply defines savings as the difference between today's income and what is spent on consumption today.

$$p_2 C_2 = M_2 + S + Si \equiv M_2 + S(1 + i) \qquad (2)$$

Equation 2 states that what is spent for consumption tomorrow equals income tomorrow plus the amount saved plus interest on the amount saved. If savings is negative, then debts contracted today must be paid tomorrow together with the interest owed on these debts.

Combining equations 1 and 2, we obtain the budget constraint for the consumer:

$$p_2 C_2 = M_2 + (M_1 - p_1 C_1)(1 + i) \text{ or}$$

$$p_1(1 + i) C_1 + p_2 C_2 = M_1(1 + i) + M_2.$$

Suppose we also define d as the percentage rate of increase in price of the consumption good between today and tomorrow so that

$$d = \frac{p_2 - p_1}{p_1},$$

which implies in turn that

$$p_2 = p_1(1 + d).$$

This means that we can write our budget constraint as

$$p_1(1 + i) C_1 + p_1(1 + d) C_2 = M_1(1 + i) + M_2.$$

Plotting this budget constraint on the consumer's indifference map, we have the graph in figure 11-4. As usual, the budget line is located by finding the intercepts along the C_1 and C_2 axes. If $C_2 = 0$,

$$C_1 = \frac{M_1(1 + i) + M_2}{p_1(1 + i)}$$

while if $C_1 = 0$,

$$C_2 = \frac{M_1(1 + i) + M_2}{p_1(1 + d)}.$$

Whatever the interest rate, one alternative that is always available to the consumer is to set savings, S, equal to zero. Hence for any value of i, the point

$$\left(\frac{M_1}{p_1}, \frac{M_2}{p_1(1 + d)} \right)$$

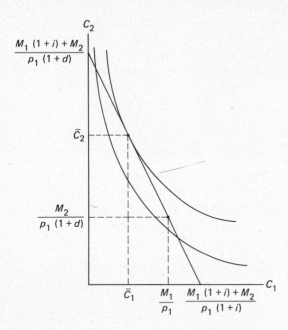

FIG. 11-4   *Choice as to timing of consumption*

always lies on the budget line. Finally, the slope of the budget line equals

$$-\frac{C_2 \text{ intercept}}{C_1 \text{ intercept}} = -\frac{1+i}{1+d}.$$

The term

$$\frac{1+i}{1+d}$$

can be interpreted as the *real cost in terms of consumption tomorrow of increasing consumption by one unit today.* If I want to increase consumption today by one unit, I have to increase my expenditures today by p_1 dollars. This means I decrease money available for spending tomorrow by $p_1(1+i)$, since I lose the interest I could have earned if I had refrained from spending today. The number of units of consumption tomorrow that I give up equals the decrease in money available tomorrow divided by the price per unit tomorrow $p_2 = p_1(1+d)$; hence the real cost is

$$\frac{p_1(1+i)}{p_1(1+d)} = \frac{1+i}{1+d}.$$

Utility Maximization and the Choice between Consumption Today and Consumption Tomorrow

The consumer chooses in such a way as to maximize utility, resulting in the usual tangency condition in figure 11-4 at the bundle $(\bar{C}_1, \bar{C}_2)$. At a utility-maximizing point, we have the condition that the *marginal rate of time preference is equal to the real cost in terms of consumption tomorrow of increasing consumption by one unit today.* It is important to note that with a perfect lending market every consumer faces the same interest rate i. Suppose we also assume that expectations as to future prices are identical for all consumers. Then every consumer will adjust his spending stream so as to satisfy

$$MTP = -\frac{\Delta C_2}{\Delta C_1} = \frac{1+i}{1+d};$$

hence the *marginal rate of time preference will be the same for every consumer.* Equating the marginal rates of time preferences across consumers means that those consumers with relatively "patient" preferences will tend to save more (as in figure 11-4) or borrow less than they would with "impatient" preferences. At any interest rate, an impatient consumer is allocating a larger fraction of income to current consumption than would the same consumer with patient preferences.

The Effects on Saving of a Change in the Interest Rate As the interest rate increases, the budget line rotates about the point

$$\left(\frac{M_1}{p_1}, \frac{M_2}{p_1(1+d)}\right),$$

since this bundle is always available, whatever the interest rate. The result of an increase in the interest rate (from i_0 to i_1) is shown in figure 11-5. At the interest rate i_0, the bundle $A = (C_1^0, C_2^0)$ is chosen. An increase in the interest rate to i_1 rotates the budget constraint in a clockwise direction about the point

$$\left(\frac{M_1}{p_1}, \frac{M_2}{p_1(1+d)}\right).$$

The bundle chosen with $i = i_1$ is $D = (C_1^1, C_2^1)$.

The substitution effect is illustrated in figure 11-5 by the move from A to B: an increase in the interest rate leads to the substitution of consumption tomorrow for consumption today along the indifference curve I_0. The reason for this is that at a higher interest rate, consumption today is more expensive than before in terms of foregone interest income. The alternative to one more unit of consumption today is to save the expenditure and have available for consumption tomorrow this saving, plus interest. As the interest rate increases, the opportunity cost of consuming today increases.

Both C_1 and C_2 are assumed to be normal goods. For an individual with positive savings,

$$\left(C_1^0 < \frac{M_1}{p_1}, \text{ hence } S > 0\right),$$

such as in figure 11-5, an increase in the interest rate acts like an increase in income. Hence the income effect moves the individual in the direction of consuming more both today and rection of consuming more both today and

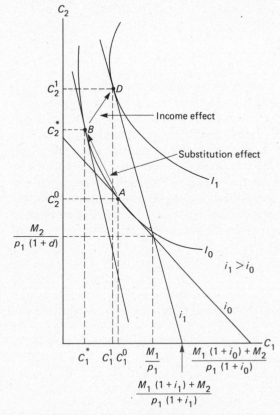

FIG. 11-5 *The income and substitution effects of an increase in the interest rate—positive savings*

tomorrow, as indicated in the move from B to D.

For a positive saver (a "lender"), the effect, on savings, of an increase in the interest rate is ambiguous. The substitution effect acts to increase savings while the income effect acts in the opposite direction. If the substitution effect dominates the income effect, then an increase in the interest rate leads to a fall in consumption today and hence an increase in savings. This case is pictured in figure 11-5, since $C_1^1 < C_1^0$, which means

$$\frac{M_1}{p_1} - C_1^1 > \frac{M_1}{p_1} - C_1^0,$$

so that savings are higher at i_1 than at i_0. If the income effect dominates, then an increase in the interest rate leads to a fall in savings.

If the consumer is a borrower ($S < 0$), then an increase in the interest rate acts like a fall in income. For the borrower, both the income effect and the substitution effect act in the same direction—to decrease borrowing as the interest rate increases. The case of a borrower is shown in figure 11-6. Since

$$C_1^0 > \frac{M_1}{p_1} , \ S < 0.$$

The substitution effect (A to B) leads to the substitution of C_2 for C_1 along the indifference

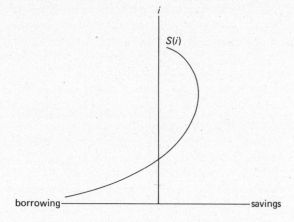

FIG. 11-7   *The supply of savings curve*

curve I_0. With C_1 and C_2 both normal goods, the income effect (B to D) acts to decrease both C_1 and C_2. Hence $C_1^1 < C_1^0$ and borrowings decrease as the interest rate increases.†

The Supply of Savings Curve   In figure 11-7, the curve $S(i)$ plots savings as a function of the interest rate. Presumably, for sufficiently low values of i, the consumer will become a borrower, and the $S(i)$ curve falls to the left so long as the consumer is in the "borrowing range" of the interest rate. As i increases beyond the borrowing range, the consumer saves positive amounts. If the interest rate is sufficiently high, the income effect may dominate the substitution effect, perhaps resulting in a backward bending $S(i)$ curve.

The $S(i)$ curve gives the amount of current savings for the consumer as a function of the interest rate. Positive savings in the current

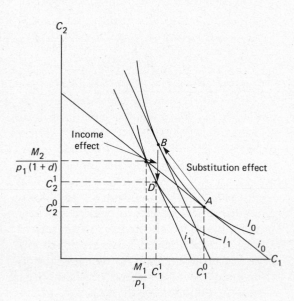

FIG. 11-6   *The income and substitution effects of an increase in the interest rate—borrower*

†Unfortunately, this straightforward conclusion concerning the responsiveness of the amount borrowed to the interest rate holds in this simple form only for the case where two periods (today and tomorrow) are involved. For many-period models, more complicated conditions hold.

period means that the consumer is adding to the stock of his assets (or reducing his liabilities), while negative savings means that the consumer is either liquidating some of his assets or is issuing notes (borrowing). In other words, savings measures the *change* in the consumer's *equity* (which equals assets less liabilities). This means that there is a further decision implied for the consumer by the act of saving—namely, how to adjust his asset portfolio, given his changed equity position.

Expectations and Futures Markets

Before looking at the way in which the consumer chooses from among alternative assets, we should examine a little more closely the notion of expectations as to the future on the part of consumers. In our discussion of the choice between saving and spending, it was assumed that the consumer has a set of expectations concerning the level of his income in the next period, M_2, and the price p_2 that will prevail in that period. Where do these expectations come from, and what does it mean to say that the consumer is certain about future market conditions? Furthermore, why should it ever be the case that the expectations of all market participants as to the future structure of prices are the same?

The device by which expectations about the future are made certain, and are made identical for all market participants, is the futures contract. By a *futures contract* in a commodity we mean a contract that specifies delivery at a given future date of a specified number of units of the commodity, at a guaranteed price to be paid at the future date. For example, on the "futures" market for wheat you might enter into a futures contract on May 1 in which you, as seller, guarantee to deliver 100 bushels of

wheat on September 1 at a price of $4 per bushel to be paid to you on September 1 by the purchaser of your futures contract; or you might buy such a contract.

On the futures market for a commodity, individuals with different beliefs as to the price of a commodity in the future period enter into contracts with one another. I might believe that the price of wheat three months from now will be $4.50 a bushel, and you might believe that the price will be $4.25. You would be willing to sell futures contracts in wheat at a futures price above $4.25, and I am willing to buy such contracts at prices below $4.50. The equilibrium market price for futures contracts that will be established is one that clears the market for such contracts—in our example, some price between $4.25 and $4.50 per bushel. Detailed consideration of the futures market will be deferred until chapter 16, which deals with uncertainty, since uncertainty plays a major role in the operation of the futures market. For our purposes, the important thing about the futures market is that individuals operating in this market can, through the purchase and sale of futures contracts, convert uncertainty about future prices and incomes into certainty.

We will assume that futures markets exist for all goods and services. The effect of this assumption is that, in making plans covering future periods, both consumers and firm managers can implement these plans by their dealings today in the futures market. Thus, when we say that the consumer expects with certainty that the price of a consumption good tomorrow will be p_2 dollars, what we mean is that the consumer can today buy, for delivery tomorrow, as many units of the good as he wishes, at the guaranteed price of p_2 dollars to be paid tomorrow. Each market participant faces the same prices in the futures market; hence "expectations" as to prices in the future are the same across all market participants, and are "certain."

In reality, organized futures markets exist for only a handful of staple commodities such as wheat, corn, soybeans, cotton, pork bellies, and silver. Because of the absence of futures markets, uncertainty is introduced into the decision problems of consumers and firm managers. This constitutes a major source of inefficiency in the allocation of resources within a society, and consequently the question of the reasons for the lack of adequate futures markets is of interest to economists.

For such markets to exist, minimum requirements appear to be (1) well-defined and enforceable property rights to the goods being traded; (2) large numbers of potential buyers and sellers; (3) a relatively homogeneous commodity; and (4) limited risks from natural, technological, political, and social changes in the society as they impinge on the commodity. If these conditions do not exist, the transactions costs become excessive; buyers and sellers find it advantageous to bear uncertainty rather than to participate in the futures market. Clearly, for a large number of commodities, transactions costs preclude the development of organized futures markets. Still, there is evidence that the number and scope of organized futures markets is expanding because of the gains to be achieved from mitigating uncertainties.

The Market for Assets

In regard to the market for assets, we are interested in seeing both how the consumer decides what kinds and amounts of assets to hold, and how the prices of such assets are related to the incomes that the assets earn. The major assets that are available for ownership include titles to resources such as land and mineral deposits; titles to capital goods including buildings, machinery, and inventories; shares of stock in business firms; and "ownership" of human capital, in the form of skills acquired by the consumer through education and training. While each of these classes of assets has its own identifying features, common to all assets is the ownership claim to the stream of income that the asset provides over time. To explain how the stream of income is related to the price of the asset providing the income, we will take a brief excursion into some elementary notions of business mathematics.

Discounted Present Value and Compound Interest

Suppose that the interest rate on money deposited in a savings and loan account is 6 percent, compounded annually. Then $100 invested today is worth $106 one year from now. If the $6 interest and the original $100 deposit are left in the account, 6 percent is paid on $106 during the second year, or $6.36, and so the deposit grows to $112.36 in two years.

Let A be the amount deposited at time 0 (today), and let i be the annual rate of interest compounded once a year. Let B_t be the value of the amount on deposit at time t, where t is the number of years that have passed from time 0. Then

$$B_1 = A(1 + i)$$
$$= \text{value of deposit at time 1,}$$
$$B_2 = [A(1 + i)](1 + i) = A(1 + i)^2$$
$$= \text{value of deposit at time 2,}$$
$$\vdots$$
$$B_t = A(1 + i)^t$$
$$= \text{value of deposit at time } t.$$

In particular, if $A = \$100$, $i = .06$, then $B_1 = \$106$, $B_2 = \$112.36$, and so on. (Note that $i = 6$ percent means i can be written as $i = .06$). The formula $B_t = A(1 + i)^t$ enables us to calculate the value for any year in the future of A dollars invested today at an annual compound interest rate of i percent, with compounding taking place once a year.

Suppose we now reverse the process. Assume that you are offered a contract that pays, say, r_1 dollars one year from now, r_2 dollars two years from now, and in general r_t dollars t years from now. Given that the annual interest rate is i percent compounded once a year, how much is such a stream of income worth to you *today?* To put it another way, how much would you have to invest today at i percent interest to obtain the income stream r_1 in one year, r_2 in two years, and so on?

A dollars invested today provides B_1 dollars in one year, where $B_1 = A(1 + i)$. To obtain B_1 dollars one year from now, you would have to invest

$$\frac{B_1}{(1 + i)} \text{ today.}$$

For example, to obtain $106 one year from now with an interest rate of 6 percent, you have to invest

$$\frac{\$106}{(1.06)} = \$100 \text{ today.}$$

To obtain B_2 dollars two years from now requires an investment of

$$\frac{B_2}{(1 + i)^2} \text{ today,}$$

and in general to obtain B_t dollars t years from now, you must invest

$$\frac{B_t}{(1 + i)^t} \text{ dollars today.}$$

Thus the amount that would have to be invested today to obtain the income stream r_1 in one year, r_2 in two years, . . . , r_t in t years is given by

$$\frac{r_1}{(1 + i)} + \frac{r_2}{(1 + i)^2} + \cdots + \frac{r_t}{(1 + i)^t}.$$

We refer to this sum as the *discounted present value (DPV)* of the income stream r_1, r_2, . . . , r_t. Let *DPV* denote discounted present value. Then

$$DPV = \frac{r_1}{(1 + i)} + \frac{r_2}{(1 + i)^2} + \cdots + \frac{r_t}{(1 + i)^t}$$

Discounted Present Value and Constant Earning Streams

Even using log tables, it is not easy to calculate *DPV* given the income stream r_1, r_2, . . . r_t and the interest rate i. For one special case, however, it is possible to obtain a simple formula relating *DPV* and the interest rate. This is the case where there is a constant stream of income of r dollars per year, paid for the next T years. Thus at an interest rate of i percent per year, *DPV* is given by

$$DPV = \frac{r}{(1 + i)} + \frac{r}{(1 + i)^2} + \cdots + \frac{r}{(1 + i)^T}.$$

Multiplying both sides by $\frac{1}{(1 + i)}$, we obtain

$$\frac{1}{(1 + i)} DPV = \frac{r}{(1 + i)^2} + \frac{r}{(1 + i)^3}$$

$$+ \cdots + \frac{r}{(1 + i)^T} + \frac{r}{(1 + i)^{T+1}}$$

When we subtract the second equation from the first, most terms on the right-hand side cancel out, leading to

$$\left[1 - \frac{1}{(1 + i)}\right] DPV = \frac{r}{(1 + i)} - \frac{r}{(1 + i)^{T+1}}$$

or

$$DPV = \frac{r}{i}\left[1 - \frac{1}{(1+i)^T}\right].$$

In particular, suppose that an asset promises an income of r dollars per year into the indefinite future. This is the case where T gets indefinitely large.

Now with i positive, as T gets large so does $(1+i)^T$; in fact, the term

$$\frac{1}{(1+i)^T}$$

goes to zero as T goes to infinity. Thus it turns out that with an interest rate of i percent per year, a constant stream of r dollars of income per year, beginning one year from now and extending into the indefinite future, has a discounted present value given by

$$DPV = \frac{r}{i}.$$

For example, a bond paying $6 per year forever has a DPV of $100 if the interest rate is 6 percent, and a DPV of $200 if the interest rate is 3 percent.

The Valuation of Assets

To return to the problem of the consumer as asset holder, we now see that applying the formulas of the last section we can associate with any asset its discounted present value. This value will vary depending upon the amounts and timing of income generated by the asset, as well as the rate of interest.

In making his choice as to which assets to hold, the consumer is assumed to be motivated solely by the size and timing of the income time streams that assets generate. Is there any general rule that governs his choices? The following remarkable result, due originally to Irving Fisher, indicates the role played by DPV in choices among assets:[†]

> Whatever his time preferences with respect to consumption, the consumer facing a perfect lending market chooses among assets solely on the basis of their discounted present values, using the market interest rate to discount income.

Another way to put this result is as follows:

> Any two assets with the same discounted present values must sell for the same price, given that there is a perfect lending market.

Recall that by the term *perfect lending market* we mean a market for loans in which any consumer can borrow or lend as much as he wishes at the going market rate of interest. The assumption of a perfect lending market extends the notion of perfect competition from markets in commodities to markets in loans.

The argument underlying the Fisher propositions can be illlustrated as follows. Suppose that the market rate of interest is 6 percent and that there are two assets, with asset #1 providing $106 at the end of the first year and $112.36 at the end of the second year, following which no income is received. Then DPV for this asset is given by

$$DPV_1 = \frac{\$106}{(1.06)} + \frac{\$112.36}{(1.06)^2}$$
$$= \frac{\$106}{1.06} + \frac{\$112.36}{1.1236} = \$200.$$

Suppose that asset #2 pays $212 at the end of one year and no income thereafter. Then

$$DPV_2 = \frac{\$212}{1.06} = \$200.$$

[†]I. Fisher, *The Theory of Interest* (New York: Macmillan, 1930).

Consider a consumer who is impatient; he much prefers consuming one year from now to consuming two years from now. The Fisher result asserts that the consumer would be indifferent between asset #1 and asset #2, despite his impatience. Why is that? Suppose he owns asset #1 and wishes to spend $212 on consumption at the end of year one. He receives $106 in income at the end of year one. He adds to that another $106, which he borrows at the end of year one at 6 percent interest, repaying this with $112.36 he receives at the end of year two. Thus ownership of either asset permits the consumer to spend $212 on consumption at the end of year one. Similarly, if a consumer owning asset #2 wished to spend $106 at the end of year one and $112.36 at the end of year two, then at the end of year one he would spend $106 and lend the remaining $106 of the income from asset #2 at 6 percent interest to provide himself with $112.36 to spend at the end of year two. The same argument applies, whatever the time preferences of the consumer.

Since every consumer is indifferent between any two assets with the same discounted present values, it follows that these assets have the same price. In fact, Fisher established the following stronger result:

Given that there is a perfect lending market, the price of any asset is equal to the asset's DPV.

This statement follows almost immediately from the argument we have given. Suppose that asset #1 sells for more than $200. Then any consumer with $200 can lend out $100 for repayment one year from now and $100 for repayment two years from now, both at the interest rate of 6 percent, obtaining $106 at the end of the first year and $112.36 at the end of the second year. Clearly, no one would pay

more than $200 for asset #1, since the income stream associated with the asset can be duplicated by lending out $200.

If the asset sells for less than $200, it makes sense for any consumer to buy the asset by borrowing the purchase price of the asset (say $195). With $195 he purchases a time stream of income that is enough to pay off a loan of $200; hence there is a costless profit available to him. Since every consumer will take advantage of such an opportunity, the price of the asset is forced up to $200.

We thus arrive at a simple and straightforward answer to the question of how the consumer goes about choosing which assets to hold. Given that lending markets are perfect, in equilibrium each asset must sell at a price equal to its discounted present value. Under such circumstances, *the consumer is completely indifferent as to the types of assets he holds, regardless of his time preferences with respect to consumption.* An alternative way of saying this is that *in equilibrium on the asset market, investment in any asset yields a rate of return equal to the market rate of interest.*

This analysis applies to all assets for which a market exists in the economy. For capital goods or resources, the time stream of income associated with such assets is the stream of net rentals that the asset earns. For a share of stock in a business firm, the time stream of income is the stream of earnings per share of the firm. We put to one side for the moment the valuation of human capital; while markets exist for the services of human capital, there is no market on which the *asset* human capital is bought and sold. Human capital will require separate treatment.

An Example from Professional Sports

In 1959, Bill Veeck, the greatest of all sports entrepreneurs, bought the Chicago White Sox baseball team. In the course of his negotiations for purchase of the team, he came across a method of "sheltering" (avoiding) taxes on income from the team that has since been used by just about every owner who has acquired a sports team since 1959. In order to use the tax gimmick, it is necessary to acquire at least roughly 75 percent of the stock of a team. It is ironic that because of a dispute between the two main owners of the Sox, Veeck was not able to acquire enough stock to employ the gimmick he discovered.

The idea is simple. When a new owner acquires a sports team, he acquires membership in a sports league, a monopoly right to present games in the city in which the team is located, a share in the television revenues from the national contract of the league, a right to participate in the annual draft of new players, and a number of other valuable rights. He also acquires the player contracts owned by the team. The practice of the Internal Revenue Service is to allow the owner of a team to treat player contracts as a depreciable asset, like a building or a machine, with the cost of such contracts written off against taxable income over a period ranging from three to five or six years. No other asset of a team, other than the stadium if owned by the team, is depreciable.

When a team is sold, the assets are all sold as a unit; the new owner cannot acquire the television contract, for example, without acquiring player contracts and all the rest. The buyer or seller has the option of assigning as much or as little of the purchase price to each asset acquired as he wishes (subject only to review by the IRS or the court or by both). There is an enormous incentive to assign as much of the purchase price as possible to the player contracts, since they represent a depreciable asset.

To indicate the potential gains associated with writing off player contracts against taxable income, consider the following example. Team X is admitted to the National Football League as an expansion team, paying $8.5 million to join the league. For this amount, they acquire, among other things, the right to participate in the NFL television contract, paying $1.1 million per team per year. They also acquire 42 players from the other teams in the league, most of whom are old or second or third stringers. The owners of Team X assign $50 thousand to all of the nondepreciable assets of the team (including the television contract) and the rest of the purchase price, $8.45 million (less $700 thousand in deferred interest), to the 42 players. This means that there is a $7.75 million asset on the books of Team X that can be written off over a five-year period, roughly $1.55 million per year, in depreciation expenses.

An average NFL team earned $945 thousand before taxes in 1973, according to a report made public by the NFL owners. Assume for convenience that Team X makes $1 million before taxes. Assume also that the owners of the team are in the 70 percent marginal tax bracket; that is, each additional dollar of income costs 70 cents in taxes. The contrast between the case where depreciation of player contracts is allowed and the case where it is not is as follows.

If player contracts were not permitted to be
(continued on page 195)

depreciated, then the team would show an income before taxes of $1 million per year, giving an after-tax income to the owner of $300 thousand per year. Assuming the team earned this amount every year into the future, then with a discount rate of 10 percent, the team would be worth only $3 million ($300 thousand ÷ .1).

With depreciation of $1.55 million per year, the team shows an income before taxes of minus $550 thousand per year ($1 million − $1.55 million in depreciation). This means that the owner can use the $550 thousand loss of the team as a deduction from his income from other sources. Since his marginal tax rate is 70 percent, he saves $385 thousand per year in taxes (.7 × $550 thousand). The after-tax income of the owner from the team thus is $1,385 million ($1 million from the team plus $385 thousand tax savings on other income). After five years, income is subject to taxes; so from the sixth year on, the owner receives just $300 thousand after taxes. What is the value of the team with depreciation, assuming a 10 percent discount rate?

The formula is the following:

$$DPV = \frac{\$1.385M}{(1.1)} + \frac{\$1.385M}{(1.1)^2} + \frac{\$1.385M}{(1.1)^3}$$
$$+ \frac{\$1.385M}{(1.1)^4} + \frac{\$1.385M}{(1.1)^5} + \frac{\$3.0M}{(1.1)^5}$$

The first five terms give the present value during the five years of contract depreciation, while the last term takes the $3 million DPV figure for income without tax sheltering and discounts to the present. The DPV turns out to be roughly $7.12 million. The tax shelter has added $4.12 million to the value of the team, assuming a 10 percent rate of discount.

Now the paradoxical question. Is the tax shelter an advantage to an individual buying a sports team? The answer is no! A new owner gets no particular advantage from the tax shelter because the price of the team will be bid up to the point where the rate of return after taxes from the team will be the same as the rate of return that could be earned elsewhere in the market. The gainers from the discovery of the tax shelter are the owners who had teams before Bill Veeck discovered the gimmick!

Profit Maximization and Discounted Present Values

The theory of the competitive firm outlined in chapters 6, 7, and 8 was based on the assumption that firms are operated so as to maximize the net cash flows (profits) of the firm for the current period. This assumption must be revised to reflect the approach taken in the present chapter.

We continue to assume that consumers holding stock in a firm exercise effective control over the policies of the firm and that consumer stockholders are interested only in the incomes they can derive from their holdings. Decisions taken by the firm manager today may involve selling and buying commitments into future periods. What criterion will the firm manager adopt in making such intertemporal decisions? Clearly, the answer is that the firm will be operated in such a way as to *maximize the discounted present value of net cash flows for the firm.*

Why is this? Because decisions based on the criterion of maximizing DPV of the firm's net cash flows will in turn maximize the market value of each stockholder's holdings of the firm's stock. As we have seen, this procedure, combined with lending or borrowing operations in a perfect lending market, permits each stockholder to attain the most preferred time stream of consumption from his holdings.

In the special case where each period is simply a repeat of the previous period, the criterion of maximizing *DPV* of net cash flows reduces to the criterion of maximizing the value of net cash flows for the current period. We will take this as our "standard" case so that we will not have to rework the entire theory of the firm developed earlier. But when there are important variations over time, the theory of the firm has to be reformulated explicitly in terms of maximizing *DPV* in order to capture the essence of such intertemporal influences on the firm's operations.

Assets, Savings, and Rentals of Assets

The consumer actually makes three related decisions concerning assets. First, he decides how much to increase or decrease the total value of his net assets (his equity or wealth) through his decision as to how much to save. This decision depends on the market rate of interest, present and future prices for consumer goods, his present and future income, and his preferences with respect to the timing of consumption.

Second, he decides what kinds of assets he will hold, given his current wealth. As we have just seen, in equilibrium each asset sells for a price equal to the *DPV* of the earnings stream associated with the asset. Under this condition, the consumer is indifferent concerning his portfolio of assets. The decision as to the kinds of assets to hold is completely independent of the consumer's time preferences with respect to consumption. Such time preferences deter-

mine the change in value of his asset holdings, not the distribution of wealth over various assets.

Third, the consumer decides on the uses to which his assets are put. If he owns title to capital goods or natural resources, he rents such assets out at the highest rentals available. In turn, the rents that are earned by such assets determine the market price of the asset, since each one sells for the *DPV* of rentals that it commands. As we have seen in chapter 10, the rental earned by a unit of a capital good or resource is the marginal revenue product of services of the asset. This marginal revenue product then enters into the valuation of the asset through the *DPV* formula.

What goes on can be summarized as follows. When the consumer holding title, say, to a capital good, enters the market today, he contracts for the rental of the services of the capital good over future periods. Suppose these rentals are r_1 in the first period, r_2 in the second period, and so on, where the rentals are *net*; that is, these are payments above the depreciation of the capital good due to use of the good. Suppose there is a natural aging of the good (depreciation that occurs independently of the use of the good), so that at the end of T periods, the good has no further productive value. Then the capital good generates an income time stream $r_1, r_2, \ldots, r_T$. The market value today of the capital good is given by the *DPV* formula,

$$DPV = \frac{r_1}{(1+i)} + \frac{r_2}{(1+i)^2} + \cdots + \frac{r_T}{(1+i)_T}$$

= price of capital good.

Thus there is a direct link between the rental markets for capital goods and the asset market, where titles to capital goods are bought and sold and the price of capital goods is determined. But more than this, there are direct links between the rental markets for capital goods, the asset market where titles to existing capital goods are bought and sold, and the market for newly produced capital goods. We turn to the last market now.

The Market for Newly Produced Capital Goods

When consumers in the aggregate engage in positive savings, part of the income generated by economic activity in the society is diverted from the purchase of consumer nondurable goods and services to investment in newly produced capital goods (at least in a full employment economy). We continue to assume that consumers as savers invest directly in newly produced capital goods. This assumption bypasses the important role played in the real-world economy by financial intermediaries such as commercial banks, mutual funds, savings and loan associations, and investment banks. Such intermediaries collect individuals' savings, and invest them directly or indirectly in capital goods. Financial intermediaries exist because of economies of scale in investment activities related to the transactions costs involved in the purchase and rental of capital goods. When such transactions costs are negligible, savers invest directly in newly produced capital goods.

In the short run, capital goods are produced under the typical cost conditions implied by the law of variable proportions; the marginal cost curve of the firm producing a capital good is the firm's supply curve of the capital good, subject to the usual qualifications concerning the decision to shut down. Thus, the market supply curve for any type of capital good is obtained by summing the marginal cost curves of firms producing the good, as in figure 11-8. We use the symbol I to denote number of units of a newly produced capital good (an "investment good") and thus to distinguish such goods from the rental services of existing capital goods, which we have denoted by K throughout this text. s_I is the supply curve of a typical firm engaged in manufacturing investment goods, so that s_I is the marginal cost curve of the firm, above the minimum of AVC. S_I is the industry supply curve, with $S_I = \sum s_I$.

There are various kinds of capital goods, each with its own production costs and hence its own market supply schedule. With equilibrium on the asset market, each newly produced capital good sells for a price equal to the DPV of the income stream of net rentals associated with the good. To keep things as simple as possible, assume that there is only one kind of capital good produced, and that the capital good earns a constant net rental r each period into the indefinite future. Then

$$DPV = \frac{r}{i}, \text{ and } p_I = DPV = \frac{r}{i},$$

where p_I is the market price per unit of the newly produced capital good.

Equilibrium in the market for the newly produced capital good can be expressed as follows. We convert the supply curve S_I of units of the capital good into a supply curve relating the *value* of investment goods produced to the interest rate, in order to make the S_I function comparable with the $S(i)$ savings curve. The point is that savings available to purchase capital goods are expressed in dollars as a function of the interest rate, while the S_I curve gives

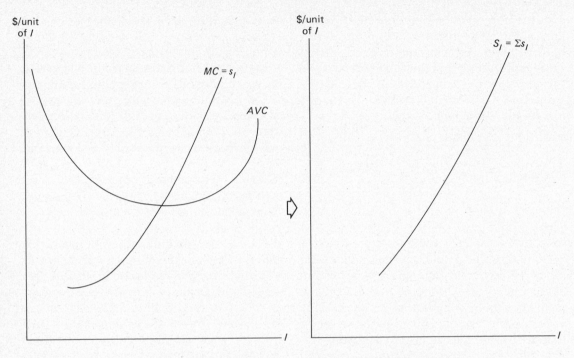

FIG. 11-8 *Supply of newly produced capital goods*

the number of units of the capital good available as a function of the price of that good, p_I. We have to convert S_I into dollar amounts in order to have the same units apply to both schedules.

The Demand and Supply for Newly Produced Capital Goods

The process of converting the supply curve of capital goods, plotted against the price of capital goods, into a curve that relates the value of capital goods produced to the interest rate is shown in the four-quadrant diagram, figure 11-9. In quadrant II, we plot the condition for equilibrium in the asset market: price equals

DPV. Given a constant rental of r_0 dollars per year per unit of the capital good, the equilibrium condition becomes

$$p_I = \frac{r_0}{i} \text{, or } p_I \cdot i = r_0.$$

The resulting curve in quadrant II is a rectangular hyperbola.

In quadrant III, the supply curve of newly produced capital goods S_I is plotted against the price per unit of a capital good, p_I. In quadrant IV, output of newly produced capital goods is converted into value terms by the relationship $V = p_I \cdot I$, where V is the value of such goods.

We wish to derive the curve $V(i)$, which appears in quadrant I and relates the value

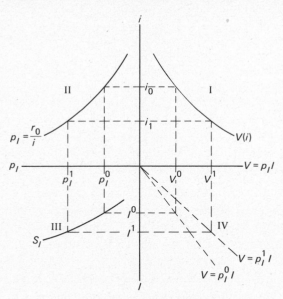

FIG. 11-9   *Deriving the V(i) curve*

leads to an increase in the *DPV* of the income stream generated by a capital good and hence an increase in its price. Since S_I increases as p_I increases, $V(i)$ slopes downward to the right.

Equilibrium in the market for newly produced capital goods occurs when demand equals supply. The demand (in value terms) for newly produced capital goods is the savings of consumers, while the supply is represented by the $V(i)$ curve. Hence equilibrium is determined by the intersection of $S(i)$ and $V(i)$, as indicated in figure 11-10. This figure shows how the equilibrium values of the interest rate and the value of newly produced capital goods (equals savings) are jointly determined by the $S(i)$ and $V(i)$ curves. Given the equilibrium values $\bar{i}, \bar{V}$, then the equilibrium price per unit of the capital good, $\bar{p}_I$ is solved from the relation

$$\bar{p}_I = \frac{r_0}{\bar{i}} .$$

In turn, this permits us to determine the equilibrium output of capital goods in physical terms, $\bar{I}$, from

$$\bar{I} = \frac{\bar{V}}{\bar{p}_I} .$$

of newly produced capital goods to the interest rate. To derive this curve, begin with the interest rate i_0. At this interest rate, equating *DPV* to p_I as in quadrant II implies that $p_I = p_I^0$. At the price p_I^0 per unit of the capital good, I^0 units of the capital good are supplied, using the supply curve S_I of quadrant III. Thus V is determined by the relation $V^0 = p_I^0 \cdot I^0$, from quadrant IV. Hence the value of output of newly produced capital goods, given the interest rate i_0, is V^0, and this represents one point on the $V(i)$ curve. A similar operation produces the value V^1 associated with the interest rate i_1. Carrying this out for all values of i results in the $V(i)$ curve sketched in quadrant I.

The $V(i)$ curve is interpreted as the value of newly produced capital goods that would be forthcoming as a function of the interest rate. With a given net rental for the services of capital goods, the curve slopes downward to the right, because a decrease in the interest rate

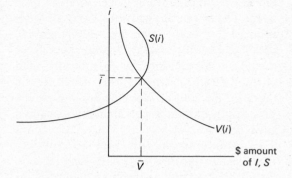

FIG. 11-10   *Equilibrium in the market for newly produced capital goods*

Savings-Investment Equilibrium— Comparative Statics

All equilibrium prices in a competitive economy are simultaneously determined, and all markets are linked to one another. Still, the savings-investment market is of special interest because the market rate of interest plays such a central role in directing economic activity between consumption and the accumulation of capital. The foregoing analysis of the market for newly produced capital goods shows that the level of production of these goods in an economy depends on the time preferences of consumers between current and future consumption, their expectations as to the rate of inflation, the marginal cost of producing capital goods, and the rentals that capital goods earn as inputs in the production process.

It is particularly interesting to trace the consequences for the economy of changes in the underlying factors that shape the $S(i)$ and $V(i)$ curves. For example, assume that preferences of consumers with respect to the timing of consumption become more impatient. Using the four-quadrant diagram of figure 11-9, we can trace out the results as in figure 11-11. The increase in impatience is reflected in the shift to the left of the $S(i)$ curve to $S'(i)$. At every value of i, consumers are less willing to save than before. This increase in impatience has the effect of increasing the equilibrium value of the interest rate from $\bar{i}$ to $\bar{i}'$, which lowers the price per unit of capital goods and results in a fall in output of newly produced capital goods from I to I'.

In contrast, assume that there is an increase in the marginal cost of producing capital goods. Figure 11-12 traces out the consequences. The increase in production costs shifts the S_I curve

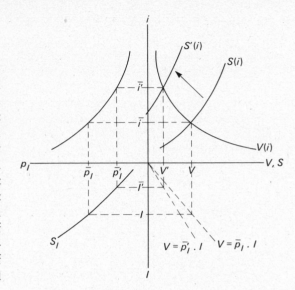

FIG. 11-11   *Effect of an increase in impatience*

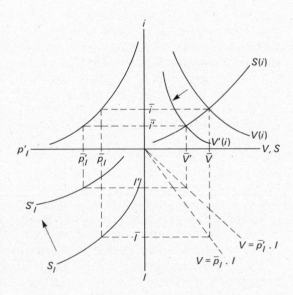

FIG. 11-12   *Effect of an increase in the marginal cost of producing capital goods*

to S'_1, resulting in a shift of the $V(i)$ curve to $V'(i)$. The result is a fall in the interest rate from $\bar{i}$ to $\bar{i}'$, an increase in the per unit price of capital goods, and a decrease in the number of units of the capital goods produced.

In a similar fashion, the effects of a change in the rental rate per unit of capital can be traced out, or the effects of a change in the expected rate of inflation.†

Human Capital and the Leisure-Consumption Choice

The decision of a consumer to acquire skills in order to increase his stock of human capital is a special kind of investment decision. His time preferences and wealth position, together with the market rate of interest, determine how rapidly he will accumulate assets through saving. Since all assets sell for their discounted present value, the consumer should be indifferent among them, including human capital. But we run into a problem at this point, because by law, no market exists in human capital, at least since slavery was abolished. A market exists in the *services* of human capital, labor time, but not in the asset that provides these services.

At any point in time, the consumer can compare the rate of return that he can earn by investing a part of his wealth in further training with what he earns by investing in other assets. All other assets sell at their dis-

counted present values. In other words, investment in such assets earns precisely the market rate of interest, i. So long as an additional dollar invested in human capital earns in excess of i percent, the consumer furthers his own interests by engaging in the investment, that is, in pursuing his training further.

Investment in training generally results in an increase in income over an extended period of time, and the question then comes up: What do we mean by "the rate of return from investment in human capital"? To make this clear, we introduce the concept of the *internal rate of return* on an investment.

Suppose that the cost of an asset is B dollars and that the asset generates a stream of income of r_1 , . . . , r_t dollars in periods $1, \ldots, t$. Then the *internal rate of return from that asset is defined as the largest number δ that satisfies the following equation:*

$$B = \frac{r_1}{(1 + \delta)} + \frac{r_2}{(1 + \delta)^2} + \cdots + \frac{r_t}{(1 + \delta)^t}$$

In other words, *the internal rate of return δ is the largest number such that, when used as a discount rate, it sets the discounted present value of an asset equal to its cost.* For assets traded on competitive markets, the cost of the asset equals its market price; assuming a perfect lending market, δ turns out to be equal to i, the market rate of interest. But since human capital is not priced on the market, a dollar's worth of additional investment in training this period may yield an income time stream with an internal rate of return larger than i. The rule for optimal investment in human capital on the part of any consumer is to *invest that sum in the current period such that the internal rate of return δ on the last dollar invested*

---

†Our comparative statics analysis ignores the fact that changes in the market for capital goods generally have effects on the rental rate r. We have ignored such effects to keep this analysis as simple as possible.

in human capital equals i, the market rate of interest.

By following this rule, the consumer guarantees that he is choosing among alternative assets—stocks, titles to capital goods and resources, and human capital—in such a way as to maximize the value of his asset holdings. By borrowing and lending in a perfect lending market he can convert this maximal wealth position into the most preferred time stream (pattern) of consumption available to him.

Investment in Consumer Durable Goods

Finally, we should say something about the decision to buy a consumer durable good, such as a house. A house or a car or any other consumer durable good can be thought of as an asset that yields a stream of services to the consumer over time. The appropriate value to attach to such services is their opportunity cost; for example, the services of a house for a year should be valued at the amount that the consumer would be willing to give up to obtain these services for this period of time.

The rule for investing in a consumer durable then is the same as that for investing in a capital good: the consumer durable good should be purchased so long as the *DPV* of the stream of services from the good (using opportunity cost to measure the value of services) is at least as great as the market price of the good. Allocation of funds to the purchase of consumer durable goods should be carried to the point where the last dollar invested in consumer durables yields the market rate of interest as the rate of return, again using opportunity cost to measure the value of the services obtained from the consumer durable.

Summary

Each consumer has a preference ranking over time streams of consumption. The law of diminishing marginal rate of time preference is assumed to characterize the indifference map of the consumer. Choices as to the timing of consumption by a consumer reflect his time preferences, his current and expected future income, the level of the interest rate, and current and expected future price levels. An increase in the interest rate leads to income and substitution effects on consumption and saving. The substitution effect always leads to less current consumption; the direction of the income effect depends upon whether the consumer is a borrower or a lender. For a consumer with a two-period horizon who is a borrower, an increase in the interest rate reduces borrowing, but the effect on lenders is ambiguous. For lenders, an increase in the interest rate increases saving when the substitution effect dominates, and leads to a decrease in saving when the income effect dominates.

Given a perfect lending market, each asset sells at a price equal to the *DPV* of the income stream of the asset, using the market rate of interest as the discount rate. Equivalently, every asset sells at a price such that investment in any asset yields a rate of return equal to the market rate of interest.

In a competitive economy, the equilibrium value of the interest rate is such that the savings by consumers at that interest rate are equal to the value of newly produced capital goods forthcoming at that interest rate. The interest rate changes in response to changes in (1) prospective rentals of capital goods, (2) price and income expectations of consumers, (3) marginal costs of producing capital goods, and (4) tastes of consumers so far as impatience is concerned.

Investment in human capital and in consumer durable goods follow the same general rules as investment in capital goods. The consumer should allocate his funds to investment in either human capital or durables to the point where the last dollar invested yields a rate of return equal to the market rate of interest.

Problems

1. In the United States, by far the largest harvest of corn occurs in the Midwest in August of each year. The annual pattern of corn prices (dollars per bushel) appears as follows:

August	November	February	May	August
$2.00	$2.09	$2.18	$2.27	$2.00

   How do you explain this pattern of corn prices? How might the pattern differ for other crops?

2. You expect interest rates to fall from 9 percent to 6 percent. Suppose that a ninety-day Treasury bill is selling to yield 9 percent, as is a one-year Treasury note. Which would you buy and why? What is your speculative profit from buying a bill or a note, assuming each is selling for $1,000?

3. Analyze the effects, on saving behavior of a consumer (both as lender and as borrower), of a change from a world of stable prices to one in which prices are expected to increase.

4. Use your analysis in problem 3 and the four-quadrant diagram involving $S(i)$ and $V(i)$ to determine how a change from stable prices to inflation affects the equilibrium value of the interest rate.

5. Calculate the market equilibrium values for the following assets, assuming the market rate of interest is 10 percent.

   a. An acre of land yielding $100 per year in rent after all expenses indefinitely into the future.

   b. A bond that pays $100 interest per year for two years, and is paid off at $1000 at the end of two years.

   c. A share of stock that currently earns $10 per year, with earnings expected to increase at a 6 percent rate indefinitely into the future.

   d. A building that will earn $100 per year for two years and then will earn $50 per year indefinitely into the future.

12
General Equilibrium
of a Competitive Economy

We are finally in a position to complete the first job we set out to do: to describe how a perfectly competitive economy works. In this chapter, we will see first how flow markets and asset markets interrelate and then how activities on these markets jointly determine what goods are produced in the economy, how they are produced, and who gets them.

To keep things in focus, you may find it helpful to review figures 1-1 and 1-2, which depict the structure of markets in a competitive economy. Thus far, we have looked at each of these markets in isolation—the rental market for capital goods and resources, the labor market, the market for consumer goods, the market for newly produced capital goods, and the asset markets. Conditions have been derived that characterize equilibrium in each of these markets. When prices are such that all of these markets are *simultaneously* in equilibrium, then we say that the perfectly competitive economy is in a state of *general equilibrium*. This is the topic of the present chapter.

General Equilibrium—A Definition

A general equilibrium of a competitive economy occurs for a set of prices when commodity bundles and asset portfolios of consumers to-gether with input-output choices of firms satisfy the following conditions.

1. Each consumer maximizes his utility, subject to his budget constraint, treating prices as given; as a part of that process, he distributes his asset holdings and supplies services of capital goods and resources he owns in such a way as to maximize the DPV of his holdings.

2. Each firm maximizes the DPV of net cash flows over the input-output combinations available to it as specified by the firm's production map, treating prices as given.

3. The resulting supplies and demands are such that all markets in the economy are simultaneously cleared; that is, market demand equals market supply in each market in the economy.

If the economy is in a state of *long-run general equilibrium*, then two other conditions hold.

4. Each firm in the economy earns only normal profits on its operations; there are no excess profits earned anywhere in the economy.

5. No reproducible capital good or resource earns a quasi-rent.

This formal definition provides a starting point in our investigation of general equilibrium, and its implications for the production of goods and services and the distribution of them among consumers. We begin by examining the way in which the level of income for the society is determined.

Measure of Income and Output for a Competitive Economy

As earlier chapters indicate, all of the income earned in a competitive economy goes to consumers. Consumers supply all of the labor time, own all of the capital goods and resources, and hold title to all of the shares of firms in the society. Let M denote income for a typical consumer. Then M is given by

M = wage income + rental income
    + profits (based on ownership of shares)
    + interest income on notes held
    − interest cost on notes outstanding.

All income earned by a consumer is spent, either on consumption goods and services; or on newly produced capital goods, consumer durables or human capital ("savings"). Thus

$$M = c + s$$

where c represents expenditures on consumption and s represents savings.

If we sum income earned over all consumers, we obtain a measure of gross income for the economy as a whole. Let GI denote gross income, which is given by

$$GI = \text{wages} + \text{rentals} + \text{profits}.$$

Interest income for the economy as a whole is zero, since interest earned by one consumer always represents an interest cost for some other consumer in the society.

Gross national product (GNP) is defined as the value of all *final* goods and services produced in the economy. It is obtained by summing expenditures of all consumers; hence

$$GNP = C + \mathcal{I}$$

where $C = \Sigma c$ is aggregate expenditures on consumption goods and services and $\mathcal{I}$ is the value of all newly produced capital goods for the society.[†] Because savings of consumers are invested in newly produced capital goods,

$$S = \mathcal{I},$$

where S is aggregate savings for the economy (that is, $S = \Sigma s$). Then it follows that

$$GNP = GI.$$

National income, NI, may be defined as the net income earned for the economy—that is, gross income less expenditures incurred to offset wear and tear due to use of capital goods (depreciation). To obtain NI, we replace rental income in GI by *net* rental income (rental income less depreciation). Thus,

$$NI = \text{wages} + \text{net rental income} + \text{profits}.$$

Similarly, net national product, NNP, is GNP less depreciation so that

$$NNP = C + \mathcal{I}_N$$

where $\mathcal{I}_N$ is the value of *net* output of newly produced capital goods, with

$$\mathcal{I}_N = \mathcal{I} - \text{depreciation}.$$

Hence $NI = NNP.$

With asset markets in equilibrium, investment in any asset yields a rate of return equal

---

[†]*GNP* excludes the value of intermediate products and raw materials used up in the process of producing final goods (consumer goods and services and newly produced capital goods) because of double counting problems.

to the market rate of interest. Let W denote the aggregate nonhuman wealth of the economy. That is, W is the value of all capital goods and resources (including resources invested in organizing firms). Then NNP can also be written as

$$C + \mathcal{I}_N = NNP = \text{wages} + Wi = NI$$

where i is the market rate of interest.

Thus a distinction can be drawn between wage income and "property" income; national income is the sum of these. Historically, wage income accounts for about 70 percent of NI, with property income accounting for the remaining 30 percent.

We can relate certain of these measures to the operation of a competitive economy through the economy's production possibility set.

Edgeworth-Bowley Production Box for the Economy

Suppose that two goods, labeled X and Y, are produced in the economy. To keep things within the confines of two-dimensional graphs, assume that there are two firms, with production maps as in figure 12-1.† L_X, K_X refer to labor and capital allocated to the production of X, and L_Y, K_Y refer to labor and capital allocated to the production of Y. Each of the firms is assumed to operate under constant returns to scale with isoquants bounding convex sets. In other words, the law of diminishing marginal rate of substitution between inputs holds for both X and Y. As drawn, the isoquants reflect the fact that X is more *capital-intensive* than Y: given any wage/rental ratio, the cost-minimizing capital/labor ratio in producing X

---

†Alternatively, each industry has many firms with identical production maps.

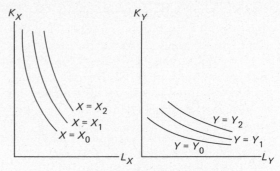

FIG. 12-1   *Production maps for X and Y*

is larger than the capital/labor ratio in producing Y. Equivalently, Y is more *labor-intensive* than X.

Assume that there are L_0 units of labor and K_0 units of capital available to the economy. We construct an Edgeworth-Bowley box diagram (fig. 12-2) to indicate how these amounts of capital and labor will be allocated between the production of X and Y in a competitive economy. The box has length L_0 and height K_0. The southwest corner of the box represents the origin for X, while the northeast corner is the origin for Y. The production maps for X and Y are superimposed on the box. As the arrows indicate, labor and capital used in the production of X are measured from the X origin, while labor and capital used in the production of Y are measured from the Y origin.

Any point in the box such as the point A can be regarded as an allocation of the L_0 units of labor and K_0 units of capital between the production of X and Y. Thus at A, $\bar{L}_X$ units of labor and $\bar{K}_X$ units of capital are allocated to the production of X, with $\bar{L}_Y$ labor and $\bar{K}_Y$ capital being used in producing Y. With that allocation, output of Y is Y_2 units and output of X is X_1 units.

Clearly, the allocation of capital and labor between X and Y at the point A is inefficient: more X *and* more Y can be produced by reallo-

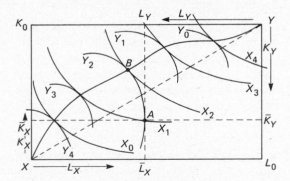

FIG. 12-2   *Edgeworth-Bowley box diagram*

cating the L_0 units of labor and K_0 units of capital available to the economy. In particular, by moving toward the northwest (allocating more capital to X and more labor to Y), we can get on higher isoquants for both X and Y. For example, moving from A to B results in the same output of Y but a larger output of X.

The efficient allocations of capital and labor for the economy lie on the curve that goes through the tangencies of X and Y isoquants. Each such allocation is efficient in the sense that it is not possible to increase the output of X without decreasing the output of Y (and vice versa), given that labor available to the economy is L_0 and capital available is K_0. For example, B is efficient. Any movement away from B that increases Y decreases X; and any movement that increases X decreases Y.

We have drawn a dotted line between the X and Y origins. Points on that line represent allocations of capital and labor to X and Y such that the capital/labor ratios in both X and Y are K_0/L_0. Points above the dotted line (in particular those on the efficient curve) indicate that K_X/L_X is greater than K_0/L_0, while K_Y/L_Y is less than K_0/L_0.

If X is more capital-intensive than Y, then any efficient allocation of capital and labor between

X and Y will involve a larger capital/labor ratio in the production of X than in the production of Y, assuming both goods are produced in positive amounts.

Tangency of isoquants in the Edgeworth-Bowley box diagram is equivalent to the condition that the ratio MP_L/MP_K in producing X equals the ratio MP_L/MP_K in producing Y. If all firms in an economy face competitive input markets, then

$$\frac{MP_L}{MP_K} = \frac{w}{r}$$

for each firm, since costs are minimized at any output level. But with competitive input markets, w and r are the same for all firms. It follows that so long as input markets are competitive, the economy will operate at an efficient production mix, that is, at a point representing a tangency of isoquants in the Edgeworth-Bowley box diagram.

The Edgeworth-Bowley diagram is the basic tool involved in the construction of the production possibility set for the economy.

The Production Possibility Set for the Economy

Consider again an economy with fixed amounts L_0 and K_0 of labor and capital. The production possibility set for an economy producing the two goods X and Y is the set of all combinations (X, Y) that are technologically feasible, given the fixed amounts L_0, K_0 of resources available to the society. Figure 12-3 depicts the production possibility set for a society.

The outer boundary of the production possibility set is called the *production possibility curve* or the *transformation curve* for the economy. Any point on the transformation curve represents an efficient output of X and Y, since it is not possible to increase the output of Y

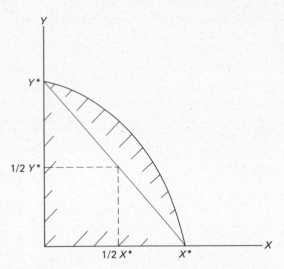

FIG. 12-3   *The production possibility set*

Y if all resources in the society (L_0, K_0) are devoted solely to the production of Y. Similarly, the intercept X* gives the maximum possible production of X when all resources are devoted just to the production of X. We are assuming that both X and Y are produced under constant returns to scale. This means that allocating half as much inputs to X (or Y) results in half as much output. Hence if we allocated $\frac{1}{2}L^0$, $\frac{1}{2}K^0$ to Y and $\frac{1}{2}L^0$, $\frac{1}{2}K^0$ to X, we can obtain the point $\frac{1}{2}X^*$, $\frac{1}{2}Y^*$ indicated on the dotted line drawn between X* and Y*. Constant returns to scale mean that we can always do at least as well as the outputs on that dotted line.

But if certain inputs are better at producing one output than another, then the economy can do better than simply move down the dotted line between X* and Y*. In the case we are examining, X is relatively capital-intensive while Y is relatively labor-intensive. In moving from the point Y*, increasing the output of X while decreasing the output of Y can be accomplished most efficiently by withdrawing proportionately more capital than labor from the production of Y, economizing on the factor specialized to producing Y. By allocating disproportionate amounts of labor to the production of Y and disproportionate amounts of capital to the production of X, output combinations can be achieved that are superior to those lying on the dotted line leading to the characteristic "bulge" in the society's production possibility curve. Again, this is reflected in the efficient curve in the Edgeworth-Bowley box, which lies above the dotted line representing equal factor intensities for the two products.

In industries where there are increasing returns to scale, the production possibility curve might bulge inward rather than outward, as can be seen in the case where Y is produced under

without reducing the output of X (and vice versa) along the transformation curve. Thus, going back to the Edgeworth-Bowley box, the combinations (X_0, Y_4), (X_1, Y_3), (X_2, Y_2), (X_3, Y_1), and (X_4, Y_0) will all lie on the transformation curve. In fact, each and every point between X* and Y* on the economy's transformation curve is an output combination that represents a tangency of isoquants in the Edgeworth-Bowley box. Points not on the transformation curve involve inefficient allocations of capital and labor; given any such interior point of the possibility set, there are feasible output points where more of both X and Y can be obtained.

As drawn, the production possibility set "bulges" outward between the intercepts on the X and Y axes. This configuration reflects certain characteristics of the technology and deserves to be explained in detail.

The intercept of the production possibility curve on the Y axis, Y*, gives the output of increasing returns and X is produced under constant returns. Allocating $\frac{1}{2}L_0$ and $\frac{1}{2}K_0$ to X allows the economy to achieve $\frac{1}{2}X^*$, but increasing returns to Y means that $\frac{1}{2}L_0$, $\frac{1}{2}K_0$ yield less than $\frac{1}{2}Y^*$. Whether specialization of inputs more than offsets this inward bulge when there are increasing returns to scale depends upon the particular technologies for producing X and Y. In a competitive economy, of course, increasing returns to scale are excluded as a possibility.

The Marginal Rate of Transformation for the Society As we move along the production possibility curve, the slope $\Delta Y/\Delta X$ of the curve becomes steeper and steeper. For a one unit increase in the output of X, the society has to sacrifice more and more units of Y, the larger is the output of X. When the output of X is small, the society can shift out of the production of Y large amounts of K, the factor specialized to X, without much loss in terms of Y. Beyond some point, however, in order to increase the output of X further, it becomes necessary to shift to the production of X proportionately more labor, a resource that is good at producing Y and poor at producing X. Thus as the output of X expands, the cost of adding a unit of X to output increases, where that cost is measured in terms of units of Y given up by the economy.

We refer to the absolute value of the slope of the production possibility curve as the *marginal rate of transformation of X into Y (MRT)* for the society—that is,

$$MRT = -\frac{\Delta Y}{\Delta X}.$$

In the typical case, the slope becomes more and more negative as X increases; that is, the production possibility set is a convex set. Or we can say that the society faces *an increasing marginal rate of transformation of X into Y.*

Maximizing GNP

Returning to the measures of output of a competitive economy, the following result holds:

Let L_0, K_0 be the fixed amounts of labor and capital available to the society. At a competitive equilibrium, the value of *GNP* for the society is maximized over the production possibility set associated with L_0, K_0 amounts of labor and capital.

The idea behind this assertion is basically very simple. Under competitive conditions, the firms producing X and Y maximize profits, treating the prices of inputs and outputs as fixed. Assuming independence among firms, the production of X is not affected by operations involved in producing Y, and conversely. Profits in producing X are

$$\pi_X = p_X X - wL_X - rK_X$$

while profits in producing Y are

$$\pi_Y = p_Y Y - wL_Y - rK_Y$$

Each firm independently maximizes profits, with the result that $\pi_X + \pi_Y$ is maximized as well. But with L and K fixed at L_0, K_0, at a competitive equilibrium we must have $L_X + L_Y = L_0$ and $K_X + K_Y = K_0$, since all markets must be cleared. Thus

$$\pi_X + \pi_Y = p_X X + p_Y Y - wL_0 - rK_0.$$

Because L_0 and K_0 are fixed, maximizing $\pi_X + \pi_Y$ amounts to maximizing *GNP*, where

$$GNP = p_X X + p_Y Y.$$

This maximization takes place over the feasible set of (X, Y) combinations, which in turn

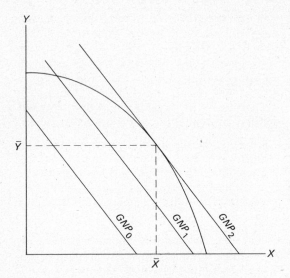

FIG. 12-4   *Maximizing GNP over the production possibility set*

At a competitive equilibrium, the marginal rate of transformation of X into Y equals the ratio p_X/p_Y. Equivalently, at a competitive equilibrium, the cost to the society (in terms of units of Y given up) to increase the output of X by one unit is equal to the number of units of Y that exchanges for one unit of $X(p_X/p_Y)$.

What we have arrived at, then, is the conclusion that prices at a competitive equilibrium accurately reflect the underlying production costs to the society, and that it is not possible to increase the value of output, given the competitive prices, beyond that achieved by the competitive system.

The Competitive Equilibrium— A Graphical Picture

In a many-consumer economy with production, two-dimensional graphs are simply too restrictive to capture all that is going on at a competitive equilibrium. To indicate at least a part of the picture, let us consider a one-consumer economy, operated as a competitive system, where all profits as well as all earnings of labor and capital go to the consumer. The economy produces two goods, X and Y, using capital and labor. Suppose that capital and labor are available in the fixed quantities K_0 and L_0. Then income M for the consumer is given by

$$M = wL_0 + rK_0 + \pi_X + \pi_Y.$$

$\pi_X + \pi_Y$ in turn is given by

$$\pi_X + \pi_Y = p_X X + p_Y Y - (wL_0 + rK_0);$$

hence $M = p_X X + p_Y Y.$

In brief, the budget line for the consumer is the economy's GNP.

At a competitive equilibrium (fig. 12-5), the consumer maximizes utility subject to his budget constraint, profits are maximized in both

is simply the production possibility set for the economy. We show this graphically in figure 12-4. For given prices p_X, p_Y, $GNP = p_X X + p_Y Y$.† The combinations of X and Y associated with values of GNP of GNP_0, GNP_1, GNP_2 are indicated by the straight lines. The slope of any line along which GNP is a constant is $-p_X/p_Y$. A maximum of GNP over the production possibility set occurs at $(\overline{X}, \overline{Y})$ where the "iso-GNP" line is tangent to the production possibility curve, with $GNP = GNP_2 = p_X \overline{X} + p_Y \overline{Y}$.

Because of the tangency condition, we also have the following result.

_____

†Of course at a competitive equilibrium, prices p_X, p_Y, w, and r are all determined by the market-clearing conditions. But given the equilibrium prices, GNP is maximized over the production possibility set, as indicated in figure 12-4.

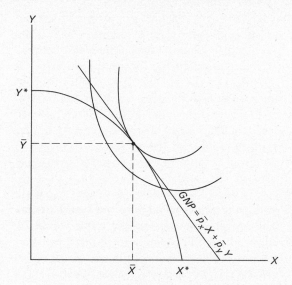

FIG. 12-5 *Competitive equilibrium*

the production of X and the production of Y, and all markets are cleared. The situation shown in figure 12-5 can be described as a competitive equilibrium characterized by outputs $(\overline{X}, \overline{Y})$ and prices $(\overline{p}_X, \overline{p}_Y)$. Given the indifference map of the consumer and given the production possibility set for the economy, then at the prices $(\overline{p}_X, \overline{p}_Y)$ the *GNP* line is such that the consumer maximizes utility by choosing the bundle $(\overline{X}, \overline{Y})$, while profit-maximizing firms will produce the same bundle $(\overline{X}, \overline{Y})$. In brief, at the prices $(\overline{p}_X, \overline{p}_Y)$, utility maximization and profit maximization are consistent with one another in the sense that the markets for X and Y are both cleared.

At any other ratio of prices for X and Y, the *GNP* line would have a different slope, and hence the profit-maximizing output point would not be the same as the utility-maximizing point, so that markets would not be cleared. This means that for the case pictured in figure 12-5, the competitive equilib-

rium is *unique* in the sense that only at the price ratio $\overline{p}_X / \overline{p}_Y$ and the outputs $(\overline{X}, \overline{Y})$ does a competitive equilibrium occur. At a competitive equilibrium, the price ratio between X and Y is determined, but not the absolute prices of the two goods. If $\overline{p}_X = \$1$, $\overline{p}_Y = \$3$ is an equilibrium pair of prices, so is any positive multiple of these, for example, $\overline{p}_X = \$5$, $\overline{p}_Y = \$15$.

Tangency of the consumer's indifference curve to the transformation curve implies that the marginal rate of substitution *MRS* between X and Y for the consumer equals the marginal rate of transformation *MRT* between X and Y for the economy. *What the consumer is willing to give up (in terms of units of Y) to obtain one more unit of X equals the cost to the society (in terms of units of Y) of increasing the output of X by one more unit.*

The production possibility set for the economy is determined by the technology (the production maps for X and Y), together with the amounts of L and K available to the economy. Given the production possibility set, the preference map of the consumer determines the output mix $(\overline{X}, \overline{Y})$ and the price ratio $\overline{p}_X / \overline{p}_Y$ that occur at a competitive equilibrium. This mix of outputs in turn determines the allocation of capital and labor services between producing X and Y, which in turn determines the marginal revenue products of these inputs. Since $MRP_L = w$ and $MRP_K = r$, this means that the wage rate and the rental rate are determined as well, which together with profits determines the income of the consumer.

Admittedly, we have not taken the asset market into consideration. We simply do not have enough leeway in a two-dimensional graph to incorporate savings, investment, and asset decisions. But the graph at least illustrates certain features of the competitive equilibrium under highly simplified assumptions.

The Competitive Equilibrium—
A Change in Tastes

Staying with our simple one-consumer two-good diagram, suppose that there is a change in tastes such that at every price ratio p_X/p_Y, the consumer prefers more of good X. What can we say about the new equilibrium relative to the old?

Figure 12-6 shows the change in equilibrium. The shift in consumer tastes is indicated by the steeper sloping solid indifference curves relative to the original curves. The consumer is willing to give up more Y to obtain a unit of X than previously. Predictably this shift in tastes leads to a new equilibrium $(\overline{X}', \overline{Y}')$ where the amount of X produced and consumed is greater than at $(\overline{X}, \overline{Y})$, while the output and consumption of Y has declined.

At the new equilibrium, the slope of the GNP line is steeper than before, meaning that p_X/p_Y

is larger than at the old equilibrium—the price of Y has fallen relative to the price of X. This change has repercussions on the factor markets as well. Y is more labor-intensive than X; hence the effect of the change in tastes has been to shift the demand curve for labor to the left, and the one for capital to the right. The wage rate w falls relative to the rental rate r, and a larger percent of the society's income takes the form of property income rather than wage income.

In a more comprehensive model, we could follow the implications into the asset markets. The higher rental for capital goods would increase the DPV of such goods at a constant interest rate and would thus encourage an increased output of capital goods, which in turn would tend to lower the rental over the long run. Such changes in capital stocks would in turn shift the production possibility curve outward to the right as the economy moves toward a long-run equilibrium.

The use of the production possibility curve approach substantially simplifies the graphics of the competitive equilibrium. But it should be pointed out that the supplies of labor services and services of capital goods in general depend upon prices just as do the supplies of outputs. This dependence has been suppressed in our treatment thus far, but will be taken up later in this chapter. One way to think of the production possibility set approach is this. At a competitive equilibrium, prices of inputs and outputs determine the supplies of inputs that will be forthcoming. It is these supplies that we use as the fixed amounts L_0, K_0 of input services in constricting the production possibility set.

In a one-consumer economy, certain crucial aspects of the competitive equilibrium are suppressed. In particular, the question "who gets

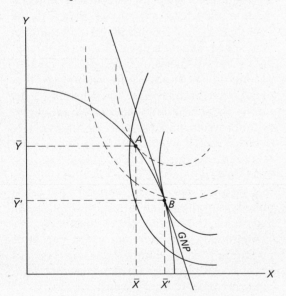

FIG. 12-6   *Competitive equilibrium—
a change in tastes*

the goods that are produced" requires explicit examination in a somewhat more general framework.

Income Distribution and the Competitive Equilibrium

Probably the most controversial aspect of a private ownership economy is the distribution of income among the members of the society. In our functioning economy, income is distributed in a highly skewed fashion, with the bulk of the population getting only a relatively small fraction of total income. Things are not quite so ideal as in a competitive system; monopoly, government influence, plain crookedness, racial and sexual discrimination, and other factors distort the distribution of income. But what happens in a competitive system? In particular, what can be said about the distribution of income among individuals at a competitive equilibrium?

In a perfectly competitive economy, each factor of production is paid the marginal revenue product that it produces, wherever it is employed. All labor of a certain type earns the same wage rate, for example. Thus if all income in the society were earned by labor, and if each consumer had the same tastes with respect to leisure-consumption alternatives, and if all labor were of the same type, then income would be distributed equally among all members of the population. In reality, however, there are other factors of production besides labor; tastes do differ among individuals with respect to leisure and consumption; and there are wide differences in the skills of different laborers. These factors lead to disparities in the distribution of income in a competitive economy.

Consider first the factors of production other than labor—such as the services of capital goods and the services of land. These factors contribute to output just as labor-time does, and payments to the owners of them represent a part of the total income stream earned by individuals in the society. To a certain extent, ownership of assets like capital goods and land is a matter of being born into the right family. If you are unlucky, you begin with nothing. Of course that is not the end of the story; accumulation of assets by individuals through savings decisions reflects not only their initial endowment of assets but also their preferences between current and future consumption. Hence over time, we will find "property income" (income derived from sale of the services of resources and capital goods) being concentrated in the hands of those who start with lots of assets and/or those who are most willing to sacrifice present consumption for future consumption. There is no question but that the disparity in asset holdings among individuals constitutes a major source of inequality in the income distribution in any private ownership society.

Secondly, those who prefer more leisure to consumption than others, given the same wage rate for labor and the same holdings of wealth, will have lower incomes. But this fact is really somewhat misleading. After all, a comprehensive measure of "income" should include the benefits derived from leisure as well as from consumption, and there is no implication that people who prefer leisure to consumption are therefore less "well off" than people who have higher money incomes. In fact, if an individual freely chooses more leisure and thus less income, he is certainly better off than if he were forced somehow to reverse his choice; his choice in and of itself *reveals* that he is better off with more leisure and less income.

Finally, certain individuals possess skills that have a higher market value than the skills possessed by other individuals. Some of these are inherent in the individual. No matter how hard someone tries, he simply cannot duplicate the innate skills of another person. In such a case, the gifted individual is earning an economic rent, and any such rent represents a source of disparity in the distribution of income among individuals. On the other hand, differences in skills can also reflect differences among individuals in their stocks of human capital, derived through investment in training and education.

As we have seen, in a competitive world with perfect lending markets, each individual invests in his own human capital to the point where the last dollar invested earns an internal rate of return equal to the market rate of interest. What this amounts to saying is that, independently of the attitudes of individuals as to the choice between present and future consumption, all of the income-earning possibilities inherent in one's own human capabilities (including leisure as a form of income) will be exploited as fully as with any other asset, so long as we stay within the confines of a perfectly competitive model. Any major differences that arise among individuals of roughly equal earning potential would reflect only the preferences of the individuals between leisure and income, with the more leisure-prone individual setting his investment in human capital at a lower level than the more consumption-prone individual. Imperfections in capital markets that restrict the amount that can be borrowed to finance investment in human capital represent important qualifications to the conclusions derived here in the context of the competitive model, of course.

Euler's Theorem and Income Distribution

Relative to the issue of income distribution in a perfectly competitive economy, there is a mathematical theorem that offers some insights into the way in which a competitive system allocates its rewards. We first state the theorem and then indicate the applicability to payments to factors of production.

Euler's Theorem: Suppose that
$$y = f(x_1, \ldots, x_n)$$
is a function that is positively homogeneous of degree k, that is,
$$f(ax_1, \ldots ax_n) \equiv a^k(x_1, \ldots, x_n),$$
for any positive constant a. Then the following rule holds:

$$kf(x_1, \ldots, x_n) \equiv \frac{\Delta y}{\Delta x_1} \cdot x_1$$
$$+ \frac{\Delta y}{\Delta x_2} \cdot x_2 + \ldots + \frac{\Delta y}{\Delta x_n} \cdot x_n. \quad (1)$$

Consider an economic interpretation of Euler's theorem. Let y be output of some good by a firm and let $x_1, \ldots, x_n$ be the amounts of inputs #1, #2, ..., #n employed in producing the good. Thus $f(x_1, \ldots, x_n)$ is the production function of the firm, stating the amounts of output that may be derived from various efficient combinations of inputs employed by the firm. $\Delta y/\Delta x_1$ is then the marginal product of input #1, representing the increase in output from adding one more unit of input #1, with a similar interpretation for all other $\Delta y/\Delta x_i$.

Thus Euler's theorem states that
$$k \cdot y = MP_1 \cdot x_1 + \ldots + MP_n \cdot x_n, \quad (2)$$

where y is the output associated with inputs $x_1, \ldots, x_n$. If we multiply on both sides of this equality by p, the price per unit of output, we obtain

$$k(py) = (pMP_1)x_1 + \ldots + (pMP_n)x_n. \quad (3)$$

That is,

$$k(py) = MRP_1x_1 + \ldots + MRP_n x_n. \quad (4)$$

In a competitive system, each input is paid its marginal revenue product. Hence the right-hand side of equation 4 gives total payments to factors employed by the firm. The left-hand side is equal to k, the degree of homogeneity, times the revenue of the firm. Hence we have

$$k(TR) = TC.$$

Thus we can conclude:

1. If the firm operates under constant returns to scale, so that $k = 1$, then revenue for the firm equals total payments to the factors of production employed by the firm.

2. If $0 < k < 1$, so that the firm operates under decreasing returns to scale, then total payments to factors are less than revenue of the firm.

3. If $k > 1$, so that the firm operates under increasing returns to scale, total payments to factors exceed revenue of the firm.

Case 1 is sometimes summarized by the statement "under constant returns to scale, there is exhaustion of total product." This means that in a competitive economy, constant returns to scale imply that all revenues earned by the firm are allocated to the factors of production employed by the firm. In contrast, under decreasing returns, the firm earns a profit

above payments to factors, while under increasing returns, the firm suffers a loss after paying factors on the basis of the values of marginal products of factors.

Euler's theorem thus provides another way to view the problem of increasing returns to scale in a competitive environment. If a firm operates under increasing returns, then adopting a competitive pricing policy with respect to both output and the inputs hired by the firm would force the firm out of business. Increasing returns to scale are again judged incompatible with a competitive system of markets.

In long-run equilibrium, each firm sets output at the minimum of $LRAC$, and so each firm operates under "constant returns to scale in the small," and the industry supply curve reflects constant costs. Hence case 1 is appropriate for the analysis of long-run competitive equilibrium, and it follows that the distribution of receipts either by the firm or by the industry is completely accounted for by the fact that each factor of production is paid its marginal revenue product. Thus there is no "unexplained residual" to account for, no receipts of the firm that are not automatically allocated to factors of production in return for services rendered by such factors. In this sense, it may be said that the competitive model explains not only how prices and outputs are determined for all goods and services, but also how incomes of individuals are generated and, taken together with the asset holdings of individuals, why the distribution of income among individuals is what it is.

Because industries differ in their factor intensities, the distribution of income depends in part on the pattern of production in the economy; and this pattern in turn depends on the tastes of consumers, the distribution of asset holdings and of income among consumers, and the stocks of assets the economy possesses. It is of the essence of the competitive model that incomes, production, and asset holdings are all simultaneously determined by the market mechanism, operating within an environment characterized by the preferences of consumers and the technology available to firms.

The Role of the Asset Markets in General Equilibrium

Thus far in this chapter we have concentrated on the flow markets of the economy because the goods and services desired by consumers are produced and exchanged on these markets, and the basic driving force underlying the competitive economy is the satisfaction of consumer wants with respect to such goods and services. On the other hand, assets are a necessary evil so far as the functioning of the economy is concerned. Assets are not desired by consumers for their own sakes, but instead are a kind of intermediate good useful to consumers as a vehicle for altering their pattern of consumption over time.

The special role that the asset markets play in the competitive system is to link short-run equilibrium with long-run equilibrium. At a short-run equilibrium, the pattern of output for the economy determines the rental rates of various kinds of capital goods and resources, and determines the wage rates to skilled laborers. Equilibrium on the asset markets means that prices of capital goods and resources adjust to these rentals in such a way as to equalize the rate of return on investment in any such asset, with all assets earning the market rate of interest. For simplicity, assume that net savings are zero, so that the economy is simply replacing assets that wear out but not adding to its stock of assets.

In the configuration of prices of assets that emerges from the short-run equilibrium, those assets earning high rental rates sell for high prices, while those earning low rentals have correspondingly low prices. The high prices of the favored assets lead to an increase in output of such assets, through the operation of the market for newly produced capital goods. Recall that in that market, output is set at the point where the marginal cost of production equals the price of the capital good; with high prices, output is increased to satisfy this equilibrium condition. Assets with low prices tend to be produced in lesser quantities. With zero net savings, stocks of capital goods with low rentals and correspondingly low prices are allowed to fall as production of such goods fails to meet depreciation of the existing stock. Stocks of capital goods with high rentals increase as production exceeds replacement needs.

This is all part of the pattern leading to the long-run equilibrium where reproducible assets sell at prices that equal the minimum *LRAC* of production of such assets. Admittedly, long-run equilibrium is like a phantom: we are always approaching it, but never quite get there. But the adjustment toward long-run equilibrium reflects a real tendency in the economy as incentives are in the process of being exploited, and the asset markets play crucial roles in this process.

A One-Input, One-Output Competitive Economy

An alternative graphical picture of the one-consumer competitive economy can be developed for the one-input, one-output case. Consider a world in which there is a single consumption

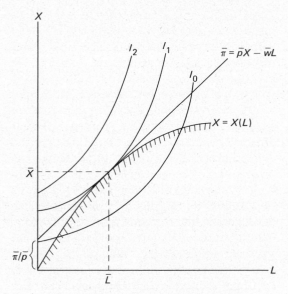

FIG. 12-7 *Competitive equilibrium—
one-input, one-output case*

good that is produced using labor only. Figure 12-7 indicates the properties of a competitive equilibrium for such a world. X is the consumption good and L is labor. The curve $X = X(L)$ is the production function for the firm; as shown, the production function exhibits decreasing returns to scale. The consumer's indifference map over consumption and labor is superimposed on the production map of the firm.

At the prices $\bar{p}$ per unit of X and $\bar{w}$ per unit of L, the firm maximizes profits $\pi = \bar{p}X - \bar{w}L$ by choosing the input-output combination ($\bar{L}$, $\bar{X}$). The intercept of the $\bar{\pi}$ line along the X axis gives profits in terms of units of the consumption good, namely $\bar{\pi}/\bar{p}$.

The consumer maximizes utility subject to his budget constraint. Because profits are allocated to the consumer, the budget constraint can be written as $pX \le wL + \bar{\pi}$. The budget constraint is satisfied as an equality in the case

where more X is preferred to less, and less L is preferred to more (fig. 12-7). Setting π at its maximum value $\bar{\pi}$, the consumer's budget line becomes the line $\bar{\pi} = \bar{p}X - \bar{w}L$. At a competitive equilibrium the choices of the consumer are consistent with the choices of the firm. The consumer chooses to supply $\bar{L}$ units of labor and to consume $\bar{X}$ units of the consumption good; hence markets for both labor and the consumption good are cleared, as indicated in the graph. Figure 12-7 gives a simple graphical picture of the simultaneous determination of output and input levels at a competitive equilibrium.

The Pure Exchange Economy

Think of a world in which, at the beginning of each day, each consumer receives an allotment of goods, coming to him "like manna from heaven." He then enters the marketplace to trade with other consumers. Afterwards, he returns home to consume the bundle he has acquired. This process is repeated the next day.

The world described is a *pure exchange economy*, since no production takes place there. The only market activity is the exchange of goods, one for another, on the part of consumers.

By suppressing production, it is possible to use simple Edgeworth-Bowley diagrams to show how a pure exchange world with two consumers and two goods operates. We also suppress intertemporal problems by assuming that each consumer plans only over a one-period horizon. Alternatively, we may think of a two-commodity world in which one commodity is "consumption today" and the other is "consumption tomorrow." Then two-period intertemporal problems can be investigated in terms of the approach taken in this section.

Most of what we can say about a pure exchange economy extends in a natural fashion to more complicated systems.

The Edgeworth Box and the Pure Exchange Economy

Our two consumers are identified as Mr. A and Mr. B, with the two goods being labeled X and Y. (X^A, Y^A) is an allocation of the two goods to Mr. A, and (X^B, Y^B) is an allocation to Mr. B. The initial allotments (before trade takes place) are labeled $(X_0^A, Y_0^A), (X_0^B, Y_0^B)$. Indifference maps for Mr. A and Mr. B are of the usual type, as shown in figure 12-8.

We construct the Edgeworth box diagram associated with this economy as follows. The length of the box is given by the amount of X available to the economy, that is $X_0^A + X_0^B$. The height of the box is the amount of Y

available, $Y_0^A + Y_0^B$. The southwest corner of the box is the origin for Mr. A, and the northeast corner is the origin for Mr. B. The indifference maps for the two consumers are plotted in the box (fig. 12-9).

X^A and Y^A increase in the directions indicated by the arrows outside the box, as is true for X^B and Y^B. Each point in the box has four dimensions, indicating the allocation of X and Y to both Mr. A and Mr. B. In particular, the initial allocation (X_o^A, Y_0^A), (X_0^B, Y_0^B) is indicated by the point C. Given that $X_0^A + X_0^B$ units of X and $Y_0^A + Y_0^B$ units of Y are available to the economy, the box consists of all of the final holdings allocations (allocations after trading) that are feasible for the economy.

In a competitive organization of the pure exchange economy, each consumer treats the prices of X and Y as given and maximizes utility subject to his budget constraint.

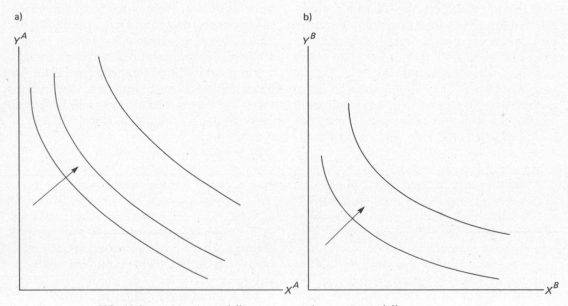

FIG. 12-8   a. Mr. A's indifference map   b. Mr. B's indifference map

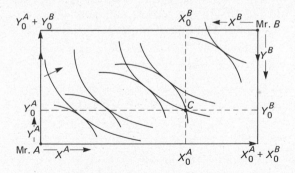

FIG. 12-9   *Edgeworth box diagram*

Competitive Equilibrium in a Pure Exchange Economy

The budget constraint for Mr. A is determined by his initial allocation (X_0^A, Y_0^A); he is free to choose any bundle (X^A, Y^A) that costs no more than the value of his initial allocation. Hence the budget constraint for Mr. A can be written

$$p_x X^A + p_y Y^A \leq p_x X_0^A + p_y Y_0^A.$$

Similarly, Mr. B's budget constraint becomes

$$p_x X^B + p_y Y^B \leq p_x X_0^B + p_y Y_0^B.$$

Assuming more is preferred to less, the utility-maximizing bundles chosen by Mr. A and Mr. B will satisfy their budget constraints as equalities.

Then a competitive equilibrium occurs in the pure exchange economy at the prices $\bar{p}_x$, $\bar{p}_y$ and with final holdings $[(\bar{X}^A, \bar{Y}^A); (\bar{X}^B, \bar{Y}^B)]$ under the following conditions.

1. $(\bar{X}^A, \bar{Y}^A)$ maximizes utility for Mr. A over the bundles satisfying $\bar{p}_x X^A + \bar{p}_y Y^A \leq \bar{p}_x X_0^A + \bar{p}_y Y_0^A$.

2. $(\bar{X}^B, \bar{Y}^B)$ maximizes utility for Mr. B over the bundles satisfying $\bar{p}_x X^B + \bar{p}_y Y^B \leq \bar{p}_x X_0^B + \bar{p}_y Y_0^B$.

3. $\bar{X}^A + \bar{X}^B = X_0^A + X_0^B$ and $\bar{Y}^A + \bar{Y}^B = Y_0^A + Y_0^B$ (that is, the total quantity of each good taken off the market equals the amount brought to the market, so that both markets are cleared).

Let us see what this amounts to graphically. First, the budget constraints for Mr. A and Mr. B appear as in figure 12-10, where $M^A = \bar{p}_x X_0^A + \bar{p}_y Y_0^A$, $M^B = \bar{p}_x X_0^B + \bar{p}_y Y_0^B$. Note that for any prices (p_x, p_y) the budget line for Mr. A goes through the initial holdings point (X_0^A, Y_0^A), just as every budget line for Mr. B goes through (X_0^B, Y_0^B). This configuration must be so, since one alternative that is always available to a consumer is to go home with the same bundle he brought to the market. Further, both consumers face the same prices; hence the slopes of the two budget lines are the same.

To illustrate a competitive equilibrium in the Edgeworth box, we transfer the budget lines for Mr. A and Mr. B to the Edgeworth diagram (fig. 12-11). The budget line for Mr. A turns out to be the budget line for Mr. B as well, if the Edgeworth box is turned upside down. The initial holdings point is C. At D a competitive equilibrium occurs because at that point Mr. A maximizes utility subject to his budget

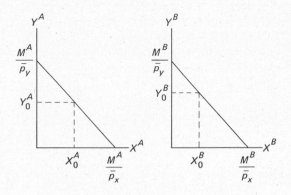

FIG. 12-10   *Budget constraints*

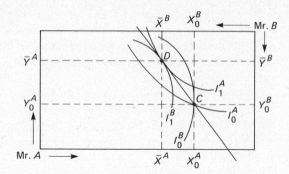

FIG. 12-11   *Competitive equilibrium
in a pure exchange world*

constraint, as does Mr. B. Markets are cleared because Mr. A gives up $X_0^A - \overline{X}^A$ units of X to obtain $\overline{Y}^A - Y_0^A$ units of Y, while Mr. B gives up $Y_0^B - \overline{Y}^B (= \overline{Y}^A - Y_0^A)$ units of Y to obtain $\overline{X}^B - X_0^B (= X_0^A - \overline{X}^A)$ units of X.

In order for markets to clear, the final holdings point must occur where the indifference curves for both Mr. A and Mr. B are tangent to the common budget line at a common point. Another way of saying this is that *at a competitive equilibrium, the marginal rates of substitution between any two commodities must be the same for all consumers, assuming that both consume positive amounts of both goods.*

Note also that at the competitive equilibrium, each consumer is better off than at his initial holding point. Trades in a competitive system are voluntary; no one engages in them unless he is made better off through trading. In particular, it is *not* the case that there are gainers and losers when trade occurs; both parties are gainers.

Walras's Law

Two characteristics of market excess demands in a competitive economy are particularly easy to identify in the context of a pure exchange economy. The first of these is *Walras's law*:

> At any set of prices, the aggregate value of excess demands is zero.

Let $E_X (p_X, p_Y)$, $E_Y (p_X, p_Y)$, denote excess demands for goods X and Y in a pure exchange economy, at prices p_X, p_Y for the two goods. Then

$$E_X (p_X, p_Y) = X^A (p_X, p_Y) + X^B (p_X, p_Y) - (X_0^A + X_0^B), \text{ and}$$

$$E_Y (p_X, p_Y) = Y^A (p_X, p_Y) + Y^B (p_X, p_Y) - (Y_0^A + Y_0^B)$$

where $X^A (p_X, p_Y)$ denotes the utility-maximizing amount of X for Mr. A, given prices p_X, p_Y, and similarly for the other symbols.

When more is preferred to less, then given any prices p_X, p_Y, both Mr. A and Mr. B satisfy their budget constraints as equalities. That is,

$$p_X X^A (p_X, p_Y) + p_Y Y^A (p_X, p_Y) = p_X X_0^A + p_Y Y_0^A, \text{ and}$$

$$p_X X^B (p_X, p_Y) + p_Y Y^B (p_X, p_Y) = p_X X_0^B + p_Y Y_0^B.$$

Adding the two budget constraints we obtain Walras's law:

$$p_X E_X (p_X, p_Y) + p_Y E_Y (p_X, p_Y) = 0;$$

that is, the aggregate value of excess demands is zero at any prices p_X, p_Y.

Walras's law also holds in the case of an economy with production, borrowing and lending, and saving. The importance of Walras's law is that if all except one market in the economy is in equilibrium (excess demand in all but one market equals zero), then the last market must be in equilibrium as well. Similarly, if there are markets with positive excess demands, then there must also be markets in which excess demands are negative.

Homogeneity of Excess Demand

The second characteristic of market excess demands in a pure exchange competitive economy is the *homogeneity property:*

In a pure exchange competitive economy, market excess demands are homogeneous of degree zero in all prices.

Homogeneity follows directly from the fact that if we multiply prices p_X, p_Y by any positive constant, then we do not change the budget constraint for either Mr. A or Mr. B. Since preference maps are independent of prices, both Mr. A and Mr. B choose the same utility-maximizing bundles under any positive multiple of prices p_X, p_Y as under prices p_X, p_Y. Hence excess demands as defined in the previous section are homogeneous of degree zero in prices as well.

Homogeneity carries over to long-run competitive economies with production and savings in the sense that if all prices, excluding the interest rate, are multiplied by any positive constant, excess demands are unchanged.†

When there are consumers who are net borrowers or lenders, homogeneity no longer holds since debts are specified in money terms and any unanticipated increase in the level of commodity prices benefits debtors and hurts creditors, and conversely for a fall in commodity prices. Excess demands are thus affected by unanticipated equal proportionate changes in commodity prices in a credit economy.

When homogeneity of degree zero in prices holds, as in the pure exchange economy, the absolute level of prices is irrelevant; individual and market excess demands depend only on

relative prices. Thus in the two-commodity pure exchange world, market opportunities and final holdings are determined only by preferences of consumers, initial endowments, and the price *ratio* p_X/p_Y.

Existence of the Competitive Equilibrium

No discussion of the competitive equilibrium would be complete without at least some mention of the problem of guaranteeing that a set of prices exists such that all markets in the economy are simultaneously cleared at that set of prices. In terms of counting equations and unknowns, simultaneous market clearing means that excess demand for each good equals zero, where each excess demand is a function of all prices in the economy. With n goods, there would be n equations (excess demand for each good $= 0$) and n unknowns (the n prices). Actually, by Walras's law, our n equations are not independent: at most, $n - 1$ excess demands are independent in the sense that, if $n - 1$ markets are cleared, then the nth market must be cleared as well. But then we care only about relative prices (at least in a noncredit economy), and so there are $n - 1$ unknowns as well, say

$$\frac{p_1}{p_n}, \frac{p_2}{p_n}, \ldots, \frac{p_{n-1}}{p_n}.$$

But simply counting equations and counting unknowns does not guarantee that a solution exists to the system of equations. We will not attempt to look in detail at the way in which the existence of a solution to the market-clearing problem can be guaranteed. Recent work by Arrow, Debreu, McKenzie, and others provides the assurance that under rather general conditions, prices always exist that result in

---

†The restriction to long-run economies is to guarantee that all firms operate with zero fixed costs so that doubling prices also doubles profits.

simultaneous market clearing.† These general conditions amount to the following assumptions: (1) consumers obey the axioms of modern utility theory; (2) firms operate under constant or decreasing returns to scale (with production maps of the form discussed in chapter 6); (3) externalities and indivisibilities are absent; and (4) each consumer holds amounts of goods desired by other consumers in sufficient quantities that he can more than survive on the basis of these holdings. In addition, certain technical mathematical conditions that guarantee that maximizing conduct is possible must hold.

This theoretical work assures us that we are not dealing with a logically invalid system; all of our subsidiary assumptions concerning consumers, firms, and markets can be tied together to form a consistent whole in the notion of the competitive equilibrium.

---

†See G. Debreu, *Theory of Value* (New York: Wiley, 1959) for a succinct mathematical summary of the problem of existence of a competitive equilibrium. Also see J. Quirk and R. Saposnik, *An Introduction to General Equilibrium Theory and Welfare Economics* (New York: McGraw-Hill, 1968).

Summary

In a competitive economy there is general equilibrium when consumers maximize utility and firms maximize profits, treating prices as given, with the resulting demands and supplies being such that all markets are simultaneously cleared. At a competitive equilibrium, the value of *GNP* is maximized over the production possibility set for the economy. The production possibility set consists of all feasible output mixes for the economy, for given amounts of available inputs. The outer boundary of the production possibility set is the economy's transformation curve, derived from the efficient production points in an Edgeworth-Bowley box diagram. At a competitive equilibrium, the ratio of prices of X to Y equals the marginal rate of transformation of Y into X.

The distribution of income in a competitive economy depends upon the distribution of asset holdings (including human capital) among consumers, rental and wage rates for resources and labor, and consumer preferences with respect to leisure and consumption. By Euler's theorem, constant returns to scale imply that income earned by factors of production exhausts the revenues of firms—there is no "unexplained residual."

Walras's law holds in a competitive economy; that is, the aggregate value of excess demand is zero at any set of prices. In a long-run competitive economy with no borrowing or lending, excess demands are homogeneous of degree zero in all prices.

Problems

1. Show that under constant returns to scale in producing X and Y, if both industries have the same factor intensities, then the transformation curve for the economy is a straight line.

2. Show that if there are decreasing returns to scale in producing X and Y, the production possibility set will "bulge" even if factor intensities are the same in the two industries.

3. In a two-person, two-commodity pure exchange world, interpret X as consumption today and Y as consumption tomorrow. Given a two-period horizon, show how the interest rate is determined in such a world.

4. A technological innovation occurs in the X industry. The X industry is capital-intensive relative to the Y industry. This innovation increases the output of X for any combination of K and L applied to X. X and Y are both produced under constant returns to scale. Assuming no change in the indifference map of the consumer in a one-consumer world, show graphically the change in the competitive equilibrium. Analyze the effects in terms of consumption of X and Y, relative prices of X and Y, relative prices of K and L, and the distribution of income between K and L.

III
Market Imperfections

13
Welfare Economics, the Competitive Equilibrium, and Market Imperfections

Welfare economics is concerned with ethical issues. Economists are called upon not only to predict the consequences of a certain policy or actions, but also to assist in arriving at value judgments as to whether the action is "desirable." To do this, they need an ethical criterion against which to measure desirability. This chapter summarizes the approach that economists take to such ethical issues.

The Individualistic Utilitarian Ethic

Underlying essentially all of modern welfare economics is the utilitarian notion that *actions are to be judged solely on the basis of their consequences.* A "good" action is one that has "good" consequences, and a "bad" action is one with "bad" consequences. This is certainly not a universally accepted criterion for judging actions; for example, most religions deem certain actions to be sinful, regardless of their consequences. Similarly, courts are concerned not only with the consequences of an action, but also with the motivation and intent of the individual committing it.

Thus we begin with a controversial postulate.

But the economist goes further. In determining what the consequences of an action are, he uses as his measure the impact of the action as reflected in the preferences of the individuals making up the society. For example, in a one-person society, action A is judged "more desirable" than action B if the individual affected by the action regards the consequences of action A as more preferred than the consequences of action B.

This approach is fundamental to the economist's view of welfare economics. His personal preferences concerning the consequences of an action are irrelevant; it is the preferences of the individuals making up the society that count. In this sense, the economist can be described not only as a utilitarian, but as an *individualistic utilitarian*. He does not attempt to judge what is good for people, but accepts their own judgments as to what is good for them. For him there is no "social good" above and beyond the "individual goods" reflected in the preference rankings of individuals; all ethical judgments in welfare economics rest on individual preferences. Individual consumers are assumed to be the best judges of their own interests.

States of the Economy

The specific ethical problems of interest to economists relate to actions that affect the production and distribution of goods and services in the economy. Under the utilitarian approach, we identify the alternatives under study with their consequences. In order to measure these consequences, we introduce the notion of a "state of the economy."

By a *state of the economy*, we mean a listing that shows (1) for each consumer the amount of each good or service he receives and the amounts of labor services he supplies, and (2) for each firm the amount of each input consumed and the amount of each output produced. The concept of a state of the economy summarizes essentially all of the economically relevant information needed to characterize the consequences of a proposed action. Positive microeconomic theory enables us to identify with a proposed action the state of the economy that would be attained, given that action. For example, state of the economy *A* would hold if an excise tax were used to raise revenue, and state of the economy *B* would hold if an income tax were used to raise the revenue. The economist's judgment as to which of the two alternatives is "better" then rests upon the rankings of *A* and *B* in the preferences of the members of the society.

The Unanimity Principle and Pareto Optimality

Things are simple enough when we consider a one-person economy. Between two states of the economy *A* and *B*, the state preferred by the single individual is judged "better" by the economist than the less preferred state. But in a world with many individuals, the utilitarian approach is faced with the problem of aggregating over individual preferences, which often are in conflict with one another. There is a nice ring to the utilitarian slogan "the greatest good for the greatest number," but the fact is that no ethical philosopher has yet found a completely satisfactory way of identifying the "greatest good" when individual preferences are in conflict. Economists have been no more successful than philosophers in resolving the problem of conflict of preferences. As we shall see, modern welfare economics simply bypasses this problem.

The approach adopted by economists rests upon the *unanimity principle:*

Between two states of the economy A and B, A is to be judged "better" than B if everyone in the society either prefers A to B or is indifferent between A and B, and for some individual(s), A is strictly preferred to B.

Suppose that *A* is judged better than *B* under the unanimity principle. Then we also say (equivalently) that *A* is *Pareto-superior* to *B*.† Using the notion of Pareto superiority, a *Pareto-optimal* state of the economy is defined as follows:

Given a set of states of the economy (A, B, C, . . .), suppose that there exists a state W in that set with the property that no other state in the set is Pareto-superior to W. Then W is said to be a Pareto-optimal state for the set (A, B, C, . . .).

Because of the backward way of defining a Pareto-optimal state of the economy, it may be worthwhile to illustrate the notion. Suppose there are three states of the economy, *A*, *B*,

---

† The term *Pareto superior* refers to the Italian sociologist, engineer and economist, Vilfredo Pareto, whose work had a major influence on modern welfare economics.

and C, to be evaluated for an economy with three individuals, Mr. 1, Mr. 2, and Mr. 3. The preference rankings for the individuals are assumed to be the following:

Mr. 1:
  A preferred to B, and B indifferent to C
Mr. 2:
  A preferred to B, and B preferred to C
Mr. 3:
  B preferred to A, and A preferred to C

We assume that each person's preferences are transitive. It follows that A is Pareto-superior to C and B is Pareto-superior to C. On the other hand, the unanimity principle does not apply between A and B. (When the unanimity principle does *not* apply, we say that the two states are *Pareto noncomparable*.) We can conclude that both A and B are Pareto-optimal states relative to the set (A, B, C) because neither B nor C is Pareto-superior to A, and neither A nor C is Pareto-superior to B. Note that if we are at state A, a change to state B makes Mr. 3 better off while Mr. 1 and Mr. 2 are worse off; a change from A to C makes everyone worse off. This illustrates another way to describe a Pareto-optimal state of the economy:

If the economy is at a Pareto-optimal state, then a change to any other attainable state that makes one consumer better off must make some other consumer worse off.

If the economy is at a non-Pareto-optimal state, then there exists an attainable state such that no one is worse off and some consumer(s) is better off.

Suppose we change the example as follows:

Mr. 1:
  A preferred to B, and B indifferent to C
Mr. 2:
  B preferred to C, and C indifferent to A

Mr. 3:
  C preferred to A, and A indifferent to B

Verify that A, B, and C all are Pareto-optimal states in the set (A, B, C).

The examples are intended to illustrate one basic point. When preferences are in conflict within a society, we will typically find *several* alternatives in a set of states of the economy being Pareto-optimal. The phraseology involved in the term "Pareto optimality" is loaded. To say that a state of the economy is a Pareto-optimal state is *not* to make a very strong statement. After all, the only states in a set that are not Pareto-optimal for the set are states that are "worse" under the unanimity principle than some other state in the set. (In the first example, only C fails to qualify as a Pareto-optimal state).

Efficiency and Equity

The basic approach of welfare economics is straightforward. Policy A is judged "better" than policy B if and only if the state of the economy achieved under A is Pareto-superior to the state of the economy achieved under B. Equivalently, A is better than B if and only if *no one* strictly prefers the state achieved under B to that achieved under A, while at least one person prefers the state under A to that under B. Given the individualistic utilitarian ethic underlying welfare economics, it is hard to argue with this criterion.

It follows almost as a matter of course that in evaluating the way an economic system functions, a minimum ethical requirement for satisfactory performance is that the economic system achieve Pareto-optimal states of the economy. If not, there is an attainable state of the economy that is unambiguously better (Pareto-superior) relative to the state achieved. As earlier comments indicate, this is not a very severe requirement to impose in judging economic systems.

Pareto optimality can be thought of as an *efficiency* property as applied to any economic system. We should always be at a Pareto optimum because, if not, we can make some people better off while no one is worse off. Clearly, it is inefficient to be at a non-Pareto-optimal state of the economy.

But asserting that only Pareto-optimal states are "desirable" does not mean that *all* Pareto-optimal states are desirable. After all, a Pareto-optimal state of the economy might be one where one individual gets all of the goods and services but the rest of the population gets nothing. Chances are that all of us would agree that such a situation is inherently *inequitable*, and we would universally reject any economic system that generated only such one-sided (but Pareto-optimal) outcomes. Ideally, our ethical rules should provide us with a way of making comparisons among Pareto-optimal states on the basis of equity considerations. Modern welfare economics, however, does not provide such a standard for comparing Pareto-optimal states; equity considerations are treated as beyond the scope of the analysis of welfare economics. This is the "bypassing of conflicts of preferences" mentioned earlier. In effect, welfare economics carries us up to the point where equity considerations become crucial and then says, now use religion, politics, ethics, or what have you to make any further comparisons.

The problems involved in issues of equity are both subtle and difficult, as illustrated by the famous paradox of majority voting.†

Paradox of Majority Voting   In a democratic society, conflicts of preferences concerning so-

cial and political issues are typically resolved through a voting mechanism; between two alternatives, the one receiving the most votes is adopted by the society. As straightforward as this method of resolving conflicts of preferences is, it raises certain problems. Consider a society consisting of three individuals, Mr. 1, Mr. 2, and Mr. 3, deciding among three alternatives, A, B, and C. Each individual is assumed to possess a complete transitive preference ranking over the alternatives, with preferences as follows:

Mr. 1: A preferred to B, B preferred to C
(and A preferred to C)

Mr. 2: B preferred to C, C preferred to A
(and B preferred to A)

Mr. 3: C preferred to A, A preferred to B
(and C preferred to B)

When presented with the alternatives A and B, the electorate votes in A (2 votes to 1); between B and C, B wins (2 votes to 1); but between A and C, we have C winning (2 votes to 1)! Thus, for the preferences of the example, majority voting leads to an intransitive ranking of alternatives, which amounts to saying that the alternative that wins out depends upon the way the agenda (pairing of alternatives) is selected. If A is paired against B, with the winner being paired against C, then C is chosen in the election; if A is paired against C, with the winner paired against B, then B is chosen; and if B is paired against C, with the winner paired against A, then A wins. Among other things, this paradox offers an explanation for the power of committee chairmen (who select agendas) in the Congress.

The Arrow Impossibility Theorem

Problems such as intransitivity arise not only in majority voting, but also in other techniques

---

†K. Arrow, *Social Choice and Individual Values* (New York: Wiley, 1951).

for making choices for a society when preferences are in conflict. In fact, there is a general result, first established by Kenneth Arrow and known as the *Arrow impossibility theorem*.†

Consider any mechanism for making choices among alternatives in a society, this mechanism to be responsive to the preferences of the members of the society. Each member of the society is assumed to possess a complete and transitive preference ranking over alternatives. If interpersonal comparisons of utility are excluded, then the only mechanism that leads to a complete, transitive ranking of the alternatives for all possible (complete, transitive) preference rankings of the members of the society, is a dictatorship.

In brief, what the Arrow theorem asserts is that given any mechanism (such as majority voting) for translating individual preferences into a social preference ranking, it is possible to find examples of individual preferences such that the resulting social preference ranking violates the completeness property or the transitivity property, except for the single case where the social preference ranking is determined by the preferences of one individual in the society (the "dictator"). (Note that the unanimity rule leads to a transitive ranking of alternatives but it is not complete, since if two consumers differ with respect to a pair of alternatives, no ranking for them is defined.)

By restricting itself to the cases in which the unanimity principle applies, welfare economics avoids the problems indicated by the Arrow theorem. This avoidance might suggest that welfare economics is a completely sterile exercise. Actually, there are some rather interesting conclusions that follow from the approach of modern welfare economics, limited though it is as an ethical creed. It is particularly important

as a tool in evaluating market imperfections. But a natural starting point is to see what welfare economics has to say about the perfectly competitive economy.

Pareto Optimality and the Competitive Equilibrium

Consider any society, with its given stocks of natural and human resources, and its stocks of capital goods. Together with the technological know-how available to the society, these stocks define for the society a *feasible set* of states of the economy. A society's feasible set is defined as the *collection of states of the economy that are achievable by the society within the constraints imposed by the technology and the society's resources*. States of the economy belonging to the feasible set will differ from one another both in terms of the pattern of production of goods and services and in the way these goods and services are distributed among the members of the society. Given the feasible set for the economy and the preference maps of all consumers, the unanimity principle can be used to determine which states of the economy are Pareto-optimal.

From the point of view of welfare economics, economic systems can be characterized as devices for choosing states of the economy from the society's feasible set. In particular, if the perfectly competitive system is used to organize the economy of a society, then certain states of the economy can be identified as competitive equilibrium states; that is, states in which utility-maximizing choices of consumers and profit-maximizing choices of firms are consistent in the sense that all markets are cleared. Given the model of the competitive economy developed in the earlier chapters, then the following propositions can be established.

---

†Arrow, *Social Choice and Individual Values.*

I. *The competitive equilibrium is efficient;* that is, every competitive equilibrium occurs at a Pareto-optimal state of the economy.

II. *The competitive equilibrium is unbiased;* that is, any Pareto-optimal state of the economy can be achieved as a competitive equilibrium, given the appropriate redistribution of wealth among the individuals in the society.

Proposition I states that the competitive mechanism passes the test of efficiency, which we have already pointed out represents a bare minimum requirement for any "desirable" system of organizing the economy. While it is comforting to know that the competitive system does not waste resources, on the other hand just to be at a Pareto-optimal state of the economy is not all that assuring; certain Pareto-optimal states could be highly undesirable on equity grounds.

Proposition II introduces a new dimension into our discussion of the performance of an economic system. Given that a particular Pareto-optimal state is judged most desirable on equity grounds, the unbiasedness property asserts that the competitive economy can always achieve such a desired state, given the appropriate distribution of wealth.

This proposition is of some importance in evaluating policy proposals to achieve goals desired on equity grounds. Direct interference with the market mechanism through the use of taxes, subsidies, controls, and the like to achieve an equitable distribution of income often involves a cost in efficiency in the Pareto sense; that is, the economy ends up at a non-Pareto-optimal state. Proposition II asserts that any desired equity goals can be achieved through redistribution of wealth, without loss of efficiency, by permitting the system of markets to function without interference so long as the basic assumptions underlying the competitive model are satisfied. This means that,

in principle at least, we can separate equity considerations from efficiency considerations in evaluating economic policy proposals. The society can implement any standards of equity it wishes by once and for all lump-sum taxes on wealth holdings, coupled with a redistribution of such holdings among consumers. The competitive market mechanism then operates to guarantee that the pattern of production and consumption associated with this distribution of wealth is efficient; that is, it results in the attainment of a Pareto-optimal state of the economy. There is no need to "trade off" equity for efficiency.

Now admittedly there is a real difficulty here. An important qualification to the joint attainment of equity and efficiency is that markets are perfectly competitive. If there is monopoly power, or if there are externalities in production or in consumption, or if property rights to goods are not well defined, or if markets for some goods do not exist—if these or similar imperfections occur, then there is no guarantee that a free market system will produce an efficient allocation of resources. In the face of such imperfections, generally interference with the market mechanism is needed to ensure that the economy will perform efficiently.

Beyond this, it is not easy to devise a method for redistribution of wealth that preserves efficiency. Such a method must not distort the incentives of consumers or firm managers in the sense that their consumption and production choices violate the efficiency conditions. Needless to say, problems with devising a lump-sum method of redistributing wealth significantly limit the applicability of the propositions above.

In the next section, we show how propositions I and II may be established for a simplified model of a competitive economy, the "pure exchange" economy discussed in chapter 12.

Pareto Optimality in a Pure Exchange Economy

In a pure exchange economy, the set of feasible states of the economy is the Edgeworth box. Given an initial endowment of X_0 units of X, Y_0 units of Y, the Edgeworth box for a two-consumer economy is as shown in figure 13-1. Any point in the Edgeworth box diagram (such as the points C, D, E, F) represents an allocation of the X_0 units of X and Y_0 units of Y between the two consumers. Thus at C, Mr. A is assigned the bundle (X_A^*, Y_A^*) while Mr. B has the bundle (X_B^*, Y_B^*) where

$$X_A^*, + X_B^*, = X_0, \ Y_A^* + Y_B^* = Y_0.$$

Is C a Pareto-optimal state? Clearly it is not. At the point D, which is also a feasible allocation of the endowment (X_0, Y_0), Mr. B is on a higher indifference curve (I_1^B versus I_0^B), while Mr. A is on the same indifference curve (I_2^A) as at the point C. Thus D is Pareto-superior to C.

Consider D. Any change from D that puts Mr. A on a higher indifference curve also puts Mr. B on a lower indifference curve; and any change that puts Mr. B on a higher indifference curve puts Mr. A on a lower indifference curve. To make one person better off, the other must be made worse off—one characterization of a Pareto-optimal state of the economy.

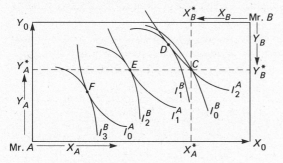

FIG. 13-1   *Edgeworth box diagram*

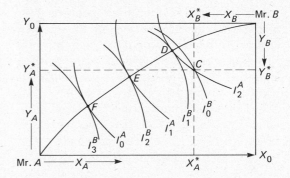

FIG. 13-2   *Pareto-optimal states in a pure trade economy*

Applying the same argument, it follows that the set of Pareto-optimal states for the pure trade economy consists of all allocations that occur at tangencies of indifference curves, as along the curve through D, E, F in figure 13-2. Hence we have the following proposition:

At a Pareto-optimal state of the economy, the marginal rate of substitution between X and Y is the same for all consumers consuming positive amounts of the two goods.

The Competitive Equilibrium and Pareto Optimality in a Pure Exchange Economy   Pareto optimality identifies the states of the economy that are efficient in the sense that no attainable state is Pareto-superior to a Pareto-optimal state. Pareto optimality is specified purely in terms of the preference rankings of consumers over feasible states. This concept is as well defined in a world without property rights as it is in a private ownership economy. In particular, there is no presumption in the notion of Pareto optimality that goods are allocated among consumers according to a pricing mechanism.

In the competitive economy private property rights exist to commodities, and owners are free to dispose of their commodities as they wish, subject only to the constraints imposed on their choices by prices prevailing in the market. Figure 13-3 depicts a competitive equilibrium in a pure exchange economy. Given the initial allocation (X_A^0, Y_A^0) to A and (X_B^0, Y_B^0) to B, a competitive equilibrium occurs at $(\bar{X}^A, \bar{Y}^A)$, $(\bar{X}^B, \bar{Y}^B)$. This equilibrium satisfies two conditions: (1) both consumers face the same prices and maximize utility subject to their budget constraints; and (2) markets are cleared. As the graph indicates, the competitive equilibrium occurs at a tangency of indifference curves. But this means that a competitive equilibrium is also a Pareto-optimal state, as asserted in proposition I.

To prove unbiasedness of the competitive equilibrium (proposition II), note that any Pareto-optimal state of the economy in the interior of the Edgeworth box is at a tangency of indifference curves. Whatever is the initial distribution of X and Y between Mr. A and Mr. B, introduce a lump-sum tax that leaves Mr. A and Mr. B at the desired Pareto-optimal state. Because indifference curves are tangent at the Pareto-optimal state, there exists a price line that can be drawn through the Pareto-

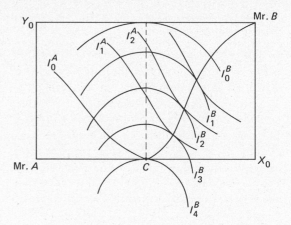

FIG. 13-4   *Arrow's exceptional case*

optimal state such that each consumer in maximizing utility chooses to stay at this state. This procedure establishes proposition II: any Pareto-optimal state can be achieved as a competitive equilibrium, given the appropriate redistribution of wealth.

There are certain exceptional cases in which proposition II does not hold. These cases violate one or more of the conditions mentioned at the end of chapter 12 relative to the existence of a competitive equilibrium. One such exception is called Arrow's exceptional case (fig. 13-4).† The point C on the boundary of the Edgeworth box is a Pareto-optimal state, as can easily be verified. (Pareto-optimal states that occur on the boundary of the Edgeworth box need not satisfy the tangency condition.) At C, Mr. B is satiated with respect to X; and at C Mr. A's initial endowment consists only of units of X. The only price line that will keep

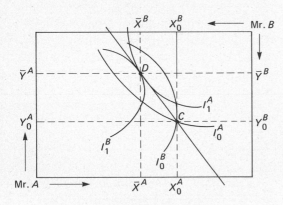

FIG. 13-3   *Competitive equilibrium in a pure exchange economy*

†K. Arrow, "An Extension of the Basic Theorems of Classical Welfare Economics," in *Proceedings of the Second Berkeley Symposium on Mathematical Statistics and Probability*, ed. J. Neyman (Berkeley: University of California Press, 1951).

Mr. B at *C* is the line that lies on top of the *X* axis of the box (with price of *X* of zero). At any positive price for *X*, Mr. B wants to give up *X* to obtain more *Y*. But with a price of *X* of zero, Mr. A wants to consume more *X* and will move to the right along the *X* axis. No competitive equilibrium exists with the initial endowment point *C*. On the other hand, if Mr. A has any units of *Y* in his initial endowment, then the exceptional case vanishes.

The Competitive Equilibrium and Pareto Optimality with Production

At a Pareto-optimal state, the marginal rate of substitution between any two commodities must be the same for all individuals consuming the goods in positive amounts; we refer to this as *efficiency in exchange*. A comparable condition characterizes the employment of inputs at a Pareto-optimal state in an economy with production. We say there is *efficiency in pro-* *duction if the economy is on its transformation curve.* As the analysis in chapter 12 indicates, this occurs if and only if inputs are allocated among industries in such a way that *the marginal rate of substitution between any two inputs is the same for all firms employing them.*

Figure 13-5 illustrates a Pareto-optimal state in a one-consumer economy with production. The output combination $(\bar{X}, \bar{Y})$ represents a Pareto-optimal state because there is no other feasible state of the economy where the consumer is on a higher indifference curve. The set of feasible states for the consumer are the consumption bundles that lie in the production possibility set. Efficiency in production implies that output occurs at some point on the economy's transformation curve. But it is only at $(\bar{X}, \bar{Y})$ that the mix of outputs is such that utility for the consumer is maximized and a Pareto optimum is achieved. Clearly, the competitive equilibrium occurs at the Pareto-optimal state, as indicated in figure 13-6.

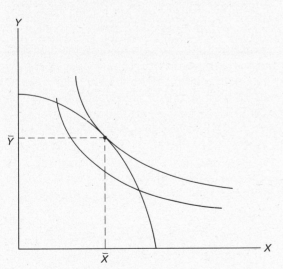

FIG. 13-5 *Pareto optimality with production*

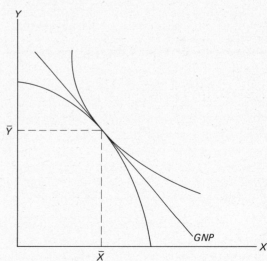

FIG. 13-6 *Competitive equilibrium*

Marginal Cost Pricing and Pareto Optimality   The slope of the economy's transformation curve, $\Delta Y/\Delta X$, measures the cost to the society in terms of units of Y forgone, to increase the output of X one unit. At a competitive equilibrium, the slope of the transformation curve is set equal to the slope of the *GNP* line:

$$- \frac{p_x}{p_y}.$$

So long as there are no externalities in production and so long as input markets are competitive, then

$$\frac{\Delta Y}{\Delta X} = - \frac{MC_x}{MC_y}.$$

If it costs \$2 to produce an additional unit of X and \$1 to produce an additional unit of Y ($MC_x = \$2$, $MC_y = \$1$), then increasing the output of X one unit means that the resources transferred out of the Y industry result in a loss of two units of Y. But this is simply $\Delta Y/\Delta X$, hence

$$\frac{\Delta Y}{\Delta X} = - \frac{MC_x}{MC_y},$$

when input markets are competitive and externalities are absent. Note that we also could have derived this result from the profit maximization conditions $p_x = MC_x$, $p_y = MC_y$, coupled with the fact that the slope of the transformation curve equals $-(p_x/p_y)$.

Because the competitive equilibrium occurs at a Pareto-optimal state, another efficiency condition must hold at a Pareto optimum:

If input markets are competitive, if there are no externalities, and if one or more output markets are competitive, then Pareto optimality requires that each produced good sell at a price equal to its marginal cost.

Under the conditions specified, at a Pareto optimum we must have the price ratio p_x/p_y equal to MC_x/MC_y. If x is produced competitively, then

$$p_x = MC_x;$$

hence for optimality,

$$p_y = MC_y$$

as well. This is referred to as the *marginal cost pricing* requirement for Pareto optimality.

There are some interesting implications of the marginal cost pricing rule. For example, the short-run marginal cost of seating an additional customer at a baseball game is essentially zero. The marginal cost pricing rule says that so long as the game is not sold out, the ticket price should be zero! (Of course, in the long run, the capital representing the stadium will not be replaced unless revenues cover cost, and the long-run marginal cost of staging a baseball game includes the costs of maintaining the stadium.) Also, consider the following common situation. On a railroad track from A to B, trains run full from A to B, but on the "backhaul" from B to A, there is excess capacity. Marginal cost pricing implies that the freight rate from B to A should be less than the rate from A to B, even though the distance travelled is identical. So long as the qualifications hold—competitive input markets, absence of externalities, competition in one or more output markets—the marginal cost pricing rule is a powerful tool in discovering possible sources of inefficiency in the economy.

Market Imperfections and Inefficiency

The competitive system scores about as well as is possible, in terms of the Pareto criterion.

This system presupposes, however, a world of certainty, with markets for all goods, absence of market power, and no externalities. When the assumptions underlying the competitive model are violated, we say that "market imperfections" are present. In chapters 15 through 19 we will study certain general classes of imperfections, from two points of view. First, we are interested in the impact of imperfections on the pattern of production and distribution of goods within an economy. This is the study of imperfections from a positive, or scientific, point of view. Second, we are interested in evaluating the welfare implications of imperfections in terms of the Pareto criterion, the normative aspect of our investigation into imperfections. To the extent that the presence of a market imperfection means that the economy ends up at a non-Pareto-optimal state, there is a "welfare loss" for the society. This issue leads naturally into how such welfare losses can be eliminated, by appropriate public policies.

The welfare losses due to market imperfections can be identified loosely as the result either of *inefficiency in production* or *inefficiency in distribution*. By inefficiency in production, we mean a situation in which the economy operates in the interior of its production possibility set. When there is inefficiency in production, it is possible to increase the outputs of all goods by a reallocation of resource services among industries. Inefficiency in distribution occurs when the economy is on its transformation curve, but the "wrong" set of outputs is being produced, in the sense that all consumers can be made better off by changing the output mix for the economy.

As we shall see, the existence of market power in the input markets leads to inefficiency in production. Externalities can create difficulties in terms of both production and distribu-

tion inefficiencies. When inefficiency in either sense exists, the job for the policymaker is to find a corrective policy that leads to a Pareto-superior situation—ideally, one that is also a Pareto-optimal state.

General Equilibrium and Welfare Economics—A Methodological Comment

Before turning to an examination of the tools available to the economist to identify Pareto-superior states of the economy when market imperfections are present, it might be well to make a few comments about the use of *partial equilibrium* theory and *general equilibrium* theory in economics. As the term implies, partial equilibrium theory involves the study of a restricted subset of the economic system—a single consumer or a single firm, an industry, several related markets, and the like—in isolation from the rest of the economy. General equilibrium theory studies the operation of the economy as a whole, explicitly taking into account interrelationships among all markets and market participants.

Viewing economic theory as a purely scientific enterprise, partial equilibrium theory can be justified on the basis of the verified predictions that it produces. For a wide range of problem areas, the links between a given segment of the economy and the rest of the system can be ignored with no appreciable loss in terms of accuracy of predictions. So long as accuracy of predictions is not damaged, it is more efficient to concentrate resources on a rather precise modeling of a specific industry than to attempt to study the entire system into which the industry is linked. On the other hand, there are certain problems in which the system has to be studied as a whole if acceptable standards of accuracy are to be achieved in the analysis. The choice between partial and general equilibrium theory in the scientific use of economic theory is made on pragmatic grounds: which one works better in producing verified predictions.

The situation is quite different in welfare economics, that is, in the use of economic theory to arrive at ethical evaluations of the operation of an economic system. The basic criterion used in welfare economics is the notion of Pareto superiority as a ranking device to judge the desirability of various states of the economy. This criterion is phrased in terms of the preference rankings of *all* the consumers in the society; *only* when there is unanimity can any definite statement be made as to the relative desirability of alternative states of the economy. This means that in welfare economics, we are forced to employ a general equilibrium approach to problems; it is essential that we know the effects of a proposed action on *every* individual in the society. In regard to problems in welfare economics, to be right about 99.99 percent of the consumers and wrong about .01 percent of them is no different in principle than to be right about .01 percent of consumers and wrong about 99.99 percent of them. Total accuracy in this sense is the inevitable limitation of using a welfare criterion that bypasses problems of equity.

Pareto Superiority and Revealed Preference

It is clear that there are real problems posed for the implementation of the rules of welfare economics by the requirement that policy 1 is to be judged better than policy 2 only if each consumer is at least as well off under 1 as under 2, with at least one consumer better off. There is first the problem of determining the impacts of policies 1 and 2 on the patterns of income and consumption for the society, and second, the problem of determining whether individual consumers are better off, worse off, or indifferent under one policy relative to another.

As it turns out, the revealed preference approach offers a straightforward method for attacking the second of these two problems. Let p_x^1, p_y^1 denote the prices that prevail under policy 1, with p_x^2, p_y^2 the corresponding prices under policy 2. (X^1, Y^1) is the bundle chosen by a consumer under policy 1, while (X^2, Y^2) is the bundle chosen under policy 2. Given that a consumer satisfies the axioms of modern utility theory of chapter 6 and given that the two bundles differ, then the consumer is better off under policy 1 than under policy 2 if

$$p_x^1 X^1 + p_y^1 Y^1 \geq p_x^1 X^2 + p_y^1 Y^2;$$

that is, 1 is better than 2 from the consumer's point of view if (X^1, Y^1) is revealed preferred to (X^2, Y^2). If this criterion holds for each and every consumer, then it is clear that policy 1 is to be judged "better" than policy 2, because policy 1 leads to the attainment of a Pareto-superior state relative to that achieved under policy 2.†

But we can say more than this. Suppose that the *only* information we possess concerning consumer preference maps is that the preference maps all satisfy the axioms of modern utility theory. Then it turns out that the only case in which we can prove policy 1 is "better" than policy 2 is when *for each consumer, the*

---

†This assumes (as in chapter 5) that there are no consumer externalities, and so the consumer's preferences depend only on what he himself consumes.

bundle chosen under 1 is revealed preferred to that chosen under 2. That is,

$$p_x^1 X^1 + p_y^1 \geq p_x^1 X^2 + p_y^1 Y^2;$$

for each consumer, the bundle chosen in 2 must still be available in 1, and, for at least one consumer, the bundle chosen under 1 is different from that chosen under 2.

The intuitive reason for this is clear. If for some consumer, the bundle chosen in 2 is not available in 1, then for an appropriately chosen indifference map, the consumer would prefer the bundle in 2 to that in 1, which contradicts Pareto superiority. Since our lack of information as to preferences admits all possible indifference maps (consistent with the axioms of modern utility theory), we have to require that the bundle chosen in 2 be available under policy 1.

To illustrate how the revealed preference approach can be applied to a practical problem, consider the issue of whether to use an income tax or an excise tax to finance a given level of government expenditures.

The Welfare Economics of an Income Tax versus an Excise Tax

Consider a two-consumer, two-good economy in which markets are competitive. The consumers are Mr. A and Mr. B, while the goods are X and Y. There are fixed amounts of resources, with a production possibility set of the usual type, giving feasible outputs of the two goods.

The government wishes to acquire X_G^0 units of good X, and considers raising the required funds for purchase of these units by imposing either an income tax with a flat rate or an excise tax on Y. The government pays the market price per unit of X purchased.

Let (X_A, Y_A), (X_B, Y_B) denote the bundles chosen by Mr. A and Mr. B, while p_x, p_y denote prices, and M_A, M_B are the incomes of Mr. A and Mr. B.

We wish to show that an income tax is better than an excise tax on Y in the following restricted sense. Given the commodity bundles chosen by Mr. A and Mr. B under an excise tax, replacing the excise tax with an income tax *together with a redistribution of income between Mr. A and Mr. B* can make both A and B better off than they would be under the excise tax. Thus what we will really be comparing is an excise tax versus an income tax coupled with a redistribution of income.

To establish this result, begin with an income tax of α percent. Under such an income tax we have

$$p_x^0 X_A^0 + p_y^0 Y_A^0 = (1 - \alpha) M_A^0$$

$$p_x^0 X_B^0 + p_y^0 Y_B^0 = (1 - \alpha) M_B^0$$

where the superscript "o" identifies prices, incomes, and consumptions under the income tax.

Market clearing implies

$$X_A^0 + X_B^0 + X_G^0 = X^0$$

$$Y_A^0 + Y_B^0 = Y^0$$

where (X^0, Y^0) is the output mix under the income tax.

Because the economy is competitive, *GNP* is maximized over the production possibility set, that is,

$$p_x^0 X^0 + p_y^0 Y^0 \geq p_x^0 X + p_y^0 Y$$

for any feasible output combination (X, Y).

Under an excise tax on Y, a new set of outputs, prices, and consumptions occurs. Denote these by the superscript "1". Hence

$$p_x^1 X_A^1 + p_y^1 Y_A^1 = M_A^1$$

$$p_x^1 X_B^1 + p_y^1 Y_B^1 = M_B^1$$

with

$$X_A^1 + X_B^1 + X_G^0 = X^1$$

$$Y_A^1 + Y_B^1 = Y^1.$$

Because *GNP* was maximized at (X^0, Y^0) under prices (p_x^0, p_y^0), it follows that

$$p_x^0 X^0 + p_y^0 Y^0 \geq p_x^0 X^1 + p_y^0 Y^1.$$

From the market-clearing conditions, this can be rewritten as

$$p_x^0(X_A^0 + X_B^0 + X_G^0) + p_y^0(Y_A^0 + Y_B^0)$$
$$\geq p_x^0(X_A^1 + X_B^1 + X_G^0) + p_y^0(Y_A^1 + Y_B^1).$$

Eliminating X_G^0 from either side and combining, we have

$$(p_x^0 X_A^0 + p_y^0 Y_A^0) + (p_x^0 X_B^0 + p_y^0 Y_B^0)$$
$$\geq (p_x^0 X_A^1 + p_y^0 Y_A^1) + (p_x^0 X_B^1 + p_y^0 Y_B^1),$$

or equivalently,

$$(1 - \alpha)M_A^0 + (1 - \alpha) M_B^0$$
$$\geq (p_x^0 X_A^1 + p_y^0 Y_A^1) + (p_x^0 X_B^1 + p_y^0 Y_B^1).$$

What this result shows is that given any bundles (X_A^1, Y_A^1), (X_B^1, Y_B^1) chosen by Mr. A and Mr. B under the excise tax, there is an assignment of incomes (M_A^0, M_B^0) under the income tax such that for those incomes, (X_A^0, Y_A^0) is revealed preferred to (X_A^1, Y_A^1) and (X_B^0, Y_B^0) is revealed preferred to (X_B^1, Y_B^1), since

$$(1 - \alpha)M_A^0 = p_x^0 X_A^0 + p_y^0 Y_A^0 \geq p_x^0 X_A^1 + p_y^0 Y_A^1$$

$$(1 - \alpha)M_B^0 = p_x^0 X_B^0 + p_y^0 Y_B^0 \geq p_x^0 X_A^1 + p_y^0 Y_B^1.$$

Under this assignment of incomes, the income tax can be judged better than the excise tax, since it leads to a Pareto-superior state of the economy.† After-tax incomes can be assigned to consumers so that each could, if he wished, buy the bundle he chose under the excise tax.

Compensation and Pareto Superiority

It is important to make it clear just what has been established in the foregoing comparison. Our result says that if we replace an excise tax with an income tax, the government obtaining X_G^0 units of X in each case, then we can assign incomes to consumers in such a way that each consumer is better off under the income tax than under the excise tax. In general it is *not* true that simply changing from an excise tax to an income tax will make each and every consumer better off; typically some consumers will be better off and some will be worse off. But what we have shown is that those who gain in the change from the excise tax to the income tax are so much better off because of the change that we can redistribute income from the gainers to the losers and still have everyone better off under the income tax than under the excise tax.

Suppose that the government can finance the construction of a nuclear power plant with either an excise tax on cigarettes or an income tax. Since 50 percent of the adult population does not smoke cigarettes, the burden of the excise tax falls almost entirely on the other half of the population. Nonsmokers would of course support the excise tax as a financing vehicle.

---

†Note that $\dfrac{p_x^1}{p_y^1} \neq \dfrac{p_x^0}{p_y^0}$ since the excise tax is imposed only on good Y.

So long as at least one consumer consumes positive amounts of both X and Y, then the bundle he chooses under the income tax will differ from that under the excise tax, and so the revealed preference result can be applied.

What our argument says is this. Replacing the excise tax with an income tax would make smokers better off and nonsmokers worse off. Smokers gain so much by the change that we can use a lump-sum tax to reduce their incomes under the income tax, transfer this to nonsmokers, and make everyone (smokers and nonsmokers) better off than they would be under an excise tax on cigarettes. (This ignores the externalities associated with cigarette smoking, of course.)

Assuming transactions costs were negligible, we can conceive of this result (a change from an excise tax to an income tax) taking place through negotiations between smokers and nonsmokers. Smokers could "bribe" nonsmokers to vote for the income tax by promising to pay them enough so that the nonsmoker would still be able to purchase the bundle he chose under the excise tax. Our argument shows that there are enough gains for smokers that it is in their interest to offer high enough bribes and nonsmokers to accept such bribes so that the income tax gets voted in, assuming of course that the agreements as to voting could be policed.

Another way of characterizing our result is that in moving from an excise tax to an income tax, the gainers from the change can compensate the losers. If the compensation is actually paid, then the change is to a Pareto-superior state of the economy. But it is important that the compensation actually be paid; if there is no redistribution of income from gainers to losers, we are stuck with two Pareto noncomparable policies.

The Compensation Principle   It is important to emphasize that gainers must actually compensate losers if the unanimity rule is to apply to the evaluation of policies. This is admittedly a very restrictive condition, and economists have attempted to devise rules that bypass the difficulties associated with it. One such rule is known as the *compensation principle*, developed in the 1930s by Nicholas Kaldor and J. R. Hicks:

Policy A is to be judged better than policy B if the gainers under A can more than compensate those who lose in changing from B to A.

Note that the compensation principle does not require that compensations actually be paid (in which case A would be Pareto-superior to B), but only that they *could* be paid.

The fundamental objection to the ranking of alternatives using the compensation principle is that in A some people are better off and some people are worse off than in B. To assert that A is better than B then implicitly compares individual utilities and assigns a higher weight, in terms of welfare, to the gainers in A than to the losers. But there are other objections as well. As it turns out, the compensation principle can lead to the peculiar situation in which A is judged better than B, *and* B is judged better than A! This was first pointed out by Scitovsky, and can be illustrated very simply.†

Suppose that under policy A, the economy produces two units of X and one unit of Y; and under policy B, the economy produces one unit of X and two units of Y. There are two consumers, Mr. 1 and Mr. 2, with preferences as follows. (The first component is units of X, the second is units of Y.)

Mr. I: (1,1) preferred to (2,0), (2,0) preferred to (1,0)

---

†T. Scitovsky, "A Note on Welfare Propositions in Economics," *Review of Economic Studies* 9 (1941).

Mr. 2: (1,1) preferred to (0,2), (0,2) preferred to (0,1)

In states A and B assume output is distributed as follows:

	A	B
Total Output	(2,1)	(1,2)
Mr. 1	(2,0)	(1,0)
Mr. 2	(0,1)	(0,2)

Is A better than B under the compensation principle? The answer is yes, because if Mr. 1 gives Mr. 2 one unit of X, then we have a new state, say C, where the allocation is given by Mr. 1 (1,0), Mr. 2 (1,1). In state C, Mr. 2 is better off than in state B, while Mr. 1 is just as well off as in B. Applying the compensation principle, state A is better than state B.

Is B better than A? Again the answer is yes. Given the state B, let Mr. 2 give one unit of Y to Mr. 1. We obtain a new state D, with Mr. 1 having the bundle (1,1) while Mr. 2 has (0,1). Since Mr. 1 is better off in D than in A, while Mr. 2 is just as well off as in A, B is judged to be better than A under the compensation principle.

This means we can reject the compensation principle on the purely logical ground that it does not provide a well-defined criterion for judging as to which of two states is "better." Various attempts to patch up the compensation principle have resulted in comparable kinds of difficulties.

Consumer's Surplus and Welfare Economics

In chapter 5, the concept of consumer's surplus was introduced. Consumer's surplus is defined as the difference between what a consumer would be willing to pay to obtain a certain number of units of a good, and what he actually pays to obtain these units. Consumer's surplus can be depicted graphically as the shaded area in figure 13-7, where the demand curve for X is the income-compensated demand curve. Note that along demand curve D the price of Y is held constant at p_y^0, and the consumer remains on the indifference curve I_0. In contrast, along the observed demand curve, p_y is fixed at p_y^0 and income is held fixed at some value M_0.

Consumer's surplus provides a measure of the gains to the consumer from being able to purchase $\bar{X}$ units at the price $\bar{p}_x$, assuming that p_y is fixed. Thus consumer's surplus has relevance for welfare economics, particularly in measuring how much gainers would be willing to pay to obtain a specified number of units of a commodity. However, there are some severe limitations to the use of consumer's surplus in welfare economics.

To illustrate, suppose the government wishes to decide whether or not to install a dam on the Mississippi River. The alternatives are of

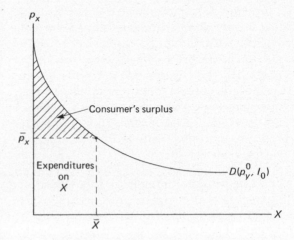

FIG. 13-7   *Consumer's surplus*

the "all or nothing" type—either a dam or no dam. The total cost of the dam is estimated, as are the services that the dam will provide. For simplicity, assume a one-person economy, and let $\bar{X}$ denote the services to the consumer from the dam, while $\bar{p}_x\bar{X}$ is the cost of the dam. Then, because there is a positive consumer's surplus area as in figure 13-7, the gains from the dam exceed its costs, and this surplus provides a welfare justification for building the dam.

Even in the one-consumer case, however, there is a qualification to be noted. Building the dam involves increasing demands for construction materials, laborers, and so on; hence prices of other commodities will be affected by an affirmative decision. All of these price effects have to be taken into account in evaluating the cost of the dam, if an unambiguous answer is to be arrived at as to the welfare implications of the decision to build the dam. But, in principle at least, it is possible to determine the general equilibrium effects of the dam construction, and having weighed these properly, consumer's surplus can be calculated and used as a criterion in evaluating the project.

Applying consumer's surplus analysis to real-world problems is much more complicated. To begin with, compensated demand curves are rarely known; instead, investigators have access at most to observed demand curves for commodities. Using the observed demand curve for a consumer to estimate consumer's surplus is valid, as noted in chapter 6, only if the income elasticity of demand for *every* good is unity. But in most cases, all that is available is the market demand curve for a commodity rather than the demand curves of all the individual consumers in the society. Using the market demand curve as the basis for arriving at welfare judgments means that what is being measured is *consumers'* surplus (note the placing of the

apostrophe), that is, the sum over all consumers of the area under the market demand curve. There is no way of telling which consumers gain and which lose from such a calculation, and of course the problems remain of using the incorrect observed demand curve rather than the compensated demand curve. And the general equilibrium problems remain as well—that is, the problems associated with the fact that other prices do change when changes are introduced into the market for a given commodity, say commodity X.

The conclusion to be derived from all this is that consumer's surplus is at best a very ambiguous measure of welfare. Conclusions derived from consumer's surplus analysis should be treated as highly tentative until they are verified by other approaches that explicitly take into account all of the issues discussed in this chapter. In particular, unless it can be shown that a policy results in a Pareto-superior state of the economy, support for the policy rests upon an implicit weighting of individuals in the society which assigns a higher weight to gainers than to losers.

Second Best and Welfare Economics

Finally, some comments should be made about what is known as "second-best" issues. Perhaps certain inefficiencies are built into an economic system, in the sense that they are beyond the control of economic policymakers. For example, a state-sponsored monopoly is established for political or military reasons, and this monopoly charges a price that differs from the marginal cost of production. Given such a built-in inefficiency, how should the economic system operate to achieve a desirable pattern of production and distribution of goods and services? This is a question of "second best";

ideally, we would reform the state monopoly and impose a pricing scheme on it that equates price to marginal cost, then permitting the rest of the economy to operate as a competitive system. Given the constraint (monopoly price greater than marginal cost), however, we must look for the next best way of organizing the economy, that is, the second-best way.

It can be argued that in a certain sense this issue is specious. If transactions costs are negligible, and if the economy is not at a Pareto optimum, then it is possible to bribe the operators of the state monopoly to change their policy to marginal cost pricing, with everyone being better off after this change, following appropriate redistributions of wealth. (This argument will be spelled out in more detail in chapter 17.) But if transactions costs are excessive, this alternative may not be available.

To be explicit, assume that X is produced by a state monopoly which buys its inputs in competitive markets and charges a price p_x that is larger than MC_x, the marginal cost of producing a unit of X. Y is produced by a competitive industry, with $p_y = MC_y$. This violates the marginal cost pricing rule for Pareto optimality.

What is a second-best solution to this problem? Given that we cannot change the pricing policy of the state monopoly, consider imposing a tax of t dollars per unit on the competitive industry producing Y. Then since Y is produced and sold in a competitive market, in equilibrium $p_y = MC_y + t$. Choose t so that

$$\frac{p_x}{MC_x} = \frac{MC_y + t}{MC_y}.$$

Then the price ratio will equal the ratio of marginal costs of production MC_x/MC_y, and a Pareto optimum is achieved.

What this simplified example illustrates is that in the face of built-in inefficiencies, generally policies must be adopted that interfere with the pricing and/or input-output policies of the competitive sector of the economy. And there are situations in which the built-in inefficiencies preclude the attainment of a Pareto optimum, whatever are the policies employed with respect to the competitive sector.

As important as such second-best problems may be in reality, our approach in the chapters that follow will be to assume that they can in fact be eliminated by negotiations, bribes, or other devices. Most of our attention in dealing with imperfections will be centered on cases in which the rest of the economy is assumed to operate competitively and only the industry isolated for study exhibits imperfections.

Summary

Modern welfare economics evaluates policies on the basis of the states of the economy achieved under them. States of the economy are ranked using the unanimity principle. If no one prefers state A to state B and at least one person prefers B to A, then B is said to be Pareto-superior to A. A state of the economy W is said to be Pareto-optimal relative to some set of states if W belongs to the set and there is no state in the set that is Pareto-superior to W. When there is a conflict of preferences among the members of a society, generally the feasible set of states for the society contains a number of Pareto-optimal states.

The competitive equilibrium has the properties that (I) every competitive equilibrium is a Pareto-optimal state; (II) every Pareto-optimal state is achievable as a competitive equilibrium, given the appropriate distribution of wealth among consumers. Property I is referred to as the *efficiency* property of the competitive system, while II is referred to as the *unbiasedness* property of the competitive system. Because of these properties, it is possible in a competitive economy to separate efficiency from equity issues by choosing the distribution of wealth (using lump-sum transfers), and then permitting the competitive system of prices to determine the allocation of resources for that distribution of wealth.

Policy A can be judged Pareto-superior to policy B if under A every consumer has available to him the bundle chosen as optimal under B, with market prices different in the two situations. In the absence of knowledge of the indifference maps of consumers (except that they satisfy the axioms of modern utility theory), this condition is necessary as well as sufficient in determining the Pareto superiority of A over B.

Problems

1. During the oil crisis in 1975, President Ford announced a plan to impose a tax on gasoline, the proceeds of the tax to be returned to consumers in the form of lump-sum grants. Show that there is no way of redistributing the proceeds of the tax among consumers such that each consumer is as well off as he was before the imposition of the tax. (Assume a competitive economy, and assume that consumers ignore the effect of grants on the cost to them of purchasing gasoline. Resources in the economy are assumed to be in fixed supply.)

2. A basic theorem of international trade theory is that in the absence of transportation costs, free international trade among competitive economies is efficient in the sense that free trade leads to a situation in which if world output of one good is increased, world output of some other good must be decreased.

   Assume a two-country world, each with fixed stocks of K and L, and each producing goods X and Y. Define the world production possibility set as the set of all feasible output mixes of X and Y, assuming that the fixed stocks of K and L in the two countries are immobile between countries. Show that if an output mix (X, Y) lies on the world transformation curve, then the slope of the transformation curve at the output mix for the first country equals the slope of the transformation curve at the output mix of the second country. Using the fact that GNP is maximized over each country's production possibility set, show that free international trade leads to efficient world production.

3. Discuss the merits of a 100 percent inheritance tax to finance government expenditures versus a graduated income tax. What possible inefficiencies are introduced by the first that are not present in the second (and vice versa)?

4. When there is a "conflict in preferences," welfare economics leaves the choice among Pareto-optimal states to ethics, politics, or religion. Are there any logical problems with deciding among Pareto-optimal states by using the rule of majority voting?

5. In the two-person two-commodity Edgeworth box case, interpret X as consumption today and Y as consumption tomorrow. Derive the marginal condition for Pareto optimality in a two-period horizon economy, and show that the perfectly competitive economy satisfies this condition at a competitive equilibrium.

6. Advertising expenditures result in a change in preferences on the part of consumers. Is there any way for welfare economics to judge whether such advertising expenditures lead to a Pareto-superior state?

Market Power

The theory of a perfectly competitive economy is based on the assumption that no market participant possesses any market power. Chapters 14 and 15 are concerned with the consequences for the economic system when one or more decision makers possess market power. Chapter 14 takes up the cases of a pure monopoly and a pure monopsony; while in Chapter 15, price leadership, monopolistic competition, duopoly, and oligopoly are discussed. The problem of market power is analyzed both from a positive and from a normative point of view: what are the effects of market power, and how are these effects related to welfare losses for the society? Special attention is given to price discrimination, the Averch-Johnson effect, and the elements of game theory.

14
Monopoly

The most obvious market imperfection that arises in an economic system is the existence of market power, with firms or suppliers of inputs being price makers rather than price takers. In fact, market power is so common that no one except an economist uses the term *competition* in the narrow sense to refer to an industry in which all firms are price takers. In common parlance, a "competitive" industry is one in which firms cut price on one another and compete in advertising and quality improvements in their products. The term *monopoly* has a different meaning to the economist than to the noneconomist as well. For the economist, a monopoly is a one-firm industry in the technical sense that the monopolist can set the price of his product without having to take into account the responses of firms selling similar or related products.

The restricted definition of the term *monopoly* as it is used in economic theory serves to isolate for analysis a single special case in the exercise of market power. It is the simplest of such cases, because it ignores the "strategic" aspects of decision making when market power is present. There are strategic elements present in decision making if the choices by one decision maker lead to reactions by other decision makers, and these reactions have to be taken into account by each decision maker. For example, the choice by the U.S. Defense Department of a missile deployment must take into account the fact that any deployment will produce a countering deployment by the Russians, and conversely. In a world where there is an entire spectrum of commodities, differentiated from one another by brand labels, advertising, and quality variations, with substitutability within and across industrial lines, most market power situations involve at least some strategic elements.

Our approach amounts to considering first (in this chapter) the simplest cases in the exercise of market power, reserving to the next chapter the difficult problems associated with strategic decision making. To keep the terminology as clear as possible, we will refer to the one-firm industry case as "pure monopoly."

Pure Monopoly

A pure monopoly exists when an industry consists of only one firm: the pure monopoly firm is the only producer and seller of the industry's product. A distinguishing characteristic of the pure monopoly is that the firm acts as a price maker in its decision making rather than as a price taker, as in the case of the perfectly competitive firm. The demand curve facing the pure monopolist is the industry demand curve. In the "typical" case the demand curve is downward sloping to the right; charging a higher price for output results in a fall in the number of units sold. Let X denote the output of the monopolistic firm, and let $TR(X)$, $TC(X)$ denote the total revenue and total costs respectively, associated with the output level X. Then the profits that accrue at an output X, $\pi(X)$, are given by

$$\pi(X) = TR(X) - TC(X)$$

where $\qquad TR(X) = p(X) \cdot X.$

Price per unit of output is written as $p(X)$ to indicate that the price that can be charged by the monopolist, p, is related to the output that can be sold, X, by the firm's demand curve, as illustrated in figure 14-1. The demand curve, $D(p)$, enables the monopolist to determine the number of units that can be sold at each price and vice versa. Thus X_1 units can be sold at p_1, X_2 at p_2, and so on, so that $p_1 = p(X_1)$, $p_2 = p(X_2)$, and so on.

We will continue to employ the simplifying assumption of a world in which each period is a repeat of the previous period. This means that the criterion of DPV maximization is equivalent to the criterion of profit maximization in each period. In particular we assume that the monopolist chooses price and the corresponding output to maximize profits. The rationale for this assumption is the same as in the case of the competitive firm; the owners of the monopolistic firm are concerned only with the income they can derive from their ownership interest and consequently the manager of the firm is charged with maximizing that income.

We have already seen that the competitive firm chooses an output level to maximize profits by equating marginal revenue to marginal cost, assuming that marginal cost is rising and that price is above the minimum of average variable cost. Things are a little more complicated in the case of the monopoly firm, but much the same principles apply. It is convenient to begin by looking at the revenue side of the profit picture for the monopolist.

Monopoly Revenue

At any level of output, revenue for the monopoly firm is equal to price times the number of units of output. Returning to the monopolist's demand curve, revenue is identified with the areas shown in figure 14-2. Revenue at output X_1 equals $p_1 \cdot X_1$, which is the area of the rectangle labeled TR_1. Similarly, revenue at X_2 is represented by the area of the TR_2 rectangle.

In general, what is the relationship between output and revenue or output increases? Does it increase (as in the case graphed), decrease, or what? The answer depends on the elasticity of the demand curve. If at a given level of output demand is elastic, then an increase in output (fall in price) leads to an increase in revenue; if demand is inelastic, an increase in

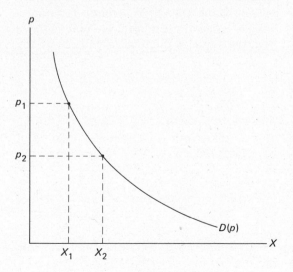

FIG. 14-1   *The demand curve of a pure monopolist*

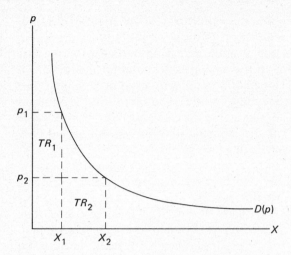

FIG. 14-2   *Monopolist's demand and total revenue*

The argument is straightforward. If demand is inelastic, then decreasing output increases the revenue of the firm (X is greater than $\bar{X}$); but decreasing output also decreases the costs of the firm, so that profits increase if output is decreased. Thus the monopoly firm cannot maximize profits at an output X if the demand curve is inelastic at X. In terms of the total revenue curve, profit maximization implies that $X < \bar{X}$.

Monopoly Average and Marginal Revenue Average revenue is defined as revenue per unit of output. Thus average revenue at an output X, $AR(X)$ is given by

$$AR(X) = \frac{TR(X)}{X} = \frac{p(X) \cdot X}{X} = p(X).$$

The demand curve facing the monopoly firm is thus the firm's average revenue curve, since at any output level, the price associated with that output level by the demand curve is also the firm's average revenue. In terms of the total revenue graph (fig. 14-3), average revenue at X is also equal to the tangent of the line drawn from the origin to the total revenue curve (fig.

output (decrease in price) results in a fall in revenue; and if demand is of unitary elasticity, revenue remains unchanged when output increases.

Generally speaking, we expect the demand curve to be more elastic at high prices than at low prices, because at high prices other goods become better substitutes for the good in question. Since output is related inversely to price, the total revenue curve for the monopolist appears as in figure 14-3. $\bar{X}$ represents the point of unitary elasticity along the demand curve, with demand inelastic for X greater than $\bar{X}$ and elastic if X is less than $\bar{X}$. That is, demand is inelastic at low prices and elastic at high prices.

Given that costs increase with the level of output, one conclusion can be derived immediately:

A profit-maximizing monopoly firm will never operate at a price and level of output such that the demand curve is inelastic at that output.

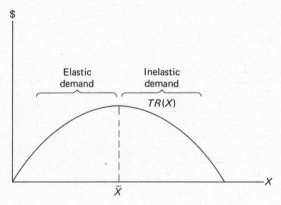

FIG. 14-3   *The monopoly total revenue curve*

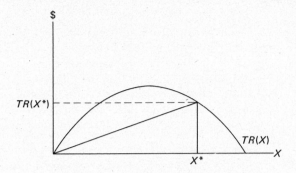

FIG. 14-4   *Average revenue for the monopoly firm*

14-4). Thus average revenue at X^*, $AR(X^*) = TR(X^*)/X^*$, which is the tangent of the line drawn from the origin to the $TR(X)$ curve at X^*.

Marginal revenue at X, $MR(X)$ is the change in revenue brought about by increasing output at X by one unit; that is,

$$MR(X) = \frac{\Delta TR(X)}{\Delta X},$$

where $\Delta TR(X)$ is the change in the revenue associated with a change in X of ΔX. $MR(X)$ can also be interpreted as the slope of the revenue function $R(X)$ at the point X, as in figure 14-5. $MR(X^0)$ is then equal to the slopes of the line AB, which is tangent to $TR(X)$ at X_0.

Note that at $\overline{X}$ where total revenue is a maximum and the demand curve is of unitary elasticity, the slope of the TR curve is zero, that is, $MR(X) = 0$. For X less than $\overline{X}$, marginal revenue is positive; for X greater than $\overline{X}$, marginal revenue is negative.

For a small change in X, ΔX, MR is given by

$$MR = \frac{\Delta TR}{\Delta X} = \frac{p\Delta X + X\Delta p}{\Delta X} = p + X\frac{\Delta p}{\Delta X}$$

where $\Delta p/\Delta X$ is the slope of the demand curve. In particular, if the demand curve is a straight line of the form $p = a - bX$, then the slope of the demand curve is $-b$, and MR can be calculated directly from the formula as

$$MR = p + X\frac{\Delta p}{\Delta X}$$
$$= (a - bX) - bX$$
$$= a - 2bX.$$

Plotting MR on the same graph as the linear demand curve we obtain figure 14-6. The intercepts of the AR and MR curves along the price axis are identically equal to a, while the X intercept of the MR curve lies halfway between the origin and the X intercept of the AR curve. Because both the AR and the MR curves are straight lines, we simply draw lines through the intercepts to construct these curves. In the case of a straight-line demand curve, the point of unitary elasticity occurs at the midpoint of the demand curve (at $\overline{X} = a/2b$) and $MR = 0$ at that output. Note also that marginal revenue

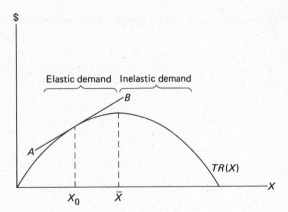

FIG. 14-5   *Marginal revenue of the monopoly firm*

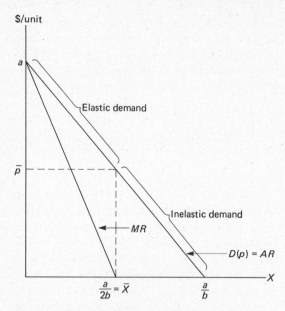

FIG. 14-6 *Average and marginal revenue—
linear demand curve*

is positive in the elastic portion of the demand
curve and negative in the inelastic portion of
the curve.†

*Marginal Revenue and Elasticity of De-
mand* Recall that elasticity of demand η_D at
the output X is defined as the percent change
in quantity demanded divided by the percent
change in price so that

$$\eta_D = \frac{\dfrac{\Delta X}{X}}{\dfrac{\Delta p}{p}} = \left(\frac{\Delta X}{\Delta p}\right)\left(\frac{p}{X}\right).$$

_____
†Recall that demand functions linear in prices and income
violate homogeneity of degree zero; hence the linear demand curve for the monopolist is shown only to illustrate
the concepts of AR and MR in a simplified context.

On the other hand,

$$MR = \left(\frac{\Delta p}{\Delta X}\right)X + p.$$

Thus there is a simple formula that applies to
all demand curves, whether they are straight
lines or not, relating η_D to MR. This is obtained
by solving for $\Delta p/\Delta X$ in the expression for η_D.
This gives

$$MR = p\left(1 + \frac{1}{\eta_D}\right) = AR\left(1 + \frac{1}{\eta_D}\right).$$

It is easy to verify that when

$$0 > \eta_D > -1$$

(demand is inelastic), MR is negative;

$$\eta_D = -1$$

(unitary elasticity) implies $MR = 0$;

$$\eta_D < -1$$

(elastic demand) implies MR is positive.

Profit Maximization and Monopoly

If the monopoly firm buys its inputs in competitive factor markets, then the cost curves for
the monopolist are derived in exactly the same
manner as those for the competitive firm, using
the approach in chapter 7. Profit maximization
implies that the monopoly firm will minimize
the cost of whatever output it decides to produce, and inputs will be hired in amounts such
that the ratio of the marginal products of any
two inputs will equal the ratio of their unit
costs. In figure 14-7, we derive the cost curve
of the monopolist and plot costs against output
for the short-run case of a U-shaped average
cost curve.

In figure 14-7a, costs for the monopoly firm

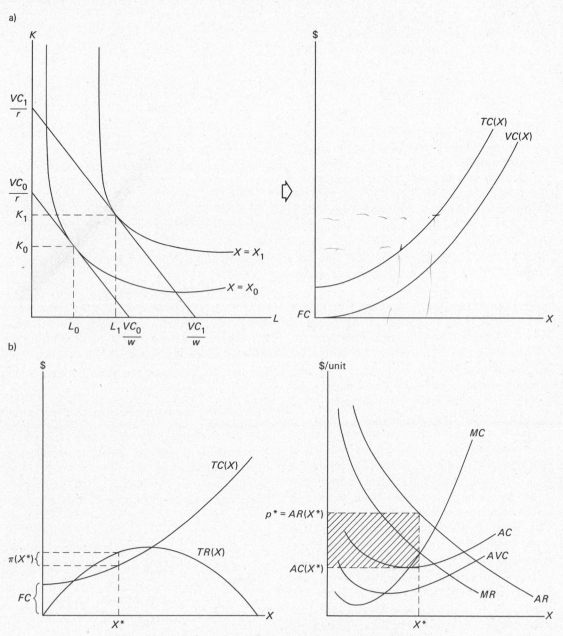

FIG. 14-7   a. *Short-run cost curves of the monopoly firm*
b. *Short-run profit maximization for the monopoly firm*

are derived as in the case of the competitive firm. In particular, at the output X_0, K_0 units of capital and L_0 units of labor are employed, with

$$\frac{MP_L}{MP_K} = \frac{w}{r} .$$

The same condition holds at (L_1, K_1), the cost-minimizing input combination to produce X_1 units of output.

The total cost curve $TC(X)$ is transferred to the total revenue graph on the left in figure 14-7b. At any output X, profits $\pi(X) = TR(X) - TC(X)$ is the vertical distance between the $TR(X)$ and $TC(X)$ curves. Profits are a maximum at X^* where marginal revenue, the slope of the TR curve, equals marginal cost, the slope of the TC curve.

The same situation is depicted in terms of average and marginal curves in figure 14-7b. At X^* marginal cost equals marginal revenue. The price charged is given by p^*, the price associated with X^* on the demand curve. Profits are represented by the shaded area, being equal to per unit profits $(AR(X^*) - AC(X^*))$ times X^*, the number of units produced.

Is there any qualification to the rule that the monopoly firm chooses the output level where $MR = MC$? The answer is that the monopolist will of course choose a positive output only if he can cover his variable costs. If price is so low that it is less than average variable costs, then the profit-maximizing output is zero units —the monopolist will shut down his plant. This outcome can arise only if the demand curve is below the AVC curve at every output level (fig. 14-8). Note that at X^* in figure 14-8 where $MR = MC$, p^* is less than average variable costs, because AR lies below AVC for every X. If the firm shuts down, it loses its fixed costs; if it operates, it loses its fixed costs plus part

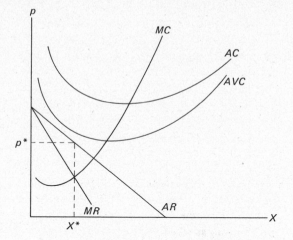

FIG. 14-8   *The shut-down decision*

of its variable costs as well. The profit-maximizing decision is to close the plant, when $AR < AVC$ for every output level. If there is *any* output level at which $AR > AVC$, then the firm will continue to operate at some such level, since its losses are less than its fixed costs.

Monopoly Demand for Factors of Production

Assume that the monopolist hires his inputs in competitive markets. In other words, the inputs employed by the monopolist are also employed in other industries, with the monopolist's demands for inputs being only a negligible fraction of the total demands for them. Because the monopolist is a cost minimizer at any output level he chooses to produce, inputs, say capital K and labor L, are hired to the point where

$$\frac{MP_L}{MP_K} = \frac{w}{r} ,$$

where r is the rental rate per unit of capital and w is the wage rate per unit of labor. In choosing an input mix to produce a given level of output, the monopolist duplicates the actions of a cost-minimizing, perfectly competitive firm. With the same technology and the same factor prices, the costs curves of a competitive firm and a pure monopoly would be identical.

However, in determining the level of output to produce and thus the number of units of capital and labor to hire, the monopolist takes into account the fact that each additional unit of output produced causes a fall in the market price of the firm's product. Recall that profit maximization implies that inputs are hired to the point where the last unit of each input hired adds as much to revenue as it does to cost (marginal revenue product of any input is set equal to its marginal cost).

For the perfectly competitive firm, this means that capital and labor are each hired to the point where

$$MRP_K = p \cdot MP_K = r$$

$$MRP_L = p \cdot MP_L = w.$$

(Thus, since capital can be rented for r dollars per unit, r is the marginal cost of capital. An additional unit of capital increases output by MP_K, the marginal product of capital, and this sells for p dollars per unit. Hence $p \cdot MP_K$ is the marginal revenue product of capital.)

For the monopoly firm purchasing inputs in a perfectly competitive input market, w and r are the marginal costs per unit of labor and capital respectively, just as they are for the competitive firm. But the marginal revenue products of labor and capital are somewhat more complicated than for the competitive firm. The marginal revenue products in the case of monopoly are given by

$$MRP_K = MR \cdot MP_K = \frac{\Delta TR}{\Delta X} \cdot \frac{\Delta X}{\Delta K}$$

$$MRP_L = MR \cdot MP_L = \frac{\Delta TR}{\Delta X} \cdot \frac{\Delta X}{\Delta L}$$

Adding one unit of capital (with labor fixed) increases output by an amount given by MP_K. But adding one unit to output for the monopolist firm increases total revenue by the amount MR. Hence for the monopolist, $MR \cdot MP_K$ is the marginal revenue product of capital and $MR \cdot MP_L$ is the marginal revenue product of labor. It follows that for the monopolist, inputs K and L are hired to the point where

$$MR \cdot MP_K = \left(p + X \frac{\Delta p}{\Delta X} \right) \cdot MP_K = r$$

$$MR \cdot MP_L = \left(p + X \frac{\Delta p}{\Delta X} \right) \cdot MP_L = w$$

Given that the monopoly firm faces a downward sloping demand curve, then $MR(X)$ is always less than $p(X)$, as given by the demand curve, for every output X. To verify this, recall that

$$MR(X) = p(X)\left(\frac{1}{\eta_D} + 1 \right)$$

where η_D, the elasticity of demand, is negative. This means that the monopoly firm hires fewer units of labor and capital than would be the case if it treated price as a constant, as perfectly competitive firms do. This conclusion is related to a systematic distortion in the allocation of resources in an economy with a monopolistic industry as contrasted with a perfectly competitive economy.

Welfare Losses Due to Monopolies

It has long been recognized in the common law that monopoly power leads to a misallocation of resources in the economy. As a starting point in identifying the source of this misallocation, we consider a simplified case. Assume that a product could be produced either by a monopolistic firm or by a competitive industry, both having the same cost curves. There are good reasons to believe that this is unrealistic, since monopolies often arise because of cost advantages due to scale of operations. But as a crude first approximation, this assumption permits us to see what the effects of monopoly power are. Figure 14-9 shows the cost-revenue situation for the short-run case of a U-shaped cost curve.

The monopoly maximizes profits by choosing the price-output combination $A = (X_1, p_1)$, where $MR = MC$. Under competition, the market price and output are set at the point where the industry supply curve (the MC curve) crosses the demand curve, which means that the competitive industry operates at the point $B = (X_2, p_2)$. The effect of monopoly

power is to restrict output (X_1 is less than X_2) and to increase price (p_1 is greater than p_2). In addition, profits are higher under monopoly than under competition, since at A profits are maximized, given the demand curve $D(p)$. Because output is less under monopoly than under competition, input hiring is restricted as well. Thus the distribution of income under monopoly shifts in the direction of higher profits for the owners of the monopoly firm with smaller earnings within the industry for the inputs K, L used in producing the industry's output. Hence monopoly control of an industry distorts price, output, and the distribution of income, as compared to the case of a competitive industry with the same costs.

Pareto Optimality and Monopoly

The comparison of the output and pricing policies of a monopolist with a hypothetical competitive industry with the same cost curves suffers from two defects. First, there is no assurance that costs under a competitive organization of the industry would be identical to those of the monopolistic firm. Second, the analysis is partial equilibrium in nature, ignoring the impacts on other industries and the input markets of a change from monopoly to competition. As was emphasized in chapter 13, issues concerning *welfare losses* require treatment in a general equilibrium framework.

We can show that with monopoly control of the X industry (and with other markets operating competitively), the economy is not at a Pareto optimum. Consider the production possibility set for a one-consumer economy. As constructed in chapter 12, the outer boundary of that set, the "transformation curve" for the economy, is derived by plotting all the combinations of outputs (X, Y) such that there are

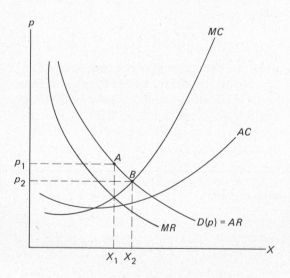

FIG. 14-9   *Short-run price-output policies—monopoly and competition*

tangencies of isoquants in the Edgeworth-Bowley box diagram. Tangencies of isoquants occur at points where the cost minimization condition

$$\frac{MP_L}{MP_K} = \frac{w}{r}$$

is satisfied. This condition is satisfied both for the monopolist and for the competitive industry, given competitive input markets. So long as input markets are perfectly competitive and externalities are not present, the economy will always operate on its transformation curve.

Consider the case of a one-consumer economy. Under perfect competition in the output markets, the economy achieves the point B as in figure 14-10. The slope of the *GNP* line expresses the ratio of the competitive prices p_x/p_y, with the joint tangency of the indifference curve and the transformation curve guaranteeing that markets are cleared.

How do things differ when a monopolist controls industry *X*? Because the monopolist operates in competitive input markets, the

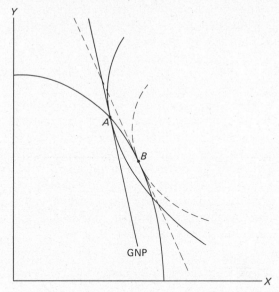

Note: A = monopoly situation; B = competitive situation

FIG. 14-11   *Monopoly control of X*

economy will still be on its transformation curve. On the other hand, the monopolist charges a higher price for good *X* than would be charged if *X* were produced competitively. The consequence is shown in figure 14-11.

The equilibrium under monopoly control of *X* is at *A*, where the *GNP* line is steeper (the p_x/p_y ratio is greater than under competition). Markets still clear, so there must be a tangency at *A* between an indifference curve and the new *GNP* line. The production of *X* has been cut back with the resources released from *X* being used to increase the output of *Y*. The economy still satisfies production efficiency (*A* is on the transformation curve), but the output mix violates Pareto optimality because, with the resources available to the economy, the consumer could achieve a more preferred point, namely *B*, without violating the resource limitations. The same general conclusion carries

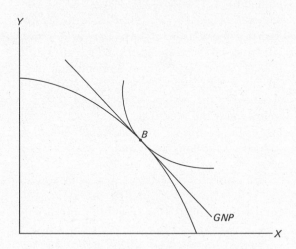

FIG. 14-10   *Competitive equilibrium*

over to economies with many consumers.†

Thus there is a *welfare loss* under monopoly as indicated by the fact that the consumer is on a lower indifference curve than could be achieved given the technology and the resources available to the economy.

The existence of this welfare loss represents the economic justification for government ownership, control, or regulation of monopolies. Of course, there are other possible justifications for controlling monopolies, in particular the distortions that are introduced into political activities by the power of monopolies. Our interest here, however, is in the purely economic aspects of monopoly power.

The Size of the Welfare Losses Due to Monopoly

The analysis of the last section establishes that when monopoly exists in one industry in an economy, the other industries being competitive, then the economy is not a Pareto-optimal state. Thus there are welfare losses arising from the existence of a monopoly. But how important are such welfare losses? This is a very controversial issue in economics. Studies by several prominent economists dating back to

---

†There is one qualification concerning the many-consumer economy. Monopoly leads to a non-Pareto-optimal result. However, the competitive solution is not necessarily Pareto-superior to the monopoly solution. Generally, shifting from *A* to *B* along the transformation curve means that some individuals are injured (including the owners of the monopoly firm) while others are benefited (especially those who are consumers of *X* and the owners of factors specialized to the production of *X*). The fact that the monopoly solution is not Pareto-optimal means that a change to the competitive solution, *with appropriate compensation to losers,* is Pareto-superior. If the compensation is not paid, then generally the monopoly solution *A* and the competitive solution *B* are Pareto noncomparable.

the mid-1950s claim that the welfare losses due to monopoly power are insignificant, with estimates as low as one-tenth of 1 percent of U.S GNP. The final answer is not in yet; recent studies dispute the earlier claims, indicating that losses might range up to 7 or 8 percent of GNP.†

The question itself is an interesting one, however, as is the measure of welfare loss employed in the various studies, which is based on consumers' surplus. To keep things as simple as possible, suppose we continue to think in terms of a one-consumer world. Again for simplicity, assume that there are constant costs for a monopolized industry producing good X. The measure of the welfare loss due to monopoly employed in the various studies is the area of the triangle ABC in figure 14-12.

The demand curve $D_X(p_y, I_0)$ is the compensated demand curve of the consumer with p_y constant and the level of indifference I_0 constant as well. Constant costs imply the straight line $MC = ATC$ curve. Under monopoly, the point $A = (p_M, X_M)$ is chosen while under competition, $C = (p_c, X_c)$ occurs. At A, consumer's surplus is the area underneath the demand curve from p_M up. But at A profits (the area of the rectangle $p_M ABp_c$) also go to the consumer. At C, under competition, there are no profits, and consumer's surplus is the area under the demand curve from p_c up. It follows that the area ABC is a measure of the loss to the consumer from monopoly power in industry X, so long as p_y and I_0 are held constant.

The estimates of welfare loss due to monopoly power involve estimating the areas ABC for various industries in which monopoly

---

†A. Bergson, "On Monopoly Welfare Losses," *American Economic Review* 63 (December 1973).

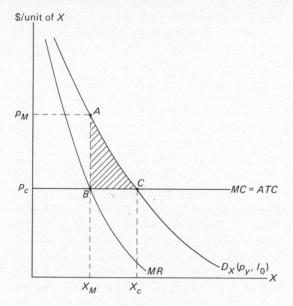

FIG. 14-12 *Welfare loss due to monopoly*

power exists. Clearly the estimates will be affected mainly by the elasticity of the demand curve; the more elastic the curve, the smaller the area *ABC*.

A basic difficulty in getting good estimates of elasticity of demand is that the demand curve to be estimated is the compensated demand curve rather than the observed demand curve, as noted in our discussion in chapter 5 and chapter 13. Moreover, since this is a partial equilibrium approach to a general equilibrium problem, interpreting any results obtained is difficult. That is, we need to consider the impact of monopoly on other markets. Finally, once we leave the one-person world and think in terms of a many-consumer economy, the equity effects of monopoly power cannot be ignored if one is to arrive at any conclusion relative to the *significance* of the welfare losses due to monopoly. It is perhaps not surprising

that the issue of "how important are the welfare losses due to monopoly" remains unresolved within the economics profession.

Natural and Artificial Barriers to Entry and Monopoly Power

Our discussion thus far has been in terms of short-run monopoly power. If there were no barriers to entry into any industry, then it is clear that monopoly power would be purely a short-run phenomenon. After all, if the monopolist sets price above the competitive level and restricts output to maximize profits, the excess profits that result would create incentives for entry into the industry, until price is forced down to the long-run competitive level where $p = $ minimum *LRAC*. Monopoly power can persist only if there are natural or artificial barriers to entry into the industry.

By *natural barriers* to entry into an industry we mean the barriers that arise because of the technological characteristics of the industry, while *artificial barriers* are those created by the social, political, or economic institutions of the society. A natural barrier to employment as a major league baseball player is that you must be able to hit or field or pitch; an artificial barrier that operated very effectively up to 1947 was that you had to be white. Artificial barriers include patents and copyrights, control of an essential raw materials source and licensing requirements of a governmental or quasi-governmental body. A natural barrier to entry is the presence of increasing returns to scale in an industry, which permits large firms to undercut any smaller prospective entrant, making entry unprofitable. Increasing returns to scale will be treated in the next section, which deals with the case of "natural" monopolies.

While natural barriers to entry provide explanations for such traditional monopolies as gas, electric, and water utilities, artificial barriers are much more pervasive in our society. Beginning with the passage of the Interstate Commerce Commission Act of 1887, a bewildering array of governmental regulatory agencies have come into existence, each chartered to "protect the public interest." The list of industries being regulated is almost endless—railroads, trucking firms, airlines, cab companies, telephone companies, television and radio stations, the securities markets, banks, savings and loan associations, liquor stores, bars, to name a few. In many of these cases, regulation came only after the firms in the industry asked for help in correcting such "abuses" as price wars and other forms of "unfair" competition. Unfortunately, the agencies have been only too successful in stabilizing the regulated industries, and a particularly effective method of achieving this is to limit entry into the industry. Government possesses the power of enforcement that can make barriers to entry really effective in a way that is difficult, if not impossible, for firms to achieve by themselves. The fact that barriers are artificial does not mean that they are not every bit as important as natural barriers.

The "Natural Monopoly" Case

When there are increasing returns to scale, the industry is called a "natural monopoly." Increasing returns are often associated with the presence of "lumpy" inputs, such as highly specialized machinery and equipment. In principle, it is possible to produce steel in your backyard, as Red China has recently demonstrated; but the technology associated with producing ten tons of steel per year is quite different from the open-hearth furnaces and electric furnaces used to produce steel in the millions of tons per year. There is a technical problem of "scaling" machinery to output levels. Generally speaking, it is not possible to construct an efficient machine of one-tenth the scale of a given machine in order to produce one-tenth the output per year; instead, completely different machinery is needed. The superior efficiency of the machinery designed for large output levels produces the "lumpiness" that leads to increasing returns to scale.

With increasing returns to scale, there is a natural barrier to entry into an industry. A firm operating under increasing returns and facing competitive input markets can undercut any firm producing a smaller output level, since per unit costs fall as output increases. This means that with increasing returns, the monopoly firm can charge prices that generate excess profits without entry occurring. Any prospective entrant faces the problem that the monopolist can "squeeze" him out by lowering price in the short run to the level where the entrant takes losses, only to raise the price again to the monopoly level once the entrant has been bankrupted.

The best known examples of natural monopolies are public utilities such as electric power companies, natural gas pipelines, telephone companies, and water and gas companies. Most of these are regulated firms, with price and output being subject to state or federal controls, or are owned and operated by a government body. Controls are imposed on the privately owned utilities because of the welfare losses that occur when monopolistic pricing and output setting takes place, coupled with the fact that even in the long run, market forces are inadequate to ensure the elimination of monopoly abuses. But there are special problems that arise in regulation of natural monopolies if the Pareto criteria are to be satisfied.

Regulation and Natural Monopolies

At a Pareto optimum, prices of goods must be proportionate to their marginal costs of production, assuming that input markets are competitive. In a perfectly competitive industry, the price per unit of output is set equal to marginal cost; hence at a Pareto optimum with all other firms operating competitively, the price and output of a natural monopoly industry must be such that price and marginal cost are equated as well.

Figure 14-13 shows the situation of a natural monopoly industry under unrestricted monopoly control, at a Pareto optimum, and under "rate of return" price regulation. With increasing returns to scale over all output levels, ATC falls as output increases, with MC less than ATC at all output levels. The unrestricted monopolist chooses the profit-maximizing combination $A = (X_0, p_0)$, satisfying the condition $MR = MC$. Pareto optimality is violated since $p_0 > MC$ at X_0.

In fact, Pareto optimality requires that output be set at X_2 with price of p_2 at the point labeled C; $p_2 = MC$ at X_2. But because MC is below ATC, the firm would suffer a loss equal to $X_2 \cdot [AC(X_2) - p_2]$ where $AC(X_2)$ is AC evaluated at X_2. The amount of the loss is shown as the shaded area on the graph. Under a regulatory policy that aims at attaining Pareto optimality, a subsidy equal to this loss would have to be paid to the firm in order to keep it in business. If the firm does not cover its average costs in the long run, the firm goes out of business of course.

The political problems associated with subsidizing natural monopolies (plus the difficulties of determining true marginal costs) have led in practice to "average cost pricing"—that is, regulation that results in the price output combination B, where the regulated firm earns only normal profits. Average cost pricing regulation automatically means that there are welfare losses for the society—output of the regulated industry is less and price is higher than at a Pareto optimum. But things are even more distorted than this.

The Averch-Johnson Effect   The typical way in which average cost pricing is implemented by regulatory commissions is to set rates for such natural monopolies as power and light companies so that the regulated firm earns a "fair rate of return" on its invested capital. There are problems with the concept of a "fair" rate of return, but generally it can be interpreted as the regulatory commission's approximation to "normal profits." Even more problems arise because of the way in which the regulatory commissions determine the "rate base"—the invested capital on which the utility is to earn a "fair" rate of return.

As a practical matter, the utility regulatory commissions restrict the rate base for a utility to the physical plant and equipment used in the regulated activities of the utility—such as generating equipment and transmission lines

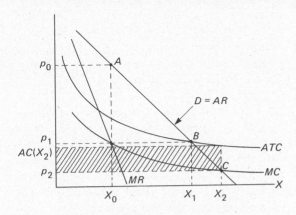

FIG. 14-13   *Pricing policies and the natural monopoly firm*

for power utilities, and switching stations and telephone networks for telephone companies. This restriction produces a systematic bias in the choice of inputs by utility companies in favor of inputs that qualify for inclusion in the rate base, and against those (such as labor) that do not qualify. In the literature of regulated industries, this bias is referred to as the Averch-Johnson effect (A-J effect), after the two economists who first studied it in a systematic way.†

The A-J effect may be illustrated as follows. The regulated firm rents K units of capital services each period, each unit of such services requiring a stock of one unit of a capital good to supply such services. The value of the capital goods required to provide the K units of capital services per period is then Kp_l, where p_l is the price of a unit of a capital good. As we have seen from chapter 11, $p_l = r/i$. The regulatory commission allows a rate of return of ρ percent per dollar of capital goods employed by the firm, so that the allowed profits of the firm are ρKp_l. Renting one more unit of capital services thus increases the rate base of the regulated firm, at the same time that it adds to the rental costs of the firm. Hiring one more unit of capital services increases costs by r dollars and increases revenue by $\rho r/i$. So long as ρ is greater than i, the cost to the firm of adding a unit of capital services is some amount r^* less than the market rental r. In effect, rate of return regulation leads to a decrease in the per unit cost of capital services, and this decrease leads to a substitution of capital for other inputs (such as labor). This substitution increases the average and marginal costs of the firm for every level of output, as shown in figure 14-14.

---

†H. Averch, and L. Johnson, "Behavior of the Firm under Regulatory Constraint," *American Economic Review* 52 (December 1962).

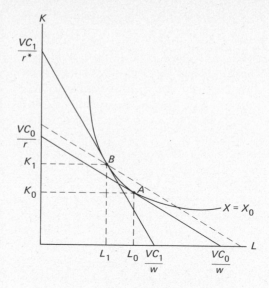

FIG. 14-14   *Cost minimization for the regulated firm*

In the absence of regulation, the firm produces X_0 units using the input combination $A = (L_0, K_0)$ with a variable cost of VC_0. Under regulation, the isocost line is steeper since the net cost per unit of K to the firm has fallen to $r^* < r$, and the firm chooses the input combination $B = (L_1, K_1)$ substituting capital for labor. Note that the variable cost associated with B at prices w per unit of L and r per unit of K, is higher than variable cost at A, as indicated by the dotted line through B.

Since this effect holds at every output level, the ATC and MC curves of the firm are shifted upward, as shown in figure 14-15. The effect of rate of return regulation is to shift AC and MC upward to AC' and MC', resulting in a fall in output from X to X' and a rise in price from p to p'. The A-J effect results in the use of inefficient production methods, plus a further movement away from the Pareto-optimal output where $MC = p$.

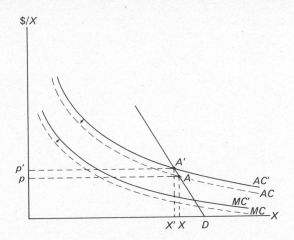

FIG. 14-15   *Price and output
for the regulated firm*

Pure Monopsony

The term *pure monopsony* refers to the case in which there is only a single buyer in the market for some commodity; it corresponds to the case of pure monopoly on the selling side of a market. Like pure monopoly, the case of pure monopsony is quite rare, but the conditions characterizing it are approximated in many real-world situations. Monopsony typically arises in the market for inputs, but there are cases in which it occurs in the market for finished products as well. For example, pure monopsony is approximated in an input market in the case of an industrial firm located in a small town, when the firm dominates the market for certain specialized types of labor; monopsony occurs in an output market when a rural cooperative buys all of the output of an electric generating plant for distribution among its members.

It is possible to distinguish between the selling and buying characteristics of a firm. Thus,

an industrial firm might be a pure monopsonist in the local market for labor, but sell its product in national or international markets where conditions approach the perfectly competitive norm. Similarly, a monopolistic seller might be located in an area where its demands for inputs are infinitesimal relative to the total market demands, and hence it could also be a perfectly competitive purchaser of inputs.

The relevant characteristic of the pure monopsonist is that he takes into account the effect of his actions on the price of the input he is purchasing. Consider the case of a firm that is a pure monopsonist in the local market for labor, while the firm's product is sold in a perfectly competitive market. If the firm were perfectly competitive both in buying inputs and in selling its product, then labor would be hired to the point where $pMP_L = w$. Acting instead as a pure monopsonist in the labor market, the situation is as depicted in figure 14-16.

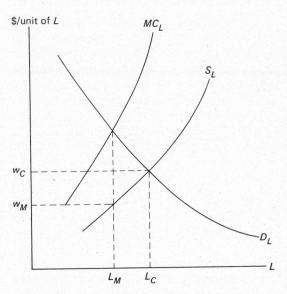

FIG. 14-16   *Monopsony in the labor market*

D_L and S_L refer to the demand and supply of labor respectively, while MC_L is the marginal cost of labor, defined as the increase in labor costs to the firm from hiring one more laborer. The supply curve of labor is taken to be upward sloping, and the demand curve for labor by the firm is downward sloping for the reasons referred to in chapter 8. Under competitive conditions, the market for labor would be cleared at the wage rate (w_C) where the demand for labor equals the supply of labor, with L_C units of labor being hired.

When the firm is a monopsonist in the market for labor, it is cognizant of the fact that an increase in the number of units of labor hired increases the wage rate, since the firm faces an upward sloping supply curve of labor. To maximize its profits, the firm hires the number of units of labor such that the marginal revenue product of labor equals marginal cost. Because the firm sells its output in a perfectly competitive market, the marginal revenue product of labor is simply $p \cdot MP_L$. But the firm is a monopsonist in the market for labor. The marginal cost of labor is no longer w, as in the perfectly competitive case. Instead the firm takes into account that hiring one more unit of labor increases the wage that has to be paid to all units of labor previously hired, as indicated by the upward sloping supply curve S_L.

Assume that labor is the only variable input.

$$MC_L = \frac{\Delta(wL)}{\Delta L}$$

is calculated as follows.

$$MC_L = \frac{\Delta(wL)}{\Delta L} = \frac{w\Delta L + L\Delta w}{\Delta L} = w + L\frac{\Delta w}{\Delta L}$$

where $\Delta w/\Delta L$ is the slope of the supply curve of labor, S_L. In particular if S_L is linear,

$$w = a + bL$$

with

$$\frac{\Delta w}{\Delta L} = b,$$

then $MC_L = (a + bL) + bL = a + 2bL.$

MC_L and S_L have the same intercept on the w axis, with MC_L rising twice as steeply as S_L.

The interpretation of the expression

$$MC_L = w + L\frac{\Delta w}{\Delta L}$$

is as follows. Adding one unit of labor increases costs not only by the amount of the wage that has to be paid to that unit of labor (w), but also by the amount of the raise Δw to the new higher wage rate that every laborer previously hired now gets; this increase accounts for the additional term $L(\Delta w/\Delta L)$. Because S_L is upward sloping, $\Delta w/\Delta L$ is positive. Hence MC_L is above the supply curve of labor at every level of L.

Returning to figure 14-16, hiring labor to the point where $MC_L = p \cdot MP_L$ means that the monopsonist chooses to hire L_M units of labor. What does he pay each unit hired? We read this off S_L. To hire L_M units of labor, the firm has to pay w_M dollars per unit. We thus arrive at the following conclusion.

Under monopsony with an upward sloping supply curve of the input, price paid per unit of the input is lower than would be the case under perfect competition, and fewer units are hired.

In the market for labor, monopsony results in a lower wage rate and in fewer laborers being hired than would be true under perfect competition.

As in the case of monopoly, monopsony leads to a non-Pareto-optimal allocation of resources in the economy. In contrast to the monopoly case, under monopsony the production efficiency condition

$$\frac{MP_L}{MP_K} = \frac{w}{r}$$

is violated so that the economy ends up at an interior point of its production possibility set, below the transformation curve. This means that it is possible to increase the output of all goods in the economy, by reallocating resources so that more labor is allocated to that industry where there is a monopsony with respect to labor, with other inputs being freed to increase output elsewhere.

Graphically, the monopsony solution appears as in figure 15-17. With a monopsony with respect to labor in industry X, the allocation of labor and capital to industry X violates the efficiency condition

$$\frac{MP_L}{MP_K} = \frac{w}{r}.$$

Thus, the economy is not on its transformation curve. Markets are cleared at $(\overline{X}, \overline{Y})$, but GNP is not maximized over the production possibility set. An appropriate reallocation of capital and labor would permit the attainment of a higher indifference curve; hence Pareto optimality is violated.

Monopoly Power and Unions

Just as there exist monopsonists with market power on the buying side of certain input markets, there also exist input markets where there are monopolists on the supply side. The best known monopolists on the supply side of input markets are labor unions, which restrict entry into the labor markets they control, and bargain with employers for wages and fringe benefits

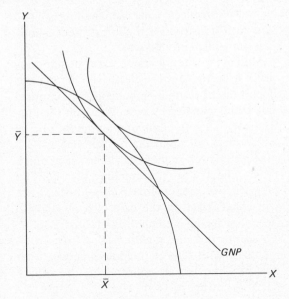

FIG. 14-17 *Monopsony equilibrium*

for their members. The traditional justification for encouraging the growth of unions has been that monopsony power on the part of employers requires monopoly unions to protect the interests of laborers. Whatever the validity of this "countervailing power" argument, the fact is that for a number of categories of labor skills, unions or labor organizations possess monopoly control of supply.

There is no generally accepted economic theory of union behavior. This is hardly surprising, since the union is a collective organization much like the society itself. The union members have diverse preferences even with respect to matters concerned solely with the labor market, and so there is no single "will of the members" that governs union decision making. As the Arrow paradox of majority voting shows, even if each union member has a complete, transitive preference ranking over alternatives, collective decision making can still lead to intransitivities if the preference rankings are sufficiently diverse.

Moreover, when a union faces a monopsonistic firm, we have the classic case of one monopoly facing another—monopoly on the supply side being matched by monopsony on the buying side. This is *bilateral monopoly,* one of many unsolved problems in economics. As a practical matter, economists do not have much to say about what the outcome of a conflict between two monopolists will be. Instead, we will concentrate on the case of a monopolistic union facing a competitive industry.

Assume that the preferences of the union members with respect to choices between leisure and income are reflected in the supply curve S_L in figure 14-18, while D_L is the demand curve by the competitive industry for the services of labor. The MR_L curve is constructed as with demand curves for outputs. At any value of L, MR_L is the increase in expenditures on labor when an additional laborer is hired. Such expenditures are a maximum at L_1 where the demand curve D_L is of unitary elasticity.

In the absence of union control, the competitive market solution occurs at $A = (L_0, w_0)$ where $S_L = D_L$. Consider in contrast the case where the union acts to maximize income for its membership. Clearly, this occurs at $B = (L_1, w_1)$, since D_L is of unitary elasticity at this point. The effect of union control has been to increase the wage rate (from w_0 to w_1) and to decrease the hiring of labor (from L_0 to L_1) as compared to the competitive solution. There is more income available in total for laborers, and fewer laborers share this income.

Admittedly, we have taken an extreme case. The dissatisfaction of unemployed members will certainly have some effect in deterring the

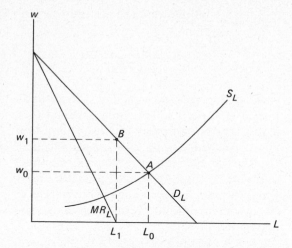

FIG. 14-18   *Union control of the labor market— income maximization*

union from a simple income-maximizing strategy. But it is important to note that *any* strategy on the part of a union designed to increase the wage rate above the competitive level results in a decrease in employment and hence results in some disaffected workers. It is the existence of workers who would be willing to work at the competitive wage but are excluded from jobs at the union determined wage rate that necessitates restrictions on memberships on the part of unions. These workers constitute the "long-run" problem for a union; the more effective the union is in raising the wage rate, the more potential workers there are who would be willing to take jobs at less than union scale, and hence the greater chance that nonunion firms will appear in the industry.

Monopoly power exercised by a union results in a non-Pareto optimum just as it does in the case where monopoly power is exercised by a firm. The loss of efficiency occurs in part because at the margin workers are not indifferent between leisure and consumption; at the union wage, there are workers who would like to work additional hours or enter the union but cannot because of restrictions on entry into union jobs.

Price Discrimination and Monopoly

Returning to the case of a monopoly firm, thus far we have been dealing with the case of a product for which there is only a single market. In fact there are important real-world instances in which the monopolist finds it possible to segregate the markets in which his product is sold and to engage in discriminatory pricing. Despite the loaded terminology, discriminatory pricing is not necessarily a bad thing; in fact it might be required in order to attain an optimum allocation of resources.

For example, consider the sale of telephone services. During the peak usage period (8 A.M. to 5 P.M. weekdays), telephone exchanges tend to operate at or near capacity, while off-peak traffic constitutes only a negligible load on telephone facilities. Certainly any policy requiring that the same rates be charged at all times of the day makes no economic sense. Similar peak/off-peak problems arise with electricity, gas, and water utilities; seasonal demands for motel rooms and resorts; scheduling golf courses and swimming pools; and backhauls of railroads and highway carriers. The point is that peak and off-peak services are really distinctly different products, and an efficient pricing system will reflect the different marginal costs that are involved in supplying these services.

There is one fundamental condition that must be satisfied before price discrimination among markets can take place: secondary markets in the product must not exist. For example, a monopolist could hardly sell a product at $1 per unit to one group of individuals and at $2 per unit to another group if it were possible to establish a market in which the $1 purchasers could sell at a profit to the potential $2 purchasers. For this reason, we will take the case of peak/off-peak pricing of nontransferable services (such as telephone communications) as our leading example.

Assume that there is a peak demand schedule $D_1(p_1)$ where p_1 is the price changed during peak hours, and a demand schedule $D_2(p_2)$, with p_2 the price during off-peak hours. The demand schedules are graphed in figure 14-19.

For simplicity, both types of demands are taken to be linear, and $D_1 + D_2$ represents the sum of the two demands. ($D_1 + D_2$ equals D_1 for $p \geq \hat{p}$ and is the horizontal sum of the two curves for $p \leq \hat{p}$.) We also are assuming that peak demand is not affected by the off-peak price, and vice versa. Actually there typically is some substitution possible so far as peak and off-peak demands are concerned, but we will ignore this problem here.

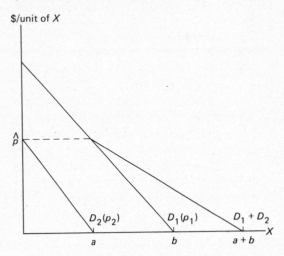

FIG. 14-19 *Peak $(D_1(p_1))$ and off-peak $(D_2(p_2))$ demands*

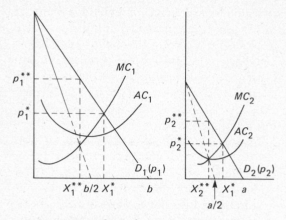

FIG. 14-20   *Independent costs* $C_1(X_1)$, $C_2(X_2)$

The profit-maximizing monopolist sets p_1 at the level where $MR_1 = MC_1$, and p_2 where $MR_2 = MC_2$ (the subscripts refer to peak and off-peak marginal revenues and costs respectively). Consider first the case where production costs can be separated so that there is a cost function $C_1(X_1)$ for peak production and a second cost function $C_2(X_2)$ for off-peak production, both independent of one another (fig. 14-20).

As long as costs are independent, we can treat peak and off-peak services as separate products. The competitive solution is to set price and output so that $p_1 = MC_1$, $p_2 = MC_2$, while the monopoly solution sets $MR_1 = MC_1$, $MR_2 = MC_2$ with the usual suboptimality results. (Again we are assuming that costs are identical under competition or monopoly.)

Note that with independent costs, the competitive solution involves price discrimination between peak and off-peak services, with the peak price p_1^* greater than the off-peak price p_2^*. Monopoly prices p_1^{**} and p_2^{**} are higher than competitive prices, of course.

A somewhat more interesting case is that in which costs depend on the sum of outputs $X_1 + X_2$. If costs depend only on total output,

then marginal cost is the same for both peak and off-peak output and the competitive solution is to charge the same price. The monopoly solution is derived from figure 14-21. D_1, D_2 and $D_1 + D_2$ are drawn as in the earlier graphs. Since D_1 and D_2 are linear, the marginal revenue curves MR_1 and MR_2 are straight lines drawn from the p intercepts of D_1 and D_2 to points lying halfway between 0 and the X intercepts. Hence MR_1 cuts the X axis at $a/2$ and MR_2 cuts the X axis at $b/2$. $MR_{1+2} = MR_1$ above the p intercept of D_2, and cuts the X axis midway between zero and X intercept of $D_1 + D_2$, at $(a + b)/2$.

Under perfect competition, the point $A = (\overline{X}, \overline{p})$ would be achieved, where the competitive supply curve, MC, is equal to $D_1 + D_2$. There is no price discrimination, because there is no difference in cost in serving either peak or off-peak demands.

With monopoly control of the industry, output X^* is chosen so that X^*, $MC = MR_{1+2}$. This occurs at B. The output chosen is allocated between peak and off-peak by setting peak output equal to X_1^* such that $MC^* = MR_1$ with X_2^* such that $MC^* = MR_2$. Hence the monopolist chooses the points $C = (p_2^*, X_2^*)$ and $D = (p_1^*, X_1^*)$. Note that the competitive output $\overline{X}$ is greater than output X^* under monopoly control, with a lower price as well.

When cost is a function of total output only, discriminatory pricing results in inefficiencies. On the other hand, when costs are separable between peak and off-peak, generally discriminatory pricing is required to achieve a Pareto optimum.

Summary

Under pure monopoly, output is lower and price is higher than under perfect competition. This results in a welfare loss in that too few resources are

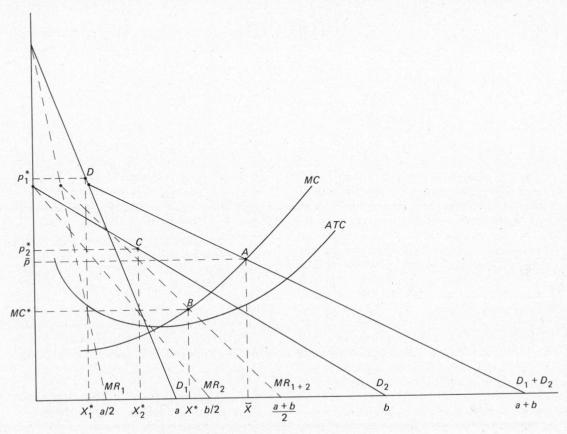

FIG. 14-21   *Peak/off-peak pricing—common costs*

devoted to output of the monopolized industry and too many are devoted to the competitive sector. While the economy satisfies the conditions for production efficiency in the sense that the economy is on its transformation curve, Pareto optimality is not achieved due to the distortion in the mix of outputs. Optimal regulation of the monopoly would involve fixing price at the level of marginal cost; in fact, regulation actually uses a variant of average cost pricing or "rate of return" pricing that deviates from the marginal cost criterion. The use of a rate base for setting prices in regulated industries leads to a substitution of capital for labor by the regulated firm that further distorts the allocation of resources

(known as the Axerch-Johnson or A-J effect).

With pure monopsony, the production efficiency conditions are violated and the economy operates off its transformation curve. Thus it is possible to produce more of all goods by a reallocation of resources, and hence Pareto optimality is not achieved.

The pure monopoly case is an idealized situation. It can be maintained either by strong natural barriers to entry or by artificial barriers such as government restraints and control of raw material sources. The next chapter takes up somewhat more common patterns of industrial organization—monopolistic competition and oligopoly.

Problems

1. The L.A. Rams of the National Football League play their games in the L.A. Coliseum. Assume that the owner of the Coliseum, the City of Los Angeles, rents the stadium to the Rams for a fee that includes the cost of ushers, parking attendants, and other employees, and that the fee is independent of the attendance at Ram games during the year. Analyze the effect, on the ticket price charged by the Rams, of a doubling of player salaries.

2. Show that if there is a monopsonist in a local labor market, then introducing a labor union can result in increases in the wage rate as well as in the number of laborers employed.

3. An electric utility produces kilowatt hours (kwh) of power according to the cost curve $TC(X) = \$5 + \$3X$, where X is thousands of kwh produced. The demand for power by consumers, X_C, is given by $X_C = 100 - 10p_C$, where p_C is the price per thousand kwh to consumers. The demand for power by industry, $X_I = 200 - 5p_I$, where p_I is the price per thousand kwh to industry.

   a. Determine the competitive output and prices p_C, p_I.
   b. Determine the monopoly output and prices p_C, p_I.

4. A monopolistic labor union faces a monopsonistic firm in the labor market. Indicate the range of wage rates and employment levels within which the equilibrium wage and employment might fall.

5. Given a demand curve for industry output $D(p) = 50 - 5p$, assume constant costs of $6 per unit. Calculate the size of the welfare loss if the industry were operated as a monopoly. What is the loss as a percentage of the value of output under competitive conditions?

15

Imperfect Competition

Pure monopoly and perfect competition lie at the two extremes of the spectrum of market power. In either of these extreme cases—total market power or total absence of market power —it is relatively straightforward to spell out the implications of self-interest for market conduct, and to describe how markets respond to such conduct. As we move toward the more realistic cases that lie between these two extremes, problems arise in specifying "reasonable" rules of conduct that are consistent with furthering self-interest for market participants. Such rules of conduct are quite sensitive to the specific characteristics of the market structure of an industry. The simple theories of perfect competition and pure monopoly no longer apply. Instead we find a number of alternative scenarios of market conduct, each with its own basic appeals and flaws.

The approach we will take in this chapter is to consider first the theory of industries where there is market power but strategic behavior is relatively unimportant. (Recall that strategic behavior is behavior by a decision maker that takes into account the reactions of other decision makers). This theory covers the case of monopolistic competition, and the case of an industry with a *price leader*, a dominant firm in an industry with many small firms. We then turn to problems of duopoly and oligopoly, where strategic behavior is the essential ingredient of the market structure problem.

The Theory of Monopolistic Competition

We have seen in chapter 14 that if there is free entry into an industry, a monopoly position cannot be sustained in the long run. If the monopolist attempted to set price at a level such that the firm earns more than normal profits, then entry by other firms would force price back down to the competitive level. Long-run monopoly requires either natural or artificial barriers to entry into the industry.

This argument assumes that the firms in an industry produce a *homogeneous product* in the sense that consumers are completely indifferent as to the identity of the firm producing the product. With a homogeneous product, the output of one firm is a perfect substitute for the output of any other firm in the industry; hence all units of the output of the industry sell for the same price. But when we turn to industries as they operate in reality, we find *product differentiation* brought about by trade names, advertising, packaging, and other marketing devices. Because firms possess enforceable property rights to their brand names and to certain of their other marketing devices, product differentiation is an artificial barrier to entry for potential competitors. The theory of monopolistic competition tries to describe the behavior of an industry where such barriers exist, under simplified conditions.

The theory depends upon three basic assumptions.

1. The industry consists of a large number of
small firms, each producing its own differentiated product.

2. Each firm ignores the effects of its actions
on the decisions taken by other firms. (Thus
we exclude strategic behavior by assumption.)

3. New firms producing close substitutes for
the products of existing firms can enter the
industry.

The last two assumptions give a competitive
flavor to the industry. Since each firm is the
sole producer of its own product, however, each
firm has some monopolistic characteristics.
This combination of features accounts for the
label *monopolistic competition* bestowed on
this model by Edward Chamberlain, the Harvard economist who developed the theory of
industries selling differentiated products.†

Strictly speaking, since each firm produces
a differentiated product, the notions of "industry output" and "price per unit of industry
output" are not well defined. However, as a
practical matter, we will assume that products
of different firms are close enough substitutes
that not too much violence to logic is done
by defining industry output X as the sum of
the outputs of all firms and industry price P
as the weighted average of prices charged by
firms in the industry. Thus

$$X = \Sigma x \text{ and } P = \frac{\Sigma px}{X}$$

(equals total industry revenue divided by industry output).

---

†E. Chamberlain, *The Theory of Monopolistic Competition*,
7th ed. (Cambridge: Harvard University Press, 1956).

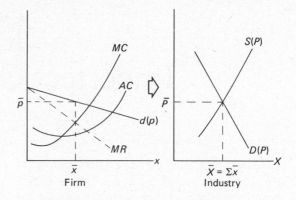

FIG. 15-1   *Monopolistic competition*

Demand Curve and Elasticity

Figure 15-1 shows industry demand $D(P)$ and
the demand curve $d(p)$ and cost curves of a
typical firm operating in an industry under
monopolistic competition. The firm diagram
looks much like the diagram for pure monopoly. The firm sets price and output to equate
MR and MC. There is nothing new in this.
However, the demand curve facing the firm,
$d(p)$, is more elastic than is the industry demand curve $D(P)$. This variation reflects the
fact that there are available more close substitutes for the firm's output than for the output
of the industry. These substitutes are of course
the products produced by the other firms in
the industry.

The elasticity of the firm's demand curve
depends on advertising, packaging, and all of
the other marketing and sales devices that can
be employed to enhance the distinctiveness of
the firm's product, together with the engineering and production inputs that result in
"inherent" physical differentiation of the product. The more distinctive the firm's product
(that is, the fewer close substitutes available),
the more inelastic its demand curve $d(p)$. The

positioning of $d(p)$ depends in part on the number of firms in the industry; the more firms there are, the less is each firm's "share" of industry demand.

Equilibrium—Short Run and Long Run

Under monopolistic competition short-run equilibrium occurs when each firm chooses a profit-maximizing price and output and the resulting choices are consistent with market clearing for the industry. The graphs shown in figure 15-1 illustrate such an equilibrium.

In the case depicted in figure 15-1, the typical firm in the industry earns short-run excess profits. This aspect encourages entry into the industry by firms producing close substitutes for such products. In fact, it is natural to assume that entry will continue so long as there are any excess profits earned in the industry. Long-run equilibrium under monopolistic competition can then be defined as in the case of perfect competition—namely, a situation in which there is no incentive either for entry or exit with respect to the industry, with the "typical" firm earning just normal profits, as shown in figure 15-2.

In order for excess profits to be zero in the long run, price must equal $LRAC$. Since the firm faces a downward sloping demand curve $d(p)$, the zero profit condition means that $d(p)$ must be tangent to $LRAC$ at some output $\bar{x}$ lying to the left of x^*, where the minimum of $LRAC$ occurs. Clearly, profits are maximized at $\bar{x}$ since at any other output, price is below $LRAC$; hence profits are negative except at $\bar{x}$. Thus $MR = LRMC$ at $\bar{x}$ as shown in figure 15-2. There is no incentive for further entry since excess profits are zero.

The adjustment to long-run equilibrium occurs as follows. With the typical firm earning excess profits in the short run, entry takes place.

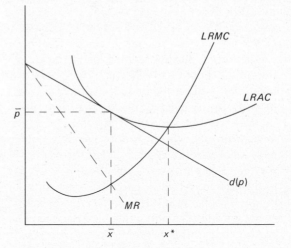

FIG. 15-2   *Long-run equilibrium of the firm— monopolistic competition*

The increase in number of firms in the industry tends to shift the demand curve $d(p)$ to the left and to increase the elasticity of the demand curve, since a wider range of close substitutes for the firm's product have appeared on the market. The shifting of $d(p)$ to the left continues until all excess profits have been squeezed out of the industry.

Welfare Losses

At long-run equilibrium, the equilibrium price $\bar{p}$ is above $LRMC$. This position indicates that the conditions for Pareto optimality are violated; monopolistic competition leads to welfare losses for the society. The losses occur because market power is being exercised by each firm, limited as this market power is in the long run. Just as in the case of pure monopoly, consumers in the society can be made better off by increasing the output of the industry, taking into account compensation paid to the owners of factors specialized to that industry. Note also that in long-run equilibrium, each firm operates with excess capacity ($x < x^*$).

One other possible source of inefficiency should be noted as well. Each firm has an incentive to make its product distinctive so as to shift its demand curve to the right and increase revenue earned at any output. One device for achieving this is to advertise. The purpose of advertising is to change the underlying preference maps of consumers, as well as to provide information as to the properties of the product being advertised. In terms of traditional welfare economics, there is little that can be said concerning welfare losses or gains relating to changes in preferences directly. However, there is a simple issue involved in the question as to whether or not advertising accomplishes these goals in an efficient manner.

A portion at least of advertising expenditures represents "defensive" advertising, that is, advertising that is required simply to maintain a firm's market demand curve in location, given the attempts by other firms to shift consumers to their products. Thus it is possible to conceive of a situation in which considerable sums are spent by profit-oriented firms, with no net change in the distribution of sales among firms—all advertising then would be simply defensive advertising. Such a situation is clearly inefficient. To the extent that defensive advertising occurs, resources are wasted. Casual empiricism suggests that a substantial portion of advertising is defensive, and monopolistic competition leads to welfare losses beyond those associated with market power per se.

Summary

We have outlined only in the broadest terms the ideas underlying the theory of monopolistic competition. There are any number of modifications to the basic theory that have been developed in the economic literature. A particularly important result that follows from the theory is that market power need not lead to excess profits, even given artificial barriers to entry such as brand names and advertising.

We next turn to the examination of another type of market structure—the case of a dominant firm industry.

The Dominant Firm

Consider an industry producing a homogeneous product in which there is one large firm and a collection of smaller firms. While the large firm is not a pure monopolist in the sense used in the last chapter, still it is assumed to dominate the industry in that it sets the price for the industry: any price set by the dominant firm is taken by all other firms to be given, beyond their control. The other firms in the industry are assumed to be so small individually that each ignores the effects of its actions on the price of the industry's output and on the decisions taken either by the dominant firm or by other smaller firms in the industry.

Demand and Supply Curves

Let $D(p)$ denote the industry demand curve, and let $S(p)$ be the supply curve of output in the aggregate for the small firms in the industry. Because the small firms act like perfect competitors, $S(p)$ is the sum of the marginal cost curves of such firms. $D(p)$ is assumed to be downward sloping while $S(p)$ is upward sloping under short-run conditions, as indicated in figure 15-3.

The dominant firm then sets price so as to maximize its own profits, taking output of the small firms as given by $S(p)$. This amounts to constructing a demand curve for the dominant

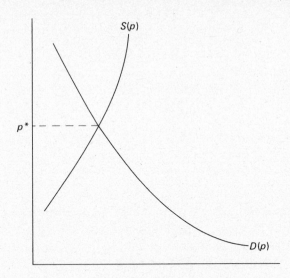

FIG. 15-3   *Industry demand D(p) and small firms' supply S(p)*

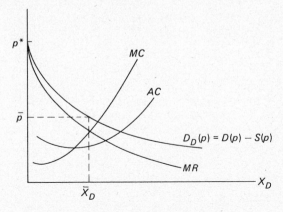

FIG. 15-4   *Choice of price $\bar{p}$ and output $\bar{X}_D$ for the dominant firm*

in the costs of the smaller firms in the industry. Changes in marginal costs of such firms shift the $S(p)$ curve, which in turn affects the profit-maximizing price and output for the dominant firm.

firm, $D_D(p)$, by horizontally subtracting $S(p)$ from $D(p)$ at each value of p. Figure 15-4 indicates the profit-maximizing choice by the dominant firm.

The demand curve for the dominant firm intersects the price axis at p^*; at any price of p^* or above, the small firms will supply all of the output demanded. For p less than p^*, $D_D(p)$ is the difference between quantity demanded for the industry and quantities supplied by small firms. Thus $D_D(p)$ is flatter sloping than $D(p)$. The dominant firm chooses price $\bar{p}$ and its own output $\bar{X}_D$ to maximize profits over its *own* demand curve $D_D(p)$ by equating marginal revenue to marginal cost. At the price $\bar{p}$, the small firms supply $\bar{X}_S = S(\bar{p})$, as shown in figure 15-5.

The major difference between this case and the pure monopoly case is that the dominant firm is affected not only by the forces that shift the industry demand curve, but also by changes

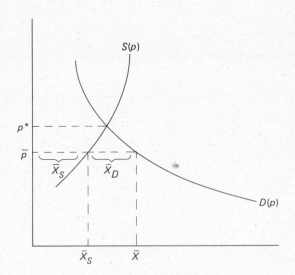

FIG. 15-5   *Industry equilibrium with a dominant firm*

Long-Run Demand and Supply

Suppose that the dominant firm has certain cost advantages over smaller firms due to patents or protected access to a low-cost raw material source, but it has no direct control over the entry of small firms into the industry. In the long run, entry will occur so long as small firms are earning excess profits; hence the long-run $S(p)$ curve is perfectly elastic at that price $\hat{p}$ such that excess profits for small firms are zero. Then the long-run situation is as shown in figure 15-6.

The $D_D(p)$ curve is perfectly elastic at $\hat{p}$ up to the output $S(\hat{p})$. The dominant firm can sell no units at $p > \hat{p}$ since small firms will supply the entire market at a price of $\hat{p}$. For prices below $\hat{p}$, smaller firms are forced out of the industry ($\hat{p}$ = min $LRAC$ for smaller firms) and the dominant firm becomes a monopolist. MR_D for the dominant firm is $\hat{p}$ for outputs up to $S(\hat{p})$; beyond $S(\hat{p})$ the MR_D curve is associated with the industry demand curve $D(p)$; in particular if $D(p)$ is linear, then MR_D will intersect the X axis halfway between the origin and the X intercept of $D(p)$.

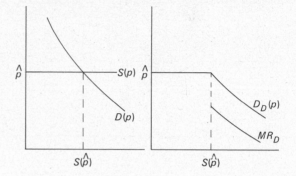

FIG. 15-6 *Long-run dominant firm industry*

Long-Run Equilibrium

What price and output will be chosen by the dominant firm in the long run? To begin with, price cannot be above $\hat{p}$ since small firms would enter the industry and supply the entire industry demand at any price above $\hat{p}$. Three cases emerge as possibilities (fig. 15-7).

Case 1: The profit-maximizing choice of the dominant firm is the price $\hat{p}$ with output $\bar{X}_D$.

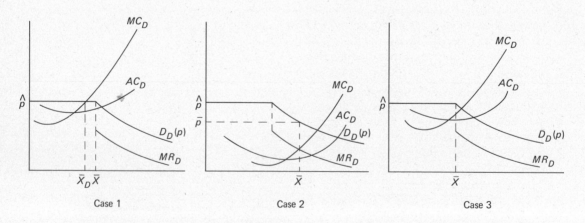

FIG. 15-7 *Long-run equilibrium with a dominant firm*

The smaller firms supply the output $\bar{X} - \bar{X}_D$ and earn normal profits.

Case 2: The cost advantage of the dominant firm converts the industry to a pure monopoly in the long run. The profit-maximizing price $\bar{p}$ is less than $\hat{p}$, which in turn equals the minimum of $LRAC$ for smaller firms.

Case 3: MC_D of the dominant firm does not equal MR_D at any output. Profit maximization implies that the industry is a monopoly with price at $\hat{p}$ and there are no small firms in the industry.

Cases 1 and 3 are both "borderline balanced" in the sense that if there is any lag in adjustment of price by the dominant firm to changes in costs of smaller firms, then there will be entry into the industry followed by price cutting by the dominant firm forcing smaller firms to fail. Further, in case 3 the fact that the dominant firm is a monopolist may encourage the firm to set price above $\hat{p}$ to capture short-run gains; when entry occurs in response to such higher prices, the dominant firm punishes entrants by price cuts.

Clearly, the stability of these cases is quite sensitive to the quality of information available to the dominant firm both with respect to the industry demand curve and the costs of the smaller firms. Given inadequate information, the dominant firm may find it advantageous to "sample" price sensitivity by experimenting with various price policies, introducing additional instability into the industry.

Strategic Behavior and Market Structure

Pure monopoly, perfect competition, and monopolistic competition are similar in that each firm makes its decisions ignoring the reaction to those decisions by other firms in the economy. This situation can be contrasted with industries in which there are several large firms, each of which knows that its decisions will produce responses by the others. Economists use the term *oligopoly* (few sellers) to refer to such industries. With oligopoly, strategic behavior comes to the fore; each firm in making decisions operates under certain assumptions as to what the responses of the other firms will be. For the remainder of this chapter, we will deal explicitly with such situations. The principles involved can be illustrated in the case of a simplified *duopoly* (two sellers) industry.

Duopoly—The Cournot Model

Consider an industry in which there is initially only one producer. For simplicity, assume that marginal costs are zero and that the demand curve facing the monopolist is a straight line of the form $x = a - bp$ where x is quantity demanded and p is the price. Then the profit-maximizing output level is $x = a/2$, where total expenditures on the product are a maximum.

Suppose now that a second firm (also with zero marginal costs) enters the industry. This change converts the industry from a monopoly to a duopoly (a two-firm industry). What kind of strategy might the second firm pursue in the presence of the first firm? One of the earliest of the mathematical economists, Auguste Cournot, suggested that the second firm might assume that the first firm would maintain its output at $a/2$ and would match any price cut initiated by the second firm in its efforts to break into the market.

The situation facing the second firm is shown in figure 15-8. Since firm #2 takes the output $a/2$ of firm #1 as given, the demand

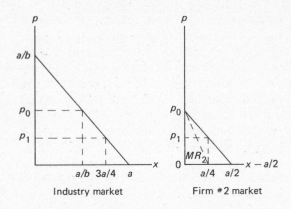

FIG. 15-8 *Cournot duopoly—demand facing firm #2*

curve facing firm #2 is the industry demand curve less $a/2$ at every value of p. Then firm #2 maximizes its revenue by choosing output at $a/4$, with corresponding price p_1. Firm #1 matches the price cut by lowering price to p_1 while maintaining its output at $a/2$.

But now firm #1 has a decision to make. Given that firm #2 is selling $a/4$ units, what output should firm #1 pick? Suppose it assumes that firm #2 will maintain its output at $a/4$ (and thus will match any price changes with firm #1). Then the demand curve facing firm #1 is of the form shown in figure 15-9. Clearly, firm #1 picks an output of $3/8\ a$, and now it is firm #2's time to adjust. Where does such a process lead?

Let x_1 denote the output of firm #1 and x_2 the output of firm #2. Then the process we have been describing is one in which

$$x_1 = \frac{1}{2}(a - x_2),$$

while

$$x_2 = \frac{1}{2}(a - x_1).$$

Define an *equilibrium* for the duopoly industry

as an output pair (x_1, x_2) such that these two conditions are simultaneously satisfied. That is, each firm chooses a profit-maximizing output assuming a fixed output of the other, and these profit-maximizing choices are consistent with one another. Substituting for x_2, we have

$$x_1 = \frac{1}{2}\Big[a - \frac{1}{2}(a - x_1)\Big]$$

$$= \frac{1}{2}\Big(\frac{1}{2}a + \frac{1}{2}x_1\Big) \text{ or } \frac{3}{4}x_1 = \frac{1}{4}a,$$

hence $x_1 = \dfrac{a}{3}$

By symmetry,

$$x_2 = \frac{a}{3}$$

also. To check this solution, note that if $x_1 = a/3$, then the revenue-maximizing choice for firm #2 is $a/3$ and when firm #2 has an output of $a/3$, firm #1 maximizes its revenue at $a/3$ as well.

The solution to the Cournot duopoly problem then is an industry output $(x_1 + x_2)$ of

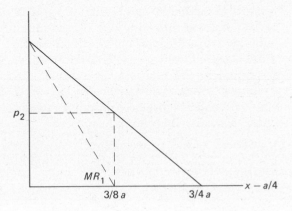

FIG. 15-9 *Cournot duopoly—demand facing firm #1*

$(2/3)a$ with a price of $a/3b$. This is an equilibrium in the sense that so long as each firm believes the other is going to maintain its output at $a/3$, neither firm has an incentive to change its own output or its price.

An "n"-firm Industry

The Cournot approach can be applied to a many-firm industry as well. Suppose that there are n firms in an industry, each of which assumes that the other $n - 1$ will hold their outputs fixed when the firm itself adjusts its output. If $x_1, x_2, \ldots, x_n$ denote the outputs of firms #1, #2, $\ldots$, #n, then the profit-maximizing output choice for firm #1 is given by

$$x_1 = \frac{1}{2}\left(a - \sum_{i=2}^{n} x_i\right).$$

Now we know by the symmetry of the problem that at an equilibrium,

$$x_1 = x_2 = \ldots = x_n$$

(every firm has the same output). Thus if x = industry output so that

$$x = \sum_{i=1}^{n} x_i$$

we will have

$$x_1 = x_2 = \quad \ldots \quad = x_n = \frac{x}{n}.$$

When we substitute in the expression above,

$$\frac{x}{n} = \frac{1}{2}\left(a - \frac{(n-1)\,x}{n}\right).$$

Therefore, $\dfrac{x}{n}\left(1 + \dfrac{(n-1)}{2}\right) = \dfrac{1}{2}\,a$

or $$x = \frac{n}{n+1}\,a,$$

with $$x_1 = x_2 = \ldots = x_n = \frac{1}{n+1}\,a.$$

(Note that when $n = 2$, we obtain our earlier solution

$$x_1 = \frac{a}{3}, \ x_2 = \frac{a}{3}, \ x = \frac{2}{3}a.)$$

The Cournot approach has the interesting property that it correctly describes the two polar cases—pure monopoly and perfect competition. In the monopoly case ($n = 1$), the profit-maximizing output is $(1/2)a$, while under perfect competition with free entry, n approaches infinity so that $x = a$; that is, price is driven down to zero, which is marginal cost. Does it make any sense in the intermediate cases of duopoly and oligopoly? The kind of reaction that suggests itself is this. When there are only two sellers, the Cournot solution says that output is at $(2/3)a$. This means that industry profits are less than they could be—in fact industry revenue (and profits) are a maximum at $a/2$. Why don't the two firms simply get together and agree to split the market, with each producing $a/4$ units? Both firms would be better off than at the Cournot solution where output for the industry is $(2/3)a$.

There are problems, of course, some of them legal. Any joint agreement to restrict output would make the firms subject to antitrust prosecution. There are the practical difficulties of enforcing such an agreement, since if either firm is convinced that the other will restrict output to the $a/4$ level, then the optimum solution for either of them is to expand output.

The same argument holds if there are more than two firms in the industry. It is to the advantage of the firms in the industry that output be restricted to the monopoly level, with the market split among all firms. Every firm stands to gain from the formation of an industry-wide cartel. But once the cartel is formed and industry output is restricted to $a/2$, then it is to every firm's advantage to cheat on the cartel agreement, and to expand output. In fact, the history of cartels suggests that they are highly unstable organizations, unless there is real power vested in the cartel to punish violators of the cartel agreement. Needless to say, the more effective the cartel is, the closer output is to the monopoly output and the further the economy is from a position of Pareto optimality.

Spatial Duopoly—The Hotelling Paradox

Another aspect of duopoly behavior is captured in the following simple example, first described by Hotelling.†

Consider a beach, with people distributed evenly from one end to the other. Two hot dog stands, both charging the same price per hot dog, are to be located along the beach. The cost to a customer of buying a hot dog is the purchase price plus the implicit cost of traveling to the stand (and back). Assume that tastes and income are identical for all consumers, including their tastes for hot dogs and traveling. To best serve the public, the two stands should be located so as to minimize the average distance traveled to obtain a hot dog. This means that we should split the length of the beach into four equal segments and locate the hot dog stands as in figure 15-10. What we have represented in the diagram is the "centralized" solution to the hot dog stand location problem. If a central planner (say the manager of the beach) were locating hot dog stands, they would be located as shown in the diagram.

†H. Hotelling, "Stability in Competition," *Economic Journal* 39 (1929).

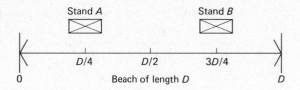

FIG. 15-10   *Optimum location of two hot dog stands*

Now suppose that a decentralized price system is at work, with stands A and B being owned by profit-maximizing firms free to locate at any points on the beach. Suppose to begin with that the stands are located as in the diagram. Will the price system work to maintain the stands at these locations? No chance. In fact, if you were the owner of stand A, you would realize that in effect you have a captive audience located between the points 0 and $D/4$, and that you are really only competing with stand B for those people located between $D/4$ and $3D/4$. Thus you can increase your sales and hence your profits, by moving to the right. (We continue to assume that the price charged per hot dog is the same for both stands.) But the owner of stand B will of course make the same calculation, and will realize that profit incentives should move him to the left. Thus we end up with the price system's solution to the hot dog stand location problem—both stands are located at $D/2$. This location increases the average distance that has to be traveled by hot dog customers, and thus is an inefficient solution to the problem.

There is a real paradox in this situation. The number of hot dogs that will be purchased in total depends on the distance that must be traveled by customers. The duopoly solution involves longer traveling distances on the average; hence sales for each hot dog stand are less than if they remained in their original locations. With each hot dog stand owner acting in his own self-interest, both are worse off.

What does this imply? Well it implies that there is now an incentive for the two firms to reach an agreement for splitting the market between them. If the agreement is really enforceable, then, given this enforceable agreement, stand *A* would locate at *D*/4 and stand *B* would locate at 3*D*/4. Everything is fine, except that now there is a premium that can be earned by cheating on the agreement, and so the optimal solution turns out to be unstable.

This simple model has some rather interesting real-world applications. Think about the fact that at busy intersections, there are often gasoline stations on all four corners, even though you may have to go miles to find another station. There is also the well-known phenomenon of "competition" in television programming. With several channels, one might expect diversity of offerings, different kinds of programs on different channels, each specialized to its own brand of entertainment. Instead, *every* commercial channel puts on the *same* kind of program, *at the same time!* Each channel is trying to reach the mass "average" audience, rather than trying to satisfy tastes at the extremes. Of even more importance, it is becoming clear that in a two-party system, both parties tend to move toward the middle. When the Republicans nominate a Goldwater or the Democrats nominate a McGovern, there is disaster for the party. The Hotelling paradox is at work throughout our society.

Concentration of resources at the center of mass of a market is generally an inefficient way to allocate these resources, but with a limited number of firms in the industry, the profit motive leads to such a concentration. The "lumpiness" of firms is the source of the difficulty; as the number of firms approaches the continuum, demands are satisfied not only at the center of the market, but also at the extremes.

Oligopoly and the Nash Equilibrium

In our two examples of duopoly industries, we have employed a notion of equilibrium that is different in certain respects from that involved in the case of a competitive economy. When strategic considerations are important, each decision maker bases his choices on certain assumptions he makes about the choices of other decision makers. Generally speaking, these assumptions turn out to be incorrect; other decision makers will react in ways not contemplated by the given decision maker. Equilibrium in a strategic situation occurs when the choices of all decision makers are jointly consistent—each firm behaves in the way that other decision makers expect it to behave, and all decisions are consistent with one another. We refer to such an equilibrium as a *Nash equilibrium*, after the mathematician who first formalized this concept.

To illustrate, there is a Nash equilibrium in the Cournot duopoly model when each firm chooses an output of *a*/3 units, assuming that the other firm will also choose *a*/3 units. As we have seen, such choices by the two firms are jointly consistent with individual profit maximization. Similarly, there is a Nash equilibrium in the Hotelling model when both hot dog stands are located at the center of the beach. Each hot dog stand owner expects the other to remain fixed in location and maximizes profits by remaining at the center of the beach; these two decisions are jointly consistent with one another.

The Nash equilibrium is an extremely useful device for analyzing oligopolistic behavior

282 III/Market Imperfections

within a given market structure, as we have seen. It should be mentioned, however, that at a Nash equilibrium there might well be incentives for the firms to change the market structure, say to a cartel arrangement; so there is no guarantee that a Nash equilibrium for a given market structure once established will persist in the face of incentives to change that structure.

Thus far we have considered a few examples of strategic behavior in simplified settings. We next turn to a general theory of strategic behavior—game theory.

Game Theory and the Minimax Principle

Strategic decision making appears in many of our social activities. The classic case is the game of poker, where payoffs are determined partly by chance, that is, by the run of the cards. But payoffs are also determined by betting strategies, with bluffing playing an important part in the strategy of every top-notch poker player. Bluffing amounts to the creation of uncertainty for one's opponents and, if skillfully used, can overwhelm pure chance in the determination of the payoffs from the game.

Because strategic elements appear in many parlor games, it is not surprising that John von Neumann and Oskar Morgenstern adopted the term *game theory* to describe the theory of decision making in strategic situations in their pioneering volume, *The Theory of Games and Economic Behavior*, which appeared in 1944.†
A *game* can be described as a decision-making situation in which the payoffs to any partici-

pant in the game depend not only on his own choices but also on the choices of the other participants. Game theory is fully developed for the simplest case, that of a two-person, zero-sum game, and we will begin by examining this case. As the term implies, in this type of game there are two decision makers: what one person wins the other person loses, and thus the sum of the winnings (one person's gain plus the other's loss) is zero for any pair of decisions by the participants.

The Two-Person, Zero-Sum Game

Let the two persons participating in the game be labeled Mr. A and Mr. B, and assume that Mr. A has choices A_1, A_2, A_3 available to him, while Mr. B has choices B_1, B_2, and B_3. We can summarize the payoffs associated with each pair of decisions in a *payoff matrix*, as in table 15-1. Entries in the matrix are interpreted as payoffs received by Mr. A, or equivalently as amounts paid out by Mr. B, since what A wins, B loses. Thus if Mr. A chooses A_3 and Mr. B chooses B_2, A pays B \$1; if A chooses A_1 and B chooses B_3, then B pays A \$4.

The problem we are interested in is: What is a "rational" strategy for making choices in a game situation? From A's point of view, the best payoff occurs if he chooses A_2 and B chooses B_3, in which case A wins \$8. But if B knows A is going to choose A_2, B will pick

†J. von Neumann, and O. Morgenstern, *The Theory of Games and Economic Behavior* (Princeton: Princeton University Press, 1944).

TABLE 15-1   *A Payoff Matrix*

A＼B	B_1	B_2	B_3
A_1	+3	0	+4
A_2	−4	−2	+8
A_3	+4	−1	−3

B_1 and A will lose \$4. But if A knows that B is going to choose B_1, A's best strategy is to pick A_3, which means that B will retaliate by choosing B_3, and so on. Needless to say, there are real strategic problems in making choices.

Von Neumann and Morgenstern have suggested the following rule of "rational" conduct in a game situation:

Each decision maker should expect the worst and should do as well as he can, assuming the worst will occur.

This rule is known as the *minimax principle*, and is applied to our game as follows. Mr. B associates with each of the alternatives B_1, B_2, and B_3 the worst outcome (his maximum loss): \$4, \$0, and \$8, respectively. Given a choice from among B_1, B_2, and B_3, he picks B_2, which has the minimum of the maximum losses. Thus Mr. B is a minimaxer over losses to him. Mr. A does the same. The worst outcome under A_1 is \$0, under A_2 (minus \$4), under A_3 (minus \$3). Mr. A picks the alternative with the best of the worst outcomes, A_1. Mr. A is a maximiner. Both A and B are following the minimax principle.

The situation is shown in table 15-2. B picks the alternative that minimizes his maximum loss, which is alternative B_2. A picks the alternative that maximizes his minimum gain, that is, alternative A_1. Thus we arrive at the pair of choices (B_2, A_1) where the payoff is zero. The solution we have obtained for this particular game turns out to be a saddle point of the game. A *saddle point* is a pair of strategies for Mr. A and Mr. B such that, if A knows B's choice, he can do no better than his saddle point choice, and if B knows A's choice he likewise can do no better than his saddle point choice. Knowing that B has chosen B_2, the best choice available to A is A_1; knowing that A has chosen A_1, B can do no better than B_2.

TABLE 15-2 *Minimax and the Payoff Matrix*

B \ A	B_1	B_2	B_3	Minimum gain to A
A_1	+3	0	+4	0
A_2	−4	−2	+8	−4
A_3	+4	−1	−3	−3
Maximum loss to B	+4	0	+8	

When a saddle point occurs, the game is *solved* in the sense that neither Mr. A nor Mr. B has any incentive to change his strategy, however many times the game is played. A saddle point is thus a *Nash equilibrium* for the game. An example of a real-world game with a saddle point is tic-tac-toe, where the minimax strategies are quickly learned, and that's the basic reason why the game is dull.

The Dominance Principle   There is one important qualification that should be noted to our discussion thus far. A rational decision maker will never choose an alternative that gives worse results, whatever decision is taken by his opponent, than he would obtain with another available alternative. Consider the game matrix in table 15-3.

The entries in the matrix are again payments by B to A. Note that from Mr. B's point of

TABLE 15-3 *The Dominance Principle*

B \ A	B_1	B_2	B_3
A_1	+2	+3	−4
A_2	−1	0	+5
A_3	+1	+1	+3

view, alternative B_2 is strictly inferior to B_1 in the sense that whatever Mr. A chooses to do, Mr. B is at least as well off under B_1 as under B_2, and he is strictly better off under B_1 if A chooses A_1 or A_2. B_1 is said to *dominate* B_2.

The minimax criterion applies only to the alternatives that are *not* dominated; hence B_2 is excluded from B's choice set in applying the minimax rule. The dominance rule ("choose only from among undominated strategies") is the simplest of the rules for making decisions in strategic situations.

Mixed Strategies and the Minimax Theorem
Most games do not possess saddle points. For example, consider the game shown in table 15-4. As between alternatives B_1 and B_2, the minimax strategy for Mr. B is to choose B_1 and the maximin strategy for Mr. A is to pick A_2. But if B chooses B_1 over and over again, A will switch to A_1, which will cause B to shift to B_2, and so they are back in the strategy box.

There is a simple rule that can be applied to determine when a zero-sum game has a saddle point.

There will be a saddle point if and only if the maximum entry in some column is also the minimum entry in its row of the payoff matrix (assuming only nondominated strategies appear in the payoff matrix).

TABLE 15-4   *A Payoff Matrix with No Saddle Point*

B \ A	B_1	B_2	Minimum gain to A
A_1	+2	-3/2	-3/2
A_2	-1	+3	-1
Maximum loss to B	2	3	

Returning to table 15-1, note that the 0 entry associated with strategies A_1, B_2 satisfies this saddle point rule. It is the maximum entry in the B_2 column and the minimum entry in the A_1 row.

When a payoff matrix does not contain a saddle point, as in table 15-4, the minimax rule is extended to cover *mixed strategies* for the participants in a game. We refer to the alternatives B_1 and B_2 available to Mr. B or the alternatives A_1 and A_2 for Mr. A in table 15-4 as *pure strategies*. By a mixed strategy, we mean probability mixes of the form $(p, 1 - p)$ where p is the probability with which B_1 is chosen, and $1 - p$ is the probability with which B_2 is chosen. In other words, we admit the possibility that Mr. B may decide to flip a coin and choose B_1 or B_2 on the basis of the coin flip. Thus he has other possible choices than simply between B_1 and B_2. Why might flipping a coin be a "rational" way for Mr. B (or Mr. A) to make choices? Intuitively, it gets around the strategic problem that, in extended plays of the game, if Mr. B picks out some strategy (say B_1 and then two plays of B_2, repeated ad infinitum), Mr. A may discover this sequence and use his knowledge to punish Mr. B by choosing the appropriate counter-strategy (A_1 followed by two plays of A_2, and so on). It will be impossible for Mr. A to determine what Mr. B is going to choose on each play of the game if Mr. B does not even know himself until the coin is flipped.

We interpret the entries in the payoff matrix as dollar gains to Mr. A (and losses of dollars for Mr. B). Assume that both Mr. A and Mr. B are interested in maximizing their average payoffs from repeated plays of the game. Then we can interpret the minimax rule as follows, for games where mixed strategies are used.

Let v denote the average payoff in dollars from B to A, from Mr. B's point of view. Mr.

B wants the average payoff v to Mr. A to be as low as possible, subject to the conditions that if Mr. A chooses strategy A_1, then on the average he will receive no more than v dollars, and if he chooses strategy A_2, again he will receive on the average no more than v dollars. In other words, Mr. B wants to ensure that Mr. A can never earn more on average than v dollars, regardless of what strategy he employs.

Let w denote the average payoff from B to A, from Mr. A's point of view. Mr. A wants the average payoff to himself w to be as large as possible, subject to the constraint that if Mr. B picks strategy B_1, then on average Mr. A will receive at least w dollars, and if Mr. B picks strategy B_2, again Mr. A will receive on the average at least w dollars. In other words, Mr. A will always receive an average payoff of at least w dollars, regardless of the strategy employed by Mr. B.

Let p be the probability with which Mr. B picks B_1, and let $1 - p$ be the probability with which B_2 is chosen. Similarly, q is the probability that A_1 is chosen with $1 - q$ being the probability that A_2 is chosen.

Given the payoff matrix in table 15-5, Mr. B wishes to minimize v = average payoff to Mr. A (from B's point of view) subject to

$$p(+2) + (1 - p)(-3/2) \leq v$$
$$p(-1) + (1 - p)(+3) \leq v.$$

(If Mr. A chooses A_1, B pays A \$2 p percent

of the time, and $-\$3/2$ $(1 - p)$ percent of the time. This average payment from B to A is to be no more than v. A similar interpretation applies to the second inequality, which applies to the case when Mr. A chooses A_2.)

Mr. A is interested in maximizing w = average payoff to Mr. A (from A's point of view) subject to

$$q(+2) + (1 - q)(-1) \geq w$$
$$q(-3/2) + (1 - q)(+3) \geq w.$$

(If Mr. B chooses B_1, then B pays A \$2 q percent of the time, and $-\$1$ $(1 - q)$ percent of the time. This average payment is to be no less than w. The second inequality applies when Mr. B chooses B_2.)

Because we have two independent maximizing problems, we use different symbols (v, w) to denote the average payoff to Mr. A from B's point of view, and average payoff to Mr. A from A's point of view. As it turns out, when A and B choose optimally, v will equal w, which is at least somewhat assuring.

To return to B's problem, assume that $v > 0$. Then we can divide through our two inequalities by v to obtain

$$2\frac{p}{v} - 3/2\left(\frac{1 - p}{v}\right) \leq 1 \text{ or } + 2x - 3/2y \leq 1$$

$$-1\frac{p}{v} + 3\left(\frac{1 - p}{v}\right) \leq 1 \text{ or } -1x + 3y \leq 1$$

where $\quad x = \dfrac{p}{v}, y = \dfrac{1 - p}{v}, x \geq 0, y \geq 0.$

Given these definitions for x and y, it follows that

$$x + y = \frac{1}{v}.$$

To minimize v is the same as to maximize $1/v$, and so we have converted Mr. B's problem to the following:

TABLE 15-5 *Mixed Strategies and the Payoff Matrix*

B A	B_1 (p)	B_2 (1 − p)
$A_1 q$	+ 2	− 3/2
$A_2 (1 - q)$	− 1	+ 3

$$\max \frac{1}{v} = x + y$$

subject to
$$2x - 3/2\,y \le 1$$
$$1x + 3\,y \le 1$$
$$x \ge 0, \quad y \ge 0.$$

This problem is now in the form of a linear programming (LP) problem that can be solved graphically by plotting the constraint set together with the objective function $x + y$. The crosshatched area in figure 15-11 marks the feasible set, that is, the set of values for x and y that jointly satisfy

$$2x - 3/2y \le 1$$

and

$$-1\,x + 3\,y \le 1, \, x \ge 0, \, y \ge 0.$$

The largest value for $x + y$ consistent with the constraint set is $5/3$, which occurs at the point $x = 1$, $y = 2/3$. Note that both inequalities are satisfied (as equalities) at this point. Since

$$v = \frac{1}{x + y} = \frac{1}{1 + 2/3},$$

we have $v = 3/5$,

with $p = vx = 3/5$

and $1 - p = vy = 2/5$.

By choosing B_1 with probability $3/5$ and B_2 with probability $2/5$, Mr. B can guarantee that whatever strategy Mr. A pursues, he cannot win more than $3/5$ dollars on the average.

By employing the same approach to Mr. A's decision problem, we find that the optimal choices for Mr. A are $q = 8/15$, $1 - q = 7/15$ with $w = 3/5$. Thus the minimum that Mr. B can guarantee he has to pay Mr. A on the

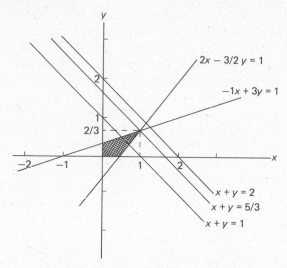

FIG. 15-11   *Solving for mixed strategies*

average, v, equals the maximum that Mr. A can guarantee he can obtain from Mr. B on the average, and the *value of the game*, the average payment from B to A, is $3/5$ dollars. (The problem for Mr. A turns out to be the *dual* to the LP problem for Mr. B, as discussed in the appendix to chapter 6.)

Suppose that Mr. A knew that Mr. B was going to pursue the mixed strategy: B_1 with probability $3/5$, B_2 with probability $2/5$. Then he still could do no better on the average than by employing his mixed strategy: A_1 with probability $8/15$, A_2 with probability $7/15$. How do we know that? Because B's strategy choice guarantees that he does not have to pay out more than $3/5$ dollars on the average, whatever is A's strategy, and A earns exactly $3/5$ dollars on the average by employing his optimum strategy. In fact, if A pursues any strategy other than his optimum one, his average payoff will fall. The argument is symmetrical with respect to *B*. Because of the similarity to the situation that holds at a saddle point (neither individual will change his strategy even if he knows the strategy of the other individual), we refer to the choices of mixed strategies by A and B as a *mixed strategy saddle point*. Note again that a mixed strategy saddle point is a Nash equilibrium.

What we have illustrated is an example of a more general result due originally to von Neumann, known as the *minimax theorem*:

Every two-person, zero-sum game has a mixed strategy saddle point.

Thus it follows that every two-person, zero-sum game can in principle be solved: mixed strategies exist such that if A announces his strategy to B, and if B announces his strategy to A, neither can do any better on the average than to pursue their announced strategies. In this sense, every two-person, zero-sum game is in principle like tic-tac-toe. The "in principle" is an important qualification, however; games like chess and checkers fit into this category, but the number of possible strategies is so enormous that no one has actually solved for the mixed saddle point strategies.

Two-Person, Nonzero-Sum Games— The Prisoner's Dilemma

Things get considerably more complicated when we turn from zero-sum games to nonzero-sum games or from two-person to *n*-person games. Unfortunately, the nonzero-sum and *n*-person games are of most interest to the economist. Consider, for example, the standard duopoly problem of two gasoline stations located near each other. Each station operator knows (1) that the demand for his product depends not only on his own price but also on the price charged by his competitor, and (2) that any pricing decision he makes will trigger a response from his competitor. So we have a game situation. But if the demand for gasoline is inelastic, then both stations are better off if they both charge the same high price than if they both charge the same low price. We have a nonzero-sum game.

There is no generally accepted rule of "rational" conduct for decision makers faced with a nonzero-sum game situation. To see the reason for this and related difficulties with such games, consider the classic "prisoner's dilemma" game.†

Two persons, Mr. A and Mr. B, are picked up by the police and charged with a crime. (It is irrelevant whether or not they committed the crime.) Each is taken into a separate room, and told the following:

> If you confess and your partner doesn't, you can turn state's evidence and we'll hold you only till the trial, say in two weeks. If your partner confesses and you don't, we'll send you up for thirty years. If you both confess, both of you will get twenty-five years. If neither of you confesses, we'll hold you both for a month and then release you.

The payoff matrix looks as in table 15-6, where the top number is A's *payoff* and the bottom is B's.

Mr. A and Mr. B are then allowed to get together by themselves to talk things over. Presumably both of them agree not to confess.

---

†For an extended discussion of the prisoner's dilemma and related games, see R. Luce, and H. Raiffa, *Games and Decisions* (New York: Wiley, 1957).

TABLE 15-6   *The Prisoner's Dilemma*

B ⟍ A	Confess	Don't Confess
Confess	A: 25 yrs B: 25 yrs	A: 2 wks B: 30 yrs
Don't Confess	A: 30 yrs B: 2 wks	A: 1 mo B: 1 mo

They are then taken back to their separate rooms for further questions, and both promptly confess, going up for twenty-five years each!

How does this happen? Look at things from A's point of view. Suppose B confesses. Then A is better off to confess—he gets twenty-five years if he confesses and thirty if he does not. So if B confesses, A should certainly confess. Suppose B does not confess, then again A is better off to confess—two weeks in jail versus one month in jail. Whatever B does, A is better off to confess. The alternative "confess" *dominates* the alternative "don't confess" for Mr. A. Because the matrix is symmetric, B is likewise better off to confess, whatever A does. If each one "follows his self-interest" and adopts the intuitively appealing dominance rule, both of them suffer disastrous consequences. The result of the decision process is a Pareto-inferior state so far as the two of them are concerned; both are better off if neither confesses.

It might be thought that the prisoner's dilemma game is something of an oddity, a theoretical possibility that really has little to do with the real world. On the contrary, most real-world duopoly or oligopoly situations actually involve a variant of the prisoner's dilemma game.

For example, return to the intersection with two gasoline stations. The demand for gasoline is inelastic, and so both operators would make higher profits if the price charged for gasoline were high rather than low. But it is not easy to make an agreement that will stick. Suppose that the cost of gasoline to each station owner is 40¢/gallon. At a price to customers of 50¢, total sales are 1,000 gallons. At a price of 60¢, total sales are 900 gallons (demand is inelastic). If both stations charge the same price, then sales are split between the two; if one station charges a higher price, all sales go to the other station. The payoff matrix looks as in table 15-7, where the decisions are the prices to be charged per gallon of gas; the top entry in each box is A's profits, the bottom entry is B's profits.

We have again a prisoner's dilemma situation. If B charges 60¢, A is better off to charge 50¢ (+$100 if A charges 50¢ vs. +$90 if A charges 60¢); if B charges 50¢, again A is better off to charge 50¢ (+$50 vs. 0). B's situation is the same; hence each station charges 50¢ and each owner earns $40 less in profits per day than if both were charging 60¢.

Cartels and the Prisoner's Dilemma

The prisoner's dilemma game represents a formalization of the proposition that in an oligop-

TABLE 15-7   *The Prisoner's Dilemma—Two Gasoline Stations*

B ⟍ A	50¢	60¢
50¢	A: +$50 B: +$50	A: +$100 B: 0
60¢	A: 0 B: +$100	A: +$ 90 B: +$ 90

olistic industry, arrangements that benefit all firms in the industry *in the aggregate* create strong incentives for individual firms to deviate from any such arrangement. And if all firms follow their individual self-interest by deviating from the arrangement, then the arrangement falls apart.

The public is protected against implicit or explicit collusion among the firms in an oligopolistic industry because of the incentives to cheat on any cartel agreement, as illustrated by the paradoxical resolution of the prisoner's dilemma. But the protection is not complete. The gains from collusion are great, and there is a long history of anticompetitive practices in oligopolistic industries in this country and abroad. From the point of view of game theory, the strategy for the industry is to change the payoff matrix to avoid the prisoner's dilemma situation. To take an extreme case, suppose that in our story of the two prisoners, at their meeting to discuss strategy prisoner A informs prisoner B that if B confesses, he will go scot-free of course, but his head will be kicked in two days after he gets on the street. This change in the payoff from confessing eliminates the dilemma—B is not likely to confess.

Sanctions that work is what is really involved in an effective cartel agreement. Formally, a cartel is a collection of individuals or firms who reach agreement as to joint actions with respect to certain economic activities such as price setting, output quotas, and market sharing. These agreements can avoid the prisoner's dilemma problem only if there is some clout behind the cartel to punish violators of the agreement and if there are resources available to police the agreement through the discovery of violators.

A major stumbling block for any cartel is the cost of obtaining information relative to the activities of its members and of potential competitors. Just as there is a demand for "swift and assured punishment of criminals" as an effective deterrent to crime, there is a need for swift and assured punishment of violators of the cartel agreement if it is to hold together. This is one reason why cartels tend to be most effective when there are only a few members; the costs of policing the cartel agreement generally preclude cartels with a large number of members. And the cartel agreement is most effective if the agreement is legally enforceable in the courts, so that fines and other sanctions imposed on members are binding.

The legal status of cartels varies from country to country and from industry to industry. Cartels are generally illegal in the United States, but there are some notable exceptions including agricultural co-ops (for example, Sunkist, which controls the California orange crop), labor unions, certain joint agreements that apply only to foreign markets for U.S. corporations, and major league baseball. Needless to say, the most effective cartels are those whose agreements are enforced by the government itself. In fact, it is difficult to give examples of cartels that have persisted and flourished over an extended period of time in the absence of direct government support for the cartel.

In the absence of government enforcement of cartel agreements, the agreements tend to be highly unstable. For this reason, economists tend to be highly sceptical about "conspiracy" theories of oligopolistic exploitation. When such exploitation occurs over the long run (as it occasionally does), most often there is government coercion involved in the cartel.

Summary

When an industry consists of a large number of small firms, each marketing its own differentiated product, the industry is one of monopolistic competition. In the long run, the demand curve facing the firm is tangent to the LRAC curve with output such that price is greater than LRMC and LRAC is above its minimum level. Added to the welfare losses due to market power are any wastes of resources associated with defensive advertising.

In an industry with a "dominant firm," this firm becomes the price setter for the industry. In the long run, cost advantages for the dominant firm result either in the industry being converted into a monopoly, or in a situation of "borderline balance" between the dominant firm and the smaller firms that remain in the industry.

An industry with a small number of firms is called an oligopoly. The Cournot approach views each firm as acting under the assumption that the other firms will maintain their output levels, matching any price changes introduced by the firm. In the case of a linear industry demand and zero marginal costs, the Cournot solution results in an equal sharing of output among firms, with industry output being greater than the monopoly output.

The Cournot model and the Hotelling model utilize a notion of market equilibrium that is common to most oligopoly theories, the concept of a Nash equilibrium. At a Nash equilibrium, each market participant makes decisions under certain assumptions as to the choices of the other market participants. When all such choices are jointly consistent with the assumptions of decision makers, a Nash equilibrium is achieved.

A special instance of a Nash equilibrium is the case of a saddle point in a game. A saddle point occurs when the minimaxing choice of Mr. A remains unchanged, given that Mr. A knows the strategy being used by Mr. B, and similarly for Mr. B's minimaxing choice. The basic theorem of game theory asserts that every two-person, zero-sum game has a mixed strategy saddle point.

The prisoner's dilemma arises in nonzero-sum games when applying the dominance rule leads to a Nash equilibrium such that each participant in the game is worse off than at another feasible outcome for the game. Applying the notion of the prisoner's dilemma to cartels, we conclude that cartels tend to be unstable unless there are governmental or quasi-governmental sanctions against cheating on the cartel agreement.

Problems

1. Given an industry demand curve $200 - 3p$, assume that the smaller firms in the industry each have short-run total cost curves given by

$$TC = 5 + 2X_S^2$$

where X_S is output of a small firm.

There are ten small firms in the industry. The dominant firm has a total cost curve of the form

$$TC = 2 + 1X_D^2$$

where X_D is output of the dominant firm.

a. Determine the short-run equilibrium price and output for the industry, together with output for the small firms and output for the dominant firm.

b. Assume that the long-run total cost curve for a typical small firm is

$$TC = 15X_S$$

while total cost for the dominant firm is

$$TC = 1 + 1X^2.$$

Determine the long-run industry equilibrium, including output of small firms and output of the dominant firm.

2. Given an industry demand curve $100 - 10p$, assume that marginal cost is zero.

a. Determine monopoly price and output.

b. Determine the Cournot solution of price and output for two firms; for three firms.

c. Determine the long-run price and output under perfect competition.

3. For the example of mixed strategies given in table 15-5, show graphically that A's optimal mixed strategy is $q = 8/15$, $1 - q = 7/15$ with $w = 3/5$.

4. Find the mixed strategies that result in a mixed strategy saddle point for the following game.

B ╲ A	B_1	B_2
A_1	$+3$	$+1$
A_2	$+2$	$+4$

(Payoffs are from B to A.) What is the expected value of the game?

5. Which organization would you expect to be a more stable cartel? Explain why.

a. The National Farmers Organization or the Mafia?

b. The NCAA (National Collegiate Athletic Association) or the NFL (National Football League)?

c. A consumer group organized to bring meat prices down or a cartel of aluminum producers?

Other Market Imperfections

There are almost unlimited applications of microeconomic theory to problems of market imperfections. In chapters 16, 17, and 18, the theory is applied to the special cases of uncertainty, externalities, and natural resources. In chapter 16, the emphasis is upon the characterization of uncertainty, consumer preferences with respect to probability distributions, and the institutions that have developed to convert uncertainty into relative certainty. Chapter 17 discusses the meaning of externalities, the need for internalization of externalities, public goods, and the scope and limitations of private negotiation and government policies designed to internalize externalities. Chapter 18 is concerned with replenishable and nonreplenishable resources, and problems of appropriability and externalities as they apply to such resources.

16
Uncertainty

As recently as seventy-five years ago, scientists thought of the universe as an orderly mechanism that operates according to a set of relatively simple, deterministic laws. Scientists believed that with patient study, contemplation, some experimentation, and a large dose of creative vision, the laws of the universe could be identified and related one to another in a comprehensive model. This view of a deterministic universe was shattered in the 1920s when physicists discovered that certain laws of the universe could be formulated only in terms of the statistical behavior of collections of subatomic particles. Einstein apparently believed to his dying day that "God does not play dice with the universe," but modern science has been forced to accept a vision of the world in which uncertainty plays an integral role. Uncertainty appears at the most fundamental level of our understanding of the workings of the physical universe.

Needless to say, uncertainty is of central importance in economic activities. It arises in strategic decision-making situations, as discussed in chapter 15. But even when strategic considerations are absent, consumers and firm managers are continually having to make decisions, the consequences of which cannot be known beforehand, and so "chance" plays at least a partial role in determining whether or not the decisions are reasonable.

In part, the uncertainty we face reflects the inherent randomness of the universe, the lack of strict deterministic laws governing physical phenomena. But uncertainty in economic affairs arises from much more prosaic sources as well. In general, there is uncertainty because we lack the requisite information to convert uncertainty into certainty. We might not have the scientific or technological know-how to obtain the information, or the market for information as a commodity may somehow be at fault. Because information is often costly to collect, process, and transmit, uncertainty can persist in certain situations simply because no one is willing to pay the price required to obtain the needed information. In such a case, continuing uncertainty would be the consequence of deliberate choices by decision makers, without any necessary connotation of suboptimality.

But there are basic problems with the market for information, relating to increasing returns in the production of information and to the appropriability of information once it has been produced. Both of these aspects of the market for information lead to difficulties in creating a market structure that preserves incentives for the production and distribution of information—incentives that are consistent with Pareto optimality. We will examine the market for information in more detail later in this chapter.

Even if the market for information worked perfectly, uncertainty would still persist in markets where the cost of information exceeds its benefits. With information markets functioning imperfectly, uncertainty looms even larger in economic affairs. Predictably, various institutions have developed to deal with problems of uncertainty. Our object in this chapter is to describe the functioning of a competitive economy in the face of uncertainty, with special emphasis on the role played by institutions designed to convert uncertainty into relative certainty.

Uncertainty and Subjective Probability

A starting point for our analysis is to look a little more closely at the notion of uncertainty. One view of uncertainty can be described as *objective*, since it regards uncertainty as a characteristic of the world that can be studied and measured without reference to the individuals affected by it. From an objective viewpoint, the probability that a given coin will come up heads on a toss can be determined by running a series of trials and calculating the relative frequency with which heads appear. In the physical sciences, *probability* always refers to objective probability.

The economist takes a *subjective* view of uncertainty, treating it as a description of the beliefs or state of mind of a consumer or a firm manager. The economic decision maker faces uncertainty if he is uncertain about the outcomes of his decisions, whether or not the world itself operates like a random process. The subjective probability that a head will come up on the toss of a coin reflects the beliefs of the decision maker, and may be different for different individuals, whatever the objective

probability of heads is. The point is that what is relevant in describing the behavior of a decision maker is what that decision maker regards as the probabilities of outcomes, since he will employ these probabilities in his own calculations and decision-making.

The subjective viewpoint regards any event as grist for the mill of probability analysis, whether that event has any objective probability attached to it or not. Thus it makes sense to ask: "What is the (subjective) probability that the sun will rise tomorrow?"—even though tomorrow's sunrise is a unique event that will never be repeated, and so the relative frequency approach is not applicable.

How can subjective probability be calculated? To indicate how one might proceed, consider trying to determine whether an individual thinks it is more probable that a coin will come up heads than tails. We offer two alternative bets to the individual.

Bet A: $1 if heads come up, $0 if tails.
Bet B: $1 if tails come up, $0 if heads.

If he chooses bet A, then we say heads has a higher (subjective) probability of occurrence for that individual than does tails, while the reverse is true if he chooses bet B. If the individual is willing to let anyone else pick A or B for him as they choose, then we regard heads and tails as equally likely from the individual's point of view, and each is assigned a (subjective) probability of $1/2$.

The calculation of subjective probabilities for an individual is thus based on the choices made by the individual among bundles promising payoffs if specified events occur. To build on this approach, we can construct "reasonable" axioms concerning the choices of individuals; these axioms imply that the individual acts "as if" he attached subjective probabilities to the occurrence of events. We will not attempt to summarize such axiom systems here, but they are widely used in the theoretical literature on decision making under uncertainty.

Our approach will be to assume that economic decision makers make choices under uncertainty on the basis of the subjective probabilities they attach to events. Once they are identified, subjective probabilities have the same mathematical properties as objective probabilities. Certain basic notions concerning probabilities are discussed in the next section.

Probability Distributions

Consider a set of events $[A, B, C, \ldots, Z]$, where associated with each event is a payoff that is received if the event occurs. Take the payoffs to be money amounts, *a* dollars if *A* occurs, *b* dollars if *B* occurs, and so on. Associated with each event is a probability that the event will occur, say $P(A), P(B), \ldots, P(Z)$. These probabilities may be regarded as either objective or subjective probabilities. In either case, probabilities are always nonnegative numbers between 0 and 1. Further, if the events $A, B, \ldots, Z$ are mutually exclusive and collectively exhaustive, then

$$P(A) + P(B) + \ldots + P(Z) = 1.$$

(Events $A, \ldots, Z$ are *mutually exclusive* if the occurrence of any one of them precludes the occurrence of any other of them; they are *collectively exhaustive* if one of the events has to occur on every trial.)

To illustrate, assume that three fair coins are tossed independently, and that you are paid $1 for each head that appears. Events, payoffs and the corresponding probabilities of payoffs appear in table 16-1. The last two columns of the table give the probability distribution over payoffs for this game; that is, the table associates with each payoff x the probability $P(x)$

TABLE 16-1 *Probability Distribution Over Payoffs*

Event	Payoff x	Probability $P(x)$
A—0 heads appear	$0	1/8
B—1 head appears	$1	3/8
C—2 heads appear	$2	3/8
D—3 heads appear	$3	1/8

with which it will occur.

Given any probability distribution over payoffs x, we can associate with that distribution its expected value $E(x)$ defined by

$$E(x) = \Sigma x P(x).$$

For the example above,

$$E(x) = \$0. \cdot \frac{1}{8} + \$1 \cdot \frac{3}{8} + \$2 \cdot \frac{3}{8}$$

$$+ \$3 \cdot \frac{1}{8} = \frac{\$12}{8} = \$1.50.$$

The expected value can be interpreted as a measure of the "average payoff" from the game. A measure of the dispersion of payoffs about the "average" payoff is provided by the *variance* $\sigma^2(x)$ defined by

$$\sigma^2(x) = \Sigma(x - Ex)^2 P(x).$$

For the example above,

$$\sigma^2(x) = (0 - 1.5)^2 \cdot \frac{1}{8} + (1 - 1.5)^2 \cdot \frac{3}{8}$$

$$+ (2 - 1.5)^2 \cdot \frac{3}{8} + (3 - 1.5)^2 \cdot \frac{1}{8} = \frac{3}{4}.$$

Another related measure often employed as a measure of dispersion is the standard deviation, $\sigma(x)$, defined as the positive square root of the variance. For our example,

$$\sigma(x) = \frac{\sqrt{3}}{2}.$$

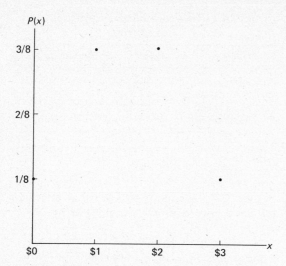

FIG. 16-1   *Discrete probability distribution over payoffs*

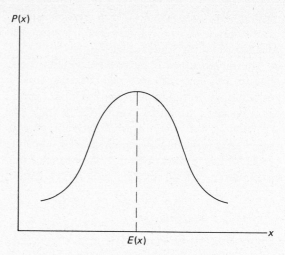

FIG. 16-2   *Continuous probability distribution over payoffs*

It is sometimes convenient to plot the probability distribution over payoffs as a graph. For the probability distribution above, the graph is shown in figure 16-1. When there is a continuous variation in payoffs, the probability distribution approaches a smooth curve as in figure 16-2. If the probability distribution is symmetrical about $E(x)$ as pictured, then the "spread" of the distribution depends on how large the variance (or standard deviation) of the distribution is. Figure 16-3 shows two symmetrical distributions with differing expected values and variances. Distribution #1 has a smaller mean (E_1) than the mean (E_2) of distribution #2, but distribution #1 has a larger variance than does distribution #2.

Assuming the existence of subjective probabilities, the problem of decision making under uncertainty amounts to the problem of choosing from among such alternative probability distributions over payoffs. The approach to this decision problem followed in most of the economic literature is the "measurable utility" approach.

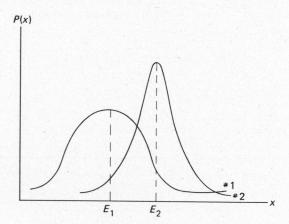

FIG. 16-3   *Distributions with differing expected values and variances*

Measurable Utility

In decision making under uncertainty, there are two dimensions to the decision problem that must be taken into account: first, the decision maker's tastes (preference ranking) with respect to possible payoffs from his decisions; and second, the decision maker's attitudes toward uncertainty. The notion of measurable utility is an attempt to capture both dimensions of the decision problem in a single concept.

To illustrate, consider two gambles.

Bet A: win $1 with probability 1/2; win $0 with probability 1/2.

Bet B: win $.50 with certainty.

Presumably every individual prefers more money to less; hence the preference rankings over *payoffs* are the same for all decision makers; that is, $1 preferred to $.50 preferred to $0. On the other hand, some individuals would choose bet A rather than bet B, while others would reverse the choice. In making choices between the two bets, individuals are expressing their tastes with respect to the two different probability distributions over payoffs (table 16-2).

Note that bets A and B have the same expected values (=$.50) but the variance of bet A is larger than the variance of bet B (1/4 versus 0). Individuals who choose B over A are averse

TABLE 16-2 *Probability Distribution Over Payoffs*

| A | | B | |
Payoff	Probability	Payoff	Probability
$0	1/2	$.50	1
$1	1/2		

to risk, while individuals who choose A over B apparently enjoy taking risks. Neither choice is "irrational"; instead each choice expresses a different attitude toward risk and uncertainty.

The idea behind measurable utility theory is this. We assume that the decision maker has a preference ranking over payoffs that satisfies the axioms of modern utility theory as discussed in chapter 5. Given such a preference ranking, utility numbers are assigned to probability distributions over payoffs in such a way that they preserve the ranking of an individual's preferences over such probability distributions: if one probability distribution is preferred to another, the first is assigned a higher utility number than the second. The individual then chooses from among probability distributions on the basis of their utilities. The method of assigning utility numbers to probability distributions can be illustrated as follows.

1. Consider a choice situation involving uncertainty, where there are n possible money payoffs $x_1, x_2, \ldots, x_n$, arranged so that $x_1 < x_2 \ldots < x_n$.

2. Given that more money is preferred to less, the utility number assigned to x_1 must be less than the utility number assigned to x_n. For concreteness, suppose we assign a utility of 0 to x_1 and a utility of 1 to x_n.

3. Next consider a gamble in which the individual receives x_n with probability p and x_1 with probability $1 - p$.

4. Assume that for some value of p between 0 and 1, the individual is indifferent between receiving x_2 with certainty and engaging in the gamble. Let that value of p be denoted by p_2. Then we assign a utility of p_2 to the money payoff x_2.

5. By performing the same experiment for $x_3, \ldots, x_{n-1}$, we obtain the utility numbers $p_3, \ldots, p_{n-1}$, which are the *measurable utilities* associated with $x_3, \ldots, x_{n-1}$.

Let's see what measurable utility does for us. Given any gamble G of the form $G = (x_n$ with probability p, x_1 with probability $1-p)$, we assign the number p as the measurable utility associated with the money payoff m such that the individual is indifferent between G and receiving m with certainty. Because the two are indifferent, this means that

$$U(G) = U(x_n \text{ with probability } p; \\ x_1 \text{ with probability } 1-p) \\ = p \equiv U(m).$$

But note that we have chosen $U(x_n) = 1$, $U(x_2) = 0$. Hence $U(G)$ could also be written

$$U(G) = pU(x_n) + (1-p)U(x_1),$$

since this also equals p, that is,

$$p \cdot 1 + (1-p) \cdot 0 = p.$$

This means that the measurable utility number associated with any gamble involving x_1 and x_n is the *expected value of utility* of the payoffs from the gamble; that is, it is the weighted sum of the utility numbers assigned to x_n and x_1, where the weights are the probabilities p and $1-p$.

Consider a gamble H of the form $H = (x_2$ with probability q, x_1 with probability $1-q)$. We will show that

$$U(H) = qU(x_2) + (1-q)U(x_1) = qp_2.$$

By our method of assigning utility numbers, x_2 is indifferent to the gamble: x_n with probability p_2, x_1 with probability $1-p_2$.

Replacing x_2 by the gamble with which it is indifferent, H becomes

$((x_n$ with probability p_2,
  x_1 with probability $1-p_2)$
    with probability q,
  x_1 with probability $1-q)$.

This can be rewritten as

$(x_n$ with probability $p_2 \cdot q$,
  x_1 with probability $(1-p_2)q + 1 - q$
$\equiv (x_n$ with probability $p_2 \cdot q$,
  x_1 with probability $1 - p_2 \cdot q)$.

The utility associated with this is

$$p_2 \cdot qu(x_n) + (1 - p_2 \cdot q)\, u(x_1) = p_2 q$$

But this is equivalent to

$$q \cdot u(x_2) + (1-q)\, u(x_1) = q \cdot p_2 + 0 = qp_2.$$

Thus any gamble can be reduced to a gamble involving only x_1 and x_n; hence the measurable utility number associated with any gamble is the *expected utility* of the payoffs from the gamble. Given any gamble involving the payoffs $x_1, \ldots, x_n$, the measurable utility number associated with the gamble is simply

$$q_1 U(x_1) + q_2 U(x_2) + \ldots + q_n U(x_n)$$

where q_i is the probability of the payoff x_i.

Some implicit assumptions have been used to derive this result. One of the most important is the assumption that *individuals are concerned only with the payoffs from gambles and the probabilities of such payoffs, but are not concerned with the process by which probabilities are generated.* This assumption implies, for example, that an individual is indifferent between playing blackjack or craps, so long as the probability of winning is the same for the two games. We can therefore replace x_2 by the gamble with which it is indifferent.

Further, it is assumed that *in a gamble involving payoffs x_1, x_n, increasing the proba-*

bility of receiving x_n *(and thus reducing the probability of receiving* x_1*) gives a preferred gamble with a higher measurable utility number*—a number assigned in such a way that the utility of any probability distribution is simply the expected utility of the payoffs, given that distribution. We have also assumed that *there is some probability p such that a gamble involving* x_1 *and* x_n *is indifferent to, say,* x_2 *with certainty.* For individuals who take moral stands against gambling, no such p, $0 < p < 1$ may exist. Finally, we have assumed that the decision maker possesses a subjective probability distribution over payoffs. (In certain cases at least, this might not hold.)

In what follows we will assume that decision makers' preferences with respect to probability distributions satisfy these assumptions so that their preferences can be represented by measurable utility numbers.

Maximizing Expected Utility

We thus conclude that under the assignment of utility numbers according to the measurable utility scheme, the measurable utility number assigned to any gamble is simply the expected utility of that gamble. This implies in turn that an individual who makes choices from among gambles in a manner consistent with his attitudes toward risk always chooses so as to *maximize his expected utility.*

For example, consider the following assignment of utilities.

Payoff x	U(x)
$0	0
$1	.3
$2	.7
$3	1

The individual is offered choices from among

A: $3 with probability .5,
   $1 with probability .5
B: $3 with probability .7,
   $0 with probability .3
C: $2 with certainty

Which does he choose? First note that B and C are indifferent; after all, the way that we arrived at the utility number .7 for the utility of $2 was by finding out that the individual was indifferent between B and C. On the other hand, bet A offers an expected utility

$$u(\$3)\,(.5) + u(\$1)\,(.5)$$
$$= 1(.5) + .3(.5) = .65.$$

Since $.65 < .7$, the individual will choose either B or C—both are indifferent and both are higher on the individual's preference scale than is option A. In fact, you should be able to show that option A is indifferent to the bet ($3 with probability .65, $0 with probability .35), and so it is clearly inferior to option B.

Attitudes toward Risk   The purpose of developing the measurable utility approach to decision making under uncertainty is to construct a numerical representation of preferences over probability distributions that expresses the attitudes toward risk or uncertainty on the part of the decision maker. It is important not to read anything more than this into the approach. An example may help clarify the uses of measurable utility.

Suppose that there is a raffle ticket offering $10 with probability .05 and $0 with probability .95. An individual is willing to pay 25¢ for the ticket. According to the measurable utility scheme, we assign a utility of .05 to 25¢, taking $u(\$10) = 1$, $u(\$0) = 0$. Suppose some other individual would be willing to pay 50¢ for the ticket; now we assign a utility of .05 to 50¢ for the second individual. Does this mean that the first individual somehow values money higher than the second individual?

The answer is no—there is no way that we can infer the valuation of money on the part of either individual from these measurable utility numbers, and we certainly cannot make comparisons between the two with respect to their preferences over money. What do the utility numbers tell us, then? They tell us precisely that the second individual is willing to pay more for a certain gamble than the first person is, and in that sense, is more willing to take risks than is the first person. The utility numbers assigned to money payoffs reflect attitudes toward risk and *not* valuations of money.

We note that under the choice of utility units, the second individual assigns an expected utility to the raffle ticket that is equal to the expected payoff from the ticket (expected payoff = $10 (.05) + $0 (.95) = .50), while the expected utility of the raffle ticket is less than its expected payoff for the first individual. This relationship suggests a way of classifying attitudes toward risk that we will employ throughout the rest of this chapter.

We say that an individual is *risk neutral* if, given any gamble G, he is indifferent between participating in the gamble G, and receiving the expected value of G with certainty. An individual is *risk averse* if he prefers the expected value of G with certainty to the gamble G; and he is a *risk lover* if he prefers the gamble G to receiving with certainty the expected value of G. These classifications of attitudes toward risk are reflected in the measurable utility numbers assigned to payoffs, in that for any money payoff strictly between x_1 and x_n the measurable utility number assigned to a risk averse individual will be higher than for a risk

neutral individual, which in turn is higher than that assigned for a risk lover. The individual who is indifferent between 50¢ with certainty and the gamble G with expected value of 50¢ is risk neutral. The individual who is willing to pay 25¢ for the gamble is risk averse.

Graphically, we can indicate the differences among these types of attitudes toward risk as in figure 16-4. Curve A is associated with a risk averse decision maker, curve B indicates a risk neutral attitude, and curve C illustrates the case of a risk lover. The measurable utility curve for a risk averse individual is strictly concave, that for a risk neutral individual is linear, while the risk lover's utility curve is strictly convex. Because choices are made on the basis of the expected utilities of gambles, we can use this graph to indicate the kind of attitudes toward risk implied by these curves.

In the case of the risk averter's curve (fig. 16-5), the utility number assigned to $2 is higher than the expected utility of a gamble in which the decision maker would receive $1 with probability .5 and $3 with probability .5. That is, $U(\$2) > .5\ U(\$1) + .5\ U(\$3)$, as

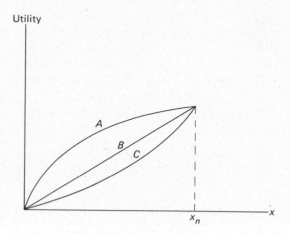

FIG. 16-4   *Attitudes toward risk*

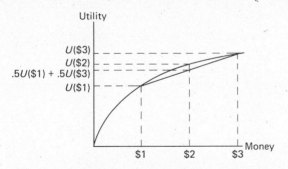

FIG. 16-5   *Risk aversion*

Payoff	Probability
$ 2	1/2
4	1/4
8	1/8
16	1/16
.	.
.	.
.	.

indicated in figure 16-5. Another way to put this is that the risk averse individual would not be willing to pay as much as $2 to engage in a bet offering an expected payoff of $2, which is, of course, the definition of a risk averse individual.

Do individuals tend to be risk averse, risk neutral, or risk lovers? This is not a new question. It was raised in a particularly intriguing fashion almost 300 years ago.

The St. Petersburg Paradox   The modern mathematical theory of probability had its beginnings in Russia during the late 1600s when the mathematician Nicholas Bernoulli became interested in the action in the gambling casinos of St. Petersburg. Among other things, Bernoulli raised the question as to whether or not gamblers are always willing to pay the expected value of a gamble in order to engage in the gamble. Bernoulli argued that this was not the case, that in fact risk aversion in some form or another shows up in most of us. To prove his point, he created the following example, which has come to be known as the *St. Petersburg paradox.*

Consider a game in which the payoffs are as follows:

and in general you will win 2^n dollars with probability $(1/2)^n$. For example, consider a game in which a fair coin is tossed and you are paid 2^n dollars if the *first* time a head shows up is on the nth toss. This is quite an interesting game; only half of the time will winnings be more than $2, only one-fourth of the time will they exceed $4, and only one-eighth of the time will they exceed $8. On the other hand, consider the expected value of the game $E(x)$.

$$E(x) = \$2 \times \frac{1}{2} + \$4 \times \frac{1}{4} + \ldots$$

$$= \$1 + \$1 + \ldots .$$

It is clear that $E(x)$ is infinity! Hence a risk neutral or risk loving individual should be willing to pay an unlimited amount of money to participate in the game.

Nicholas Bernoulli's son Daniel resolved the paradox by arguing in rather modern terms that what people look at is the expected value to them not in money but in utility, or satisfactions. He also pointed out that an extra dollar is worth more to a poor person than to a rich person. (This is the usual rationalization offered for a progressive income tax—in order to equalize the burden of a tax, the rich should be taxed proportionately more than the poor.) Consider a Bernoulli-type approach in which the utility of money payoffs is represented by the square root of the payoff, rather than the payoff itself.

In such a case the utility payoff table would look as in table 16-3. Then the expected payoff in utility terms becomes

$$\sqrt{2}\left(\frac{1}{2}\right) + 2\left(\frac{1}{4}\right)$$
$$+ 2\sqrt{2}\left(\frac{1}{8}\right) + 4\left(\frac{1}{16}\right) + \ldots$$

With a little manipulation, it can be shown that this sum is equal to

$$\frac{1}{\sqrt{2}-1} = 2.41.$$

Utility is the square root of the corresponding money amount. This means that the value of the game to the participant (the amount he would be willing to pay to engage in the game) would be only $5.76 (2.41 squared).

The Bernoulli-type utility function would appear as in figure 16-6. Note that the slope of the curve, which measures the marginal utility of money, decreases as the money payoff increases—the curve gets flatter as we move to the right along the money axis.

The graph portrays a situation that looks very much like the law of diminishing marginal utility, applied to money, and that is the way that Bernoulli interpreted it. However, that is

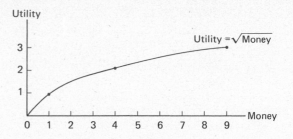

FIG. 16-6   *Bernoulli utility function for money*

not how the curve should be interpreted. Bernoulli's utility of money curve is just the risk averter's curve (fig. 16-5). "Diminishing marginal utility of money" applies *only* to decision making under uncertainty, and means nothing more nor less than risk aversion.

Risk Aversion and Economic Activity

There are various ways to interpret the notion of risk aversion. For the economist, the important thing is that, when faced with the prospect of a gamble, a risk averse individual would be willing to pay someone else to replace the gamble with an alternative that offers the expected value of the gamble with certainty. For example, if the risk averse individual is stuck with a gamble that pays $1 with probability .5 and $0 with probability .5, he would be willing to pay, say 10¢, to someone who would take the gamble off his hands and replace it with 50¢ with certainty.

Risk aversion also implies that there is a willingness to pay for insurance that will reduce uncertainty, even if it cannot be eliminated completely. If we think of the variance

TABLE 16-3   *Expected Utility—*
The St. Petersburg Game

Dollar Payoff	Utility Payoff	Probability
$ 2	$\sqrt{2}$	1/2
4	$\sqrt{4} = 2$	1/4
8	$\sqrt{8} = 2\sqrt{2}$	1/8
16	$\sqrt{16} = 4$	1/16

as measuring the dispersion of outcomes about the expected value, then the risk averse individual will typically be willing to pay something for insurance that enables him to reduce the variance of outcomes. On the other hand, the risk neutral decision maker is completely indifferent as to the dispersion of outcomes; only the expected value is of concern to him. The risk lover would actually pay to increase the dispersion of outcomes, assuming that the expected value remains unchanged.

Where there is a willingness to pay for something, there is an incentive for that something to be produced. The price system has responded to the demands of risk averse (and risk loving) individuals by creating insurance (and gambling casinos). We first turn to the role of insurance in an economy in which uncertainty is present.

The Law of Large Numbers and Insurance

We have already noted that risk averse decision makers will pay a premium to replace a gamble of given expected value with another gamble offering the expected value of the first one but with certainty. This characteristic explains the demand side of insurance. The insurance company offers its customers a guaranteed payment in the case of death, accidents, health problems, and the like, converting an uncertain financial situation for the customer into one in which payments to cover costs are guaranteed.

But we still have to explain how insurance companies, presumably owned by risk averse stockholders, would be willing to accept gambles involving uncertainty to them. The supply side of insurance involves an application of the *law of large numbers*, which can be formulated as follows.

Let $x_1, \ldots, x_n$ be the values of independent random variables having the same probability distribution, with expected value $E(x)$. Let

$$\bar{x} = \frac{x_1 + x_2 + \ldots + x_n}{n}$$

be the average of these values.† As n gets arbitrarily large, the probability that $\bar{x}$ will differ from $E(x)$ by any given amount goes to zero.

An alternative statement is this. Given a random sample of size n drawn from a population, the probability that the sample mean $\bar{x}$ will differ from the population mean $E(x)$ goes to zero as n goes to infinity.

Figure 16-7 illustrates the law of large numbers. For the case $n = 1$, $\bar{x}$ simply equals x_1, and so the curve shown for $n = 1$ is the probability distribution of the variable. As n gets larger, the probability distributions concentrate more and more about the expected value $E(x)$. In particular, as n goes to infinity, the probability distribution of $\bar{x}$ essentially collapses simply to $E(x)$ itself. For a sufficiently large sample, $\bar{x}$, the sample average, is essentially known *with certainty*.

The law of large numbers expresses a kind of increasing returns to size as far as risks are concerned. When an insurance company sells policies, in effect it is drawing a sample of size equal to the number of policies sold from some population. So long as the insurance company can get enough customers with the same underlying probability distribution of payoffs, and so long as independence is preserved, the com-

---

†$\bar{x}$ can be interpreted as the average value taken on where there are n observations from a given population.

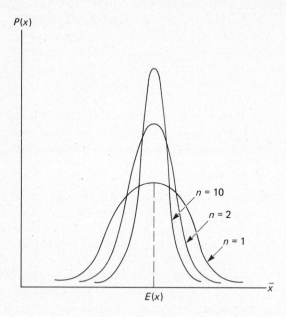

P(x)

n = 10

n = 2

n = 1

E(x)

x̄

FIG. 16-7   *Illustration of law of large numbers*

pany can be certain of the payoffs it will have to make to its customers in total, even though the payoffs to any one customer still remain uncertain. Thus the life expectancy of any one person who was born in 1900 is highly uncertain, but for a sufficiently large sample of individuals born in that year, the average life expectancy can be estimated very accurately.

The law of large numbers works only if independence and identical probability distributions are assumed. This limitation leads insurance companies to identify "risk" classes of potential customers in order to screen out individuals whose distributions differ markedly in an adverse way from the average of the population. Similarly, diversification over different geographic areas is necessary if fire and earthquake insurance companies are to avoid problems associated with lack of independence. For

the same reason, life insurance contracts used to contain a war clause that limited payments in the case of death in a war.

There is also the problem of identifying the true expected value of the population, that is, the characteristics of the underlying probability distribution. For life insurance companies, for example, premiums must be calculated today on the basis of estimates of the life expectancy of a population whose vital characteristics are still a matter of conjecture. We know that men born in 1900 tended to die, on the average, around 1967 but what will be the experience of men born in 1950?

Moral Hazard and Coinsurance   Another problem that arises in insurance is *moral hazard*. There is moral hazard when the act of buying insurance against potential losses causes the probability distribution of losses to change. To take an extreme case, suppose that you could buy fire insurance that promises to pay 110 percent of your losses in a fire. The existence of the insurance contract would provide positive incentives for you to burn down your own property. Even if the arson laws effectively precluded your setting fire to your house, at the very least one would expect you not to be quite so careful to avoid fire hazards, given that you owned such an insurance contract.

It is moral hazard that leads to insurance clauses canceling payment of life insurance in certain cases of suicide, and it is moral hazard that leads to coinsurance in most medical and health insurance as well as in automobile collision insurance. *Coinsurance* applies to a situation in which, when a loss occurs, both the owner of the insurance contract and the company issuing it are obliged to make payments in certain amounts. The $100 deductible collision insurance on automobiles is an example of coinsurance, since the owner of the car must pay the first $100 of damages in any accident in which he is at fault (details differ in no-fault states). The coinsurance provision in effect guarantees that there will be some financial loss to the insured individual if a claim is filed, which builds in incentives to avoid situations in which losses leading to claims might occur, and thus reduces moral hazard for the insurance company.

Insurance and the Optimal Allocation of Resources Briefly to summarize, insurance is feasible when there is risk aversion on the part of the population, and when it is possible for insurance companies to utilize the law of large numbers to convert uncertainty for the individual into certainty for the population as a whole. This requires in turn that the probability distribution over losses for individuals be roughly the same for most individuals, that maintaining independence among losses be possible, and that the probability distribution can be estimated to a fair degree of accuracy by the insurance company. Finally, the insurance contract, coupled with other aspects of the legal structure, must preclude any significant component of moral hazard in insurance.

If these conditions were met for all situations involving uncertainty, then insurance contracts would be available to convert a world of uncertainty into one of certainty, for anyone who was willing to pay the premium. Under competitive conditions, premiums would fall to levels where insurance companies earned the same rate of return as firms in any other industry, and the competitive system would generate Pareto-optimal equilibrium positions.

Unfortunately, these conditions are not always satisfied in situations involving decision making under uncertainty. Certain risks associated with decisions are unique to individuals, the probability distribution over losses differs among individuals, and moral hazard simply cannot be eliminated from certain situations. To add to the problem, there is a difficulty in maintaining a competitive structure in the insurance industry. Because the law of large numbers involves a variant of increasing returns to scale, effective insurance might well require companies so large that they are able to exercise market power with respect to premium charges, leading to the usual suboptimal results concerning the allocation of resources in the economy.

Thus insurance does not offer a complete solution to the problem of decision making under uncertainty. Some risks are uninsurable, and even when risks are insurable, monopoly pricing of premium charges, where it exists, leads to an excessive amount of risk bearing on the part of the population.

One other problem concerning insurance should at least be mentioned. Insurance contracts typically involve the payment of a relatively small premium today to protect against a relatively large loss at some time in the future. The larger the possible loss is and the further in the future the insurance protection is extended, the greater is the risk to the individual buying an insurance contract that the insurance company will default at time of payment. The hazards of bankruptcy of insurance companies promote concentration of insurance sales in a handful of older, larger, more conservative firms as buyers of insurance attempt to avoid default risks. Thus the built-in natural economies of scale of the law of large numbers are supplemented by the risks of default to encourage concentration in the insurance industry. In addition, regulations by the states designed to increase the safety of insurance contracts have also tended as a side effect to lessen competition in the insurance industry. Thus the possibility of noncompetitive pricing of insurance contracts is a real matter of concern in the economy.

The Futures Market

Insurance performs the function of converting uncertainty into certainty. Several other economic institutions play the role of redistributing uncertainty over the population, in particular transferring uncertainty from the risk averse to the risk lover. The futures market performs both of these functions. In the futures market, contracts are bought and sold which promise delivery of a certain number of units of a commodity, at a specified date in the future for a fixed price to be paid at that future date. The contract comes due at the delivery date, at which time the holder of the contract can demand delivery of the commodity from the individual who sold the contract.

Consider the following idealized situation. In April, a wheat farmer is engaged in planting his crops, which are to be harvested in September. The farmer has to commit himself in April to contracts for labor, fertilizer, rental of machinery, harvesting costs, and so on, without knowing what his crop will sell for in September. The futures contract enables him to remove this uncertainty by permitting him to sell today a promise to deliver x number of bushels in September. Such a contract is called a September futures contract. The price he will receive per bushel is the market price of September futures as of the day in April when he sells the contract. Through sale of the futures contract, the farmer removes the uncertainty as to what price he will receive per bushel for his crop and hence can make plans as though the future were certain, at least with respect to prices. Of course, the farmer still faces uncertainty with respect to the weather, but a major source of uncertainty has been eliminated through the futures contract.

Similarly, imagine a flour miller operating on the other side of the futures market, who must make plans in April as to his milling schedule for September, including the purchase of wheat for milling at that time. By purchasing the farmer's futures contract in April, he can eliminate uncertainty as to the price he will have to pay for wheat for September milling.

The effect of such purchases and sales has been to convert uncertainty concerning prices into certainty, for both the farmer and the miller. As with all voluntary exchanges, both the buyer and the seller of the futures contract gain from the transaction. A related operation involving the futures market involves the notion of hedging.

Hedging on the Futures Market   A hedge occurs when an individual engages in a simultaneous purchase and sale, one transaction in the futures market and the other in the cash market. To illustrate, take the case of a miller who buys cash wheat today to be milled into flour that will be sold one month in the future. (The process of converting wheat into flour takes one month to complete.) The price of flour one month from now is determined by the cash price of wheat at that future time. To eliminate the risk of price fluctuations in wheat, at the same time that the miller purchases cash wheat, he sells a futures contract to deliver wheat one month hence. The effect of these two simultaneous operations can be illustrated as follows.

April 1   cash price $3.75/bushel
        May futures $3.70/bushel

Hedge: Buy 1000 bushels cash
        @ $3.75/bushel
        Sell 1000 bushels May futures
        @ $3.70/bushel

On May 1, the miller has converted the cash wheat he bought on April 1 into flour, and he has to deliver wheat under his futures contract, which means he has to buy 1000 bushels of cash wheat on May 1 at the cash price prevailing then. The May 1 price of flour depends on the May 1 cash price of wheat. We consider the outcome for the miller based on two possible cash prices of wheat on May 1—$4 per bushel and $3.50 per bushel.

May 1   cash price $4.00/bushel

    Profit due to increase
    in price of flour:
        ($4.00 − 3.75) × 1000 = $250

    Loss due to futures
    contract:
        ($3.70 − 4.00) × 1000 = $300
    Net loss $ 50

May 1   cash price $3.50/bushel

    Profit due to futures
    contract:
        ($3.70 − 3.50) × 1000 = $200

    Loss due to fall in price
    of flour:
        ($3.50 − 3.75) × 1000 = $250
    Net loss $ 50

These figures show that whether the cash price of wheat rises or falls between April 1 and May 1, the miller takes the same $50 loss

from his hedging operation. He might be quite willing to pay $50 to remove uncertainty as to the future price of flour. After all, in the example, he could obtain a profit of $250 or a loss of $250 if he remained in an unhedged position, and for a risk averse miller this dispersion might be large enough to convince him to hedge.

The loss of $50 on the 1,000 bushel transaction occurs because the May futures price in April is 5¢ per bushel below the April cash price. If the May futures price were 5¢ per bushel above the cash price, then there would be a guaranteed $50 profit to the miller from his hedging operation, as you should verify for yourself.

The situation in which the futures price is below the cash price is the "typical" situation, and reflects the fact that there is a preponderance on the market of individuals like the miller who wish to sell futures in order to hedge against future price fluctuations. What this means is that, on the average, speculators (buyers of futures contracts) should make profits from their transactions, capturing the premium hedgers are willing to pay to avoid risks.

In brief, futures markets play the role of redistributing uncertainty from hedgers to speculators by permitting the producers and processors of commodities to hedge against future price fluctuations in the commodity. The term *speculator* has some negative connotations, but what we mean by the term is simply an individual who takes an unhedged position in the market, either as a seller or as a buyer of futures contracts. Because these contracts are freely entered into, the existence of futures markets permits the attainment of Pareto-superior states of the economy relative to a situation in which futures markets did not exist. At the same time, futures markets also act to provide a forum where speculators with differing expectations as to the future price of the commodity can engage in transactions.

Speculation and the Futures Market The futures markets perform the role of transferring uncertainty from risk averse individuals to risk neutral or risk loving individuals, as well as acting as a forum where individuals with different probability beliefs about the course of future prices of commodities can speculate on the basis of their beliefs. Farmers and others with access to wheat are not the only ones who sell futures contracts to deliver wheat, nor is it always the case that the purchaser of a futures contract is a miller who wants to take delivery of wheat at some future time.

Instead, anyone with the money can sell a futures contract in April (or May or June, for example) to deliver wheat in September, whether he produces wheat or not. Any person who sells such a contract without having the wheat to cover the contract is a *short seller* in the futures market. He goes to his broker and deposits a sum (*the margin*) equal to roughly 10 percent of the value of the futures contract he wishes to sell. Suppose that he sells 100 bushels of wheat in April for delivery in September at a price of $3.75 per bushel; then he has to deposit $37.50 (10 percent of the value of the contract—$3.75 × 100 bushels) with his broker. The broker sells the contract. Between April and September, the price of wheat futures fluctuates, and if the price starts going up, the short seller has to deliver more margin to maintain his account at 10 percent of the market price for the futures contract. Come September, the short seller in effect buys 100 bushels of cash wheat, delivers to the holder of his futures contract, and collects the money due to him. If the cash price in September is $3.50, then

the short seller has made 25¢ per bushel; if the cash price is $4, he has lost 25¢ per bushel.

Just as there are short sellers, there are *margin buyers* of futures contracts who put up 10 percent of the purchase price of a futures contract and borrow the remainder from their broker. If the cash price of wheat in September is higher than the price at which the futures contract was bought, the margin buyer makes a profit; if the September cash price is below the futures contract price, the margin buyer suffers a loss.

With short sellers selling to margin buyers, the futures market looks more like a gambling casino than a social institution for redistributing risk. Transactions between such individuals are based on the differences in their expectations as to what the price of wheat actually will be in September. If we substitute "differences in their expectations as to which is the faster horse," the similarity to gambling becomes perhaps a bit more transparent. But there is an important difference between the futures market and the race track. The existence of the futures market and the existence of speculators on that market enables risk averse individuals to transfer risks of future price changes to those speculators. As noted earlier, futures markets convert a world of uncertainty into one of certainty for individuals who are willing to pay the cost, which is the profits earned by speculators.

The Value of Information

Risk aversion leads to a search for methods to reduce the dispersion of payoffs from decisions; insurance and futures contracts are economic institutions that act to reduce or eliminate uncertainties faced by such decision makers. Another approach to reducing uncertainty is by acquiring additional information concerning the process generating the dispersion of returns. The decision to acquire information can make sense whether the decision maker is risk averse, risk neutral, or a risk lover.

For example, consider the case of a farmer who is faced with the problem of harvesting his wheat crop. The crop will mature as of a certain date in August. If the crop is subject to a heavy rain after that date, it is ruined. Hence there is a strong incentive to harvest as rapidly as possible after the maturation date. On the other hand, increasing the speed at which harvesting takes place also increases the cost per bushel of wheat harvested.

Assume that the choice the farmer faces is between harvesting the entire crop today, at a cost of $10,000, or harvesting half of it today and half tomorrow, at a cost of $2,500 per day. The harvested crop is worth $50,000. Payoffs to the farmer depend on whether or not there will be a heavy rain tomorrow, since a heavy rain will ruin any part of the crop that is not harvested. The payoff matrix to the farmer looks like table 16-4. (We assume that in harvesting over two days, half the crop is harvested today.)

Let P be the subjective probability of heavy rain tomorrow and let $1 - P$ be the subjective probability of no heavy rain tomorrow. Then the expected money payoff from decision A is $40,000, and the expected money payoff from decision B is

$$\$22,500\ P + \$45,000\ (1 - P).$$

Suppose the farmer is risk neutral; he looks only at the expected money payoff. Then A and B are indifferent at that value of P for which

$$\$22,500\ P + \$45,000\ (1 - P) = \$40,000,$$

that is, for $P = 5/22.5$. For $P > 5/22.5$, A is

TABLE 16-4   *Payoff Matrix—Harvesting Decision*

Nature Decisions	Heavy Rain Tomorrow	No Heavy Rain Tomorrow
A Harvest all today	$40,000	$40,000
B Harvest over two days	$22,500	$45,000

preferred; while for $P < 5/22.5$, B is preferred. A risk averse farmer would require an even lower value of P before he would be willing to stretch harvesting over two days.

Now assume that it is possible, at some cost, to forecast with certainty whether or not there will be a heavy rain tomorrow. The question is: How much would the farmer be willing to pay for such information? We already begin to see the paradoxical character of information as a commodity. If you know what the information is, you certainly are not willing to pay for it; if you do not know what the information is, how do you decide whether it is worth buying? Our approach is the following. We interpret the subjective probability P as the probability that the information you will receive is that there will be a heavy rain tomorrow with certainty, and $1 - P$ is the probability that the information will inform you with certainty that there will not be a heavy rain. Because P is a subjective probability, P can differ among different farmers, of course.

The expected money payoff from information as to whether or not it will rain is derived as follows. With probability P, the information will be that it is going to rain. With that information, the decision is to harvest in one day with a payoff of $40,000. With probability $1 - P$, the information is that there will be no rain; hence B is chosen with a payoff of $45,000.

Thus the expected money payoff with information is

$$\$40,000\ P + \$45,000\ (1 - P)$$
$$= \$45,000 - \$5,000\ P$$

Let x be the maximum amount that the risk neutral farmer would pay for information. x is equal to the difference between the expected payoff with information and the expected payoff without information. For a farmer with $P \geq 5/22.5$, the expected payoff without information is \$40,000; hence

$$x = (\$45,000 - \$5,000\ P) - \$40,000$$

thus $x = \$5,000\ (1 - P)$ for $P \geq \dfrac{5}{22.5}$.

Similarly, if $P \leq 5/22.5$, the farmer would choose B in the absence of information, with expected money payoff without information of

$$\$22,500\ P + \$45,000\ (1 - P).$$

Thus x can be solved for from

$$x = (\$45,000 - \$5,000\ P)$$
$$- [\$22,500\ P + \$45,000\ (1 - P)].$$

Thus $x = \$17,500\ P$ $(P \leq 5/22.5)$

We find the value of information varies with P, as in figure 16-8. The maximum value of information occurs at P^*, where $P^* = 5/22.5$, where the value of information $x = \$3,888$. This makes intuitive sense. In the absence of information, the farmer is indifferent between options A and B at P^*, and it is in just such a situation that information is most helpful in arriving at a decision. In contrast, the value of information is zero both at $P = 0$ and $P = 1$; at either extreme, the farmer is already certain in his own mind as to whether or not it is going to rain, and information is superfluous (even if the farmer's beliefs turn out to be wrong!). Between the two extremes, the

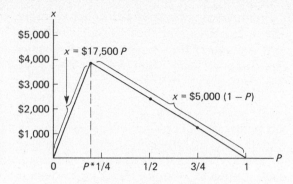

FIG. 16-8   *Value of information*

value of information rises as the subjective probability of the farmer gets closer to the crucial value P^*.

The example we have chosen is of course oversimplified; most often information is not available to convert uncertainty into perfect certainty, at any price. But even when information permits only a correction of probabilities, the same general principles apply as in the example. Information is most valuable when the decision maker is indifferent as among his alternatives, and is least valuable when subjective beliefs are at the extremes of $P = 0$ and $P = 1$. Furthermore, our example deals only with the case of a risk neutral decision maker. Needless to say, information is generally more valuable (given the same subjective probabilities) if the decision maker is risk averse than if he is risk neutral; and it is more valuable the larger are the costs of making the wrong decision.

The Market for Information as a Commodity

We have seen how one can calculate the maximum amount of money that a decision maker would be willing to pay for information. This method gives us a start at analyzing the demand side of the market for information. Turning to the supply side, the production of information generally involves the use of various resources, and hence there is a cost that can be assigned to that production.

Take the simple case of a one-supplier, one-demander market, where information as to whether it is going to rain costs, say, $2,000 to produce. We can argue that the information will be produced so long as P is between $2/17.5$ and $3/5$ (using fig. 16-8), since between these values of P the farmer would be willing to pay $2,000 or more for the information. Precisely what price would emerge depends on the relative bargaining strengths of the farmer and the forecaster in this bilateral monopoly situation.

So far so good. But now assume that we expand our example to the case of several farmers, each faced with the same decision problem as the farmer in our example. With the same payoff matrices, each of these farmers is willing to pay as much as $2,000 or more for weather information if their subjective values of P are within the range of $2/17.5$ and $3/5$. It begins to look as though our weather expert can really clean up. Furthermore, the social value of the information is accurately reflected in the prices farmers are willing to pay.

In principle, the monopolistic forecaster can go to each farmer and negotiate a price (say $2,000 each) for his information. But in fact, he runs into a difficulty. Any given farmer may well say to himself, "If he's selling it to someone else, why can't I just get in touch with that person after he's gotten the information, and get it myself for free or in any case for a good deal less than $2,000?" Since every farmer can argue the same way, the forecaster may find it difficult to sell his information for *any* positive price, even though it is worth over $2,000 to each farmer. We have come to the nub of

the problem with respect to information: *appropriability*, that is, establishing enforceable property rights.

The difficulty with information as a commodity is that while it is costly to produce, it is often essentially costless to transmit, and as a consequence its value is extremely difficult to appropriate. Once the information has been made available to even one customer, that customer becomes a potential competitor in the marketing of the information. Certain items of information, of course, may be so specialized that they are of value to only one individual or one firm, and the argument does not apply to such information. But where information is valuable to a group of individuals or firms, the "free rider" problem arises; that is, every potential buyer wants to pay no more than the cost of transmitting information, which approaches zero.

Problems with appropriability of information have led to the development of legal institutions to protect property rights to information in order to preserve incentives for the production of it. Since information has social value, preserving such incentives tends to move us toward Pareto optimality. Among the best known of the legal institutions are patents and copyrights.

But now we run into another problem. To the extent that the patent and copyright systems work, the producer of information acquires monopoly rights to the information. Like all monopolists, the information monopolist tends to restrict access to information in a manner so as to maximize profits, taking into account the effects of his actions on the price that can be charged.

Thus we find that in the absence of legal protection, not enough information is *produced*; when legal protection for information is provided, not enough is *used* due to monopoly pricing. Hence it appears that with or without legal rules to ensure appropriability, the market for information introduces welfare losses into the society.

Hirschleifer on Information

It has been pointed out by Hirschleifer that the inappropriability of information might not be so great a problem as we have indicated, and that, in fact, maybe *too much* of certain kinds of information is being produced.†

Let us return to the weather forecasting example where the free rider problem caused difficulties with the production of socially valuable information. Suppose the forecaster discovers that, for the reasons discussed earlier, no one is willing to pay a positive price for his weather information. Nonetheless, it might still pay him to invest resources to produce the information. The forecaster always has the option of going into the market and buying or selling futures contracts in wheat (assuming his forecast applies to the wheat crop), or buying or short selling factors specialized to the wheat industry, on the basis of his information. If he knows for a fact that there is going to be a heavy rain, for example, his optimum strategy is to suppress this information, and buy wheat futures, capitalizing on the increased price of wheat when rain occurs. If he knows there is not going to be rain, then the wheat crop will in fact be higher than expected (on the basis of the subjective probabilities P), and he can make money by first selling wheat futures short and then announcing his forecast. (This as-

sumes that his forecast will be believed, of course.) Alternatively, if he knows it is not going to rain, he can lease the available harvesting equipment and cash in on the demand for such equipment to bring in the unexpectedly large harvest. In other words, the value of information can be appropriated by speculative operations in markets for which the information is relevant. Information need not be salable in order to appropriate its value.

Of course this strategy applies to any weather forecaster. We might well find that there are a number of individuals engaged in producing the same information, for their private use in speculating in the grain market. We have thus identified a case in which the inappropriability of information might lead to an excess production of it, because the private gains from the information exceed the social gains. (After all, we need only one correct weather forecast, not many such forecasts.) An even more striking case, according to Hirschleifer, is horse racing; the social gains from the race are the identification of horses that are fast, for whatever that information is worth to society. The private gains from knowing beforehand which horse is fastest are far in excess of any possible social gains, and hence there is an excessive investment in acquiring information on the speediness of horses.

We are left in an ambiguous position so far as welfare losses are concerned. Too little information may be produced or too much, depending on both the extent to which speculative activities are feasible and the legal status of information so far as appropriability is concerned. There is no simple answer to this problem in general; the institutional structures of the markets for various kinds of information are crucial in arriving at welfare judgments.

---

†J. Hirschleifer, "The Private and Social Value of Information and the Reward to Innovative Activity," *American Economic Review* 61 (1971).

Default Risk and the Capital Markets

In our discussion of asset holdings, it was assumed that lending markets are perfect in the sense that each individual can borrow or lend as much as he wants at the going market rate of interest. We know that this is unrealistic, and that in fact there is a wide difference between lending and borrowing rates for a given individual, and a difference in borrowing rates among individuals and among firms. In order to see how these imperfections arise out of uncertainty, suppose we look at the problem of borrowing from the point of view of a firm whose rate of return is subject to uncertainty.

We assume that the firm has an equity (ownership interest) of m dollars. In addition, at the beginning of the year the firm issues x $1 notes payable one year later at face value ($1). Let p denote the price at which the notes are sold, so that $0 < p < $1. Then the interest rate charged the firm is given by $(1 - p)/p$, since the firm receives p dollars at the beginning of the year and must pay $1 back at the end of the year. Let A denote the value of assets of the firm at the beginning of the year:

$$A = m + px.$$

Let r denote the rate of return per dollar of assets earned by the firm, and let B denote the value of assets held by the firm at the end of the year. Then,

$$r = \frac{B - A}{A}, \text{ so that } B = A(1 + r).$$

We assume that the rate of return earned by the firm is subject to uncertainty, which can lead to difficulties for the holders of notes issued by the firm. So long as $B \geq x$, the firm

pays off its notes at face value at the end of the year. However, if $B < x$ (year-end asset value less than the face value of the notes outstanding), then each $1 note gets paid off only B/x dollars. (We are considering the case of a corporate firm, where creditors can collect only from the assets of the corporation and not from the personal assets of the owners of the corporation.) When $B < x$, we say that *default* has occurred. Let $\bar{r}$ denote the default rate of return; that is, $\bar{r}$ is such that $B = A(1 + \bar{r}) = x$. If $r < \bar{r}$, the firm defaults; that is $B < x$. Thus,

$$\bar{r} = \frac{x - A}{A} = \frac{x}{A} - 1.$$

Since $A = m + px$, $\bar{r}$ can also be written as

$$\bar{r} = \frac{x}{m + px} - 1.$$

Note that because $0 < p < 1$, every increase in the number of notes issued (assuming p is fixed), *increases* the default rate of return, assuming that the firm has a positive equity, m. As x gets large relative to the equity m, the default rate of return goes to

$$\frac{1}{p} - 1 = \frac{1 - p}{p},$$

the interest rate charged to the firm. This result agrees with our intuition; if the firm is financed almost entirely with borrowed money, then it will default if it does not earn at a rate at least as high as the interest rate it must pay for its borrowings. Equity capital m acts as a cushion for lenders, allowing the firm to pay off its debts even if it does not earn enough to meet its interest payments.

Suppose that the firm operates under *stochastic constant returns*, interpreted as a case in which the probability distribution over the

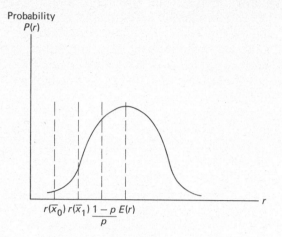

Probability
$P(r)$

$r(\bar{x}_0)\ r(\bar{x}_1)\ \dfrac{1-p}{p}\ E(r)$

FIG. 16-9   *Probability distribution
of rate of return*

rate of return is the same, whatever the value of the firm's assets is. Then the probability distribution over rate of return might appear as in figure 16-9. $\bar{r}(x_0)$ and $\bar{r}(x_1)$ denote the default rates of return associated with x_0 and x_1 \$1 notes issued, where $x_1 > x_0$. As x gets large, $\bar{r}(x)$ approaches $(1 - p)/p$. $E(r)$ is the expected rate of return.

Now suppose we look at things from a lender's point of view, that is, from the point of view of someone who owns a note issued by the firm. Let y denote the amount that will be paid at the end of the year to the holder of a \$1 note. Then

$$y = \begin{cases} \$1 & \text{if } r \geq \bar{r} \\[2mm] \dfrac{B}{x} = \dfrac{A(1+r)}{x} & \text{if } r \leq \bar{r}. \end{cases}$$

To keep things simple, suppose that there is only one lender to the firm, say a bank. Then the bank holds all the notes issued by the firm, x. Can we say anything about the number of notes that the bank will buy at the price p?

First, suppose that

$$P(r) = 0 \text{ for } r < \frac{1-p}{p};$$

that is, the firm never earns less than the rate of interest charged to the firm. Then the bank is guaranteed payment on the notes issued by the firm, and would be willing to buy an unlimited amount at the going interest rate $(1 - p)/p$. This results in a perfect lending market, which again agrees with intuition; if there is no default risk, lenders are operating in a world of certainty in terms of repayment of loans.

Second, suppose that there is some positive probability that the firm will earn at a rate less than $(1 - p)/p$ (as in figure 16-9). Then as the bank increases its purchases of notes (x increases), the probability of default increases. The probability of default is the area to the left of $\bar{r}$; as x increases, $\bar{r}$ moves to the right, and so the probability that r will be less than $\bar{r}$ increases.

However, the expected repayment to the lender per \$1 note decreases as x increases. Hence even if the banker were risk neutral, he would still tend to limit the number of notes he would buy from the firm at any fixed interest rate $(1 - p)/p$. He would limit his purchases even more severely if he were a risk averter.

What we have seen here is that uncertainty and the presence of default risk interferes with the operation of a perfect lending market. When default risk is present, there is an externality created between borrower and lender, since the debt-equity position of the firm is an element determining the payoffs from notes purchased by the lender. Further, under default risk, we no longer have anonymity of firms. Instead, notes issued by different firms are no longer perfect substitutes for one another; the name of the firm issuing the note is a crucial piece of information in assessing the value of the note.

Finally, we might mention one further externality that arises in borrowing and lending operations. When a lender buys notes issued by a firm, he is not indifferent as to the number of notes the firm issues to other lenders, since the default rate of return increases whenever the total number of notes outstanding is increased. Thus we have the development of special contractual agreements between borrowers and lenders in which the borrower agrees to limit his issuance of notes to other lenders or guarantees first priority to his assets in the case of default, as a condition for the loan. These arrangements have evolved into the complex structure of modern corporate finance, a far cry from the simplicity of the perfect capital markets we have examined in the first part of this book.

Summary

Uncertainty arises in economic decision making when information is not available to allow the decision maker to determine with certainty the outcomes associated with decisions. Under the proper conditions, uncertainty can be described in terms of the subjective probabilities that decision makers associate with events and hence with outcomes of decisions. When he makes choices under uncertainty, two aspects of the decision maker's preferences are relevant: first, his preferences with respect to payoffs, assuming they are to be received with certainty; and second, his preferences with respect to risk. Both aspects of the decision maker's preferences are reflected in the measurable utility numbers associated with payoffs. By assigning such utility numbers, the decision maker whose choices are consistent with his preferences will act to maximize his expected utility; that is, he will choose the probability distribution over payoffs that has the highest value of expected utility from payoffs.

If the decision maker would prefer the expected value of a gamble with certainty to the gamble itself, he is a risk averter; if he is indifferent between the two, he is risk neutral; and if he prefers the gamble, he is a risk lover. The risk averter's measurable utility function over money is concave; the risk neutral individual's is linear; and the risk lover has a convex measurable utility function.

Insurance arises because, on the demand side, risk averters are willing to pay a premium to avoid risks, while on the supply side the law of large numbers allows the insurance company to convert uncertainty for the individual into virtual certainty for a group of similar individuals. If all uncertain events could be insured against in competitive markets, uncertainty would not be a source of welfare losses. However, moral hazard, lack of independence among risks, economies of scale, and problems associated with default risk of insurance companies act as barriers to the attainment of Pareto optimality through insurance alone.

The futures markets permit risk averse individuals to shift risks to risk neutral or risk-loving individuals. They also perform an insurance function through facilitating hedging operations. Beyond this, futures markets facilitate speculation among individuals with different probability beliefs concerning future prices of commodities.

Information has value to all classes of individuals—risk averse, risk neutral or risk loving. The value of an item of information is a function of the difference between the expected utility of payoffs with information and expected utility without information. Information is most valuable when the decision maker is indifferent among alternatives in the absence of information; and information is least valuable when the decision maker is certain in his own mind as to the occurrence of events.

While information is costly to produce, it is often virtually costless to transmit. This difficulty with the market for information leads to problems of appropriating the value that attaches to information. Hirschleifer points out, however, that speculative operations by the producer of information can bypass the appropriability problem.

The notion of a perfect lending market makes sense in a world in which default risk is absent. When default risk is present, the market for loans loses its competitive characteristics; in particular, notes issued by different borrowers are not perfect substitutes for one another.

Problems

1. Confronted with choices among gambles, a decision maker responds as follows.

   $10 with probability 1/2, $100 with probability 1/2, is indifferent to $50 with certainty

   $10 with probability 1/3, $100 with probability 2/3, is indifferent to $60 with certainty

   What choices does the decision maker make in the following?

   a. $50 with probability 1/4, $100 with probability 3/4 versus $60 with probability 1/2, $100 with probability 1/2.

   b. $10 with probability 1/5, $60 with probability 4/5 versus $50 with certainty.

   c. $50 with probability 1/2, $100 with probability 1/2 versus $60 with certainty.

2. An individual has a measurable utility function over money payoffs of the form $U = \sqrt{M}$. He is faced with a situation in which he receives $0 with probability 1/2, $98 with probability 1/2. How much would he be willing to pay to replace this gamble with its expected value?

3. The September futures price for wheat is $4 per bushel on May 1, while the cash price is $4.15 per bushel. Assuming that a miller has to buy wheat in May to produce flour in September, with the price of flour in September dependent on the cash price of wheat in September, determine the profit or loss to the miller on a hedging operation involving 1000 bushels of wheat.

   Suppose the cash price on May 1 is $4 per bushel while the futures price is $4.15 per bushel. How does your conclusion change?

4. An automobile firm is thinking of retooling to produce a compact car for next year's market. The payoffs from this decision depend crucially on whether or not a gasoline tax of 40¢ per gallon is to be passed by Congress. Calculate the value of this information to the firm, given the following information:

   If the tax passes and if the firm retools, it will make $50 million; if the tax passes and the firm has not retooled, it loses $50 million.

   If the tax does not pass and the firm retools, it loses $100 million; if the tax does not pass and the firm does not retool, there is zero change in profits.

   What is the critical value of P (the firm's probability that the tax will pass) such that information is most valuable?

5. Explain why insurance is not available for each of the following risky situations.

   a. A firm is engaged in R & D to develop a smog-free car that gets 50 miles to the gallon and sells for $2,000. The firm would like to ensure against the possibility that it will not be able to build such a car.

   b. A student would like insurance to cover the loss in lifetime earnings if he fails to earn a college degree.

   c. The State of California wants insurance against losses to its residents if there is a major earthquake on the San Andreas.

   d. A confirmed gambler wants insurance against the possibility that the sure thing he is backing in the fourth race at Santa Anita will not win.

17
Externalities and Public Goods

There is an oil spill from the wells in the Santa Barbara channel and it takes weeks before the ocean and the beaches are cleaned up. Motel owners lose tourist business and the citizens of Santa Barbara can neither swim nor enjoy the ocean view.

A new neighbor moves in next door, and he likes to keep his lawn manicured. Your lawn, which gets mowed twice a month, takes on the look of the forest primeval. You move up your mowing schedule to once a week.

You buy a new home in a quiet residential neighborhood, blocks from the bustle of traffic. The city decides to build its new hospital right across the street from you. Weekend nights you can set your watch by the arrival of ambulances and police cars, which always announce their coming with lights flashing and sirens going full blast.

These are examples of *externalities*, a concept that has become of considerable public interest especially since the emergence of the ecology movement in the 1960s. As the term implies, an externality occurs when some activity external to a given decision maker enters into his decision-making process; that is, *an externality occurs when an activity carried on by one decision maker affects the decisions taken by another decision maker.*†

Externalities can involve either benefits or costs, carrying with them *external economies* or *external diseconomies*. If you own an apple orchard and a beekeeper sets up business next door, the beekeeper provides external economies for you by producing gratis the crossfertilization needed to maintain your orchard. If the next door firm happens to be a steel mill, then again you are provided with certain free services in the form of all the smoke and fumes you could possibly wish for, an external diseconomy that might well lead to your going out of business.

In an ultimate sense, externalities arise because we are living in a world with limited natural resources, including land and breathable air. Our activities tend to "crowd in" on the range of activities available to other people, whether we intend this or not. If it were possible to screen out the rest of the world completely from each person's sphere of activities, then externalities would vanish. But because of the growth of world population and its concentration in a relatively few urban centers, external effects have mushroomed, and there is certainly no indication that this trend will abate in the near future.

---

†Strictly speaking, we will exclude activities by other decision makers that affect a given decision maker only through their effects on market prices. For example, in a competitive environment, the choices of all other consumers and firms determine the prices a given consumer faces; this will not be considered an externality. Only activities of other decision makers that directly affect preference or production maps will be treated as externalities.

Externalities and Pareto Optimality

The problem with externalities is that while the consumer or firm producing the externality controls the rate at which his activity takes place, that rate of activity in turn produces costs or benefits for other firms or consumers in the society. Therefore, the other firms or consumers have an interest in controlling the rate at which an externality-producing activity is operated. Unless some method is devised for bringing the other consumers and firms into the decision process for operating the externality-producing activity, welfare losses result.

We have already seen that under profit maximization by firms and utility maximization by consumers, a competitive economic system generates equilibrium positions that are Pareto optimal, *assuming externalities are absent*. The qualification is important.

To illustrate, consider a world in which there is one consumer and two goods, X and Y, both produced under competitive conditions. Suppose that there is a fixed amount of labor L available to the economy, and that both industries use only labor to produce their outputs. Assume that production externalities are present in that increases in the output of Y reduce the amount of X that can be produced from any given amount of labor. (For example, the production of Y creates pollutants that reduce the productivity of labor in industry X.) To keep things simple, we assume that the output of Y is unaffected by the production of X.

The production possibility curve for the society is derived as in figure 17-1. L_x and L_y refer to labor used in the production of X and in the production of Y, respectively. The lower left-hand quadrant (quadrant III) displays the labor constraint for the economy; labor allocated to X plus labor allocated to Y equals total

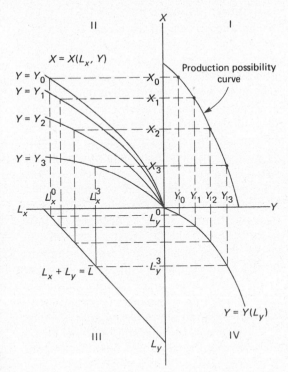

FIG. 17-1 *Derivation of the production possibility curve—externality*

labor available to the economy. In quadrant IV the $Y = Y(L_y)$ curve expresses output of Y as a function of labor used in its production and exhibits diminishing returns. Quadrant II displays the output of X as a function of labor employed in producing X, and as a function of the output of Y. There is an external diseconomy present, so that higher values for Y reduce the output of X, for any amount of labor used in producing X. Thus output of X is larger for any value of L_x when $Y = Y_0$ than when $Y = Y_1$, and so on.

With L_y^0 units of labor allocated to the production of Y, Y_0 units of Y are produced as indicated in quadrant IV. This leaves $L_x^0 (= \bar{L} - L_y^0)$ units to be allocated to X. We read off the $Y = Y_0$ curve the output X_0 associated with L_x^0. Thus the combination (Y_0, X_0) lies on the production possibility curve for the economy. With Y_3 units of output, L_y^3 units of labor are employed, leaving L_x^3 units of labor to produce X. Reading off the $Y = Y_3$ curve in quadrant II, output of X is X_3. The point (Y_3, X_3) is also on the production possibility curve, and similarly for the intermediate points.

Consider the slope of the production possibility curve (fig. 17-2), that is, $\Delta X/\Delta Y$. As Y increases from Y_0 to Y_1, X decreases from X_0 to X_1. A part of the fall in X is accounted for by the transfer of labor away from the production of X into the production of Y. But a part of the fall in X is due to the fact that an increase in the output of Y decreases the productivity of labor employed in producing X, as indicated in the four-quadrant diagram. The real cost to the economy, in terms of units of X forgone, of an increase in the output of Y is the sum of these two effects.

The inefficiencies associated with externalities arise because the firm producing Y takes into account in its decision making only those effects of its decisions that are reflected in its own costs. Increasing the output of Y by one unit involves *private* costs (costs to firm Y) equal to the wage rate of labor times the number of units of labor required to increase output by one unit. The cost to the society, the *social* cost, of increasing the output of Y by one unit equals private costs to firm Y plus the price per unit of X times the loss in output of X due to the externalities produced by firm Y.

In a competitive economy, decisions by firms are made on the basis of private costs and revenues. The firm producing Y sets its output at that level such that the marginal private cost of increasing output one more unit equals the

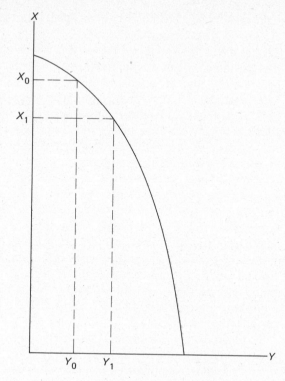

FIG. 17-2   *Production possibility set*

price per unit. Given the output of Y, the firm producing X maximizes profits in the same way. At a competitive equilibrium, the price ratio p_x/p_y equals the ratio of the marginal private costs of production of the two goods.

What this means can be seen from figure 17-3. The firm producing Y ignores the costs it imposes on the producer of X. Under profit maximization, in a competitive economy, $\bar{p}_y = MPC_y$ and $\bar{p}_x = MPC_x$, where MPC_y and MPC_x refer to the marginal *private* costs of producing Y and X. The slope of the GNP line is given by $-(\bar{p}_y/\bar{p}_x)$, which in turn equals $-(MPC_y/MPC_x)$. At a competitive equilibrium, markets are cleared under utility and profit maximization as at the point $A = (\bar{Y}, \bar{X})$ in

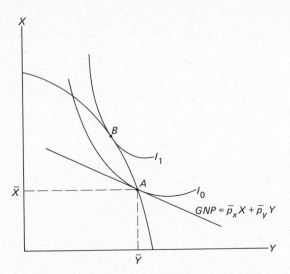

FIG. 17-3 *Competitive equilibrium—external diseconomies produced by Y*

to reduce their consumption of Y and increase their consumption of X, the price of Y to consumers must rise relative to the price of X, as indicated by the steeper GNP line through B than through A. p_x^*, p_y^* denote the prices of X and Y at the Pareto-optimal state B:

$$\frac{p_y^*}{p_x^*} > \frac{\bar{p}_y}{\bar{p}_x}$$

On the other hand, to induce the producer of Y to reduce his output from $\bar{Y}$ to Y^*, the price per unit of Y *to the producer* must fall (or his marginal private cost must rise). This paradox must be solved if the economy is to attain a Pareto optimum in the presence of externalities—the price of Y to consumers must rise and the price to producers must fall, relative to the price of X.

This paradox is resolved by *internalizing* the externality. An externality is said to be internalized when the producer of the externality treats as private costs and benefits all of the social costs and benefits that result from the

the diagram. The slope of the GNP line is flatter than the slope of the production possibility curve, $\Delta X/\Delta Y$, because

$$\frac{\Delta X}{\Delta Y} = -\frac{MSC_y}{MSC_x}$$

where MSC_x, MSC_y are the marginal *social* costs of producing X and Y. $MSC_x = MPC_x$ (X produces no externalities), but $MSC_y > MPC_y$ as noted earlier.

Clearly, A is inefficient since at B on the production possibility curve, the consumer is on a higher indifference curve than at A. B is a Pareto optimum that is Pareto superior to A.

Internalizing Externalities

The Pareto-optimal point B involves a decrease in the output of Y and an increase in the output of X, compared with the point A, as indicated in figure 17-4. In order to induce consumers

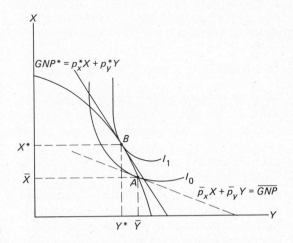

FIG. 17-4 *Internalizing externalities— competitive equilibrium at B*

externality. Once an externality has been internalized, profit-maximizing behavior by firms and utility-maximizing behavior by consumers in a competitive environment guarantees that the economy will attain an equilibrium at a Pareto-optimal state such as B.

To illustrate, a method for internalizing the externality involved in our example is to impose a per unit tax on Y equal to the costs imposed on the producer of X by the externalities created by the producer of Y. The price per unit of Y is reduced to the producer of Y, creating incentives for a decrease in its production. Since a part of the tax is shifted to consumers of Y, the price per unit of Y is increased to the consumers of Y. Assume that the price per unit of X is fixed. Then the appropriate tax is one that raises the price of Y to consumers from $\bar{p}_y$ to p_y^*. Thus the economy is moved away from the state A to the Pareto-optimal state B. The proceeds of the tax are returned to consumers in the form of lump-sum grants. Because we move to a Pareto-superior state, there is enough in the way of tax receipts to guarantee that each consumer can be made better off (including the consumers who own the firm producing Y), than when the externality is not internalized, by an appropriate distribution of the tax receipts.

Policies for Internalizing Externalities   In order for an efficient allocation of resources to be achieved, it is essential that externalities be internalized. Imposing a per unit tax on a firm producing an externality is only one of several devices that can be employed to accomplish internalization. Other devices currently employed include the absolute prohibition of activities that generate certain kinds of external effects, fines for exceeding specified levels of damage, and subsidies to producers based on their success in eliminating external effects. Thus for example, the use of high sulphur oil is prohibited in the Los Angeles basin and in certain other metropolitan areas in the country; newly produced automobiles must pass EPA (Environmental Protection Agency) tests as to emission levels before being sold in the United States; federal subsidies are paid to cities to improve sewage treatment and water purification facilities; DDT is banned for use as a pesticide; and certain cities base their industrial sewage charges on the level and composition of the wastes that individual firms discharge into the sewage system.

We have already seen that the appropriate per unit tax on Y can move the economy to the Pareto-optimal state B in figure 17-4. Establishing standards that limit the output of Y to Y^* can accomplish the same result. Given the desired output Y^*, the government agency issues licenses to produce Y (together with the right to produce the pollutants that accompany such production), the total of such licenses adding to an output of Y^*. Licenses would be auctioned off to the highest bidders. Given a competitive auction market, the marginal cost of production of Y (including the license fee) rises to p_y^*, and this cost is passed on to consumers in the form of a price of p_y^* per unit of Y. The economy moves to the Pareto optimum B, where the proceeds of the auction are distributed among consumers in such a way that each consumer is better off than at A.

There is one obvious difficulty with policies such as the per unit tax on Y and the licensing scheme: to determine what output mix and what distribution of income represents a Pareto optimum that is Pareto superior to the initial situation. Because we are dealing with nonobservables (what we actually observe is the market situation with noninternalized externalities), information is required as to both the preference maps of consumers and the technological possibilities facing firms, if a satisfactory policy is to be established. In the absence of such information, government actions can exacerbate the inefficiencies of externalities rather than correct them.

Things would be simple if any policy that resulted in reducing pollution or other such externalities were always desirable. Unfortunately, pollution typically is generated through activities that in part produce desirable consequences. Decreasing pollution involves decreasing these desirable consequences as well. In the trade-offs between pollution reduction and increasing the costs of the goods and services whose production generates pollution, problems arise for public policy. We want externalities internalized so that the marginal social cost of producing a unit of each good is equal to its marginal social benefit, not so that all activities that generate externalities are shut down. To accomplish this through standard setting, taxing, licensing, or subsidies generally requires more information than any governmental agency can acquire.

Negotiations and the Internalization of Externalities The fact that there are difficult informational problems for government agencies in implementing policies to internalize externalities does not mean that other approaches might not work. One alternative is direct negotiation between the firms or consumers affected by externalities and the producers of them. We can think of things this way. The firm producing Y in our example is really producing a joint product: output of Y, which is a consumer good, and output of a pollutant, which turns out to be an (undesirable) intermediate product in the production of X. We already know that in the absence of externalities, the system of competitive markets attains an equilibrium at a Pareto optimum. What causes the economy

to deviate from a Pareto optimum when externalities exist?

Clearly, if pollution were a product that was bought and sold in competitive markets just like other products, then again a Pareto optimum would be achieved—we would have added one more product to our list of goods and services, but nothing essential would have changed. Viewed in this way, the problem with pollution as with other non-internalized externalities is that there is "market failure"; that is, there is no competitive market where pollution is bought and sold.

Suppose there were such a market. In particular, suppose the firm producing Y sold tickets, each of which gave the holder the legal right to require the producer of Y to restrict his output by one unit, and thus to reduce his pollutants by a comparable amount. What would the demand and supply schedules for such tickets look like?

Consider first the demand for such tickets by the X firm. Let T denote the number of tickets and q the price per ticket. The profits of the X firm, π_x, are given by

$$\pi_x = p_x X - wL_x - qT$$

where $X = f(L_x, Y)$ is the production function of the X firm, with

$$MP_{L_x} > 0, \ MP_y^x < 0.$$

(MP_y^x is the decrease in output of X because of pollution when the output of Y is increased by one unit.) Given a competitive market in tickets, the X firm buys that amount of tickets such that the marginal revenue product of a ticket equals its cost; that is,

$$-p_x MP_y^x = q.$$

(Note that buying one more ticket *reduces* Y by one unit, hence the marginal revenue product of tickets is $-p_x MP_y^x$). $(-)p_x MP_y^x$ can be interpreted as the increase in cost to the X firm of an additional unit of output of Y, since MP_y^x gives the decrease in X output due to an added unit of Y, and p_x is the price per unit of X.

On the supply side, the firm producing Y finds that its profits π_y are now given by

$$\pi_y = p_y Y + qT - C(Y),$$

where $C(Y)$ is the cost of the Y firm ($C(Y) = wL_y$).

Let $\overline{Y}$ denote the profit-maximizing output of the Y firm when $q = 0$. $\overline{Y}$ can be interpreted as the Y output when there is no internalization of externalities. Then $T = (\overline{Y} - Y)$; that is, the number of tickets sold is simply the reduction in output of the Y firm from the level achieved in the absence of internalization of the externality. We can rewrite the expression for π_y as

$$\pi_y = q\overline{Y} + (p_y - q)Y - C(Y).$$

Maximizing profits, the Y firm sets marginal revenue equal to marginal (private) cost:

$$(p_y - q) = MC_y.$$

When the market for tickets is cleared, then the price per ticket q not only satisfies this condition; it also satisfies $q = -p_x MP_y^x$ from profit maximization by the X firm.

Substituting for q from the profit-maximizing conditions for the X firm we have

$$(p_y + p_x MP_y^x) = MC_y$$

or $\quad p_y = MC_y - p_x MP_y^x \ (\equiv MSC_y).$

The right-hand side of this last equation is equal to marginal private cost for the Y firm plus the increase in cost to the X firm caused by an additional unit of output of Y. Thus the right-hand side is the marginal social cost of an additional unit of output of Y.

Because $p_y = MSC_y$, the establishment of a market in tickets to restrict the output of

Y has led to a Pareto optimum. ($p_x = MSC_x$ whether the output of Y is internalized or not.)

The interesting thing about this result is that neither the X firm nor the Y firm requires information about anything other than its *own* technology and costs in order for a Pareto optimum to be established. This is a major virtue of a competitive market of course. Establishing a competitive market in pollution tickets enables the economy to attain a Pareto optimum through decentralized decision making, which is informationally more efficient than centralized direction.

The Coase Theorem In a world with zero transactions costs, all externalities will be internalized through direct negotiations between the consumers or firms producing externalities and the consumers or firms whose decisions are affected by them. In our example, the polluting firm producing Y sells pollution tickets to the firm producing X. In effect the X firm bribes the Y firm to lower its level of pollution. This example is one in which property rights to pollution are in the hands of the Y firm.

But we can conceive of other possibilities. For example, assume that the X firm has a legally enforceable right to pure water, and the activities of the Y firm result in lowering the quality of water available to the X firm. The X firm might be located downstream from the Y firm, for instance. Now it is the X firm that must be "bribed" by the Y firm if any output of Y is to result. We can think of the X firm selling tickets to the Y firm, each ticket permitting the Y firm to produce one unit of output (and the pollutants that accompany such output). What differences in outputs of X and Y occur under this set of property rights as compared to our original example?

With the X firm selling tickets, each ticket permitting the Y firm to increase output by one unit, profits for the X firm become

$$\pi_x = p_x X + qT - wL_x$$

while profits for Y firm are

$$\pi_y = p_y Y - qT - C(Y) \equiv (p_y - q)Y - C(Y).\dagger$$

The X firm sells that number of tickets such that marginal revenue equals marginal cost, with each ticket sold increasing the output of Y by one unit and hence reducing the output of X due to pollution, leading to the condition

$$p_x MP_y^x + q = 0.$$

For the Y firm, profit maximization implies

$$(p_y - q) = MC_y.$$

In equilibrium, we thus have

$$p_y = MC_y - p_x MP_y^x \equiv MSC_y.$$

Hence we arrive at the Pareto-optimal conditions that held for the case where the property rights were vested in the Y firm. In a one-consumer economy of the type pictured in figure 17-3, the Pareto optimum is unique. Thus the same output mix is achieved for the economy regardless of whether the X firm or the Y firm possesses property rights to pollution.

This result is a special case of what is known as the Coase theorem.‡ The Coase theorem, due to Ronald Coase, a leading economist in the field of law and economics, asserts that *the output mix for the economy is identical, whatever is the assignment of property rights to the X and Y firms, so long as there are zero transactions costs.*

Strictly speaking, this result is not quite correct in the case of a many-consumer economy.

If property rights to pollution are vested in the X firm rather than the Y firm, then income received from sales of pollution tickets goes to the owners of the X firm, whose income elasticities of demand might be different from those of the owners of the Y industry. With different income elasticities, the price-output mix at a competitive equilibrium will differ, depending upon where property rights are vested. For a one-consumer economy, of course, this issue does not arise.

Hence a restatement of the Coase theorem is in order, namely:

Ignoring income effects, the output mix for the economy is identical, whatever is the assignment of property rights to the X and Y firms, so long as there are zero transactions costs.

What we can conclude from this exercise is that when transactions costs are zero and when there is no market power in the market for "pollution tickets," then externalities cease to pose a special problem for the economy.† Unfortunately, for many externalities neither of these conditions holds. To illustrate, consider the problem of pollution caused by automobile exhausts. In this case there are large numbers of pollutors and pollutees. If an attempt were made to establish a market in which pollutees reached private agreements with pollutors through purchases and sales of "pollution tickets," the costs of policing agreements arrived at would far outweigh any possible benefits to the pollutees. Because of such excessive transactions costs, markets for pollution tickets do not exist. And in the case of a single polluting

---

†Note that $T = Y$ since the Y firm requires one ticket to produce each unit of output.
‡R. Coase, "The Problem of Social Cost," *Journal of Law and Economics* (October 1960).

†Strictly speaking, this is true only from an efficiency point of view; equity considerations still arise since the beneficiaries of internalization will depend on the assignment of property rights.

source, say a coal-fired power plant, the problem arises of monopoly power in the market for tickets on the part of the power plant. The plant would take into account the effect on the demand for tickets of a reduction in its output, with the usual distortion of resource allocation as indicated in chapter 14.

This is not to say that private agreements between affected consumers or firms and the producers of externalities cannot play a role in the internalization of externalities, but rather that for many forms of externalities, some alternative to markets for pollution tickets is required. To the extent that these alternatives involve government coercion, we are again faced with the difficulty that information needed to establish Pareto-optimal policies is excessively expensive to collect.

Public Goods

A particularly interesting and important instance of an externality occurs in the case of so-called "public" goods. The term is used in various ways in the economic literature, but we will use *public good* only to refer to goods or services that possess one or more of the following attributes. First, everyone in the society "consumes" the same amount of the public good; second, the marginal cost of serving another consumer of the public good is zero; third, my consumption of the public good does not decrease the amount of the good available for you to consume. Commodities that satisfy all three of these attributes we will call "pure" public goods.

An example of a pure public good is a lighthouse. All of the ships in the vicinity of the lighthouse "consume" the same services from the lighthouse, namely the light beacon; there

is no "portioning out" of the light beam to different users. The costs of the lighthouse are independent of the number of ships taking advantage of the lighthouse's services, so that adding another ship does not increase costs—marginal costs per ship served are zero. And of course the fact that one ship is using the lighthouse services leaves the same amount of services available to any other ships.

National defense expenditures are another example that is often cited to illustrate the notion of a public good. Such expenditures and the services of protection and security provided by them are consumed "in common"; there is no way to isolate the special services provided to me from those received by you. And within a fixed population, the fact that one person receives the services of defense protection does not detract from the amount of such services received by any one else in the population. On the other hand, increasing the population through annexation of more territory might reduce the security provided to any one member of the community from a given amount of defense expenditures—the marginal cost of adding another customer is nonzero. Hence national defense is not a pure public good, but it does have certain features of a public good.

Another example is "pure" information, that is, information that is costless to transmit. The information that it is going to rain tomorrow can be made available to an unlimited number of people without reducing the services such information provides to any one individual. The marginal cost of adding another customer is zero. On the other hand, it might well be the case that only a certain segment of the population is aware of the information and in this sense, the "consumption" of information can be different for different individuals in the population. Again the standards for a pure public good are not quite met, but there are "public" aspects to pure information.

Public goods need not be produced or controlled by the government, although many public goods fall into this category. The term *public* is used instead to distinguish public goods from strictly private goods such as bread, beer, and housing. Individuals consume their own portions of these goods; what one individual consumes reduces the amount available to all other individuals, and marginal costs of supplying another person are nonzero.

A television signal has certain public good properties. Once the signal has been sent over the airwaves, any individual can turn on his television set and enjoy the services provided by the signal, without interfering with the ability of other individuals to enjoy them as well. But television is operated in the United States by private, profit-oriented corporations rather than being supplied by the government. (Practices differ around the world, with television being preempted by government in certain countries, and with both government and private stations in others.) Similarly, lighthouses could, in principle, be operated as money-making enterprises rather than being provided gratis by the government. The point is that the notion of a public good still applies to the services of the lighthouse or to television signals, independently of the institutional arrangement governing the supplying of such services.

Let us return to the case of a pure public good. Just because everyone consumes the same quantity of the public good does not necessarily imply that everyone values these services identically. You might be a hawk who feels that whatever the military is getting, it needs more; and I might be a dove opposed to any expenditures on defense. But in the case of national defense expenditures, like it or not, we all consume the same amount of such expenditures in the sense that the total amount enters into each person's preference ranking, rather than certain portions that we can identify as uniquely "belonging" to given individuals. The hawk places a high value on defense expenditures, while for the dove such expenditures have negative marginal utility, but they are both stuck with the same amount to consume.

The fact that some public goods are supplied by the private sector indicates that, in certain instances at least, public goods can be appropriated and the services of such goods marketed just like other commodities. It is partly a matter of technology and partly a matter of the structure of social institutions that determines which public goods will be supplied by private firms and how charges will be levied for such goods. For example, television signals can be scrambled and sold, as in pay-television, or they can be provided free to the audience with production costs covered by advertisers, as in the non-pay-television cases. Bridges and roads come close to being public goods (assuming that crowding is absent and that maintenance costs are unrelated to traffic), yet we have both freeways and tollways, free bridges and toll bridges. (Note however that if the marginal cost of serving another customer is zero, then access charges lead to inefficiencies; too little of the public good is consumed.)

Public goods, whether pure or not, pose problems for a market economy. Intuitively, we know that these problems occur because in a certain sense such goods must be consumed "in common," but the market is organized on the basis of individual decision making rather than "consensus" decision making. Another way of putting this is to say that public goods involve *indivisibilities*: problems arise in parceling out the services of such goods among consumers. We first look at the special problems that attach to pure public goods.

Pure Public Goods

For concreteness, take defense expenditures as a pure public good (for example, by assuming that in fact the marginal cost of adding another individual to the group benefiting from such expenditures is zero). By the nature of a pure public good, it is not technologically possible to exclude any individual in the society from "consuming" the full amount of the services of national defense expenditures. There is no access charge to the services of national defense; these services are a free good for every consumer in the society. This does not mean, of course, that consumers do not have to pay taxes to support the military. National defense is a free good because each consumer obtains the same amount of services, independent of what his tax payments are.

So far so good. Given a competitive environment, Pareto optimality requires that goods be priced on the basis of marginal costs of supplying them, and this condition is certainly satisfied in the case of a public good such as national defense. But another problem arises. In the case of private goods, prices perform two distinct functions: to ration the supplies of private goods among consumers on the basis of the offers made for such goods, and to indicate to suppliers where supplies should be increased or decreased. With public goods for which there are no access charges there are no price signals to indicate whether or not "enough" of the public goods are being supplied to the people.

Pareto Optimality and Pure Public Goods

How much in the way of public goods "should" be produced in the society? Consider a two-

good, two-consumer world, with commodities X and Y and consumers Mr. A and Mr. B. If both X and Y are private goods, then Pareto optimality requires that these goods be produced and distributed among consumers in quantities such that the marginal rate of transformation between X and Y for the society equals the marginal rate of substitution between X and Y, which is identical for each consumer. Under a competitive organization of the society, this condition is satisfied when all consumers face the same prices for X and Y, with producers facing the same prices as well. In contrast, consider the case where X is a pure public good and Y is a private good.

Let Y_A, Y_B denote the amounts consumed of the private good Y by Mr. A and Mr. B, and let X_A, X_B denote the amounts consumed of the public good. Because X is a pure public good, $X_A = X_B = X$, where X is the amount of the public good produced; each consumer consumes the same amount of the public good, equal to the total output of that good. $Y = Y_A + Y_B$ is the output of the private good.

We use Samuelson's graphical approach to find a Pareto optimum for the economy.† A Pareto optimum can be thought of as a state where the utility of Mr. B is as large as possible for any given level of Mr. A's utility, given that the economy is on its transformation curve.

Mr. A is assumed to have an indifference map of the usual type (fig. 17-5). Suppose that Mr. A is at the preference level indicated by the indifference curve I_0^A. A Pareto optimum occurs when Mr. B reaches the highest indifference curve possible, given that Mr. A remains on I_0^A and given that the output of X and Y is a point on the economy's transforma-

†P. Samuelson, "Diagrammatic Exposition of a Theory of Public Expenditure," *Review of Economics and Statistics* 37 (1955).

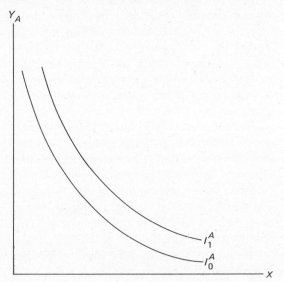

FIG. 17-5   *Mr. A's indifference map*

a)

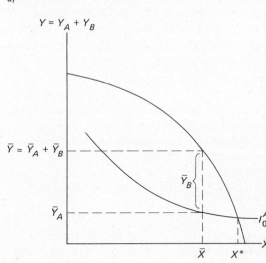

b)

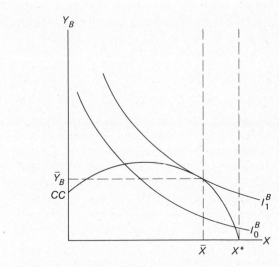

FIG. 17-6   *Deriving a Pareto optimum*
for the case of a pure public good

tion curve. A Pareto optimum is derived in figure 17-6. The indifference curve I_0^A has been plotted on the graph of the production possibility set for the economy (fig. 17-6a). For every value of X, the amount of Y available for Mr. B, given that Mr. A is on his indifference curve I_0^A, is the vertical distance between the production possibility curve and the I_0^A curve. For example, at X^*, there are 0 units of Y available for Mr. B, at $\bar{X}$ there are $\bar{Y}_B$ units available, and so on.

The curve CC in figure 17-6b plots the units of Y available for Mr. B for each value of X. At a Pareto optimum, Mr. B attains the highest indifference curve possible, given that his consumption (X, Y_B) lies on the curve CC. This occurs at $(\bar{X}, \bar{Y}_B)$, where the indifference curve I_0^B is tangent to CC. Both Mr. A and Mr. B consume $\bar{X}$ units of the public good, while Mr. A consumes $\bar{Y}_A$ units of Y and Mr. B consumes Y_B units of Y.

Note that at any value of X, the slope of the CC curve equals the slope of the production possibility curve minus the slope of I_0^A. At a

Pareto optimum, the slope of the CC curve equals the slope of I_1^B. Thus at a Pareto optimum we have the condition: slope of production possibility curve = slope of I_0^A + slope of I_0^B; or equivalently,

$$MRT = MRS_A + MRS_B$$

where MRT is the marginal rate of transformation between X and Y for the society and MRS_A, MRS_B are the marginal rates of substitution between X and Y for Mr. A and Mr. B.

If both X and Y are private goods, then the corresponding condition for Pareto optimality is

$$MRT = MRS_A = MRS_B;$$

that is, the absolute value of slope of the product possibility curve equals the absolute value of the slope of Mr. A's indifference curve, which in turn equals the absolute value of the slope of Mr. B's indifference curve.

Pricing and Public Goods

When goods are private, prices established in competitive markets perform the function of moving the economy to a Pareto optimum, subject to the usual qualifications concerning monopoly, externalities, and such. With a public good, if prices are used as a device for excluding consumers from consuming the good, then inefficiencies result. Nonetheless, in order to produce the "correct" amount of a public good, resources must be bid away from the production of private goods, and the required revenues to finance expenditures must be raised from consumers, generally through taxes or fees. The appropriate amounts to be collected from consumers, for any given distribution of wealth and income, is determined by the condition $MRT = MRS_A + MRS_B$. If we knew what consumer A was willing to give up in terms of the private good Y to obtain one more unit of the public good X (that is, if we knew MRS_A), then we could use this information to determine the tax to be assessed against A to finance the public good, and similarly for consumer B.

Unfortunately, MRS_A and MRS_B are not observed in the market when there are no access charges. We cannot, for example, charge U.S. citizens fees for the security services afforded by our missiles; everyone gets that "security" whether he wants it or not. Artificial devices to discover preferences, such as surveys and polls, suffer from the defect that so long as there is no monetary cost to the consumer because of expressing his preferences, there is an incentive to overstate the desirability of public goods. On the other hand, if the consumer is told that the tax he will bear depends on how many units of a public good he thinks desirable, there is an incentive to understate preferences.

There are difficult problems involved in devising a workable technique that provides the appropriate incentives for the discovery of the "true" preferences of consumers with respect to public goods. As a consequence, decisions made by legislative bodies as to the amounts of public goods produced are among the most controversial of political decisions.

Summary

An externality is present when the activity of one decision maker affects the choices of another decision maker. The externality is internalized when the first individual takes into account in his decision making all of the effects of his activities on the other individuals and firms in the economy. Generally speaking, externalities that are not internalized lead to welfare losses for the economy. The welfare losses can be due to inefficiency in exchange, production, or distribution.

Externalities can be internalized through taxes or subsidies, through direct regulation of output or consumption, or through setting up standards, fines, and the like. But all such governmental controls have the common flaw that information concerning individual preferences and the technologies facing firms is required to ensure that the policy measure attains a Pareto-superior state. Such information is rarely, if ever, available to the policymaker.

An alternative method of internalizing externalities is through direct negotiation between the externality-producing unit and affected decision makers. So long as transactions costs are zero and a competitive environment is maintained, such direct negotiations can solve the problem of internalizing externalities without the need for information as to preferences and technology. The Coase theorem indicates that, excluding income effects, the output mix obtained by the economy is independent of the property rights relative to externalities, if transactions costs are zero. However, transactions costs

are large for a wide range of external effects, and where they are small, market power problems can arise. Direct negotiations cannot be expected to solve all problems created by externalities.

Related to externalities are "public goods." Such goods possess one or more of the following attributes: (1) each person "consumes" the same amount of the public good; (2) the marginal cost of serving one more customer is zero; (3) the consumption by one individual does not reduce the amount available for other consumers. Problems can arise with public goods when access to the public good is restricted through a pricing charge (pay-television, for example); but the most pervasive problem relates to the choice of an optimal amount of the public good to supply in the absence of access charges. In a two-good world, the marginal rate of transformation of the private into the public good should be equal to the sum over consumers of the marginal rates of substitution between the two. But marginal rates of substitution are unobserved, creating informational problems in achieving a Pareto-optimal allocation of resources between private and public goods.

Problems

1. Given figure 17-3, indicate how the Pareto-optimal state B could be achieved through the following:

    a. a tax on Y
    b. a subsidy to the producers of X
    c. a law permitting the producers of X to sue the producers of Y for damages caused by pollution

2. Town A is located upstream on a river that runs through town B. Both towns use the river for drinking water. A plant in town A dumps its wastes into the river, increasing the costs to town B of purifying its water. Explain how negotiations could solve the problems created by the plant.

3. In a one-consumer, two-good world, the utility function of the consumer is given by

    $$U = X \cdot Y.$$

    The production functions for X and Y are

    $$X = \frac{\sqrt{L_x}}{1 + Y}$$
    $$Y = \sqrt{L_y}$$

    where $L_x + L_y = 100$.

    Derive the transformation curve for the economy, the Pareto-optimal output mix, and the output mix that would be achieved in a competitive economy if the externality is not internalized.

4. Give the arguments for and against replacing our present free television system with the following:

    a. pay-television where each program viewed would require payment of a fee set by the pay-television company

    b. pay-television as in the British system where each television set owner must pay a yearly tax, but all programs are then free

5. "There must be an optimal amount of pollution in our society. If there weren't, there would be an incentive for pollutors and pollutees to negotiate a lower level." Comment.

18

Natural Resources

Natural resource stocks are assets of the society in that they can yield streams of services to the society over future periods. But certain features of natural resources distinguish them from other assets, and these create special problems for the efficient operation of a price system. Briefly, these relate to the *replenishability* characteristics of natural resources; the *appropriability* properties of natural resources; and *externalities* that arise in the production and consumption of services from such resources.†

Replenishability and Natural Resources

It is convenient to distinguish between replenishable natural resources (such as fish populations, forests, and land), and nonreplenishable resources (such as deposits of coal or oil). These two types are sometimes referred to as "nonexhaustible" and "exhaustible" resources, respectively, but of course any resource can be exhausted if it is managed improperly. In a certain sense, every resource is in principle replenishable; but for certain resources we either do not have the know-how to accomplish the appro-

priate recycling, or it just does not pay to recycle—these we call the "nonreplenishable" resources.

For nonreplenishable resources, exploitation of the resource results in a permanent loss to the society of a part of its stock of the resource. Current consumption of oil leads to a permanent decrease in the world's stock of oil. The notion of "the world's stock of oil" is admittedly somewhat fuzzy. The figures on oil reserves used by geologists are typically stated in terms of "recoverable" reserves, but what is recoverable depends on the costs of extraction relative to the price of oil. Every $1 increase in the price of oil increases the world's recoverable reserves of oil.

In contrast, replenishable resources can be harvested on a regular basis and, under proper management, can continue to yield services at a sustained rate into the indefinite future. With the energy crisis of the past few years, we are all aware of the problems posed by nonreplenishable resources. But there are also pressing problems in such replenishable resources as the blue whale and gray whale populations, where overfishing threatens extinction of the species.

Most services of natural resources are bought and sold on markets in the economy, just as are other commodities. The kind of question one might raise concerning the relationship of the price system to nonreplenishable resources

†See V. Smith, "Economics of Production from Natural Resources," *American Economic Review* 58 (1968) for a detailed discussion of the issues raised in this chapter.

is: "What is the optimal rate at which such a resource should be exhausted, and does the price system lead to such a rate of exhaustion?" Similarly, for replenishable resources, we want to know whether the price system leads to harvesting practices that maintain the stock of the resource at a desirable level. The efficiency of the price system in conserving natural resources depends crucially on the appropriability and externality characteristics of the resource.

Appropriability, Externalities, and Natural Resources

As we have seen in chapter 17, externalities are linked to problems of appropriability. Even so, it is convenient to treat them somewhat separately. Turning first to appropriability, we say that an asset is *completely appropriable* if the owner of the asset can exclude anyone else from access to the services of the asset. The ability to enforce exclusion means that the owner of the asset can charge others for the use of it and hence can appropriate to himself any potential earnings from its services.

At the other extreme is the case of a completely inappropriable asset, often referred to as a *common property* resource, with services of the asset freely available to anyone who wishes to exploit it. These are admittedly polar cases; most assets lie somewhere between these two extremes. For the typical asset, certain services are appropriable while others are not. As is to be expected, those services will be appropriated for which the costs of enforcing exclusion are lower than the revenues that can be derived from such exclusion; this balancing of costs and revenues in turn depends in large part on the structure of institutions (such as markets and a legal system) that the society possesses for creating and protecting property

rights. Resources such as land, mines, and forests are perhaps close to the case of completely appropriable assets, while waterways and fisheries are closer to being common property resources.

The problem with common property resources is easy to identify. So long as the services of an asset are appropriable, the owner of the asset has an incentive to manage the use of the asset with a view toward its long-run earning potential. But nobody has an incentive to conserve on the use of a common property resource. After all, any benefits from practicing conservation today are freely available tomorrow to anyone who wishes to capture them, if the asset is a common property resource.

Common property resources are *free goods* in the sense that there is no access charge for use of the resources, and hence the services of the resource will be used to the point where the marginal benefit from the last unit consumed is zero. Small wonder that our lakes and streams have become dumping grounds for industrial and residential wastes, or that we are depleting the stocks of ocean fish; until an appropriate charge is levied for access to these resources, the common property characteristic of these resources invites over-exploitation.

We begin by looking at the economics of replenishable resources.

Natural Growth and Replenishable Resources

Replenishable resources are those resources for which a process of natural growth makes possible sustained harvesting, without depleting the stock of the resource. Examples of replenishable resources are fish and game populations and forests. The stocks of such replenishable resources grow over time according to biological laws relating to availability of food and water, crowding, the age distribution of the population, and the process of natural reproduction of each species.

We can represent the gross properties of the natural growth of a replenishable resource in terms of a graph as shown in figure 18-1. The size of the stock of the resource (its "population") is denoted by S and is measured along the horizontal axis, with the growth in the stock measured on the vertical axis. The graph may be interpreted as follows. For population sizes less than $\underline{S}$, the replenishable resource dies out, with growth being negative below $\underline{S}$. (Thus, there is assumed to be some crucial minimum number of whooping cranes below which whooping cranes vanish; such a crucial minimum might be, say, ten cranes.) For populations above $\underline{S}$, an increase in the population size is accompanied by an increase in its growth up to the level S^*, after which growth is positive but declining as population increases in size. For small populations there is ample food available, encouraging rapid increases in population; but as population increases, crowding occurs and the food supply is less abundant on a per capita basis, lowering the rate of growth. At $\bar{S}$, the population again reaches zero population growth, because the available food supply is completely exploited.

$\bar{S}$ is referred to as the *natural equilibrium* of the resource, since in the absence of harvesting, this number is the population size that would tend to persist. Note that $\bar{S}$ is "stable" in the sense that if S is greater than $\bar{S}$, population growth is negative, while if S is less than $\bar{S}$, growth is positive. Thus under "natural" conditions there is a tendency for population to move toward $\bar{S}$.

Because of natural growth, it is possible to harvest the resource while maintaining the size of the underlying population. Thus each year

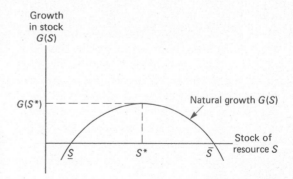

FIG. 18-1   *Natural growth curve*

we can harvest the natural growth in population $G(S)$, maintaining the population at a permanent level. The natural growth curve can thus be interpreted as telling us, for each population size, the maximum amount that can be harvested on a sustained basis without depleting the stock of the resource. The $G(S)$ curve is thus a curve that gives the sustainable yield for each population size. The harvest yield on a sustained basis is highest at a resource stock of S^*, and we refer to that yield, $G(S^*)$, as the *maximum sustainable yield* from the resource.

With this background, we can now look at the way in which a price system determines the rate of exploitation of a replenishable resource, with particular attention to the problems posed by externalities and the lack of appropriability.

The Economics of Replenishable Resources: Complete Appropriability

We begin by considering a world in which there are many stocks of a replenishable resource, each appropriated by an individual owner, and each stock with its own natural growth curve. For example, consider the case where there are hundreds of logging firms, each exploiting its own forest. Then each resource owner will make his harvesting decisions in such a way as to maximize the discounted present value (DPV) of the flow of income from his resource stock. Let S_t denote the stock of the resource held by a typical owner at time t, and let s_t denote the units harvested in the tth period. p_t and $C(s_t, S_t)$ are the price per unit of the resource harvested and the total costs of harvesting, respectively. Then the expression for DPV is given by

$$DPV = \frac{p_1 s_1 - C(s_1, S_1)}{(1 + i)}$$
$$+ \frac{p_2 s_2 - C(s_2, S_2)}{(1 + i)^2} + \ldots$$

Let ΔS_t denote the change in the stock of the resource during the tth period. Then

$$\Delta S_t = S_{t+1} - S_t = G(S_t) - s_t$$

(that is, the change in the stock in any period equals the growth in the stock during the period less what is harvested).

We assume that perfect competition prevails in the markets facing the resource owner; hence p_t is taken as a parameter by the owner. We will also assume that the marginal cost of harvesting is positive (an increase in the harvesting rate s_t increases cost C), and that the marginal cost of increasing the resource stock is negative (an increase in S_t decreases C). For example, in a fishery, given any population of fish, increasing the pounds of fish caught (s_t) increases total harvesting costs; but increasing the population of fish (S_t) makes fish easier to catch and hence decreases the harvesting costs associated with any given number of pounds of fish caught. In a forest, increasing the density of trees (up to a point at least) decreases the logging cost for a given amount of board feet produced.

Let $MC_t = \Delta C / \Delta s_t$, where MC_t is the marginal cost of harvesting. Consider now the choice of the resource owner as to his harvesting rates $s_1, s_2, \ldots$, and so on, and the associated time profile of resource stocks $S_1, S_2, \ldots$, and so on. The owner wishes to maximize DPV. This is accomplished by choosing his harvesting rates such that

$$\frac{\Delta DPV}{\Delta s_t} = 0 \text{ for each } s_t,$$

taking into account the fact that harvesting a unit today reduces the amount that can be harvested tomorrow. (This is the intertemporal equivalent of the static rule of choosing output X such that $\Delta \pi / \Delta X = 0$.)

Increasing output s_1 by an amount Δs_1 then has the following effects on DPV.

First, profits in period 1 are increased by

$$\left(p_1 - \frac{\Delta C}{\Delta s_1} \right) \Delta s_1 = (p_1 - MC_1) \Delta s_1.$$

Discounted to the present, this increases DPV by

$$\frac{(p_1 - MC_1) \Delta s_1}{(1 + i)}.$$

Second, harvesting an additional amount Δs_1 in period 1 reduces the stock at the beginning of period 2, S_2, by the same amount Δs_1. This in turn increases costs in period 2 by the amount

$$\left(\frac{\Delta C}{\Delta S_2} \right) \Delta s_1.$$

(Recall that *reducing* the stock available *increases* harvesting costs.)

Third, assuming harvesting is unchanged in periods 3, 4, . . . , then because harvesting in period 1 was increased by Δs_1, harvesting in period 2 must fall by

$$\left(1 + \frac{\Delta G}{\Delta S_2}\right)\Delta s_1.$$

That is, $\quad \Delta s_2 = -\left(1 + \frac{\Delta G}{\Delta S_2}\right)\Delta s_1,$

assuming no change in harvesting in periods 3, 4, ... (The amount harvested in period 2 decreases both because the stock at the beginning of period 2 is lower (by Δs_1) and because with a lower beginning stock, there is a different amount of growth G during the period.)

Hence the decrease in profits in period 2 is given by

$$\left[(p_2 - MC_2)\left(1 + \frac{\Delta G}{\Delta S_2}\right)\Delta s_1 - \frac{\Delta C}{\Delta S_2}\Delta s_1.\right]$$

Discounted back to the present, this changes DPV by

$$-\frac{\left[(p_2 - MC_2)\left(1 + \frac{\Delta G}{\Delta S_2}\right) - \frac{\Delta C}{\Delta S_2}\right]\Delta s_1}{(1 + i)^2}.$$

Since $\qquad \frac{\Delta DPV}{\Delta s_1} = 0$

when DPV is maximized, we conclude that

$$\frac{\left(p_1 - MC_1\right)}{(1 + i)}$$
$$-\frac{\left(p_2 - MC_2\right)\left(1 + \frac{\Delta G}{\Delta S_2}\right) - \frac{\Delta C}{\Delta S_2}}{(1 + i)^2} = 0.$$

Our special interest is in harvesting programs such that the same amount is harvested each period (sustained yield harvesting). Of course, there is no guarantee that a resource owner will choose to harvest his resource on a sustained basis, even when the resource is completely appropriable. In fact, if we consider the case where a replenishable resource was previously unexploited (say a forest in a remote corner of the world), then presumably the stock would originally be at the natural equilibrium $\bar{S}$. The first effects of human management of the resource would invariably be a reduction of the stock to the level at which sustained harvesting might take place. But we will assume for simplicity that in fact the DPV maximizing strategy is a sustained yield strategy.

Given that the resource owner chooses to harvest on a sustained basis, with the same harvest output and the same resource stock each year, then we can drop the time subscripts and simply refer to the annual harvest as s, with the sustained stock at the level S. Suppose we also assume that the price per unit of harvested output and the per unit costs of labor and capital inputs are constant in each period. Then the rather complicated expression above can be simplified to

$$(1 + i)(p - MC)$$
$$= (p - MC)\left(1 + \frac{\Delta G}{\Delta S}\right) - \frac{\Delta C}{\Delta S}.$$

Rearranging terms, we can write this as

$$p - MC - \frac{\left(-\frac{\Delta C}{\Delta S}\right)}{i - \frac{\Delta G}{\Delta S}} = 0.$$

User Cost and Sustained Yield Harvesting
Consider the condition

$$p - MC - \frac{\left(-\frac{\Delta C}{\Delta S}\right)}{i - \frac{\Delta G}{\Delta S}} = 0.$$

We interpret this condition as follows. If there were no increase in harvesting costs due to changes in the population of the resource S, so that $\Delta C/\Delta S = 0$, we would have the usual profit maximization condition: set price per unit p equal to marginal cost of harvesting, MC.

But harvesting an additional unit today involves a *user cost*—that is, a cost of using (depleting) the stock of the resource, given by $-(\Delta C/\Delta S)$. (Again recall that $\Delta C/\Delta S < 0$). Harvesting an additional unit today (with no change in harvesting rates in future periods) results in a permanent increase in harvesting costs; in each period in the future, harvesting costs are higher by the amount $-(\Delta C/\Delta S)$. We discount this increase in harvesting costs back to the present to get its DPV, by using the discount rate $i - (\Delta G/\Delta S)$.

$\Delta G/\Delta S$ is the change in the growth of the stock of the resource per unit of time due to a unit increase in the stock. Thus $\Delta G/\Delta S$ is the "natural growth rate" of the resource (its "own interest rate"). Given that a one unit increase in the stock produces a natural rate of return $\Delta G/\Delta S$, this increase must be deducted from the market rate of return i to ensure that the net yield from investing in the resource is i percent. (In effect, the annual income received from the stock changes by $\Delta G/\Delta S$ percent, given a one unit increase in S.)

DPV Maximization—The Graphics   The implications of the rule for DPV maximization can be illustrated graphically as follows. Given sustained yield harvesting, then the net cash flow π in any period is constant, where

$$\pi = ps - C(s, S).$$

(The time subscripts on s and S have been dropped because the amount harvested, s, and the resource stock, S, are the same in each period.) Then

$$\Delta\pi = p\Delta s - \left(\frac{\Delta C}{\Delta s}\right) \Delta s - \left(\frac{\Delta C}{\Delta S}\right) \Delta S$$

$$= (p - MC) \ \Delta s - \left(\frac{\Delta C}{\Delta S}\right) \Delta S.$$

Along an iso-profit curve, the net cash flow is constant; hence $\Delta\pi = 0$, which means that the slope of any iso-profit curve is given by

$$\frac{\Delta s}{\Delta S} = \frac{\dfrac{\Delta C}{\Delta S}}{(p - MC)},$$

where

$$\frac{\Delta C}{\Delta S} < 0, \ p - MC > 0.$$

Thus the iso-profit map for the appropriated replenishable resource is as shown in figure 18-2. The arrow indicates the direction of increased net cash flow, so $\pi_2 > \pi_1 > \pi_0$. The iso-profit curve labeled π_0 indicates the combinations of s and S that are associated with the net cash flow π_0.

Superimposing the growth curve of the resource on the iso-profit map, we obtain figure

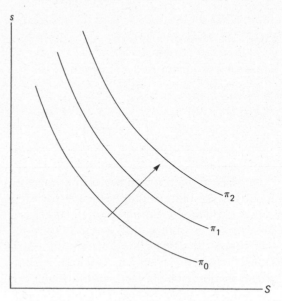

FIG. 18-2   *Iso-profit map for an appropriated replenishable resource*

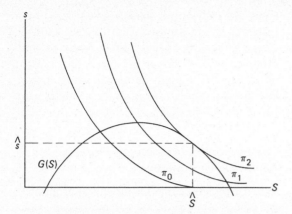

FIG. 18-3 *Natural growth and the iso-profit curves*

18-3. Now it might be thought that DPV is maximized in the sustained harvesting case at the combination $(\hat{S}, \hat{s})$ where the highest iso-profit curve π_2 is tangent to the $G(S)$ curve. But the resource stock S_t at time t yields growth $G(S_t)$ one time period later, at $t + 1$. Thus we have to adjust the iso-profit curves to reflect this one-period time lag between S and s and the consequent loss of interest earnings. This adjustment is accomplished by flattening the iso-profit curves, as in figure 18-4.

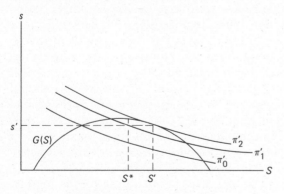

FIG. 18-4 *DPV maximization*

The iso-profit curves π_0, π_1, π_2 of figure 18-3 are replaced in figure 18-4 by the flatter π_0', π_1', π_2' curves. At every combination (s, S), we have added the interest rate i to the slope of the corresponding iso-profit curve. Hence the slopes of the new solid curves are given by $(\Delta s / \Delta S) + i$, to reflect the time lag between acquiring a stock and being able to harvest the growth of that stock. DPV maximization occurs at (S', s') where the highest new iso-profit curve, adjusted for the time lag, is tangent to the growth curve, $G(S)$.

Hence the combination (S', s') satisfies

$$\frac{\Delta s}{\Delta S} + i = \frac{\Delta G}{\Delta S},$$

or

$$\frac{\frac{\Delta C}{\Delta S}}{p - MC} + i = \frac{\Delta G}{\Delta S},$$

which reduces to

$$p - MC - \left(\frac{-\frac{\Delta C}{\Delta S}}{i - \frac{\Delta G}{\Delta S}} \right) = 0$$

as indicated in our previous discussion.

DPV Maximization and Maximum Sustainable Yield Under appropriation of the resource stock, sustained harvesting in a competitive environment does not necessarily imply that the stock will be managed so as to achieve maximum sustainable yield. In fact, if the case is as illustrated in the last section, the resource stock is larger and the annual harvest less than could be achieved at the maximum sustainable yield stock S^*. Does this mean that the price system is inefficient?

The answer is no. Under appropriation of the resource stock, optimal allocation of resources in the economy implies an annual harvest of s', as shown, rather than s*. The stock S' is such that the last unit harvested in each period sells for a price p equal to the marginal cost of producing that unit, plus the user cost discounted at the rate $i - (\Delta G/\Delta S)$. If annual harvesting were to be increased, with S' moving toward S*, then we would be allocating re- sources (labor, capital, and such) to the produc- tion of this good, although these resources have a higher value productivity in other industries in the economy. This use of resources would be inefficient in the sense that the economy would move to a Pareto-inferior state.

The influence of the interest rate on the optimal stock and harvesting rate should be mentioned. The higher the interest rate, the higher the cost (in terms of foregone income) to the resource owner of maintaining any given resource stock. Hence an increase in the inter- est rate creates incentives to decrease the stock of the resource that is held. At sufficiently high interest rates, the resource stock might be even less than S*. In terms of figure 18-4, this could occur if the interest-adjusted iso-profit curves had positive slopes.

The reason for contrasting the DPV maxi- mizing harvesting rate with the maximum sustainable yield harvest rate is that many re- plenishable natural resources (such as forests and fisheries) are managed by government agencies, for reasons we will investigate in the next section. In most (if not all) cases, the criterion adopted for resource management by these agencies is maximum sustainable yield. This approach generally results in a nonop- timum solution to the resource conservation problem. In the case of resources like fisheries and forests, it results in maintaining the stocks at less than optimal levels, as pictured in figure 18-4. For other resources, maximum sustained

yield harvesting leads to excessive stocks of the resource. Under appropriability of resource stocks, the competitive system leads to opti- mum stock and harvesting levels. But certain problems with replenishable resources necessi- tate interference with the market mechanism, particularly when appropriability is absent.

The Economics of Common Property Replenishable Resources

When a replenishable resource is appropriated, the owner of the resource will manage the stock of it to maximize its discounted present value. This means that the last unit harvested from the resource in any period must add just as much to DPV as it would if the unit were not harvested and instead were allowed to increase the stock in that period and hence increase harvests from the stock in all future periods. The owner is well aware that any harvesting done now decreases the potential future earning power of the resource. This is the inherent "conservation" of natural resources that is ac- complished under appropriability by the price system. If future demand is expected to be high, this expectation increases the value of additions to the stock today, and promotes conservation. On the other hand, if future prices are expected to be low relative to the present, this expecta- tion increases incentives for harvesting now instead of "investing" in the stock of the re- source; and incentives for conserving the re- source are weakened.

But consider what happens when a natural resource is a common property good. That is, there do not exist property rights to the stock of the resource. From the point of view of any user of the resource, the future earnings poten- tial of the resource can be ignored, since there is no way to appropriate the future earnings potential. To put it another way, user costs are treated as if they were zero.

There are many examples of the disastrous consequences when replenishable natural resources are treated as common property goods. A prime example is the slaughter of the buffalo herds in the American West, a slaughter that reached its peak during the railroad building era of the 1870s and led to decimation of the species. This is only one of a series of such incidents that have caused some anthropologists to conjecture that the disappearance of a score of large mammal species between 20,000 and 5,000 B.C. was due not to the ice age, but rather to the wanderings of man the hunter over the globe. More recently, we have the phenomenon of Lake Erie, which is reportedly "dead" or in the process of dying, as a result of indiscriminate use of the lake as a dumping ground for industrial, commercial, and residential wastes—a clear-cut case of the misuse of a replenishable natural resource because of its common property characteristics.

The problem is worldwide, and occurs in socialistic as well as capitalistic economies. Japan is in the process of destroying its off-shore fishing industry through pollution; California has lost its sardine industry because of overfishing; the lakes and rivers of Russia are being clogged with industrial wastes; and New York City is being threatened by the movement of a sea of sludge that lies some twelve miles away from Manhattan Island. It is not only exotic species such as the whooping crane that are endangered by mankind; valuable commercial resources such as the blue whale and the Chesapeake Bay oyster are also threatened.

Ocean Fisheries—A Common Property Resource   To see what happens when replenishable resources are not appropriated, consider the case of ocean fisheries. Problems of establishing and protecting property rights to ocean fish are particularly severe. In the first place, certain fish such as the salmon move vast distances during their lifetimes; even if it were possible to establish property rights to particular areas of the ocean surface, the desired objective of appropriability of the fish stock still might not be accomplished. Furthermore, the tradition of "freedom of the seas" carries with it the absence of any effective national or supra-national institutions for enforcing property rights in the open oceans.

The problems created by this lack have recently become more and more intense. Over the past twenty years, Russia and other Eastern European countries have developed fishing fleets that have moved into the traditional fishing grounds of the world, adding to already existing overfishing practices. A "bumping" process has taken place, whereby commercial fishermen of all countries have moved into previously "national" fishing areas. Thus we have incidents (familiar to us from newspaper reports) in the oceans near Iceland, in the fisheries off Ecuador, in Alaskan waters, and off the coasts of Maine and New York. There used to be stories about the "unlimited food potential" of the oceans, but marine biologists now agree that it has been vastly overrated. We may already be near the limits of ocean harvests from a sustained yield point of view.

Suppose we look at the problem of inappropriability of the ocean fish stock from the point of view of the model developed earlier. We again assume perfect competition in the sense that there are a large number of fishing firms, none having any market power. Because the fish stock is not appropriable, each fisherman treats the stock of fish as a given, beyond his control. He acts to maximize the current profits from his fishing, and ignores the future revenue potential of the fish population; hence the user cost is treated as being zero. For any fisherman, there are no costs associated with depleting the stock of fish; instead there are only the costs he incurs for capital and labor to operate his fishing vessel. In the short run, fishing firms might make excess profits from their operations; but in the long run, each firm earns only normal profits.

For simplicity, assume that each fishing firm has the same costs of harvesting, $C(s, S)$. Costs still depend on the stock of fish S, but no firm controls S. Because the stock of fish is determined in part by the decisions of other fishermen, and because the stock enters into the costs of any given fisherman, this means that there are externalities (referred to as "stock" externalities) present when the fishery is a common property resource. At a profit-maximizing catch, the firm equates price per unit of catch, p, to marginal costs of harvesting MC. Furthermore, long-run equilibrium implies that $p = C(s, S)/s$; price equals average cost. Finally, with n fishing firms, the total catch, ns, equals the growth in the stock $G(S)$ at a steady state of sustained harvesting. Thus for the industry as a whole, total catch is equal to the annual growth in the fish stock. The consequences of inappropriability may be seen from figure 18-5.

The graph contrasts the situation under appropriability (point A) with that for the common property case (point B). Under appropriability the owner takes into account the future earning potential of the fish population, and sets output at s_2 with a fish stock of S_2. When the stock is not appropriable, then equilibrium occurs where profits are zero, along the $\pi = 0$ curve. At a sustained harvest position, the catch equals the growth in stock; hence we

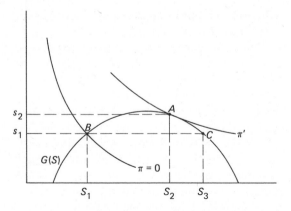

FIG. 18-5   *Common property equilibrium and equilibrium under appropriability*

arrive at the point B, where the fish stock is S_1 and the catch is s_1.[†]

Is this inefficient? The answer is clearly yes. When the fish stock is treated as a common property resource, the future rents that accrue from investing in the fish stock are ignored. The situation depicted in the graph is typical of most unregulated common property resources. Competitive pressures result in the allocation of too much in the way of capital and labor to exploitation of the resource, and the stock is maintained at too low a level. Recall that for fisheries, an increase in the population of fish reduces the cost of harvesting. Note that at C, we have the same sustained harvest, as in the common property case (B). But at C, because the stock is larger, less capital and labor

---

[†]Note that the slope of the $\pi = 0$ curve is steeper than the slope of the π' curve, which holds under appropriability. The flatter π' curve reflects the interest cost of maintaining the stock, a cost that is borne by the owner of the stock under appropriability but is ignored, of course, when the stock is a common property resource.

are required to obtain the harvest s_1 than at B. Marine biologists estimate that this is the current situation in the North Sea fishery, one of the most overexploited of the world's fishing grounds. More fish could be caught, on a sustained basis, if *fewer* ships and men were employed in North Sea fishing. This is inefficiency with a vengeance.

Policies to Internalize Stock Externalities The price system produces inefficient results when natural resources are inappropriable, and these results give rise to a demand for government intervention in the system to correct such inefficiencies. The government has adopted the goal of maximum sustainable yield in regulating replenishable resources such as fisheries. To attain this goal, the government has imposed certain regulations, including license requirements, limits on catches, limits on size of fish caught, the restriction of fishing to brief "seasons," and limits on equipment such as nets that can be used. International agreements have also been signed to implement some of these regulations.

The effects of these regulations are mixed. Charging a fee for access to the fish stock, together with a poundage fee based on catch, has the effect of converting the common property fishery to something more like an appropriated asset. If the dollar amounts were properly chosen and if enforcement were possible, then we could obtain a solution that comes close to the competitive pricing solution under appropriability. Similarly, rules specifying a minimum size for fish that can be legally caught have the effect of ensuring a viable age distribution for the fish population. In ocean fisheries, this is typically accomplished through rules as to the mesh of the nets that can be used.

On the other hand, certain of the conservationist regulations interfere directly with the efficiency of the capital and labor employed in fishing. Such regulations include the enforcement of requirements as to equipment that gives the fish a better than even chance—a sporting approach, but one that has the effect of increasing the cost of obtaining any given amount of fish caught. Another example of regulations that reduce efficiency is specifying a certain limited period as the only "season" for fishing a species. The problem with such a regulation is that it encourages investment in specialized fishing vessels of speed and capacity suited to the short fishing season, vessels that may lie idle the rest of the year. From the economist's point of view, systems of license fees and taxes on landings of fish are especially desirable, since they perform the function of restricting access to the fish stock much as private ownership would, without decreasing the efficiency of the factors employed in commercial fishing.

Finally, it should be noted that for a variety of reasons, every major fishing nation subsidizes its fishing industry. The subsidies take the form of tariffs and/or import quotas on imported fish, government financed technical programs to increase the productivity of fisheries, preferential treatment of domestic shipbuilding concerns, and even income supplements to individual fishermen. With a common property resource, it is not surprising that each country feels it has an incentive to exploit the resource as fully as possible, but as we have seen, such policies can result in grossly inefficient management of the resource from a worldwide point of view. Government subsidies to fishing firms have the effect of intensifying these inefficiencies.

The Economics of Nonreplenishable Resources—Appropriability

We next examine the way that the competitive economy operates to determine the rate of exhaustion of the world's stocks of nonreplenishable resources such as fossil fuels (coal, oil) and metals (iron, copper, zinc, for example). A first step is to see what happens under conditions of complete appropriability, so that property rights exist to each resource stock. Again we assume that there are a large number of stocks of a given resource, each independently owned and controlled, with each stock so small that resource owners ignore the effects of their decisions on the price of the output marketed.

Using the notation of the earlier sections, let s_t denote the amount of the output sold in period t and let S_t denote the stock of the resource at time t. The nonreplenishable nature of the resource is indicated by the relation

$$S_{t+1} = S_t - s_t;$$

the stock at time $t+1$ equals the stock at time t less the amount mined and sold during the tth period.

Then the typical resource owner will manage his stock so as to maximize the discounted present value of the time stream of income from his holdings of the stock, where

$$DPV = \frac{p_1 s_1 - C(s_1, S_1)}{(1 + i)}$$
$$+ \frac{p_2 s_2 - C(s_2, S_2)}{(1 + i)^2} + \ldots .$$

$C(s_t, S_t)$ are the total costs of "mining" the resource in period t. We assume that the marginal cost per unit mined ($MC_t = \Delta C/\Delta s_t$) is positive and that mining cost increases as the stock is depleted, that is $\Delta C/\Delta S_t < 0$. We also assume that the marginal cost of mining increases as the stock of the resource is depleted.

Once again, DPV maximization implies that

$$\frac{\Delta DPV}{\Delta s_t} = 0,$$

for every t taking into account that fact that increasing output in the tth period reduces the amount that can be mined in the future, and assuming that the amount mined is positive in the tth period.

An increase Δs_t in the amount mined in period t increases the net cash flow in period t by the amount

$$(p_t - MC_t)\,\Delta s_t.$$

But this increased output reduces the stock available to be mined in period $t+1$ by Δs_t. Assuming no change in mining rates in periods $t + 2, t + 3 \ldots$ and so on, the net cash flow in period $t + 1$ is reduced by

$$\left(p_{t+1} - MC_{t+1} + \frac{\Delta C}{\Delta S_{t+1}} \right) \Delta s_t.$$

The overall effect on DPV is then given by

$$\frac{(p_t - MC_t)\,\Delta s_t}{(1 + i)^t}$$
$$- \frac{\left(p_{t+1} - MC_{t+1} + \dfrac{\Delta C}{\Delta S_{t+1}} \right) \Delta s_t}{(1 + i)^{t+1}}.$$

Thus the rule $\dfrac{\Delta DPV}{\Delta s_t} = 0$ implies that

$$(p_t - MC_t)\,(1 + i) = p_{t+1} - MC_{t+1} - \frac{\Delta C}{\Delta S_{t+1}}$$

or $\quad p_{t+1} - p_t\,(1 + i)$

$$= MC_{t+1} - MC_t\,(1 + i) - \frac{\Delta C}{\Delta S_{t+1}}.$$

This last expression can be interpreted as follows. Suppose that there are no variable mining costs, and so the right-hand side of the last expression is zero. Then if the resource owner supplies positive amounts of the resource in each period, the price per unit must rise over time at a rate equal to the market rate of interest. Why? If p_{t+1} were less than $p_t(1 + i)$, it would make sense for the owner to sell his entire stock in period t and invest the money in assets earning the market interest rate. If $p_{t+1} > p_t(1 + i)$, then he would sell nothing in period t, since he could earn more than the market rate of interest by simply holding his stock for sale at $t + 1$.

The fact that variable costs of mining are nonzero complicates things, but the same basic idea holds. For example, marginal production costs in oil are close to zero, but user cost

$$- \frac{\Delta C}{\Delta S_{t+1}}$$

is positive. This means that positive output in each period implies that price rises faster than the rate of interest, since

$$p_{t+1} - p_t(1 + i) = - \frac{\Delta C}{\Delta S_{t+1}},$$

when $MC_t = MC_{t+1} = 0.$

Since each resource owner will follow this rule, the market situation will be as depicted in figure 18-6. Assuming that the demand schedule in each period is unchanged over time, market equilibrium is as shown. At time t, the market supply curve $S(p_t)$ is the sum of the supply curves of individual owners, and similarly for $S(p_{t+1})$. The $S(p_{t+1})$ curve lies to the left of the $S(p_t)$ curve because output $\Sigma s(p_t)$ in period t reduces the stock available for mining in period $t + 1$ and hence increases the user cost of mining any given output in period $t + 1$. The higher the interest rate, the further to the left is the $S(p_{t+1})$ curve. The consequence is that market price rises over time, as indicated on the graph.

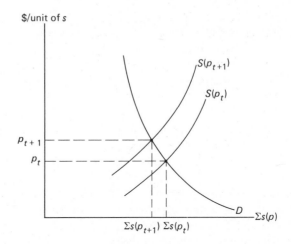

FIG. 18-6   *Price changes over time—nonreplenishable resource*

What we see here is the operation of an automatic "conservation of nonreplenishable resources" by the price system. The exhaustion of such resources over time is accompanied by a steady increase in prices, even when per unit input costs and demand are constant over time. The increase in price over time performs two functions: first, it encourages consumers and firms to find substitutes for the services of the resource; and second, it provides incentives for resource owners to limit sales in the present in order to take advantage of higher future prices. It also provides incentives for research and development activities designed to recycle "exhaustible" resources and to discover substitutes.

Economists have generally been somewhat skeptical about the forecasts of doomsday prophets—not because they are unaware of the problems of exhaustion of resources, but because the kind of cataclysm envisaged by the doomsday group ignores the role of the price system. Competitive markets cannot create more oil or more copper or more iron ore.† But the operation of these markets tends to make the transition from an oil economy to a non-oil economy much more gradual than physical scientists seem to believe. Long before we run out of oil, oil prices will be high enough that the shift out of oil into alternative energy sources will occur automatically. Not that living standards will be unaffected, but at least we will not be rushed from a 70¢/gallon gasoline economy today into a "no gas available at any price" economy tomorrow. The length of the transition period when oil prices are rising is of crucial importance, since the more time we have, the better the chance that low-cost substitutes will be discovered.

Thus far we have ignored the complicating features of externalities in nonreplenishable resources. It is time to look at this aspect of the resource problem.

Nonreplenishable Resources and Externalities

We have been dealing with the case where there is a large number of resource owners, each with his own stock of the resource. The competitive assumption is somewhat unrealistic. For example, De Beers controls most of the output of diamonds; there are only a handful of important producers of gold, iron ore, and other such minerals; and we are only too painfully aware of the concentration of market power in the oil industry.

So monopoly is a problem in many of the most important nonreplenishable resources. This problem is mitigated somewhat for nonre-

plenishable resources that are storable such as gold, diamonds, and silver, since the existing stocks are large relative to current output, and tend to be more widely dispersed in ownership than the mines are. In any case, the kinds of solutions to the problems of monopoly power discussed earlier apply here as well; monopoly is not a problem unique to natural resources.

In contrast, there are externality problems in certain nonreplenishable resources (particularly oil) that tend to exhaust such resources at too rapid rates. Drilling rights to oil are assigned on the basis of surface areas on the earth, while the pool of oil lies underground and is often difficult to locate with any exactness; therefore, when one firm discovers oil in its exploration operations, it has difficulty in establishing exclusive rights to the entire underground pool that it is tapping. Another firm can move into the same general area and, with luck, can tap into the same pool originally discovered by the first firm. This possibility, whether or not it becomes a reality, changes the strategy of the original oil firm with respect to its extraction rates of oil. There now is a positive incentive to pump out as much oil as possible as soon as possible. Once again, user cost ($-\Delta C/\Delta S$) is ignored because of common property problems. Consequently, pumping costs increase and the percent of the underground pool that will be recovered decreases.

As we have seen, if ownership rights to the entire underground pool were vested in one firm, it would adjust its extraction rate in accordance with decision rules that lead to conservation of the underground pool. In the absence of such rights, the pool of oil becomes a common property resource, and no firm has an incentive to practice conservation with respect to it.

---

†Increases in prices do have the effect, however, of increasing the stocks of "recoverable reserves," as noted earlier.

Recognition of this basic problem of externalities has led to state and federal laws designed to regulate pumping practices, with quotas being assigned to the various firms exploiting a common pool of oil. In principle, such regulations could result in extraction rates that mirror the rates that would occur under appropriability of the resource in a competitive economy. But in fact, such regulations have regularly been applied with first priority assigned to the economic well-being of the oil firms and with less attention to the long-term interests of the public. State laws are particularly subject to abuse, since if any one state promotes practices of conservation, other states can adjust their quotas to permit the firms located in them to reap short-run profits because of the limitations on production in the states practicing conservation. Beyond this, the cooperative practices that are encouraged under both state and federal laws also encourage firms to get together on pricing and marketing strategies. As often happens, government policies designed to improve the efficiency of the operation of an industry have resulted in the creation of institutions that make cartelization of an industry feasible.

Nonetheless, the problem of absence of property rights to underground pools of oil discourages conservation of this resource, and represents a clear-cut example of a breakdown in the competitive structure of prices as a device for managing an important natural resource. Although we have been less than successful in accomplishing this goal with our present practices, there may be alternatives, such as the creation of new kinds of property rights, to solve this problem. Certainly it represents an important area for further work on corrective public policies.

Consumer Externalities and Natural Resources

Producer externalities create problems for the price system in the management of our stock of natural resources because the common property nature of certain natural resources provides incentives for their overexploitation. In principle, these problems could be solved by the assignment of property rights to individual stocks of such resources and then permitting the market system to determine the rates at which the stocks are mined or harvested. However, the establishment and protection of property rights to common property natural resources is difficult to accomplish, as illustrated in the cases of ocean fisheries and oil deposits, especially since a simultaneous goal is to preserve a competitive environment in the natural resources industry. Hence various governmental measures have been adopted in an attempt to internalize producer externalities, with at best only qualified success.

In addition to the externalities that arise among producers of natural resources, important consumer externalities exist with respect to natural resources, and the problems associated with these externalities are even more complicated. We are all aware that smog is spreading over urban areas and that rivers and lakes are becoming unfit for boating and swimming, much less drinking. The common property nature of our air and waterways has led to the dumping of wastes that pollute the environment, directly reducing consumer satisfactions. In principle at least, bargaining between groups of consumers and producers could establish an "acceptable" level of pollution: bribes by consumers to producers could be mutually agreed to so that the value of clean air and water at the margin to consumers is equated to the marginal cost to producers of reducing pollution.

The policing and informational problems involved with negotiation and other devices to internalize externalities have been discussed earlier. In most cases, some governmental action is necessary to reflect correctly the preferences of consumers in their attitudes toward public goods such as pollution. If the correct actions are taken, then an optimal amount of pollution can be obtained.

Consider another aspect of the problem of consumer externalities. Decisions made by the current generation with respect to the management of both replenishable and nonreplenishable resources will determine in large part the natural environment of future generations. But future generations are not represented in the decision making that takes place through the market mechanism. The price system allocates resources in response to the preferences of consumers as reflected in their choices expressed in the market place. As we have already seen, the system operates efficiently with respect to such preferences, if the market mechanism operates like the competitive model. Future generations of consumers affect the operation of the price system only insofar as expectations about their preferences influence current decision making by the owners of resource stocks, or insofar as the present generation obtains direct satisfactions from bequeathing a legacy to their descendants.

If the present generation is highly myopic, then interest rates will be high, and high interest rates are associated with rapid exploitation of replenishable and nonreplenishable natural resources. The high interest rate reflects the reluctance of the current generation to save for the future, and in that sense the price system accurately reflects the preference pattern of consumers of the current generation. This is a classic instance of "market failure": no market exists where future generations can bargain with the present as to the allocation of resources among them. This basic problem still awaits solution. As in other cases, economic theory provides partial answers that are important and suggestive, but political and ethical considerations must be taken into account as well.

Summary

Replenishable natural resources can be harvested over time on a regular basis without exhausting them. When a replenishable natural resource is appropriated, its owner chooses a time path of harvesting that maximizes the DPV of the cash flow generated by the resource. In the special case of a constant harvesting rate over time, we say the resource is managed on a sustained yield basis. In a competitive economy, an optimal sustained yield policy is to choose the population S and the annual yield s such that

$$p - MC - \left(\frac{-\dfrac{\Delta C}{\Delta S}}{i - \dfrac{\Delta G}{\Delta S}} \right) = 0$$

where $G(S)$ is the natural growth curve of the resource. Generally speaking, such a sustained yield harvesting program does not result in the maximum sustainable yield from the population (that is, the value of S such that $\Delta G / \Delta S = 0$). Since the above rule must be satisfied at a Pareto-optimal state, maximum sustainable yield is generally not consistent with an efficient allocation of resources.

When a replenishable resource is unappropriated, then in the long run the resource is harvested at a rate whereby excess profits are zero, assuming the absence of government controls on access to the resource. This means that there is inefficiency in production; too many resources are allocated to the harvesting of the resource and the stock of the resource is at a level lower than a Pareto optimum. In general, government controls aimed at maximum sustainable yield move the economy only partway toward efficient allocation of resources, and certain regulations (such as artificially limited seasons and restrictions on technologies for harvesting) introduce new sources of inefficiency into the system.

For nonreplenishable resources, output in the current period leads to a permanent decrease in the world's stock of the resource. When such resources are appropriated with a competitive market for the resource, and assuming no discoveries of new stocks of the resource, then price rises over time in the face of a constant demand curve for services of the resource. The amount of price rise depends on the responsiveness of cost to changes in output levels and stocks, and on the market rate of interest. The higher the interest rate, the higher the rate of price increase over time. Similarly, the more costs rise with a decrease in the stock of the resource, the faster will price increase. The price system thus creates incentives for conserving the resource as the stock of it is exhausted. When the resource is unappropriated, the resource is mined on the basis of current profitability and controls on access are required to achieve a Pareto-optimal state. Finally, the notion of Pareto optimality incorporates only the preferences of the current population; a myopic population will deplete resources at a faster rate than one that places a high value on the environment in which the next generation will live.

Problems

1. The OPEC countries argue that the price of oil was below "optimum" levels when Arab oil was under the control of western oil companies. Given the history of increasing royalty payments by the oil companies and threats of nationalizing oil on the part of the Arab countries, what justification can you make for the OPEC position?

2. Suppose the growth curve of a tree looks as follows:

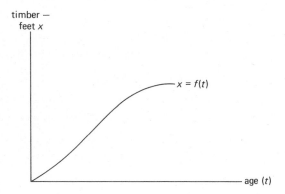

   Show that, if logging costs are negligible, then a DPV-maximizing lumber firm will cut down the tree when the rate of growth of the tree

   $$\frac{f(t+1) - f(t)}{f(t)}$$ is equal to the interest rate.

   Give an explanation for this rule. What is the effect, on the age distribution of trees, of an increase in the interest rate?

3. Construct a "model" of a DPV-maximizing farmer to determine the appropriate amount of fertilizer the farmer will use to maintain the productivity of an acre of land he has under cultivation. (Assume a sustained yield harvesting program.)

4. Discuss the role, if any, of appropriability (or lack of appropriability) and externalities in connection with each of the following.

   a. Pollution of the Missouri River by DDT fertilizers and the runoff from feed lots.

   b. "Clear cutting" practices in Oregon, Idaho, and Montana.

   c. The exhaustion of gold in the California and Nevada mines.

   d. The decrease in population for the five-year period 1970–75 in Los Angeles County.

5. Assume that there is monopolistic control of a nonreplenishable resource such as iron ore. Indicate the difference in the time path of prices and output under monopoly as compared to perfect competition with appropriability.

Epilogue

It might be worthwhile to summarize briefly where we have arrived on the basis of the last eighteen chapters, and to relate this summary to the introductory comments to the book. The two fundamental concepts underlying microeconomic theory are (1) that individuals are motivated by self-interest and act in response to it; and (2) that prices are set and exchanges occur on markets according to the law of supply and demand. Both self-interest and the law of supply and demand have specific, technical meanings within microeconomic theory, as outlined in the early chapters of this book.

The scientific content of microeconomic theory appears in the form of various testable propositions. These propositions concern the pattern of demands for goods and services by consumers and the choices of input-output mixes by firms, as well as the way in which the choices of these decision makers influence market prices and quantities through the law of supply and demand. Most of these propositions are stated in qualitative rather than quantitative form; that is, they describe the direction of change of price or quantity, rather than specifying the magnitudes of such changes. These propositions still can be empirically tested, although admittedly they lack the specificity of comparable propositions in the physical sciences. The material covered in chapters 5 through 12 is generally relevant to the propositions of microeconomic theory.

Over the past chapters, we have been concerned primarily with issues of normative economics rather than positive economics—a change in focus from a perfectly competitive economy to economic systems with market imperfections. If the world really operated as a perfectly competitive economy, the role of the government would be reduced to solving problems of equity. Frictionless markets operating in an environment without market power, externalities, or uncertainty automatically generate equilibrium states that are Pareto optimal; problems of efficiency never arise. Market imperfections lead to welfare losses associated with inefficiencies in production or exchange, and the appropriate role for government is now expanded to include problems of efficiency as well as those of equity.

Needless to say, we have only skimmed the surface of microeconomic theory and its applications to the problems of society. This text has been explicitly literary, graphical, and intuitive in approach; for a full understanding of the intricacies of the theory, a formal mathematical framework is essential. Furthermore, to apply the theory in a creative fashion to any real-world problem, a detailed understanding of the empirical reality of specific industries and markets is required.

If the nonspecialist is now more fully aware of the scope and limitations of the economist's tool kit, and if the specialist is able to build on the foundations outlined here, then the book has accomplished its purpose.

Common Symbols

AC, ATC	(short-run) average total cost	MRTS	marginal rate of technical substitution of Y for X
AFC	(short-run) average fixed cost		
AP	average product	MSC	marginal social cost
AR	average revenue	MTP	marginal rate of time preference
AVC	(short-run) average variable cost	MU	marginal utility
		NI	national income
CES	constant elasticity of substitution	NNP	net national product
		p	price per unit
$D(p)$	market demand	$P(x)$	probability of x
DPV	discounted present value	q	quantity
$E(p)$	excess demand	r	rental per unit of capital services
Ex	expected value of X	$S(i)$	savings
FC	fixed cost	$S(p)$	market supply
GI	gross income for the economy	SRAC	short-run average total cost
GNP	gross national product	SRMC	short-run marginal cost
i	interest rate	TC	total cost
K	units of capital services	TR	total revenue
L	units of labor services	TP	total product
LRAC	long-run average total cost	U	utility
LRMC	long-run marginal cost	V	value of newly produced capital goods
LRTC	long-run total cost		
LRVC	long-run variable cost	VC	variable cost
M	money income	w	wage rate per unit of labor services
MC	marginal cost		
MP	marginal product	W	value of nonhuman wealth
MPC	marginal private cost	δ	(delta) internal rate of return
MR	marginal revenue	η_D	(eta) own price elasticity of demand
MRP	marginal revenue product		
MRS	marginal rate of substitution of Y for X	η_S	own price elasticity of supply
		π	(pi) profits
MRT	marginal rate of transformation of X into Y	σ	(sigma) elasticity of substitution
		$\sigma^2(X)$	variance of X
		$\sigma(X)$	standard deviation of X

Subject Index

Name Index

About the Author

James Quirk received his B.B.A., M.A., and Ph.D. from the University of Minnesota. He has taught at St. Mary's University (Texas), Purdue, and the University of Kansas. He is presently on the faculty at Caltech. His interests are in mathematical economics, the economics of professional sports, the theory of bureaucracy, and traditional jazz.

Computer Typesetting Services, Inc., of Glendale, California, set this book in 10-point Continental. Nancy Long of House of Graphics, Palo Alto, California, prepared the technical art for it, and Kingsport Press, Kingsport, Tennessee printed it.

Sponsoring Editors	Bruce Caldwell and Robert D. Bovenschulte
Project Editor	Gretchen Hargis
Designer	Joe di Chiarro
Cover Photo	Elihu Blotnick